France in the South Pacific
Power and Politics

France in the South Pacific
Power and Politics

Denise Fisher

E PRESS

Acknowledgements

I would like to thank Peter Brown, Robert Aldrich, Hugh White, Darrell Tryon and Stewart Firth for their encouragement and strategic advice in the preparation of this book.

There are many who have provided particular inspiration. These include Marie-Claude Tjibaou, who asked me not to forget the people of New Caledonia; Déwé Gorodey, Roch Wamytan, Paul Néaoutyine, the late Jacques Lafleur, Pierre Frogier, Thierry Lataste, the late Paul de Deckker, Alain Christnacht, Jean-Yves Faberon, Nathalie Mrgudovic, Stephen Henningham, Malcolm Leader, David O'Leary, Penny Wensley AC and Frédéric Angleviel. Angela and Mike Smith, Nicole Jamieson, Véronique and Thierry Lataste, and Chantal and Bernard Attali offered ports of call along the way. Thank you too to the highly professional staff of the French Embassy in Australia, and to officials, both French and local, in Paris, Noumea, Tahiti and Matu Utu, whose warmth and support have enriched my respect, understanding and affection for those working to ensure a stable and fair future for the people of our region. I am indebted to colleagues in the Australian Department of Foreign Affairs and Trade who have enlarged and shaped my view of the world over a career of 30 years.

I appreciate the support of Jacqueline Lo and The Australian National University (ANU) Centre for European Studies, where I have been based for the last year. Peter Brown and the ANU School of Languages assisted with some early, much appreciated, research funding. Thanks too to Justine Molony and Duncan Beard for editing.

My husband Denis and three sons Damien, Adrian and Jonathan, and my late parents, Carmel and Trevor Kaine, provided valued support and interest.

Glossary and acronyms

Glossary

broussard	European long-term resident of New Caledonia living mainly on farms or in rural villages
Caldoche	European long-term resident of New Caledonia, often second and third generation
Indigénat	(native code) system confining Kanaks to designated areas, taxing them, subjecting them to punishment by administrators rather than judges, and requiring them to work on government projects, from 1887 to 1946
événements	(events) term used by the French for the civil disturbances in New Caledonia from 1984 to 1988
Kanak	indigenous people of New Caledonia, Melanesians
metropolitan	expression deriving from the French *métropolitain* meaning from the *métropole* or continental France
Mwâ Kâ	(big house) totemic monument in central Noumea
outre-mer	(overseas France) collective expression referring to all French departments, territories and collectivities overseas
régalien	(regalian) sovereign, pertaining to the French sovereign state, often referred to in the context of the Noumea Accord as the five powers retained solely by the French State by the end of the Accord (2018); i.e., defence, foreign affairs, currency, justice and public order

Acronyms

French and historic institutions

ADECAL	Agence de Développement Économique de la Nouvelle-Calédonie (New Caledonia Economic Development Agency)
AFD	Agence Française de Développement (French Development Agency)

CEP	Centre d'Expérimentation du Pacifique (Pacific Experimentation Centre): name for the French nuclear testing facility in French Polynesia
CFP	Currency of the French Pacific entities, variously translated in the early years as 'Colonies Françaises du Pacifique' or 'French Pacific colonies'; 'Change Français du Pacifique' from 1947; and, in recent years, 'Cours' or 'Comptoir' 'Français Pacifique'. It has a fixed value relative to the Euro, CFP1 = Euro.00838.
COM	Collectivités d'Outre-Mer (overseas collectivities)
COMSUP	Commandant Supérieur (commander of French armed forces)
DOM-TOM	Départements d'Outre-Mer, Territoires d'Outre-Mer (overseas departments and territories)
EFO	Établissements Français d'Océanie (French Pacific establishments, the former name for French Polynesia)
EUR	Euro
FANC	Forces Armées de la Nouvelle-Calédonie (New Caledonian armed forces (French))
IFREMER	Institut Français de Recherche pour l'Exploitation de la Mer (French Research Institute for Marine Exploitation)
INCO	now Vale INCO, multinational nickel company operating in New Caledonia
INERIS	Institut National de l'Environnement Industriel et des Risques (National Institute for Industrial Environment and Risk)
INSEE	Institut national de la statistique et des études économiques (National Institute for Statistics and Economic Studies)
IRD	Institut de recherche pour le développement (Institute for Development Research)
ISEE/ITSEE	Institut de la statistique et des études économiques/Institut territorial de la statistique et des études économiques (Institute for Statistics and Economic Studies/Territorial Institute for Statistics and Economic Studies (New Caledonia))
ISPF	Institut de la statistique de Polynésie Française (Statistics Institute of French Polynesia)
LMS	London Missionary Society
RFO	Radio France Outre-Mer, France's overseas broadcasting service
SLN	Société le Nickel (The Nickel Company), French-owned nickel company in New Caledonia
STSEE	Service Territorial de la Statistique et des Études Économiques (Territorial Service for Statistics and Economic Studies) (Wallis and Futuna)

Regional Pacific institutions

ADB	Asian Development Bank
CRISP	Coral Reef Initiative for the South Pacific
CROP	Council of Regional Organisations of the Pacific
EDF	Economic Development Fund
FFA	Forum Fisheries Agency
FRANZ	France, Australia, New Zealand Arrangements
MSG	Melanesian Spearhead Group
NFIP	Nuclear Free and Independent Pacific, anti-nuclear NGO
OCO	Oceania Customs Organisation
PACER	Pacific Agreement on Closer Economic Relations
PECC	Pacific Economic Cooperation Council
PICTA	Pacific Island Countries Trade Agreement
PIDP	Pacific Islands Development Program
PIF	Pacific Islands Forum (formerly South Pacific Forum (SPF), 1971–2000)
PITA	Pacific Islands Telecommunications Association
PPA	Pacific Power Association
PREPARE	Pacific Regional Endeavour for an Appropriate Response to Epidemics
RAMSI	Regional Assistance Mission to the Solomon Islands
SOPAC	Secretariat of the Pacific Applied Geoscience and Technology Division
SPC	Secretariat of the Pacific Community (formerly South Pacific Commission, 1947–1998)
SPF	South Pacific Forum
SPNWFZ	South Pacific Nuclear Weapons Free Zone Treaty
SPREP	Secretariat of the Pacific Regional Environment Program
SPTO	South Pacific Tourism Organisation

International and Australian institutions

ACP	EU Africa–Caribbean–Pacific developing country assistance program
ANSTO	Australian Nuclear Science and Technology Organisation
C24	Committee of 24, or Special Committee on Decolonisation within the Fourth (Political) Committee of the United Nations
CSIRO	Commonwealth Scientific and Industrial Research Organisation
EC	European Commission
EEZ	Exclusive Economic Zone
EU	European Union
FAST	French Australian Science and Technology program
FAUST	French–Australian Seismic Transect, program exploring offshore resources around New Caledonia
NATO	North Atlantic Treaty Organisation
OCT	Overseas Countries and Territories of the EU members
OECD	Organisation for Economic Cooperation and Development
STABEX	EU support for agricultural exports
SYSMIN	EU financing for mining products
UNCLOS	United Nations Convention on the Law of the Sea
UNGA	United Nations General Assembly

New Caledonian institutions

ADCK	Agence de développement de la culture kanak (Agency for Kanak Cultural Development)
ADRAF	Agence de développement rural et d'aménagement foncier (Rural Development and Land Management Agency)
ALK	Académie des Langues Kanak (Academy of Kanak Languages)
Cadres d'Avenir	('future executives') or 400 cadres ('400 executives') positive action program for training and placement of Kanak executives
NMC	Nickel Mining Company, company involved in nickel mining in the north of New Caledonia
SLN	Société Le Nickel (The Nickel Company), French-owned nickel company
SMSP	Société Minière du Sud Pacifique (South Pacific Mining Company)
SNNC	Société du Nickel de la Nouvelle-Calédonie (New Caledonian Nickel Company), company involved in nickel mining in the north of New Caledonia

SOFINOR	Société d'Économie Mixte de Développement Contrôlée par la Province Nord (Mixed Economy and Development Company of the Northern Province)
SPMSC	Société de Participation Minière du Sud Calédonien (South [New] Caledonian Mining Participation Company)
STCPI	Société Territoriale Calédonienne de Participations Industrielles ([New] Caledonian Territorial Company for Industrial Participation)
Zonéco	Program for resource assessment of New Caledonia's EEZ

Vanuatu political groups, pre-independence

MANH	Mouvement Autonomiste des Nouvelles-Hébrides (Autonomist Movement of New Hebrides)
UCNH	Union des Communautés des Nouvelles-Hébrides (Union of the Communities of New Hebrides)
UPNH	Union de la Population des Nouvelles-Hébrides (Union of the New Hebrides Population)

New Caledonian political groups

AE	Avenir Ensemble (Future Together), pro-France party
AICLF	Association des Indigènes Calédoniens et Loyaltiens Français (Association of Indigenous Caledonians and French Loyalty Islanders), 1946–1953
APLC	Alliance pour la Calédonie (Alliance for [New] Caledonia), pro-France party
CE	Calédonie Ensemble ([New] Caledonia Together), pro-France party
CNDPA	Conseil National des Droits du Peuple Autochtone (National Council for Indigenous Peoples Rights), Kanak rights party
FCCI	Fédération des Comités de Coordination des Indépendantistes (Federation of the Independentist Coordination Committees), grouping of pro-independence parties
FI	Front Indépendantiste (Independence Front), pro-independence group
FLNKS	Front de Libération Nationale Kanak et Socialiste (Kanak Socialist National Liberation Front), pro-independence group
FN	Front National (National Front), pro-France group
FNSC	Front National pour une Nouvelle Société Calédonienne (National Front for a New Caledonian Society), pro-France group
FULK	Front Uni de Libération Kanak (United Kanak Liberation Front), pro-independence

GFKEL	Groupe des Femmes Kanak et Exploitées (Group of Kanak and Exploited Women)
LKS	Libération Kanak Socialiste (Socialist Kanak Liberation) pro-independence party
MCF	Mouvement Calédonien Français (French Caledonian Movement) pro-France party
MDD	Mouvement de la Diversité (Diversity Movement), pro-France party
Palika	Parti de libération Kanak (Kanak Liberation Party) pro-independence party
PFK	Parti Fédéral Kanak (Kanak Federal Party) pro-independence party
PSC	Parti Socialiste Calédonie ([New] Caledonian Socialist Party), pro-independence party
PT	Parti Travailliste (Labour Party), pro-independence party
RDO	Rassemblement Démocratique Océanien (Democratic Oceanic Party), pro-independence party
Rheebu Nhuu	('eye of the land') Kanak-based movement to protect the environment in the wake of nickel production
RPC	Rassemblement Pour la Calédonie (Rally for [New] Caledonia), pro-France party formed by Jacques Lafleur in 2006
RPCR	Rassemblement Pour la Calédonie dans la République (Rally for [New] Caledonia within the Republic), pro-France party formed by Jacques Lafleur in 1977 and re-named R-UMP in 2004
R-UMP	Rassemblement – UMP (Rally – Popular Union Movement), pro-France party
UC	Union Calédonienne ([New] Caledonian Union), pro-autonomy 1953–1977; pro-independence party from 1977
UC Renouveau	Union Calédonienne Renouveau (Renewed [New] Caledonian Union), pro-independence party
UICALO	Union des Indigènes Calédoniens Amis de la Liberté dans l'Ordre (Union of Indigenous [New] Caledonian Friends of Liberty in Order), 1946–1953
UNCT	Une Nouvelle-Calédonie pour Tous (A New Caledonia for All)
UNI	Union Nationale pour l'Indépendance (National Union for Independence), pro-independence party
UPAE	Union Pour un Avenir Ensemble (Union for a Future Together) pro-France party
UPM	Union Progressiste Mélanésienne (Melanesian Progressive Union), pro-independence party
USTKE	Union Syndicale des Travailleurs Kanaks et des Exploités (Federation of Unions of Kanak and Exploited Workers)

Glossary and acronyms

French Polynesian political groups and expressions

Ai'a Api	(New Homeland), pro-autonomy party of Emile Vernaudon, in various alliances
Fetia Api	(New Star), pro-France party of Philip Schyle,
FLP	Front de Libération de la Polynésie (Polynesian Liberation Front), pro-independence party; precursor to Oscar Temaru's Tavini
Here Ai'a	Centre-left party
Ia Mana Te Nunaa	(Power to the People), early pro-independence party
Iorea Te Fenua	(Land and Heart), pro-France party of Jean-Christophe Bouissou
O Porinetia to Tatou Ai'a	(Polynesia is Our Country), pro-France party of Gaston Song
Rautahi	(Unity), pro-France party of Jean-Christophe Bouissou
RDPT	Rassemblement démocratique des populations tahitiennes (Democratic Assembly of the Tahitian Peoples)
Tahiti Nui	(Greater Tahiti), proposal for a Noumea-type accord for French Polynesia, and a proposed alternative name for French Polynesia
Tahoeraa Huira'atira	(People's Assembly), pro-France party led by Gaston Flosse
Tavini Huira'atira no Te Ao Maohi	Serviteur du Peuple (Polynesian People's Servant Party) pro-independence party led by Oscar Temaru
Te Aia Api	(New Fatherland), early pro-autonomy party
Te E'a Api	(New Way), early pro-autonomy party
Te Here Ai'a	(Love of Fatherland), early pro-autonomy party
Te Tiarama	pro-France party of Tahoeraa dissidents
To Tatou Ai'a	(Our Land), pro-France coalition led by Gaston Tong Sang
UPLD	Union pour la Démocratie (Union for Democracy), coalition led by Oscar Temaru comprising pro-independence and pro-autonomy parties
UT-UDR	Union Tahitienne — Union pour la Défense de la République (Tahitian Union — Union for the Defence of the Republic), early pro-France party; precursor to Flosse's Tahoeraa
UT-UNR	Union Tahitienne — Union pour la Nouvelle République (Tahitian Union — Union for the New Republic), early pro-France party

Maps

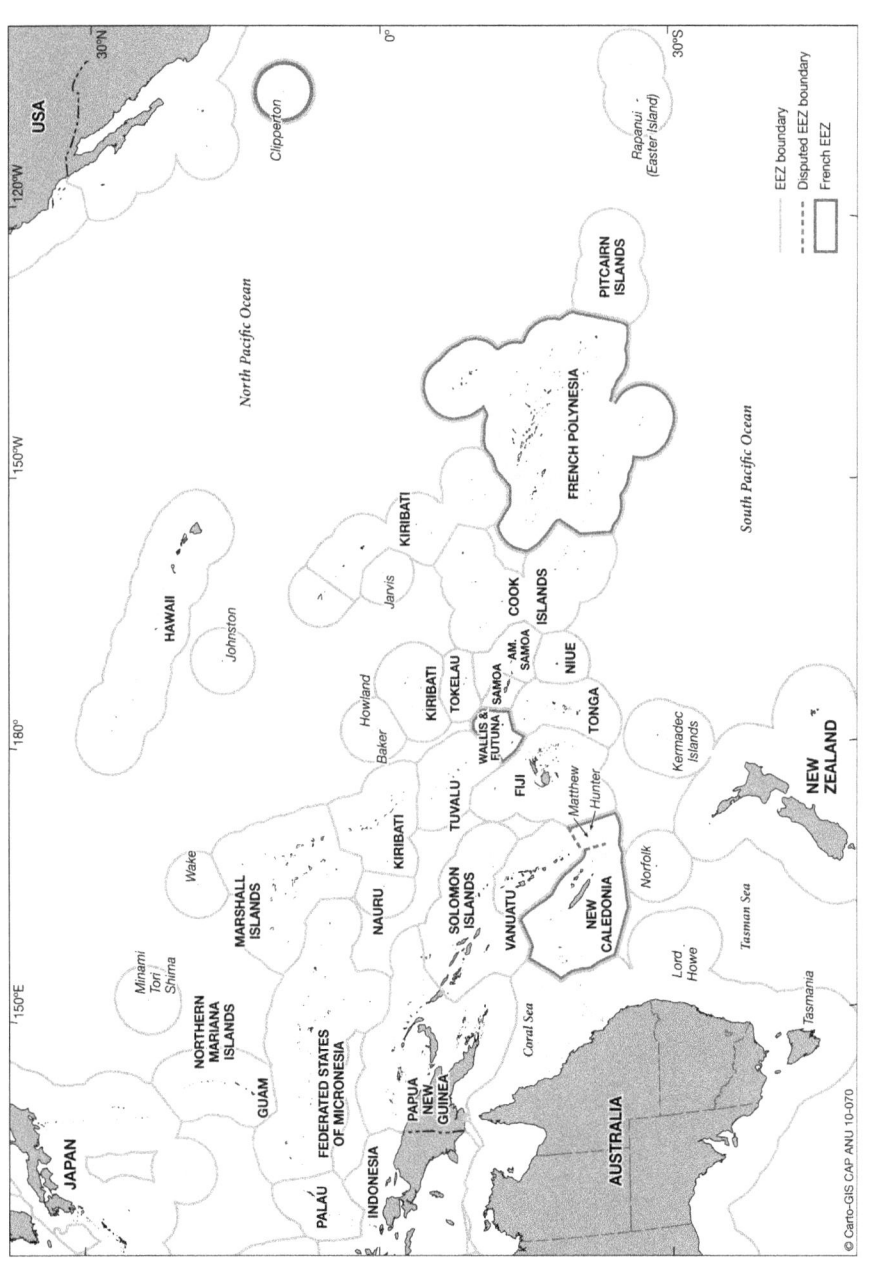

Map 1 France in the South Pacific, including Exclusive Economic Zones

Source: Cartographic & GIS Services, ANU College of Asia and the Pacific, The Australian National University

France in the South Pacific: Power and Politics

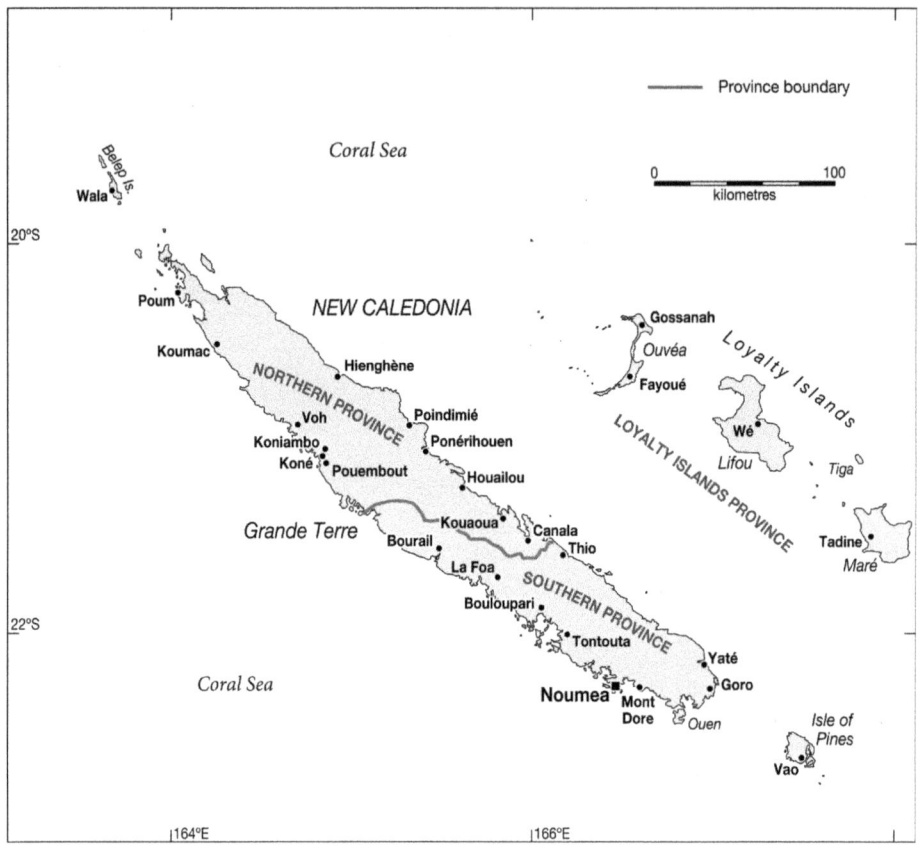

Map 2 New Caledonia

Source: Cartographic & GIS Services, ANU College of Asia and the Pacific, The Australian National University

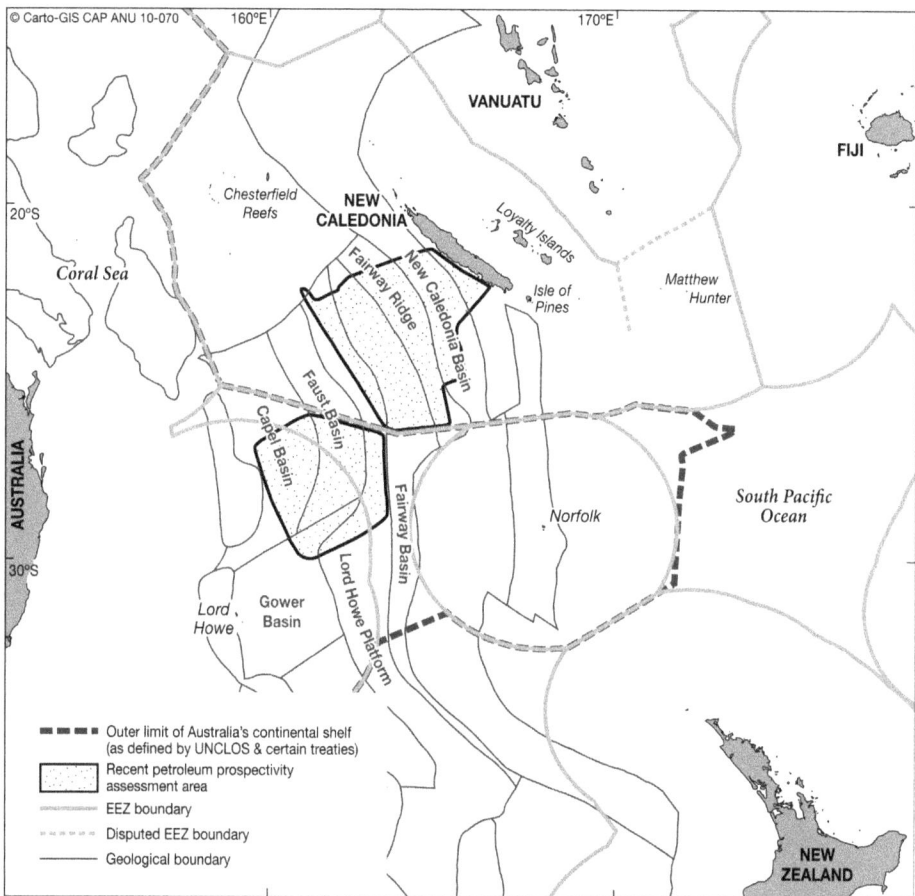

Map 3 Location of hydrocarbons off New Caledonia

Note: Shaded areas indicate areas of recent petroleum prospectivity assessment by the Geological Survey of New Caledonia and Geoscience Australia, targeting known areas of comparatively thick sedimentary accumulations with likely petroleum potential

Source: Nouzé 2009; Geoscience Australia

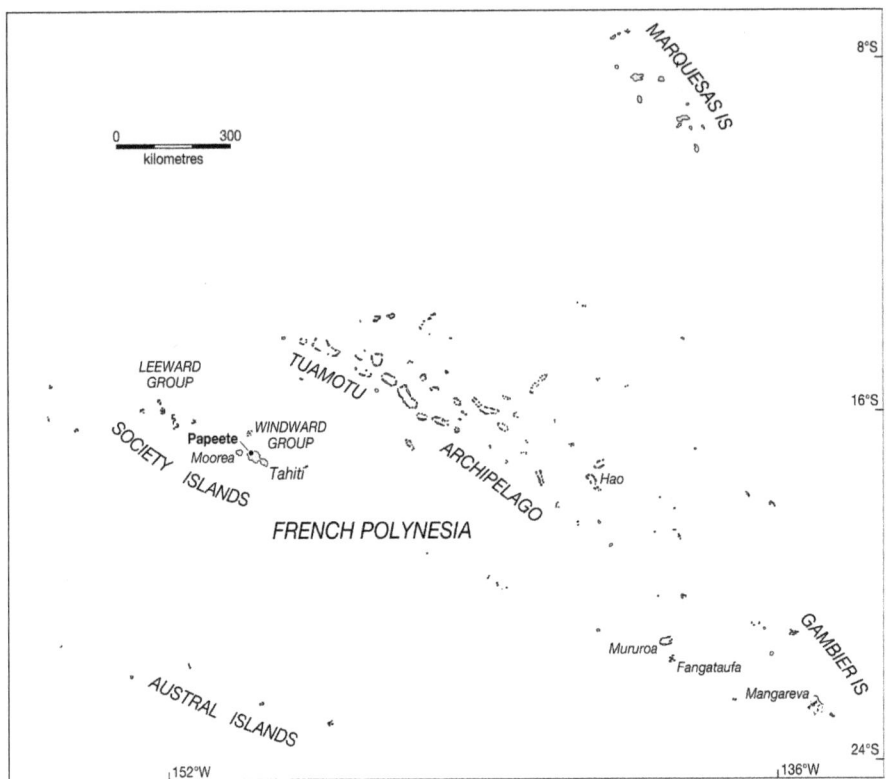

Map 4 French Polynesia

Source: Cartographic & GIS Services, ANU College of Asia and the Pacific, The Australian National University

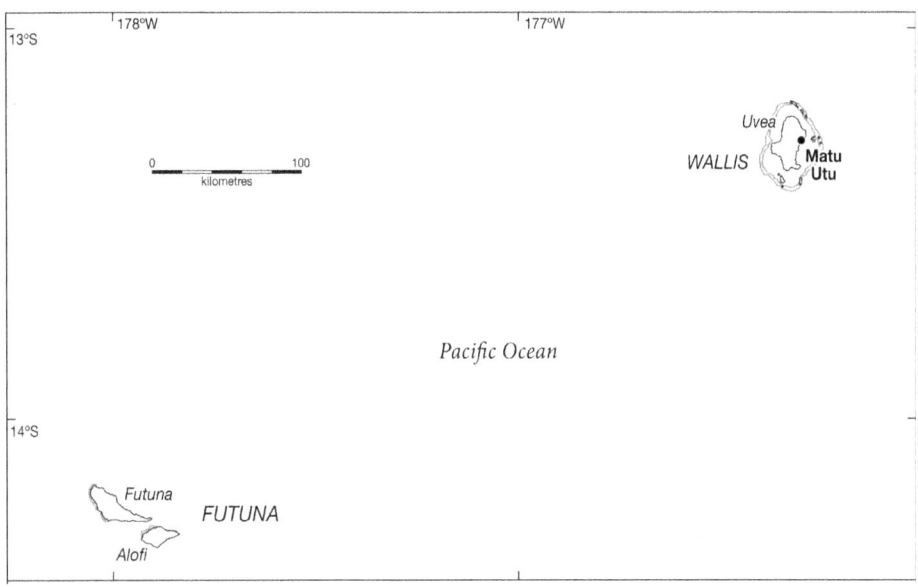

Map 5 Wallis and Futuna

Source: Cartographic & GIS Services, ANU College of Asia and the Pacific, The Australian National University

Introduction

'Nous devons gérer les révolutions que nous ne pouvons pas éviter'

'We must manage those revolutions we can't avoid'[1]

The study and awareness in Australia of France's presence and influence in the South Pacific have waned since France ended its controversial nuclear testing in French Polynesia in 1996 and seriously addressed Kanak demands for independence in New Caledonia through the Matignon and Noumea accords from 1988 to 1998.

Few Australians are aware of the fact that France, present in its South Pacific entities New Caledonia, French Polynesia and Wallis and Futuna,[2] is one of Australia's closest neighbours. New Caledonia is only two and a half hours flying time from Brisbane, but its name is less familiar to most Australians than the names of the Solomon Islands, Fiji, or even Tonga much further away. In recent years, nightly regional weather reports of the Australian television channel, SBS, regularly omitted New Caledonia from their forecasts, and presenters pointed from Sydney across to Fiji, without reference to the long cigarette-shaped main island of New Caledonia they traversed along the way. Including their maritime zones (Exclusive Economic Zones or EEZ), the three French Pacific entities stretch from east of Queensland to well over halfway across the Pacific. New Caledonia[3] and French Polynesia, respectively, bookend the South Pacific region, with Wallis and Futuna at the centre. France also possesses Clipperton Island, an uninhabited atoll southwest of Mexico, which is administered by the French authorities in French Polynesia.

For the last two decades, relative calm and stability have prevailed in the three French South Pacific entities. But in the two principal French Pacific collectivities, New Caledonia and French Polynesia, there are inherent instabilities. Administered by posted French officials, side by side with elected local governments, they each have large indigenous populations and a history of protest and violence, and are inexorably anchored in their geographic region with links to neighbouring populations. Managing expectations within France

---

1   Edgard Pisani, interview with Hugh White, then *Sydney Morning Herald* reporter, 1985.
2   With a constitutional change in 2003, under Article 74 of the French Constitution, French Polynesia and Wallis and Futuna became overseas collectivities or *collectivités d'outre-mer* (COM), and New Caledonia has a *sui generis* status as *collectivité spécifique* by virtue of section XIII of the Constitution (Faberon and Ziller, 2007, 3). They will collectively be referred to as entities or collectivities. The South Pacific region will be considered to represent the regions encompassed by the members of the Secretariat of the Pacific Community and the Pacific Islands Forum. Translations of French terms will be the author's own.
3   Which includes the islands of Walpole, Belep, Huon, Surprise, Chesterfield, Astrolabe, Bellone, and Matthew and Hunter (or Fearn), the latter claimed by both France and Vanuatu.

and the region of increasing autonomy has called for innovation and flexibility. By the 1990s, the French were providing such a response, but only after serious opposition, including violence, in New Caledonia; a prolonged campaign in French Polynesia against nuclear testing there; and, concerted regional action and international criticism. Since it stopped nuclear testing in French Polynesia in 1996, and negotiated a renewed agreement — the Noumea Accord — transferring some autonomy and deferring a vote on independence in New Caledonia, France has generally maintained a creative, innovative approach for most of the last two decades. As regional leader and close neighbour, Australia has supported and encouraged France in these efforts.

But cracks are appearing. Instability in government has characterised French Polynesian governance since 2004. Critical deadlines are approaching in New Caledonia, Australia's near neighbour. There is a new generation of leaders in France and, given the priority that France traditionally gives to its role in Europe, and its other domestic political and economic challenges, it is not certain that the solutions of the past will provide continued predictability and stability in the future. Nor even that France will remain in the region or, if so, on what terms.

Generally, very little has been written about the recent evolution of France's engagement in the South Pacific region. Strong views about the pros and cons of France's controversial engagement in nuclear testing and the decolonisation of New Caledonia generally formed the basis of English and French language academic writings in the 1980s and 1990s. Since then, much of the commentary and academic literature on contemporary France in the South Pacific has emanated from the French Pacific collectivities themselves, or metropolitan France, and most is in the French language.[4] In general, Australian academics and journalists writing on the South Pacific are restricted by language from exploring the French-language resources. This means that the complexities surrounding the French entities, and their role in the region, risk being overlooked by Australian policymakers. It also means that, for French readers, some regional perspectives, including Australian perspectives, have been represented generally from a French viewpoint. Moreover, in the recent French-language literature, the voice of indigenous people is notably absent.[5] Thus, this literature tends to favour, or assume, the continued presence of France, and to paint an unalloyed positive

---

4   A decade of analysis in English in the 1980s by Australia-based writers including journalist Nic Maclellan (often in collaboration in both languages with French academic Jean Chesneaux), John Connell, Robert Aldrich, Stewart Firth, Stephen Henningham, Stephen Bates, and Helen Fraser, abated by the mid 1990s. While Maclellan continues to write on the subject, along with Hawaii-based David Chappell and Quebec-based Eric Waddell, most recent writings are primarily in French, including by Paul de Deckker, Alain Christnacht, Jean-Pierre Doumenge and François Doumenge, Isabelle Cordonnier, Jean-Yves Faberon, Mathias Chauchat, Pierre Cadéot, Nathalie Mrgudovic, Jean-Marc Regnault, Frédéric Angleviel, and Sarah Mohamed-Gaillard.
5   Indigenous views are not prolific. They are generally reported through publications such as the daily *Les Nouvelles Calédoniennes* and *La Dépêche de Tahiti* or New Caledonia's cultural periodical *Mwà Véé*; party

picture of France and its policies in its collectivities and in the wider region. The general consensus in the recent French literature is that the bad old days are behind France, and France, with its reformed policies, is now a welcome, unreservedly positive influence in the region.[6] With its diplomatic attention focused on trouble spots elsewhere in the Pacific, the Australian Government tends to concur in this view.[7]

This book questions this assumption. Reflecting the experience of the author, an Australian former diplomat, it focuses on broad strategic positions and practical policy. It is based on an examination of the available literature, particularly the contemporary literature, but also draws on interviews with key figures in Paris, the French collectivities and in Australia, not only during the course of research, but also during a three-year posting as Australia's Consul-General in the French Pacific collectivities, based in Noumea, from 2001 to 2004. It starts with a review of the history and rationale underpinning France's South Pacific presence, and considers future directions and challenges, in the broad context of regional security. It will present for the English language reader some of the thinking evident in recent French language literature to add to understanding of contemporary French policy. Finally, it signposts areas for further attention by Australian students of international relations, in an area that has generally been neglected but that offers significant rewards in terms of its direct relevance to Australian interests.

As set out in Chapter 1, history suggests that France has as much right to be present in the region as Australia does (an assertion that was much disputed during the 1980s and early 1990s when France's policies were opposed in the region). France has been in the region as long as any other European power. It has invested significant financial, political and human resources in ensuring a continued presence. Securing the Matignon/Noumea Accords in New Caledonia and statutory reform in French Polynesia enabled France to claim, as did Louis Le Pensec, then Minister for Overseas France,[8] that its presence is based on the democratic will of the people in its Pacific collectivities, including their indigenous peoples (Le Pensec, 1990). In recent years France has sought to improve its image and engagement in the broader region.

---

websites such as Palika's journal.kanal.org; or, through cultural writings such as those by poet and politician, Déwé Gorodey. Even the views of Kanak leaders Jean-Marie Tjibaou and Paul Néaoutyine are recorded primarily in collections of their interviews (see References and bibliography).

6 Evident in the assertion by former Prime Minister Michel Rocard in a forward to Nathalie Mrgudovic's work, *La France dans le Pacifique Sud: Les enjeux de la puissance* (2008), that France had passed 'from the ranks of detested power … to one more like that of big sister' (13).

7 Then Parliamentary Secretary for Pacific Affairs Duncan Kerr, on 18 November 2008, spoke of Australia's 'strong appreciation for the role of France in the region supporting the region's security and development' and said he was 'convinced … that genuine integration is the key to a stable and prosperous future here [in New Caledonia]', media release, Department of Foreign Affairs and Trade, 18 November 2008.

8 'Overseas France' will be used as an equivalent to France's use of the term *L'Outre-mer*, or overseas dependencies.

One weakness in this argument is that the democratic will of the people in its Pacific collectivities is yet to be fully tested on the subject of their future status relative to France. Ideas about independence, decolonisation and emancipation are still evolving in the Pacific collectivities. Both French Polynesia and Wallis and Futuna look to New Caledonia to set the pace of their own future status. In French Polynesia, increasing support for pro-independence parties seeking, at the least, the autonomy measures accorded to New Caledonia, has been frustrated by pro-France pressure and marked by outbursts of violence and ongoing political instability. The tiny collectivity of Wallis and Futuna, ruled by an alliance of kings, church and State, is dependent on the continued prosperity of New Caledonia, where most of its people work. And, in New Caledonia, the democratically endorsed Noumea Accord and its suite of irreversible provisions for increased autonomy is yet to be fully implemented and is a transition measure only, on the future of which critical votes have yet to be cast.

The argument is advanced that, central to France's continued positive influence and acceptance in its collectivities and in the region, will be democratic governance there, particularly France's ability to find a long-term democratic solution to the status of New Caledonia by 2018. The provisions of the Noumea Accord come to an end by 2018, with votes to be held on the future status of New Caledonia between 2014 and 2018 (although one senior French adviser has already suggested the vote could technically be held as late as 2023, Christnacht 2011).

Regional leaders, and elements of civil society, remain wary of France. Many remember the failed policies of the 1980s and early 1990s, when France was a force for instability in the region. While cautiously welcoming France's recent positive engagement, they hold high expectations for France's treatment of its collectivities, and its contribution to the economic development of the region. Paradoxically, the post-colonial instabilities within the independent island countries of the Pacific intensify their leaders' expectations of France and its entities. This is particularly true of leaders of the Melanesian countries of Papua New Guinea, Vanuatu, Solomon Islands, and Fiji. In these Melanesian countries, important developments relating to the assertion of indigenous claims are evolving in parallel with New Caledonia's transition processes and deadlines under the Noumea Accord, creating their own uncertainties and potential for ongoing instability. Fiji, prey to government by military coup, is seeking a workable long-term democratic process to address the claims of all elements of its population, a population as ethnically divided as New Caledonia's. In the wake of internal division, the future of the Solomon Islands and the Regional Assistance Mission there is yet to be resolved permanently. Papua New Guinea has managed violent opposition to government policies in Bougainville by drawing partly upon the Noumea Accord model, providing for progressive autonomy with its own electoral deadlines falling due from 2011 to 2016, coincident with the Noumea Accord deadlines. West Papuan claims for independence from Indonesia remain a fractious issue for many regional Melanesians.

All these countries are members of the Melanesian Spearhead Group (MSG), which was formed to support Kanak claims in New Caledonia. The MSG has shifted its focus to economic issues in recent years, but it remains a forum for Melanesian expression on regional issues, and it remains watchful of outcomes in New Caledonia.[9] The Pacific Islands Forum (PIF) and the United Nations (UN) Committee on Decolonisation, while relatively dormant on the issue in recent years, retain a watching brief over New Caledonia. The positive relationships that France has fostered in the region and, by extension, the role of Europe and the effectiveness of the European Union (EU) in the South Pacific, which France has led, are all at stake as the future of New Caledonia unfolds.

Strategic benefits for France

France's Pacific presence represents a global strategic asset. Its Pacific entities are a key link in its worldwide chain of overseas possessions, with the potential for mismanagement to set off domino reactions elsewhere along the chain. Retaining a physical global presence has lent weight to France's claim to continue as one of only five powerful Permanent Members of the UN Security Council wielding a veto in the UN, at a time when the composition of that group is under discussion. Its sovereignty in the Pacific, and naval presence there, though small, mean France can bring a unique perspective to its North Atlantic Treaty Organisation (NATO) membership including its renewed participation in the High Command. As a leading EU nation, France's Pacific possessions provide an important support basis for activities such as the European space program.

Within the Pacific, the resident presence of France enables it to play a significant strategic role complementary to that of regional allies — the United States, Australia, New Zealand, and Japan — and potentially balancing the influence of newcomers to the region, such as China, at a time of global power shifts.

For France, New Caledonia represents a source of significant strategic resources such as nickel (it is believed to represent 30–40 per cent of the world's nickel and the third largest world's reserves) and potentially petroleum (there are signs of hydrocarbons in the basins off New Caledonia and Australia). New Caledonia, along with French Polynesia and Wallis and Futuna, offer France the potential

---

9   The MSG sent a visiting mission to New Caledonia in June 2010 to assess the implementation of France's promises under the Noumea Accord.

resources of their vast Pacific maritime EEZ. Together, they contribute 7.6 m. sq. km. of France's total of 11.57 m. sq. km. of EEZ. Controlling these existing and potential assets positions France at the forefront of the global marketplace, at a time when new, long-term supplies of resources and energy are in demand.

Strategic benefits for Australia and the region

The region-wide and global dimensions of France's presence have specific security implications for the region, particularly for Australia as leading power of the region. France's responsibility for the smooth administration of its three collectivities in the Pacific has meant that, for the last two decades, Australia could devote its diplomatic and development cooperation effort elsewhere in the Pacific. Broadly, as noted by the Australian Government's White Paper on Foreign Affairs and Trade, 'instability in the South Pacific negatively affects Australia's ability to protect its eastern approaches' (Foreign Affairs and Trade 2003, 20). In crude terms, if the French were to leave, there would be three more potentially fragile island economies on Australia's doorstep, and considerable demands on Australia's diplomatic energy and resources to ensure their development and stability appropriate for its domestic security.

Australia and New Zealand together could never match the over $A4.6 billion[10] per year that France has put into its Pacific entities. Without these inputs, there would be an inevitable weakening of these economies, with resultant security vulnerabilities for the region, and Australia. Whereas the populations of the French Pacific collectivities represent less than six per cent of the population of the South Pacific countries in the Secretariat for the Pacific Community (SPC), or 515,000 of a total population of 9.1 million of all SPC island member countries, they currently have the highest standard of living of the Pacific island entities, with per capita incomes exceeding those of New Zealand (SPC figures from October 2006, website <http://www.spc.in> accessed December 2008), due largely to significant French financial inflows. An unstable New Caledonia on its doorstep would impose urgent demands on Australia, within the already tenuous Melanesian 'arc of instability' that embraces its northeast shores. Weak independent states of French Polynesia and Wallis and Futuna would add further to the demands, not only on Australia and New Zealand, but on regional Pacific organisations, the PIF, SPC, and the multiple regional organisations under the Council of Regional Organisations of the Pacific (CROP).

A second related factor is the regional burden-sharing that France has provided, especially in recent years. For Australia, in whose charge the main weight of

---

10   EUR 2.65 billion in 2008 alone, see note 1 Chapter 6, explaining conversion rates.

development and security of the island states remains, the political and economic resources of a major European state, with a regional presence accepted by the wider region, are welcome contributions to the region. Apart from up to $A146 million it provides annually to numerous regional agencies and bilaterally, France, as a founding EU member, has been a prime instigator of the EU's Pacific island development assistance programs. France is well placed to improve the effectiveness and size of EU contributions to the region.

France's presence carries strategic significance in the region. While the importance of the French collectivities in protecting sea routes and providing re-supply bases has diminished with global and technological change, that role remains. Noumea provided an important staging point for Australian ships during the 2006 Fiji coup and in the evacuation of injured servicemen when a Blackhawk helicopter crashed into a destroyer at that time. The presence of several thousand skilled and trained military personnel of a western ally, at the western and eastern ends of the Pacific in Noumea and Papeete, is a regional security asset for Australia. The French were the first physically to respond to Australia's call for support in East Timor in 1999, being able to send a vessel that was already in the region.

And the future presence of France in the collectivities, if made on a clear basis of choice governed by democratic principle, would constitute a belt of western and European interest and values in the region at a time when northern Asian interests are changing, with resource-hungry China turning its attention to the South Pacific.

Global security is now determined by more than military might. It also involves good governance, successful environmental management and a predictable resource and energy supply. The French entities currently enjoy generally democratic government and a French justice system, which accommodates local custom. They are a potential vehicle for French and local scientific and technical research and collaboration addressing major global environmental issues including climate change, so critical to Pacific islanders. Their extensive maritime zones, backed by French investment, represent potentially valuable, albeit unchartered, seabed resources at a time when the world is re-thinking its long-term future energy and mineral needs.

In the broader Pacific region the predictabilities of the past are giving way to the challenges of the future. The immediate post-colonial period is behind it, and the effects of globalisation, while they present opportunities, also highlight weaknesses and vulnerabilities, as the global financial crisis has shown. Environmental issues present unique challenges for the island states. Concerns of traditional donors about governance problems, with their negative impact on the effectiveness of development cooperation that leave the island states open to the import of terrorism, raise complex security concerns. All of these factors have heightened the stark reality of the region's poverty and dependence on patron states. Meeting these challenges region-wide requires flexible approaches to cooperation and governance.

The conjunction of political and economic change within France, the effects of developments such as the global financial crisis and climate change on the wider Pacific region, and Australia's own growing strategic interest in France's democratically based presence, has led to a narrowing of the difference between the interests of France and those of Australian and other regional governments, providing scope for closer cooperation in new areas and new ways

With much depending on the *democratic* presence of France in the region, France's securing a successful, democratic outcome in New Caledonia will be the key, both to France continuing to derive strategic benefits in the region, and for Australia's ongoing regional security interests. Addressing ongoing instabilities in French Polynesia and ensuring continued tranquility in Wallis and Futuna, whose statutory framework dates from 1961, will be important. But these two collectivities look to New Caledonia as a model. And New Caledonia is in the midst of an agreed transition process, with specific deadlines for a democratic outcome, which is being watched by regional leaders. With its mineral wealth, status as France's regional base for its military and scientific research presence, and its proximity to the largest regional power, Australia, New Caledonia represents a significant strategic investment for France. As French academic Xavier Pons so eloquently put it when writing in 1991, New Caledonia's importance is that of 'its potential as a powder keg, which, if it were to explode, might contribute to destabilise the whole region' (in Aldrich 19911, 45). This remains as true now as it was then.

After the Noumea Accord?

In seeking a long-term solution to the future status of New Caledonia, French and local leaders have a range of alternatives to consider, including by drawing from the options already in operation in the Pacific island countries. Independence is not the only option and, indeed, it is seen as unlikely by many, in view of the demographic and economic realities in New Caledonia. But it is an option which some in New Caledonia will not give up lightly, having been willing to shed blood for it only 20 years ago.

With the future arrangements in New Caledonia, its pre-eminent Pacific entity, to be decided from 2014 to 2018, it is a propitious time to review elements of France's presence in the South Pacific, its official actions and policies, motivations, and its relationship with the wider region; and to reflect on future challenges, risks and options. To set this analysis in context, Part I will present a brief overview of the history of France's presence in the Pacific, from the time of the first French pirates there in the early seventeenth century; to the establishment of a colonial presence which could have easily included both Australia and New Zealand; the pivotal World War II period which engaged Australian strategic interest for the first time and when the relatively egalitarian American presence catalysed autonomy and independence demands; and the troubled post-war years when France's view of its presence as a projection of its worldwide middle power status reinforced its pursuit of policies overriding local sensitivities, creating problems to which it was required to respond.

Part II will examine the period after France's cessation of its nuclear tests (1996) and the conclusion of the Noumea Accord in 1998, a time when significant statutory change has been implemented in both French Polynesia and New Caledonia, a transition that is still in process. It will also survey France's policy towards the region as a whole, including the greater engagement of the EU there.

Part III will identify France's continuing motivations for staying in the region; some of the risks and uncertainties surrounding those interests; and the challenges for the future, including options for New Caledonia, and for how France might work with Australia and other regional countries to advance shared objectives.

Part I — France in the Pacific to the 1990s

1. The French Pacific presence to World War II

The image of the French in Australia is a complex mix of impressions. Australians see the French as a cultivated people, with a passion for perfection in knowledge and in the day-to-day elements of life whereby clothing becomes *haute couture* and food *haute cuisine*, a finely tuned sense of the romantic and the amorous, a healthy not to say excessive suspicion of all things Anglo-Saxon, an uncompromisingly juridical approach to life, an almost manic respect for the ambiguities and inflections of their own language, and a strong sense of religiosity associated with the Catholic church. There is a quixotic element to Australians' idea of the French, in whom Latin emotions are perceived to take over and at times inveterate stubbornness can give way to a disarming desire to right wrongs.

At the same time, in foreign policy circles, the image of France is that of a country single-minded in its pursuit of its national interests, to the extent that it can ride apparently roughshod, and unapologetically, over the interests of others. To the more initiate Australian, the French maintain such a pride for their own culture and their civilising mission that they have coined a phrase, *rayonnement de la culture française,* which is untranslatable in other languages but which conveys a sense of the transfiguring radiation of their culture, as if from a divine presence.

And, ultimately, France represents, for most Australians, the notions of *liberté, égalité et fraternité*, a semantic trinity that was first coined by France, to which Australians, often unwittingly, owe the basis of their own national institutions, and to which values France is held, often to higher standards than others.

In the long stretch of the history of France's presence in the South Pacific region, all of these qualities in their contradictoriness and ambiguity are present in abundance. The story is one of courage, endurance, failure, at times brilliant success, stubbornness and, overall, of extensive financial and cultural investment, all of which have led to and characterise its presence there today. To examine this history, even in a cursory way, is to embark on an adventure as gripping as the history of Australia's British ancestors in its region, and just as important for Australians to understand because it has contributed to Australia's own national character and security. This chapter will look briefly at France's presence in the Pacific from the earliest contacts, and consider pivotal events in World War II, which shaped the nature of France's contemporary presence.

Earliest French contact with the Pacific

The earliest French engagement with the Pacific dated from the speculation about a southern land posed by a French monk, Lambert, in the eleventh century, which encouraged one of the first French explorers, Paulmier de Gonneville, to look for it in 1503. He found a southern land but lost all his records in a shipwreck in the English Channel after an encounter with pirates. His mysterious voyage inspired further efforts by the French, and others, to find the southern land (see Dunmore 1978, 1997 and Sankey 1991).

In the sixteenth and seventeenth centuries the Spanish and Dutch led the quest in the Pacific. But Frenchmen were also present, from the 19 French crew of Ferdinand Magellan's expedition in 1520, to voyages by Pierre-Olivier Malherbe, Jean-Baptiste de la Feuillade and Jean-Baptiste de Gennes in the seventeenth century. French pirates travelled there in the 1680s, with names like Passe-partout ('able to go anywhere'), Hallebarde ('halberd', a lethal sixteenth century weapon), and Vent-en-panne ('reviving wind'). Even then, roving French and British buccaneers had their fallings out, underpinned by their mainly Catholic French and Protestant British differences, a sign of things to come.

By the seventeenth and early eighteenth century, French exploration in the Pacific was characterised by patriotism marked by rivalry with other nationalities, shipwrecks, a missionary spirit and, later, by a certain commercial interest. But this period was not to see the effective establishment of a French presence. At this time, only privately funded French vessels travelled to the Pacific, leading to increasingly commercial activity.[1] The French India Company operated in the Pacific from 1706, establishing a critical new southern route, around the Cape of Good Hope, between America and Africa.

Growing French activity entailed difficulties with the dominant power, Spain, with whom France had to negotiate delicately, demonstrating the primordial effect of European political events and policy, which was to be a hallmark of France's presence in the South Pacific up to the present. Officially sanctioned French trade was interrupted briefly from 1713 when the Treaty of Utrecht ended the Spanish War of Succession, but resumed with renewed hostilities against Spain. By 1720, the French India Company controlled 300 ships and, between 1698 and 1725, at least 168 French ships were known to have sailed the Pacific.

---

1   These traders included Jacques Gouin de Beauchesne (1698), Noel Danycan (1701), Julien Bourdas (1701), Nicolas de Frondat (1707) and Michel-Joseph du Bocage de Bléville (who discovered Clipperton Island in 1711, which remains French today).

This period also saw the beginnings of scientific and strategic interest in the Pacific, with voyages by scientists Louis Feuillet (who taught astronomy in Peru 1707–1712) and Amédée-François Frézier (1711–1717). The latter, an army defence specialist sent by Louis XIV to report on Spanish defences, drew the first reliable map of South America.

This was the time of the *philosophes* in Paris, who debated issues of the day in private *salons* informally sanctioned by the King. In 1756 the *Histoire des navigations aux terres australes* (*History of Navigation in the Southern Lands*) by Charles de Brosses, a shareholder of the French India Company, advocated exploration, knowledge and commerce rather than conquest; colonial establishments to provide bases for French fleets; and even suggested penal settlement as a substitute for penal punishment, all features to be taken up in subsequent years. De Brosses first coined the terms 'Australasia' and 'Polynesia' (see Bachimon 1990, 18). Much of his work was controversially pirated by Englishman John Callander in his 1768 *Terra Australia Cognita*, an act that can be seen as a precursor to future rivalries characterising the opening up of the South Pacific to Europe.

From exploration to staking French claims

The voyage by Louis-Antoine de Bougainville to the South Pacific from 1766 to 1769 is seen as a turning point for the French. It embodied many of the features of later, and even contemporary, French engagement in the region. Bougainville set out to establish a French South Pacific settlement to compensate France for the loss of Canada (he had been an aide to General Montcalm and negotiated the French evacuation after France's defeat there), setting a trend whereby French action in the Pacific would be motivated by balancing losses elsewhere (for example in Algeria and Indochina in the twentieth century, see below). He became enmeshed in rivalries back in Europe, provoking concern in Madrid and London after he successfully installed a French colony in the Falkland Islands, which was ultimately withdrawn. His 1766 voyage to the South Pacific, commissioned as a quid pro quo for the Falkland loss, led to his claim for France of the East Tuamotu islands in 1767, and then Tahiti in 1768, parts of what is now French Polynesia, when he established the quaint but symbolic pattern of French explorers making a written declaration of possession for France and burying it in a bottle. Bougainville was accompanied by a number of scientists, typical of French exploration teams. (His crew included many colourful characters, including the Prince of Orange and Nassau, and a woman disguised as a male valet. For interesting accounts of this, see Bougainville 1772, 13, 301 and Cazaux 1995).

Bougainville created the image of Tahiti and the South Pacific as a place of sensuous and free living, which endures in French minds to this day. In his own words, a young Tahiti woman from the canoes surrounding Bougainville's vessels climbed aboard 'and negligently allowed her loincloth to fall to the ground … Sailors and soldiers hurried to get to the hatchway, and never was a capstan heaved with such speed' (cited by Dunmore who noted that 'On that day the legend of Tahiti was born', 1997, 48–49). He took a Polynesian, Ahutoru, back with him to Paris, who became the motif for the Rousseauist idea of the noble savage, his native islands the new Cythera.

Symbolic of future patterns, fate and British rivalry came into play. The British had beaten Bougainville to Tahiti, as their own Samuel Wallis had anchored there less than a year before; and Bougainville only narrowly missed discovering Australia, the Great South Land. Seventh, after his return in 1769, geostrategists in London and Paris were to see Tahiti as an important logistical staging post in the Pacific quest.

Subsequent French ventures were to reflect the hallmarks established by Bougainville. Jean-François-Marie de Surville in 1769 set off in search of a 'Davis Land', partly to trump the British who had reputedly found it, and discovered what is now the Solomon Islands, but, fatefully missing what is now Vanuatu, New Caledonia, and New South Wales, and missing Britain's Captain James Cook in northern New Zealand by only a few miles (Surville 1981). Yves-Joseph de Kerguelen discovered the islands that bear his name near Antarctica in 1771 and 1773, and he planted a bottled note of possession; the Kerguelen Islands remain a French possession, uninhabited and frequented only by scientists working there.

The next great French expedition to the southern ocean, by Jean-François Galoup de la Pérouse, was as grand, epochal and fateful as that of Bougainville (see La Pérouse 1832). It too was led by an aristocrat in pursuit of the glory of the fatherland, who was on a mission of scientific discovery (but not possession, as La Pérouse believed Europeans had no right to claim lands where inhabitants had worked and buried their ancestors (Dunmore 1977, 93)). La Pérouse landed in Botany Bay on 23 January 1788, only days after the British had arrived, and was charged to report on their activities. Despite rivalries, the British co-operated in providing support where necessary, taking French papers and letters back to France for La Pérouse and giving logistical support. The French chaplain, le Père Receveur, died and was buried ashore at Frenchman's Bay, now in the Sydney suburb of La Pérouse. He was the first French person to be buried in Australia.

La Pérouse's subsequent disappearance, on the way to what was known to be New Caledonia, already discovered by Cook in 1774, became a *cause célèbre* in France. While revolutionary events in France impeded further expeditions, determination to find out what happened to La Pérouse resulted in a voyage in 1791 by Joseph-Antoine Raymond Bruny d'Entrecasteaux, also accompanied by eminent scientists (see Horner 1996). Their research papers ended up in British hands after capture in the Atlantic, to be returned to France only after the intervention of Sir Joseph Banks, an outcome to be paralleled years later with research by Nicolas Baudin (see below). Amongst the seekers of the truth about La Pérouse were George Bass, Matthew Flinders, Louis de Freycinet, Louis Duperrey and Jules Dumont d'Urville. But it was France's fate to be gazumped by the British once more as it was an Englishman, Peter Dillon, who finally established that La Pérouse had been shipwrecked at Vanikoro, in what is now the Solomon Islands. The story is again one of adventure and rivalry (recounted by Dillon 1829 and, with poetic licence, Guillou 2000).

The La Pérouse expedition and its aftermath are emblematic of the dangers, risks, mystery and adventure that characterised and motivated European exploration at the time, and demonstrate as well the unusual mix of rivalry and unity of individual French and British explorers in pursuing goals in the region.

The French exploratory presence in the Pacific diminished in the late eighteenth century and early nineteenth century, with the preoccupations of the Revolution and its aftermath. The British remained active, and British–French rivalry intensified. The eponymous Étienne Marchand, a French trader, claimed possession of the Marquesas Islands in 1791, but had been preceded by an American, Joseph Ingraham, only months before.

Baudin, accompanied by 22 scientists, was commissioned in 1798 to circumnavigate Australia, although he, too, was gazumped by the British when Matthew Flinders got to the south of the continent before him (see Baudin Legacy Project website http://sydney.edu.au/arts/research/baudin/project). His accidental meeting of Flinders at what is now Encounter Bay is another example of fortuitous, amicable, but tardy French interaction with the British (which did not prevent the French from later arresting Flinders in Mauritius). Baudin died before returning to France, and had earlier sent back one of his ships with much of the expedition's research, which was captured by the British in the English Channel and, in a remarkable repetition of La Pérouse's experience, was only released through the intervention of Sir Joseph Banks. But British unease remained, and indeed was heightened by the publication of an account of the voyage by François Péron, using French geographical names instead of British ones (Australia was '*Terre Napoléon*'). French patriotism, and nostalgia was poignantly evident in the description of a meal Péron and his fellow scientist Freycinet shared with Tasmanian Aborigines, when the Frenchmen stood up and sang the *Marseillaise* (Chesneaux and Maclellan 1992, 55; Plomley 1983*).*

As if to underline their position as second-comer, free French access to Australia from the west ceased with Britain's taking of Ile de France in 1810, particularly after Napoleon's defeat at Waterloo in 1815.

In summary, France's exploration of the Pacific in the seventeenth and eighteenth centuries was characterised by scientific interest, the patronage of the King and government, a strong sense of national mission, a complex co-operative yet rival relationship with the British, who repeatedly beat them to the punch, and remarkable displays of courage and humanity in the face of loss of life, illness and disappointment. European politics and domestic preoccupations in France shaped the timing and nature of French exploration. The French made an invaluable contribution to scientific knowledge and especially in mapping the new lands at this time. While there were private, commercial ventures, notably at the end of the seventeenth century, and a century later, by Marchand, the main motivation was national prestige. This sense of national honour was only sharpened by the dominance of the British, both in Europe and in the new Pacific lands, into the early nineteenth century.

Consolidating a regional presence: Rivalry and ambiguity

France consolidated its presence in the Pacific in the nineteenth century. Its motivations were to establish supply points for its navy; to protect its nationals, mainly missionaries; and to assert sovereignty over its settlements, including a penal settlement in New Caledonia. There were commercial interests, but these were secondary. France's pursuit of these interests was characterised by an overriding pattern of ambiguities, often arising from political circumstances back home. It was one of the first to establish settlements and claim sovereignty over them, yet, once again, it also lost out to the British and Americans on numerous occasions. Its overall approach was one of determined power and ambition, yet combined with hesitation and short-term vision (see Chesneaux and Maclellan 1992, 62).

Early in the century, and mainly when the restored monarchy was in place, the eighteenth century tradition of scientific discovery continued to drive French expeditions.[2] But these were followed by ventures with more political objectives.[3] By the late 1840s, France had established consular representatives

---

2   These included expeditions by Freycinet (1817–1820), Duperrey (1822–1825), Bougainville's son Hyacinthe (1824–1826), and Cyrille La Place (1829–1831).
3   Including by Dumont d'Urville (1826–1829 and 1837–1840), August Nicolas de Vaillant (1836) and Abel Dupetit-Thouars, (1836–1840 and 1842–1843), whose uncle had failed in his efforts to search for La Pérouse (Chesneaux and Maclellan 1992, 56–57).

in Australia to safeguard its interests there, which comprised mainly looking after a small immigrant French community and providing intelligence for Paris (Aldrich 1990, 201).

Defending the missionary presence and the Pritchard affair

France's experience in establishing a foothold in the Pacific in the early nineteenth century was a mixed one. It was driven principally by its need to protect the interests of its nationals who were Catholic missionaries. Common challenges in the various French missionary settlements were first, establishing good relations with the locals and, second, securing a place in the face of competing activity by non-Catholic European missionaries who had usually arrived there first and were overwhelmingly British — which raised related political rivalries.

While France had missionary societies (from 1625, a Congregation of the Missions and, from 1663, a *Société des Missions Étrangères* (Foreign Missionary Society) in Paris), early ignorance about the great southern land and, later, the disruptions of the French Revolution to the status of the French clergy, impeded efforts to evangelise overseas, which meant they were relatively late arrivals to the Pacific, and resented by others already there. These tended to be British or American Protestants, present through the London Missionary Society (LMS), with representatives in Tahiti, Tonga and the Marquesas from 1796, and American groups in Hawaii and archipelagos to the east.

The first French attempt at religious activity was in Hawaii, when the chaplain aboard Freycinet's ship *Uranie* baptised the Chief Minister Kalanimoku at his request in 1819 (Dunmore 1997, 127). As a group of American Congregationalists arrived soon after, a local French resident, Jean-Baptiste Rives, urged the Paris Foreign Missionary Seminary to send French Catholic missionaries in 1824. The Sacred Heart 'Picpus' fathers (named after their Paris address) sent six missionaries to Honolulu in 1827, but they were not welcomed by Queen Kaahumanu, who had already been converted by the Americans. She expelled two of the priests, and sought to do the same when another arrived in 1835. The French captain Vaillant, in Honolulu during his Pacific voyage, was able to secure a rescinding of this expulsion order. When two more missionaries arrived in 1837, they were also expelled. Despite efforts by visiting French captain Dupetit-Thouars, this time the expulsion stuck. Captain Cyrille Laplace visited in 1839 and was able to negotiate freedom of religion for Catholics, along with trade rights equal to those of the British and Americans. The Picpus fathers returned in strength, one of whom was Father Damien, known for his work with lepers. Such was the influence of the French that their consul was appointed finance minister in Hawaii in 1863 and then foreign minister. A provisional government took power in 1893, however, and demanded American annexation of the islands.

The French were to experience similar contention when French Catholic missionaries arrived elsewhere, particularly in what is now French Polynesia, where the LMS had preceded them. These events were recorded by the LMS representative in Tahiti, Rev. George Pritchard (edited by de Deckker 1983; see also Newbury 1980 and Faivre 1953) and came to be known as the Pritchard affair.

Having alienated the LMS early by successfully displacing the group in the Gambier archipelago in 1834, the Picpus fathers landed at Tahiti in 1836, where the LMS had been established since 1797. The priests courted Queen Pomaré, provoking Pritchard's ire, resulting in the Queen expelling them back to the Gambiers. Pritchard was subsequently appointed British Consul, compounding French fears that the British were using religious differences to oust them from the Pacific. The American Consul, a Belgian called Jacques-Antoine Moerenhout, who was sympathetic to the French, informed a visiting French bishop about the priests' expulsion.

French Admiral Dupetit-Thouars, when he landed in Tahiti in 1838, was tasked to 'assert the status of France as a nation "which has the means and the will to ensure that its citizens everywhere are respected"'(Dunmore 1997 136 citing the captain's instructions). He undertook some complex diplomacy to secure a positive result for France, offering Pritchard and Moerenhout asylum aboard his ship should hostilities break out; and seeking from Queen Pomaré a letter of apology to King Louis-Philippe, monetary compensation, and a gun salute to the French flag. The Queen agreed to the terms, blaming Pritchard for the problems. In the end, in a sign of the way things would evermore be done in the French Pacific, Pritchard came up with the cash compensation himself and Dupetit-Thouars supplied the gunpowder for the gun salute, as the Queen did not have these resources. Moerenhout was appointed French Consul, having lost his American appointment after Pritchard had complained to Washington. Dupetit-Thouars subsequently negotiated a favoured-nation trade agreement for France, similar to that arranged by Laplace in Hawaii. And thus French honour was preserved.

But not for long. After Dupetit-Thouars' departure a prohibition order was issued against Catholic preaching and Laplace once again came to the rescue, in 1839, negotiating a freedom of religion clause in the order. Resentments between the British-led Protestants and the French Catholic fathers persisted. Dupetit-Thouars returned to Tahiti in 1842 to reinforce French rights, this time requiring the signing of a document placing Tahiti under French protection.

The Pritchard affair was significant in that rivalry and bitterness between the French and British, which underlay the events, persisted for years, up to the present (see, for example, the injunction of the President of the French national assembly to 'turn the page once and for all on the Pritchard affair', *Assemblée Nationale* hearings on France and the Pacific States 1996).

Elsewhere, similar problems simmered. In the Marquesas, years of resistance by non-Catholic missionaries from 1797 ended in 1838 with a successful implantation of Picpus missionaries at Tahuata, again negotiated by the resourceful Dupetit-Thouars (Dunmore 1997, 140). In Tonga, attempts by the Wesleyans, present from 1822, to resist French Marist activity persisted until 1861 when Marist Father Chevron obtained an edict allowing freedom for Catholics to practice their religion. Despite similar difficulties, by mid century, Catholic missions were established in New Caledonia (from 1843, but see below), Fiji (from 1844), Samoa (from 1845), and New Hebrides (from 1848). In many cases the intervention of officials and visiting French ships was necessary to protect the missionary presence.

The establishment of a French missionary presence in New Caledonia was difficult. A formal agreement was signed by the Melanesians, accepting French sovereignty, soon after the arrival of the Marist missionaries at Balade in the north, on 1 January 1844. But the settlement was abandoned from 1847 until 1851 after attacks by Melanesians (recounted in Delbos 2000, Chapter 1), but also because of concerns in Paris about alienating Britain after the Pritchard affair (see Colonisation, below). Later missionaries survived only after France's declaration of possession of the archipelago in 1853, and further contact by French ships. Earlier attempts by the LMS to establish a foothold in New Caledonia in 1840 and 1841 had not succeeded. LMS' Samoan teachers refused to land on Grande Terre, the main island, because of the ferocity of the locals; and the Isle of Pines settlement in 1841 was troubled. The LMS was more successful in establishing a presence in the Loyalty Islands from 1841, providing a further complication for the French in later years.

Similarly, in New Zealand, in 1832, English missionaries had resisted possible French influence with the arrival of Laplace and other French explorers, and a Wesleyan group had unsuccessfully sought to oust French priests. Marist Bishop Pompallier arrived in 1838 to find Protestant missionary societies ensconced, but met little overt opposition mainly because of the size and disparate leadership of the islands (Dunmore 1997, 142). Despite his strong influence in the north, where he conducted himself as a *de facto* government, the signing of the Treaty of Waitangi in 1840 ensured British political dominance. The French were, again, gazumped by the British.

The Marists were more successful in establishing ascendancy over the British in the islands of Wallis (named after the British adventurer Samuel Wallis) and Futuna in 1837. But, nonetheless, they too met a brutal reaction from the local inhabitants. Their Father Peter Chanel was to become the first Roman Catholic Pacific martyr, and later, saint, in 1841, at the hands of the King whose son he had converted. Remorse for this act was to see the entire population convert, which strengthened France's political influence there.

French Marists were to be less successful in the Solomons, where they tried to settle in various locations from 1845 but, by 1855, had given up. They did not attempt a presence in Papua New Guinea until 1881, on Thursday Island, and 1885, at Yule Island near Port Moresby, although they were in constant dispute with the British including through the Governor of Queensland who, in 1896, referred the differences to London and Rome.

The pattern of these experiences explains much about perceptions and contributions of the French in the Pacific in the first half of the nineteenth century. Overridingly, the Catholic religion came to be identified with French interests, and Protestantism with British or at least, in French eyes, Anglo-Saxon interests. While France succeeded in establishing its own presence in some settlements (French Polynesia, New Caledonia and Wallis and Futuna), it lost out in other places (Hawaii, New Zealand, for a time in French Polynesia, Papua New Guinea), in most cases to the British. The religious animosities and resentments on both sides underlie the emotion often attaching to French perceptions of Anglo-Saxons in the Pacific, and vice versa, persisting until this day. The assertion of a political interest in order to protect its nationals became a deep-seated rationale for its presence, and one which, it will be seen, has also persisted until today.

Colonisation

French acts of possession in the South Pacific were thus not unalloyed assertions of empire. France in the nineteenth century was motivated by a mission to bring what was seen as 'civilisation' or religion to the rest of the world and to protect its own nationals, as well as by national pride and a desire to rank with other rival imperial powers. Despite the difficulties of establishing and supporting the missionary presence in the face of rivals, France was the first to establish possession, 30 years in advance of other empire-builders (1842 in Tahiti, 1853 New Caledonia, 1858 Clipperton, and 1886 Wallis and Futuna; compared for example to Britain in Fiji, 1874, Tonga 1885 and Solomons 1890; Germany in New Guinea, 1885, and Samoa 1899; the United States in Hawaii, 1898, and Samoa 1899). France was also seen by other colonising powers as a force to fear and to counter. France, however, had also encountered failure along the way. Its failures can be attributed variously to the greater strength of its rivals and poor timing arising from preoccupations at home, but also, as will be seen, to indecision and hesitation. Fewer population pressures in France at this time, as opposed to elsewhere in Europe, and the country's engagement elsewhere (including Algeria), reduced the urgent practical need for it to establish settlements in the Pacific.

Apart from being beaten to the punch, as by the British in Tasmania and New Zealand, and by the British and Americans in Hawaii, the French sought on numerous occasions in Fiji, Tonga and Samoa to support Marist missionaries, without asserting its naval presence and, indeed, the suggestion of a French protectorate in Tonga was never realised. Despite proposals for French protectorates from French advisors and missionaries in the Easter Islands in 1885, and in the north of the Cook Islands, in 1888, annexation did not occur. This was largely because of indecision in Paris, perhaps informed by hesitancy about the relative lack of return for such distant engagement.

Indecision, competing interests and preoccupations, and half-heartedness in the capital also dictated the French approach to the possessions that they did establish. Working against French expansion in the Pacific were the extreme and constant political instability and changes of government in the motherland that characterised most of the century (certainly 1815–1880); the continual priority of European politics; the importance of colonial undertakings in Africa and Indochina; the reticence of authorities towards Catholic missionaries at the end of the century; and, the relative weakness of French commercial activity in the region.

Even where France did establish sovereignty, it did so only progressively and often after bartering with Germany and Britain: a Germany which successfully established its commercial enterprises from Apia to Fiji through to the Carolinas from 1857; and a Britain lobbied by its own colonies in Australia and New Zealand to entrench itself more deeply in the region. Just as European power relationships dictated the pace of French action in the Pacific when it was a Spanish lake, so the political chessboard in Europe affected the pattern of French annexations in the Pacific.

In what is now French Polynesia, while the Marquesas were annexed in 1842, Tahiti remained a protectorate until 1880, and Paris did not confirm a declaration by Dupetit-Thouars in 1842 in the wake of the Pritchard affair, which also had engaged American interests. The Gambiers were only annexed in 1881. French sovereignty in the Leeward Islands was set aside by agreement with the British in 1847, challenged by the Germans in 1879, proclaimed in 1880, and recognised internationally over Bora Bora, Huahiné and Raiatea only in 1888. Of the Australs, France formally annexed Rapa only in 1888, Remataru in 1900 and Ruratu in 1901, to avoid difficulties with Britain (for the same reasons France held back on annexing the Cook and Easter Islands, in the end losing out to Britain and Chile respectively, see Dunmore 1997, 203–04). As will be seen, the New Hebrides remained an arena of French–British rivalry well into the twentieth century. And, in New Caledonia, France's initial hoisting of the *tricolore* when first landing missionaries in 1843 was speedily negated by the capital, wary of putting the British further offside after the strains of the Pritchard affair in Tahiti. Official annexation of the main island, Grande Terre occurred only in 1853, and effective control of the Loyalty Islands, where the LMS was active, by 1865.

New Hebrides

France's administration of the New Hebrides was shaped by the complex British–French relationship, yet more indecision, and a liberal amount of innovation.

As in Wallis and Futuna, France repeatedly declined several appeals for a French protectorate over the New Hebrides islands (proposed by the Irish trader John Higginson from 1875). The French presence consisted primarily of missionaries and large-scale planters. Britain and France, in the face of heavy lobbying by their interest groups concerned about eventual dominance by the other, agreed in 1886 to set up a Joint Naval Commission to administer the archipelago from 1888. Having no civil law to back them up, the two French and two British officers, who comprised the Commission in its early years, were largely ineffectual. Their Commission evolved into a Condominium of the New Hebrides in 1906, to administer a joint protectorate.

The Condominium arrangement was a creative solution at the time to accommodate the flagging imperial aims of both parties, who were working increasingly together back home to meet the growing German imperialist threat. The system involved ingeniously duplicative arrangements: two sets of administrators, each responsible for their own citizens; two languages; two forms of Christianity; three sets of laws applicable respectively to the indigenous people, French and British settlers; two educational systems; two police systems; and, two sets of currencies and systems of weights and measures. Although there were periods during which the British and French Commissioners did not speak to one another, and differences were addressed by a mixed tribunal whose head, at one time, was a deaf Spanish count (see Chesneaux and Maclellan 1992, 76), it proved remarkably effective over 80 years and was one of the first examples of experimental forms of government in the Pacific.

The two commissions in practice administered their own nationalities (the French, their planters, the British, primarily missionaries). The numbers involved were minuscule. Jean Chesneaux and Nic Maclellan note that the British population was only 55 (compared to the French population of 151) in 1897, 228 (401) in 1906, and 298 (566) in 1910 (1992, 77) although, by 1939, the French population was 10 times bigger than the British and centred on the island of Santo. The administration of the Melanesians took a very low second place.

But, ironically given the unique Condominium arrangement, it is in the New Hebrides that Anglo–French ambiguities of rivalry and co-operation were most acutely evident. France took its responsibility for the influence and protection of nationals far more seriously than did Britain, using land claims of French nationals to create the grounds for an eventual takeover, and employing French nationals wherever possible, even in lowly positions. Despite, or perhaps because of, these efforts, British influence became more widespread (Henningham 1992, 26–27). Because most planters were French, land disputes arising from different indigenous concepts of land ownership added to anti-French tensions amongst the local people. Although the dual, parallel nature of the Condominium arose from different concepts of the state, at times of catastrophe (for example, the 1913 eruption of the Ambrym volcano) the administrations worked well together. In an example of co-operation on the ground, after the 1929 depression, the French State subsidised the price of copra to aid its planters, but the British did not, and often local British residents channelled their goods through a compliant French neighbour (Chesneaux and Maclellan 1992, 77–78). Until the 1960s, the Condominium arrangement worked reasonably well.

French Polynesia

The progressive French annexation of what was to become, in 1880 with the appropriation of Tahiti, the Établissements français d'Océanie (French Pacific establishments, EFO), was not only the subject of international negotiation already referred to, but also of internal resistance.

From the early years of the nineteenth century, France had come to see Tahiti strategically, as an important staging post for its navy (based in South America), and a stopping-off point for what it hoped would be profitable trade, over and above the romanticised image of the island that it perpetuated, particularly once the long-planned Panama Canal was constructed. Government subsidies encouraged French whaling after 1819. In 1816, French lieutenant Camille de Roquefeuil bought sandalwood in the Marquesas, noting that 'In order to keep up a good understanding, it had been necessary to admit some young girls, who had expressed a desire to become acquainted with our people' (quoted in Dunmore 1997, 155). But such a warm welcome was not to last.

In the Marquesas, initial resistance by chiefs Iotete (1842) and Pakoko (1845) extended into guerilla activity leading to French military intervention in 1870 and 1880 (Toullelan 1990, Dening 1980). The population fell from 60,000 in 1840 to 3500 in 1902 (Chesneaux and Maclellan 1992, 70). In Tahiti, Queen Pomaré IV only reluctantly signed the French protectorate agreement in 1842 and led resistance from 1844, her forces reoccupying Tahiti in 1846. Tahiti's population had also suffered from new diseases and bloody conflict, falling from 70,000 in the 1770s to 10,000 in 1842 (Dunmore 1997, 181). Events in Tahiti had been complicated by the timing of decisions back in Europe, with Britain agreeing in 1842 to the French protectorate, notwithstanding lobbying against it by their inveterate Consul, Pritchard, leading to French Parliamentary ratification of the plan in January 1843. Rebellions occurred in the Tuamotu group, on Anaa in 1852 and the Australes at Rapa in 1887. The Leewards war was to last 10 years from 1888 to 1897 in response to French annexation attempts at Huahine, Bora Bora and Raitea. It took three warships and a force of a thousand men to bring the hostilities to an end. Underlying much of this resistance was the Protestant allegiance and identity of the people, some of whom looked to the British to take the place of the French.

By the early twentieth century, France had consolidated its position. From 1885 the administration consisted of a governor, and an elected general council of 18 members, 10 from Tahiti and Moorea, two from Marquesas, four from Tuamotus, one from Gambiers and one from the Australs and Rapa. Electors were French citizens.

France's control was complete to the point of local inertia. The population rose in Tahiti from 6400 in 1881 to 11,682 in 1902, albeit with very few (around 1000) immigrants from France (Dunmore 1997, 206). The attention of the colonial power was only mobilised when major events occurred which, once again, engaged broader national interest emanating from European political developments. Examples include a German raid against Papeete in 1914, the departure of a Tahitian battalion for World War I, and differences with Mexico over the annexation of Clipperton (for which the King of Italy, of all possibilities, was appointed arbiter in 1931, and who confirmed the French position).

An area of continuing vexation throughout the latter nineteenth century was land ownership. Polynesian practice entailed individual usage of land, within a collective lineage ownership. Protestant missionaries had enshrined these principles in the Pomaré Code of 1842, which were directly contrary to the Napoleonic principles of individual ownership. In 1863 France established an agricultural fund to do a land survey, enabling land transfers to planters and agricultural producers (Europeans, Chinese, or locals). European (overwhelmingly male) marriage into land-owning indigenous families further boosted the de facto European land transfer, leading to an influential class of 'demis', or mixed-blood people (see Panoff 1989). While Europeans were not numerous (600 in Tahiti and Moorea, in a total population of around 6000), one resident official, Gauthier de la Richerie, asserted in 1862 that sooner or later all the lands would be assigned to whites through fraudulent practices such as trading land for liquor (Chesneaux and Maclellan 1992, 72–73). With Pomaré's signing of the Annexation Treaty in 1880, the High Court oversaw land transfers until around 1935 when it ceased, by general indifference perhaps, as memories of the bloodshed of the early nineteenth century dissipated.

But French development plans in the EFO stalled. Its projects for large-scale productive plantations of cotton, sugar and coffee failed. The most profitable exports were copra, vanilla and mother-of-pearl produced, ironically, by small-scale local operations, but controlled by the big French trading houses. By the end of the century, oranges were also being exported to California and Australia. Phosphate was mined on Makatea Island from 1907. But dreams of Tahiti as a strategic commercial stopping point were foiled, when a private French venture to build the Panama Canal failed in the late nineteenth century, only for an American company later to succeed in the endeavour (Heffer 1995, 148–52). The canal's opening, in 1914, meant effective US control of the eastern access to the South Pacific. Less traffic was generated through Papeete than the French had expected, and shipping was dominated by the British.

Perhaps because of its strategic location in the centre of the Pacific, the EFO maintained links with its Pacific neighbours, Hawaii, the Cook Islands and even California. English was spoken as much as French as late as 1888 (when Robert Louis Stevenson visited) (Chesneaux and Maclellan 1992, 74–75).

The EFO were drawn into World War I during which 1088 Polynesians fought for France, and 205 lost their lives. A German ship, surreptitiously helping itself to phosphate on Makatea, was captured by the French warship, the *Zélée*, at the beginning of the war. In September 1914 two German cruisers appeared off Papeete and shelled the town, sinking the *Zélée*, before sailing away. Another German vessel went aground in Maupihaa, west of Tahiti in 1917.

European interest in visiting the EFO, hitherto confined to prominent individuals such as Paul Gauguin, Henri Matisse and Robert Louis Stevenson, grew after World War I and was actively promoted from 1924. A colonial exhibition in Paris in 1931 heightened awareness of the colonies. The making of films (*Tabou* in 1928, *Mutiny on the Bounty* in 1934) perpetuated the romantic Polynesian myth, and boosted interest in tourism.

New Caledonia

The French claim to New Caledonia, like that of French Polynesia, was characterised by difficulties with the British, and by internal resistance. In January 1843, Dupetit-Thouars dispatched Commander Julien Lafferrière to raise the French flag, and establish Bishop Guillaume Douarre and his missionaries at Balade, in the northeast of Grande Terre, New Caledonia's largest island. Robert Aldrich (1990, 24) noted that a cession of land was concluded with local chieftains, but that 'this did not effectively constitute a claim'.[4] But strains with the British over the Pritchard affair in Tahiti led the powerful new French Minister for the Navy, François-Pierre Guizot, architect of the new *entente cordiale* with the British back home, to recall Dupetit-Thouars and to have the flag at Balade lowered. In any case, Douarre and his missionaries were forced to desert Balade within 12 months owing to hostility from the local people.

The motivation for the eventual declaration by Rear-Admiral Auguste Febvrier-Despointes of French possession of New Caledonia, at Balade, on 24 September in 1853, was twofold: the establishment of a strategic base and penal settlement in the western Pacific; and forestalling British annexation (Aldrich 1990, 24–26; Dunmore 1997, 188), and indeed, a British hydrographic vessel was in waters off Isle of Pines at the time. By this time, France and Britain were allies in the Crimean War and there was no negative British reaction. Within a few days of the Febvrier-Despointes announcement, the chief of the Isle of Pines declared allegiance to France. Effective control over the Loyalty Islands, where the LMS were entrenched, only came later, Maré and Lifou in 1864 and Ouvéa in 1865 (Aldrich 1990, 26). In 1854 Captain Louis Tardy de Montravel established a settlement at a harbour called Port-de-France, which became Noumea in 1866.

As in the EFO, from where New Caledonia was administered until 1860, colonisation was a slow process, and met significant local resistance. Only 100 white settlers were in New Caledonia by 1860, mainly French but also British. The first governor of New Caledonia, Admiral Charles Guillain, oversaw the introduction of 250 convicts in 1864 and the settlement remained a penal colony until 1897. It hosted 25,000 convicts in that time, as well as 4526 deported members of the Paris Commune (the *communards*) after their 1871 uprising against the French Government in the aftermath of the Franco-Prussian War, and over 1000 Algerian Kabyle insurrectionists in 1871. In 1880 there was an amnesty for political prisoners, and only a small group, of close to 140 individuals, chose to remain.

---

4   A view not shared by all. In March 2009, Kanak leader Roch Wamytan referred to the January 1844 treaty with the customary chiefs as the basis for French nationality, not the later declaration of possession of 1853. Personal communication, 2009.

As convicts served their time and were freed with a grant of land, and as large French companies such as Ballande of Bordeaux were given land on Grande Terre, while the indigenous Kanaks were pushed towards the north and centre, indigenous discontent increased. Ownership rights were alien to Kanak concepts of land as a tribal home. An effective policy of cantonment of the Kanaks, relegating them to reserves, was introduced in 1876. By 1878 tensions erupted in a rebellion led by Chef Ataï, sparked by the encroachment on indigenous lands by European-owned cattle. The rebellion focused on settlements at La Foa, Bourail and Bouloupari on the western coast north of Noumea. In the conflict, 200 settlers and 1200 Kanaks (some engaged in intra-tribal battles) were killed, including Ataï, (see Leenhardt 1937 and Latham 1978).

Immigration from the motherland was promoted, especially by the active Governor Feillet (1894–1903). Several large families and numerous smallholders established themselves, to be known as '*broussards*' (bush dwellers). Feillet's long governorship was an aberration. He was succeeded by nine governors, or temporary occupants of the position, from 1903 to 1914, in constant rotations that were dubbed the *valse des gouverneurs* (Aldrich 1990, 314). By 1913 Kanaks were relegated to 120,000 hectares, or seven to eight per cent of the surface of the main island, with the Europeans in the bush owning or renting three times more land with a population five or six times smaller (Chesneaux and Maclellan 1992, 66). As in the EFO, successive attempts were made at large-scale cultivation of rice, maize, coffee and sugar, with little success. The Kanaks succeeded with small-scale coffee production in the 1930s. Cattle-raising, too, was successful, and both persist today.

In 1874, French engineer Joseph Garnier discovered nickel on Grande Terre. By 1877 a processing plant was established at Pointe Chaleix in Noumea and, in 1880, the Société le Nickel (SLN) was set up by John Higginson, funded by Baron Rothschild. The foundry was not successful at the time, in the face of new technical expertise and competition from Canada (Lawrey 1982). Ballande, a businessman from Bordeaux, set up the Hauts-Fourneaux de Nouméa in 1909. He established a foundry at Doniambo, just outside Noumea, in 1910 and another at Thio in 1912 (Jeffrey 2006, and <http://www.sln.nc> accessed 21 October 2008). Ballande and SLN merged in 1931.

Besides Higginson and Ballande, other influential families included Bernheim (who endowed a private library to the people of Noumea, which is still operating), Marchand, and Barrau (Aldrich 1990, 148). SLN and the large French importers dominated the economic life of the colony in the early twentieth century. Many smaller mines were established creating wealth for a few families, including the Pentecosts and Lafleurs, who remain politically and economically dominant to this day. By the turn of the century New Caledonia was the world's largest exporter of nickel and cobalt and second largest producer of chrome.

Not all of the leading figures were French. Higginson was originally Irish and James Paddon, a British trader from Australia, was a founding business trader in the colony from 1854. In the mid-nineteenth century, spoken English was more understood than French amongst the Kanaks, largely because of the work of the LMS. The first census in 1860 showed that the majority of the 432 Europeans were Anglo-Saxons (Chesneaux and Maclellan 1992, 68). The Australian influence in the livestock sector has left words such as 'station', 'stockman', 'stockwhip' and 'store', in current usage by the French in the bush even today.

A consultative General Council (*Conseil général*) was created in 1885 but was comprised solely of whites from the bush or Noumea. From 1887 the *indigénat* system was introduced, and applied until 1946, institutionalising discrimination against Kanaks. Kanaks were forbidden to leave their reserves without permission, had to pay a per head tax, and were required to provide labour for road and other public works. 'Chiefs' and 'lesser chiefs' were appointed by the French administration and were tasked with providing workers for the settlers or the mine.

Development differed between Grande Terre, and the Loyalty Islands and Isle of Pines, which were predominantly Kanak and Protestant, and where no alienation of Kanak land had been allowed. The English-speaking LMS was replaced from 1891 by evangelical missions from Paris and the Bible was translated into local languages from 1922. A French Protestant pastor and ethnologist, Maurice Leenhardt, took a great interest in the Kanaks, at times in conflict with the French administration.

As in the EFO, it took major events such as the 1878 uprising and World War I for the metropolitan power to take much notice of New Caledonia. Three battalions of indigenous infantrymen fought for France (1107 Melanesians and 1006 Europeans fought in Europe, including at Gallipoli, of whom 456 were killed). Melanesian involvement in fighting for France contributed to a further Kanak revolt in 1917 by Grand Chef Noël. Eric Waddell attributes the rebellion to a reaction against the colonial drive to recruit 'volunteers' for the European war (2008, 38). Chesneaux and Maclellan suggest that it was French losses in the war, with the knowledge that France could be defeated, that contributed to Noël's revolt (1992, 67). In the event the rebellion was easily controlled. Those Melanesians who had served in World War I were able to become French citizens, although this did not entail the right to vote (complete suffrage in New Caledonia was not attained until 1956, see Gohin 2002, point 16; and below). In 1935 these Melanesians were being included on all civil registers.

Between the wars New Caledonia reverted to its colonial torpor. John Lawrey quoted novelist Pierre Benoît who visited Noumea in 1928 and described it as 'A small town so deeply asleep that it seems dead' (1982, 7). It was enlivened by the arrival of an effective Governor, Georges Guyon, whose administration ran from 1925 to 1929 and who developed infrastructure and education, doubling those who attended school by 1939 to over 7000, of whom 3117 were Kanaks (Dunmore 1997, 223).

The success of nickel production fluctuated in line with the vagaries of world demand, as it continues to do today. The 1929 depression affected nickel prices and disrupted construction of a planned railway, which ceased after the first stage was completed from Noumea to Paita in the north. But, despite the depression, nickel and chrome production increased until the eve of World War II. In 1939 nickel production reached 370,500 tonnes (over eight times the production recorded in 1925), and chrome reached 52,388 tonnes. Since Japan was a major customer, production was temporarily disrupted in the early 1940s (see below).

With vacillating fortunes, the import of foreign labour, necessary to work the mines, also fluctuated. Indonesian, Japanese and Vietnamese workers were brought in to work on the mines early in the century. By 1929 they numbered 14,535, more than the number of European residents at that time (Ward in Spencer 1988, 82). Many of these labourers left when their contracts expired but, by 1931, there were more than 7000 Asian residents in New Caledonia out of a total population of 57,300 (Aldrich 1990, 286 and ISEE 2008; Table 4.1a, Chapter 4).

With the growth in prosperity punctuated by the Depression, a call for autonomy and dominion status was made in 1932, interestingly by a European resident, Edmond Cave, a member of the General Council, but did not gather momentum (Aldrich 1990, 314). Dunmore (1997, 223) noted that this call reflected the growing identification with New Caledonia, as opposed to France, by those Europeans who had been born there (12,600 of a total European population of 17,400 in 1936). The Melanesian population by this time was stabilising rather than declining. Atat the turn of the century, the entire population numbered around 50,000, and was mainly rural, with only 7000 living in Noumea. The numbers of Kanaks dropped from close to 45,000 in 1860 to 27,100 in the 1920s, and rose again to approximately 30,000 in 1940 (Chesneaux and Maclellan 1992, 66; Barbançon in de Deckker and Faberon 2008, 120; Aldrich 1990, 286; Lawrey, 9; and, Table 4.1a, Chapter 4).

In contrast to the EFO, in the nineteenth century New Caledonia, with its dependence on French shipping and market for its nickel, its internal preoccupation with its role as a penal settlement, and with its near neighbour the large Anglo-Saxon continent of Australia, had few links within its South Pacific islands neighbourhood. These were limited to summary links between Melanesian residents and those in the nearby New Hebrides islands, and contacts between French residents in each place.

Wallis and Futuna

Franco–British rivalry and indecision were features of French annexation of Wallis and Futuna. French missionaries had arrived in the islands from the 1830s but France did not respond to local requests for protectorate status in the 1840s, nor in the 1860s. The Queen of Wallis, Amélie, supported the French missionaries, and efforts by British evangelists to establish a presence were abandoned. France finally established a protectorate in 1886 in Wallis, and in Futuna in 1887, and then only in response to apparent efforts by the British to cultivate Amélie by inviting her to Fiji. But France only formalised annexation arrangements in 1913.

The strong traditional focus of the islands, and their overwhelming response to Catholicism, meant that it was not necessary for France to exert much colonial effort to administer it. Rather, a pattern developed of synchrony between the few colonial administrators present, the Catholic Church hierarchy, and monarchs of the three traditional kingdoms, which persists today (Aldrich and Merle 1997, Cadéot 2003, *New Pacific Review* 2003, Faberon and Ziller 2007, de Deckker in Howe et al 1994, 269).

Summary of French experience to World War II

France's activities in the Pacific from the very earliest days were motivated by national prestige, a quest for scientific knowledge, and religious proselytisation. Rivalry with other European powers, mainly the British, and the experience of repeatedly being usurped by other powers in the region, sharpened France's sense of national assertion. Commercial activity came consistently second to nationalist objectives. Domestic political challenges and alliances at home in Europe, which were complex and, at times, explosive, demanded primary policy attention and shaped the pace and energy with which France established its footholds in the Pacific. Increasingly, France became aware of the strategic importance of its Pacific colonies, particularly the EFO and New Caledonia, in serving its national purpose.

Hallmarks of the French presence included, at times, extraordinary leadership, courage, and sense of style in its commanders as much as its early privateers; in general, sophistication and deft diplomacy in a context of international rivalries; a commitment to personal hardship and sacrifice for national honour; but only sporadic application, in the Pacific, of the national sense of brotherhood, freedom and equality which evolved in the home country from the late 1700s;

a determination to suppress local opposition, backed by military strength; and, by the beginning of World War II, an element of administrative inertia even as innovative solutions, for example in New Hebrides, were being implemented.

All of these features were to inform later French policy approaches. For their part, the local people in the French archipelagos suffered loss of life and diminished populations, and fought back, particularly strenuously in New Caledonia and the outlying areas of French Polynesia.

World War II and its legacy

'La fin de la guerre est aussi la fin de l'Empire colonial'?

'The end of the war is also the end of the colonial Empire'? (Faberon and Ziller 2007, 348)

World War II challenged the political and economic role of the French in the Pacific, as it did elsewhere. The rapid defeat of the French Government in Paris and the participation of citizens from the Pacific overseas territories in combat in Europe (including the 'Guitarist' battalion, comprising 387 Kanaks and 318 Tahitians and New Hebrides locals, of whom a third died, Daly 2002) traumatised the French and local communities in the Pacific, underlining the vulnerability of their French administrators. Closer to home, the Pacific theatre itself, where other powers were the main protagonists, introduced violence and destruction of a scale unparalleled in the history of the local people. The early role of Australia, asserting its diplomatic authority independent of Britain for the first time, and the massive influx of American forces stationed in the French territories, exposed the local people to alternative administrative influences and, particularly in the case of the Americans, with relatively larger national and personal wealth than the French rulers, and new practices of economic and racial egalitarianism. It was the war and its aftermath which catalysed local independence movements in the region, including in the French territories. The wartime experience initiated a habit of regional consultation and co-operation with Britain, Australia and the United States.

Effect of World War II in New Caledonia: Relations with Australia

In New Caledonia the early days of World War II saw not only persistent suspicions of Anglo-Saxonism, but also fine examples of Anglo–French regional teamwork in adversity, reflecting similar co-operation for survival in Europe, and a new engagement by Australia. As the war progressed, the previously dependent links with Britain were loosening and Australia arguably made its first independent foreign policy decisions specifically related to New Caledonia (see below, and analysed in Fisher 2010c). As Australia became more involved in the region, the existing, deep-seated anti-British sentiment of the French and Caldoche (long-term European residents) was increasingly extended to Australia as well.

Australian and French Pacific perceptions were already mutually negative. French annexation of New Caledonia in 1853 had been coldly received in Australia, the *Sydney Morning Herald* of 2 November 1853 lamenting that 'by the laxity of the British government … the opportunity of colonising that fine group [had] been lost'. Australia was opposed to calls for French annexation of the New Hebrides, which many saw as within Australia's sphere. By the late nineteenth century, views on New Caledonia were shaped by the feeling, curious for a country itself built by convicts, that a loathsome penal settlement continued to operate in the neighbourhood, just as Australia had ridded itself of this curse. The unease was expressed in concerns that escaped convicts would make their way onto Australia's fair shores (Aldrich 1990, 224–25).

Australian perceptions of a menacing France were reciprocated by a French belief that Australia wanted to displace it in New Caledonia to conserve its economic interests (Pons 1988, 156). Against their own value systems, some French people, even officials, had a disdain for Australians typified in the report of one French diplomat who in 1936 described Australians as lacking taste, having never 'seen a fine piece of furniture, a beautiful painting, a truly elegant woman, … [nor] eaten a decent meal. In the things that interest us, the Australian public is uneducated and uneducable' (Aldrich 1990, 309). This was reflected in the title of the memoires the Comtesse de Chabrillan, wife of one French consul, '*Deuil au bout du monde*' or 'Mourning in the back of beyond' (Chabrillan 1877).

But, despite all the acrimony in the Australian press, as Lawrey indicated, 'Australasian colonists … never seriously questioned the permanency of French sovereignty over New Caledonia' (1982, 18). This belief was shaken temporarily when France fell to the Nazis in 1940.

Australia's role in installing the Free French Governor

When Paris fell in June 1940, the French Governor in New Caledonia, Georges Pélicier, was a senior colonial civil servant who, like many of his peers, saw Noumea as a brief career stepping stone, and had not engaged in the society he administered. When a central government was set up at Vichy, he was in the difficult position of determining whose interest he was to serve. Some of the Caldoches sought to benefit from the situation and to advance local autonomy. A local lawyer, Michel Vergès, promulgated a manifesto seeking a sovereign assembly to take over the governor's powers, and was promptly arrested. Pélicier's own Secretary-General, André Bayardelle, seemed to agree with Vergès, noting that the colony was too much subjected to the Ministry of Colonies 'whose initiatives were frequently untimely and cancelled out the best efforts of governors to organise the colony' (cited in Lawrey 1982, 8). At one point, a local left-wing representative called for New Caledonia to be placed under joint Australian–American protection (Burchett 1941, 197).

After a few weeks of judicious dithering, during which Pélicier even announced that New Caledonia would continue to fight at the side of Great Britain, on 29 July, responding to pressure from Vichy leader Marshal Philippe Pétain, Pélicier gazetted Vichy's constitutional laws (although he resisted pressure to cut off relations with Britain and New Caledonia's principal supplier, Australia, Lawrey 1982, 28 and Munholland 2005, 38). Many Caldoches angrily demonstrated against these laws. In the event, the General Council unanimously adopted a resolution calling for a representative assembly, expressed its disapproval of the governor, and its resolve to contact General de Gaulle. In his declining days at the helm Pélicier called for the Vichy government to send a warship to Noumea, and the *Dumont d'Urville* arrived from Papeete in late August, captained by a confirmed Vichy supporter, Commander Toussaint de Quièvrecourt. De Quièvrecourt immediately reported to Vichy that the local agitators were subsidised by Australia, whose real aim was to annex New Caledonia (Lawrey 1982, 31). On 5 September, the vacillating Pélicier, after suffering a bomb attack at his residence and the mounting anger of the masses, quietly slunk out of town with his family (an event recounted colourfully in Burchett 1941, 205). His post was taken over by the commander of local French forces, Maurice Denis.

Meanwhile, de Gaulle, then an exiled French military officer struggling to put together an alternative government in the wake of the German invasion and collapse of French resistance, moved into action. In an early indicator of his strategic vision of the role and importance of the French overseas possessions which was to characterise France's approach through many of the post-World War II years, he made his famous 18 June *appel*, or call for the support of the Empire. As Kim Munholland noted,

> Beginning as an improvised coalition of those who ... chose to continue to fight at the side of Great Britain, the Free French under de Gaulle's leadership became a political movement devoted to a defence of the French Empire from its perceived enemies and served as a Gaullist instrument for the recovery of French grandeur, prestige, and influence after the humiliation of 1940. (Munholland 1986, 547)

As such, the *ralliement*, or winning-over, of the overseas territories had great symbolic value. It also had real value, in the need, which De Gaulle also saw, to promptly neutralise potential Vichy colonial and naval power overseas (Gorman 1997 and Floyd 2007, 10). Martin Thomas, in his military history of the *ralliement* in the empire, argued that 'Control of the French empire was vital to the competing French leaderships of 1940–1944, since the empire was a physical embodiment of what limited independence remained to the Vichy regime' (Thomas 1998, 5).

De Gaulle moved early to secure the support of the New Caledonia outpost to shore up his fledgling leadership. He asked the British to assist him to replace Pélicier with a pro-de Gaulle figure. The person he had in mind was Henri Sautot, a small man with a ginger moustache affectionately known as '*Pommes-paille*' ('Straw-potatoes'), who was French resident commissioner in nearby New Hebrides. There, he had rallied the local French population speedily to the Gaullist cause. He had also worked with Australia to build a strategically important flying boat base at Vila.

Australian involvement in the installation of de Gaulle's man, Sautot, was vital. At this time, Australia's foreign policy institution was in a fledgling state. Although Prime Minister Menzies had signalled in early 1939 that Australia had its own primary responsibilities and needed its own diplomatic sources in the Pacific (Menzies 1939), in practice Australia had established diplomatic representation in only three places by mid 1940, in London, Washington and Ottawa (Foreign Affairs and Trade 2000).

To this point, at least from the armistice in June 1940, Australia had not been a disinterested bystander. On 18 June, the War Cabinet had discussed events in New Caledonia, discussions that were marked by concern that the Japanese presence in New Caledonia, associated with its ongoing purchase of nickel, posed a threat to Australian security, particularly with the Australian navy having left for the Mediterranean. This appears to be the first discussion of events in New Caledonia by the Australian Cabinet (DFAT Historical Document or HD No 399 18 June 1940). There was a broader concern about Japanese intentions in the Dutch East Indies (now Indonesia), Indochina, and Hong Kong (DFAT HD No 408 19 June 1940). The Department of External Affairs identified early that, of all the French possessions overseas, including Indochina, it was most concerned about New Caledonia. It counselled caution, and the continuing support for the Bordeaux (later Vichy) government, unless an effective resistance could be organised (DFAT HD No 440 26 June 1940). One of the early options Canberra considered, if only briefly, was an Australian takeover of New Caledonia (and then the New Hebrides), to forestall Japan, an option considered unattractive as it could provide a precedent for Japan to do the same in the Dutch East Indies (DFAT HD No 400 18 June 1940).

Immediately after the armistice, Australia (along with New Zealand) had sent a message of sympathy to Governor Pélicier. Pélicier responded by stating 'our firm resolve to co-operate with the French community throughout the whole world for the liberation of France, for which it has decided to continue the struggle by the side of the British Empire', and seeking supplies from Australia (DFAT HD No 427 and 439 24 and 26 June 1940).

Australia drew its concerns about the vulnerabilities of the French Pacific islands to the attention of Britain and the United States. London responded by expressing concern at Japanese nickel purchases from New Caledonia, and suggesting Australia send a representative to Noumea (DFAT HD No 438 25 June 1940). Washington was not responsive (DFAT HD No 464 28 June 1940). On its own initiative, Australia negotiated with the director of SLN, France's nickel producer, to purchase nickel matte, in July 1940, in order to encourage the colony to cease exporting to its major purchaser, Japan, with the primary aim of heading off on-shipment to Germany. This act was described by Lawrey as 'a matter of enlightened self-interest', since Australia had no need of nickel supplies and was acting solely to maintain a market for New Caledonia and keep it in the 'allied orbit' (Lawrey 1982, 25–26). But the action was later to backfire when the locals (incorrectly, as it turned out) accused Australia of acting unfairly as a middleman.

Australia continued to be concerned about the potential for the Japanese to benefit from the situation. It had sent an Australian called Oughton, to negotiate the purchase of chrome from New Caledonia, similarly to ensure an alternative market to Japan for the territory's chrome. Oughton, among others, reported that the Governor was showing exaggerated respect for the Japanese Consul by granting a license for the sale of nickel to Japan (DFAT HD No 70 13 August 1940, Munholland 2005, 41).

In July, the Australian Government decided to appoint Official Representative to Noumea, posting Bertram C. Ballard in the position. Ballard was a French-speaking lawyer who had been based in Vila from 1934. He was tasked to keep the Australian Government 'fully informed on political and economic conditions in New Caledonia' and assess the attitudes of 'officials, the General Council, and

Caledonians' towards both Vichy and General de Gaulle's movement' (DFAT HD No 45 undated). Ballard's office in Noumea became Australia's fourth diplomatic mission overseas, preceding its first mission in Paris by five years.

Responding to a request from de Gaulle, and because the area fell under the auspices of the Australian Naval Station, the British asked Australia to make available the aged naval vessel HMAS *Adelaide* to install Sautot. Having just dispatched Ballard, Australia took its time to respond. The situation was complex, as one of Ballard's reports showed. He described the atmospherics of a dinner party attended by the outgoing Pélicier, the incoming Denis and the visiting Fiji-based British High Commissioner for the Pacific, as 'scarcely-restrained hysteria' (Lawrey 1982, 38). Wilfred Burchett, then a freelance journalist but later to become one of Australia's well-known war correspondents, referred to the 'glacial frigidity' of this dinner and the 'Gilbertian' situation at Government House in a book he wrote about New Caledonia in the lead-up to the war (Burchett 1941, 204).

Canberra continued to bide its time. The Australian Government did not want the French administering power to be overwhelmed by protesting Caldoches, with the possibility that Australia would be asked to fill the breach, and the potential for misinterpretation and consequences elsewhere, notably in French Indochina (DFAT HD No 83 29 August 1940; see also Daly, 3). Thus Australia was concerned to ensure a working French administration in New Caledonia. There were also signs that the British were not fully aware of the complexities of the situation on the ground (see Fisher 2010c, 27). In the event, Canberra took a decision to act only after Ballard assessed that a complaisant Vichy governor was not likely and that the people would 'welcome and follow' a governor appointed by de Gaulle (DFAT HD No 110 8 September 1940).

Australia's hesitation to agree to London's request was one of the first indications, if not the first, that the Australian Government, evaluating its own, as distinct from British, interests, saw advantage in a stable French-administered allied entity on its eastern flank (Fisher 2010c).

The *Adelaide* duly escorted a Norwegian ship, the *Norden*, with Sautot aboard, consistent with de Gaulle's characteristic instructions that the operation was to be conducted as a French operation with merely contingent support from the *Adelaide*. In the early hours of the morning of 19 September 1940, the vessels approached the southern passage through the reef near Noumea. They were awaiting the agreed signal that it was safe to transfer Sautot to Noumea. This involved the quaint arrangement that the Gaullist boat to receive him off the main beach, Anse Vata, would throw overboard two kerosene tins when it was 300 metres from the *Norden*, and two more when 200 metres away (Sautot 1949, 39; Lawrey 1982, 44). Meanwhile, despite all attempts at secrecy, Sautot's planned arrival was well known in New Caledonia. Sautot himself explained, without surprise, that one of the Gaullist committee had confided the information to his mistress who, although a loyal Gaullist herself, could not restrain herself from spreading the information (Sautot 1949, 42). Ashore, the French *broussards*, or rural Caldoches, had descended on the capital from their stations and towns in the bush, to welcome the new governor. Denis, after a pitiful show of indecision during which he twice dissolved into uncontrolled sobbing, finally escaped the crowd through a back window at Government House, ultimately to be detained in the village of La Foa (Burchett 1941, 212–13).

In the event, the two vessels lumbered into Noumea harbour to see the *Dumont d'Urville* moored with guns trained fore and aft. It was later discovered that shore batteries had been given orders to open fire on the *Adelaide*, orders which were not carried out (Lawrey 1982, 46). At this point the *Adelaide*'s commander, H.A. Showers, cast diplomacy to the winds and transferred Sautot from the *Norden* onto his vessel, and the *Norden* set sail back out through the harbour. Members of the Gaullist Committee approached in their boat, gave the kerosene tin signal, and took delivery of Governor Sautot. The *Adelaide* continued to patrol, wary of the *Dumont d'Urville*, whose captain showed prudent restraint, especially since some of the *broussards* in the capital were fully enjoying their victory in the streets. There were also reports that a second Vichy vessel, the *Amiral Charner*, was on its way from Indochina to Noumea. The following day, de Quièvrecourt formally protested the *Adelaide*'s presence and threatened a showdown. With both Showers and the Vichy captain referring time-consumingly to their capitals, tensions persisted for several days. But Showers initiated a personal meeting with the French captain and negotiated the departure of Vichy-sympathising officials on a merchant vessel, and the *Dumont d'Urville*'s departure for Saigon. In view of this, the Vichy government ordered the *Amiral Charner*, en route to Noumea, back to Saigon.

The Australian Government extended economic aid and co-operation pursuant to an agreement between Churchill and de Gaulle in August 1940. But this activity was fraught with difficulties and frictions, as locals grumbled about Australian delays. At one point, Free French accusations that Australia was abusing its position as middleman in purchasing nickel (the device constructed to assist New Caledonia while preventing nickel purchase by the Germans) were being made surreptitiously to London at the same time as the Australian War Cabinet was resolving to exercise 'a generous spirit' in assisting New Caledonia in its economic problems (Lawrey 1982, 68). These kinds of differences, imbued with emotion and potential for misunderstanding, were to characterise future dealings between New Caledonia and Australia in the latter half of the century.

Australia played another role in New Caledonia at this time. While the Free French Government had been established in Noumea — a not inconsiderable achievement, especially in view of de Gaulle's failure to do this elsewhere (in Indochina, Madagascar, the Levant, the French Antilles, all of North Africa and Djibouti, see Thomas 1998, 1), the Australian Government knew the new neighbouring regime was fragile as Australia prepared for Japan's entry into the war. In February 1941 an Australian military mission visited New Caledonia. It recommended setting up an advanced operational air base there, to 'contribute materially to the defence of Australia in the event of war with Japan' (Lawrey 1982, 55), supplying two, six-inch coast defence guns for Noumea and arms, ammunition and equipment for local forces. The War Cabinet meeting, which approved these recommendations, exceptionally included a French officer, sent by Sautot, whose task appears to have been, in true Gaullist tradition, to assure the Australians that the Free French were in effective control in order to head off Royal Australian Air Force (RAAF) control of any air base established in New Caledonia (Lawrey 1982, 56). It was curious that Australian Prime Minister Menzies met de Gaulle in London to secure agreement to these arrangements only in March, some weeks after the mission had arrived in Noumea. So it is not surprising that writers at the time (Lawrey 1982, 64) record some continuing suspicion on de Gaulle's part about Australian activities. For all his efforts, Sautot was to pay a heavy price for his co-operation with Australia and, later, the Americans (see below).

These activities were a measure of the strength of Australia's concern to shore up New Caledonia. The Army Minister, P.C. Spender, even pronounced, perhaps unwisely, that, economically, New Caledonia should be regarded as 'part of Australia'; and, for the purpose of granting export licences, should be 'treated on the same basis as an Australian State or Territory insofar as purchases from Australia are concerned' (see Lawrey 1982, 56).

A flying boat base was duly established on the Ile Nou with a small RAAF detachment, two guns were installed on Ouen Toro hill in Noumea (where they remain today as a memorial), and a small artillery detachment remained to train local troops in using them (Smith 2001). Australia provided shipping and support for the French Pacific Battalion, which, with its Tahiti contingent, sailed for the Middle East in May 1941. The RAAF surveyed and began construction of three landing fields, at Tontouta (which is now the international airport), Plaine des Gaiacs in the north, and Koumac on the northern tip of Grande Terre. And, from December 1941 to July 1942, an Australian company led by D.G. Matheson was sent to New Caledonia to prepare for guerilla activity and to deny the enemy useful assets such as nickel mines including, if necessary, by demolition. They were based in Bourail, north of Noumea (Garland 1997, Chapter 2). They trained local Home Guards including Melanesians, (of whom they spoke highly in their reports) and later, US infantrymen (see Appendix in Lawrey 1982, 123–24).

Australian soldiers thereafter were primarily active elsewhere in the Pacific and in Europe, while the Americans and New Zealanders worked out of New Caledonia.

De Gaulle's reflexive policy approach, imbued with suspicion about British (and for his followers in Noumea, Australian) designs on France's colonial empire and informed by the prevalence of the Vichy regime in many colonial capitals (see Thomas 1998), was to centralise his authority. He had already imposed controls relating to national pride, such as that Australian aircraft were to be employed only subject to local French approval and the numbers and roles of resident Australian personnel were to be limited, leading to a feeling in Australia that his attitude saw 'ingratitude becoming a duty' (Lawrey 1982, 58–59). An instruction soon came to Canberra from London that all dealings with Sautot, which would have previously been referred to Paris, should be referred to de Gaulle's headquarters in London, not simply as a safeguard for Sautot but to underline to Australia, which London saw as diplomatically inexperienced, not to take advantage of the situation to arrogate to itself more political control in Oceania (Lawrey 1982, 62).

It is interesting that what led London to impute 'diplomatic inexperience' to its former colony was in fact the latter's asserting its own interests and assessments at the time, perhaps more a mark of diplomatic coming of age. Australia's measured and calculated diplomatic activity from its early watchfulness over the nickel market with Japan, its establishment of its own representative in Noumea, its role in installing Sautot, and its follow-up military shoring up of New Caledonia's defences in its own interests, as distinct from those of Britain, were all the more impressive in that it took place well before the fall of Singapore and Pearl Harbour.

Effect on Australian–French–New Caledonian links and embryonic Australian diplomacy

The development of Australian–French–New Caledonian relations at the beginning of the war set the pace for future relations and perceptions, notably the suspicions and counter-suspicions of future years. While some Australians had called for British hegemony in the Pacific to protect Australian security interests many years before, it was only at this time that Australia, for the first time, appreciated the strategic importance of effective *French* administration of its near neighbour, New Caledonia, as a direct element in its own security (this strategic significance and consequence for policy was enunciated by Burchett at the time, 218 *et seq*). Australia's constant evaluation of its own, as opposed to British, interests, throughout these uncertain days was a critical developmental step. The pre-eminence of British interests for Australia until then was no doubt weighted against the fact that the United States at this stage had not entered the war and still had not recognised the de Gaulle government, even by the time General Alexander Patch arrived in Noumea in 1942. The Australian Government's establishment of one of its first diplomatic missions in Noumea in August 1940 reflected the significance of having its own links with New Caledonia, and the latter's important role in the development of Australian diplomacy and foreign policy in their earliest years. Australia's experience of its dealings with New Caledonia at the time, with its complex layers of formal links to central French headquarters (at this time in London but later Paris), to Noumea, and on the ground with local Caldoches and Kanaks, and its relations with Tahiti on a secondary level, was to leave an indelible imprint on Australian policy-making circles (see Fisher 2010c, 31). It represented one of Australia's first involvements in regional multi-lateral co-operation, with Britain, France, the United States, and New Zealand, which was to build into the formal institution of the South Pacific Commission (later called Secretariat for the Pacific Community) based in Noumea. From this point, Australia's relationship with France in the Pacific, particularly New Caledonia, would be run from Canberra, and not from London.

The Sautot episode and the Australian advance defence mission are also important as they boosted the image of Australia, albeit one tinged with suspicion, in the eyes of many of the resident population, building on the identification the European residents were beginning to show towards a sense of their own interests in their own region and with their own geographic neighbour.

Finally, the installation of the Free French Government in New Caledonia represented one of the first successful 'rallyings' of French colonies to the Free France cause. Whereas Thomas argues that the various responses by France's other colonies to de Gaulle's call for support can be explained by a number of exogenous factors, the early response by the Pacific collectivities strengthened their status and place in the post-war Empire, even if Australia's role in it was for the most part conveniently forgotten.

Effect of World War II on independence movements in French territories: US 'invasion'

But, for the people of France's Pacific colonies, it was the American presence during the war that radically changed their expectations. Senior French officials in the early 2000s privately confided that it was the Americans during the war, not the French, who brought the French Pacific islands into modernity (Personal communication 2002).

And the American presence in the French Pacific was not small. Noumea as the main base, and the New Hebrides air bases at Efate and Espiritu Santo, served as bastions of the US counteroffensive after the battles of the Coral Sea and Midway. 22,000 US personnel were based in New Caledonia, with 2600 on Wallis, 4300 at an air base constructed in the New Hebrides and over 4000 at a refuelling base at Bora Bora and a meteorological station at Raiatea in French Polynesia (Dunmore 1997, 234 and de Deckker 2003a, 63). The United States used the uninhabited French possession, Clipperton, as a meteorological and radio base (Aldrich 1990, 30).

Effect of US presence in New Caledonia

The impact of the American presence in Noumea was huge. At one point in 1942, over 100,000 American and New Zealand personnel were there. They outnumbered the population of New Caledonia at the time (60,000) and boosted the population of Grande Terre by nearly 100 per cent. Around 1 million US soldiers were said to have transited there during the war (see Lawrey 1982, 98 and Le Borgne 2005, 18).

The Americans were arguably more respected than the French administration in the early war years, mainly owing to the dubious behaviour of the French High Commissioner appointed by de Gaulle. Governor Sautot's easy manner with the Americans and Australians had created concerns for French leaders, so far away in the formal European environment. De Gaulle appointed High Commissioner Georges Thierry d'Argenlieu to keep Sautot's feet to the fire and ensure that French sovereignty would be appropriately defended. D'Argenlieu was an entirely different character to Sautot. He was a former World War I naval officer who had become a Carmelite monk and headed the Paris Carmelite province until his mobilisation in 1939. He proved to be zealous to the point of obstruction in asserting French rights, focusing on form rather than substance and at one point delaying allied construction of needed airfields. He also devoted his energies to ousting the much-loved Sautot, finally arresting him and sending him to New Zealand, and then London, at a time when New Caledonia was under direct Japanese threat (Sautot 1949, 176). He promoted suggestions that Sautot supporters were Australian agents (Lawrey 1982, 109–10). At the time both the Australian High Commissioner in London and the Prime Minister had been concerned at d'Argenlieu's appointment, since he 'had no knowledge of the Pacific' and his colonial experience had been in the West Indies (DFAT HD August 1941) — it was this kind of background which was to create difficulties for French officials in the region 40 years later. Munholland (2005) attributed to these experiences of rigid French policy adherence the seeds of future differences between France and the United States after the war. Another observer from the time, Jean le Borgne, wrote of de Gaulle's misunderstanding of the humiliation of Sautot inflicted by d'Argenlieu (2005, 18). Sautot's own account is a harrowing tale of devotion to a cause and deeply felt betrayal and misunderstanding (Sautot 1949).

For their part, French concerns about American long-term designs were not entirely without foundation. The strategic importance of New Caledonia was made very clear early in the war. Anthony Eden referred to New Caledonia as a place of the highest strategic importance. Roosevelt, who was interested in the contribution New Caledonia could make as a US commercial aviation layover point in the South Pacific from 1935, repeatedly asserted in 1943 and 1944 that New Caledonia should not remain French after the war, but rather should be a trustee territory of the UN (Lawrey 1982, 121; Weeks 1989, 189). The US Navy General Board, and a US senator touring the region, noted the strategic importance of New Caledonia for the Americans and recommended cession by the French to the United States (Munholland 2005; Weeks 1989, 191). By the end of the war a group of New Caledonians themselves proposed that the colony become American (Mrgudovic 2008, 74). There never was, however, a coherent US strategy for the annexation of New Caledonia, and the United States lost interest in the idea at the end of the war (Weeks 1989, 185 and 196).

The local people responded warmly to the Americans' pragmatism and democratic values. In contrast to the French, who extracted free labour from the Kanaks under the *indigénat* scheme, the Americans paid local labourers. Notwithstanding racial segregation in the US army, the behaviour of white and black GIs, as equals and at ease with each other, made an impression. The US military command favoured the study of indigenous languages, in contrast to the French approach (Chesneaux in Spencer et al 1988, 61). According to John Lawrey (1982), who was working in the Australian diplomatic mission in Noumea at the time, the impact of the numerous hale and hearty, well-equipped Americans, cheerily sharing their rations of chocolate and chewing gum, was overwhelming. The economy of the archipelago was boosted hugely by US consumption. The fact that it was the Americans, not the French, who supplied the military materiel to defend the archipelago, weakened the authority of the French, for whom the inflexible d'Argenlieu, as described, was a poor representative. The practice at the end of the war, of dumping vast quantities of equipment in local waterways (this occurred in Wallis, New Hebrides at aptly named Million Dollar Point, and New Caledonia) rather than export it or leave it for local use or perhaps misuse, simply reinforced the wonder at American wealth and profligacy. One US jeep escaped this fate and is still used, today, in Noumea, on significant anniversaries of the war, when it is driven around by a jubilant group of Caldoches in the guise of World War II officers and a blonde Monroe-look-alike nurse in vintage uniform.

The war and Americans in the EFO, New Hebrides and Wallis and Futuna

As in Noumea, in the EFO, the confusion following the fall of Paris in 1940 saw demands for more autonomy, which persisted throughout the course of the Pacific war. In Papeete, the Free French Committee organised a referendum, with the results falling overwhelmingly in favour of Free France over Vichy. One of their number, a returned local serviceman from World War I, Pouvanaa a Oopa, led a push for more autonomy and independence. An attempt was made to arrest him in 1941 but not carried through (Chesneaux and Maclellan 1992, 80; Faberon and Ziller 2007, 314). During the war he was a vocal critic of the local administration and rationing system (Dunmore 1997, 243) and this boosted his political profile.

While the American presence was not as pervasive in the EFO as in New Caledonia, the wealth and economic boost they represented changed Bora Bora, where they ran a fuel depot. The island was mythologised and represented as Bali Hai in the James Michener novel *Tales of the South Pacific* (1946), which was later turned into a Hollywood film, *South Pacific*, leaving a lasting legacy as a tourist paradise. The values the Americans represented, of racial equality and modernism, complemented the push for autonomy already underway and vocalised by Pouvanaa and his followers.

In the New Hebrides, during the course of the war, 100,000 Americans passed through Efate where they had established an airstrip, huts and recreation base. The main impact of the American presence was the revival of an existing cargo cult on the island of Tanna, the John Frum movement. The tiny island of Uvea in the Wallis group hosted two airfields. Such was the attachment of the islanders to the influx of well-off US soldiers that a call was made (but not taken up) for annexation before the Americans left in 1946.

The effect of the American presence and management of the war from the French colony, New Caledonia, had broader repercussions for the French Pacific colonies than social change. One consequence of the Pacific war for France was recognition of the strategic role of the French Pacific presence in regaining national prestige. The early rallying to de Gaulle by the French territories there left an important legacy, one that de Gaulle had doubtless foreseen in his early efforts to secure their support. The war resulted in the dominance of the Americans in the Pacific as a whole, not simply in their continental littoral presence but with island territories of their own, mainly north of the Equator. This prevailing strength was to make the Pacific Ocean an 'American lake' for most of the rest of the century (Heffer 1995, 250). For France, struggling to re-establish its national prestige within the western alliance, its Pacific presence was a strategic instrument as French leaders sought to entrench France's right to a seat at the high table of the United Nations (UN) Security Council in the wake of the war.

A second effect of the US role in France's territories during the war was that it catalysed demands there for more political rights from France. But now the demands were being made of a France for whose credibility the American experience called into question, not only its military capacity to defend its colonies but the values of liberty, fraternity and equality that France professed to represent (Mrgudovic 2008, 75). De Deckker (2003a, 63) directly attributed to the influence of the Americans the introduction of voting rights in the Defferre law of 1956 (see next chapter; also Le Borgne 2005, 18). There is little doubt that, in New Caledonia, the budding demands for more autonomy, which had already been noted in proposals amongst the European residents in the Cane (1932) and Vergès (1940), were compounded by a growing Kanak demand for change arising from their contact with Americans, and arguably Australians and New Zealanders, during the war. In Tahiti, Pouvanaa's demands were more extreme and curtailed immediately by the French. But, notwithstanding the social impact of the Americans and the calls for greater autonomy, it is undeniable that all through the war and beyond, the prevailing culture in all the colonies remained French.

A third determining feature of the Pacific war for the French territories was its reinforcement of the primacy of New Caledonia over the other French colonies in strategic and regional importance. Its location, relatively developed infrastructure and sophistication, and responsiveness to modernity, underpinned successful US-led prosecution of the Pacific war.

Another enduring characteristic of the American presence in New Caledonia in the Pacific war was the habit of co-operation and consultation between the Free French in London and Noumea, the British, the Americans, New Zealanders and Australians, even though such co-operation was fraught with misunderstanding, prejudice, and the need for delicate diplomacy. This wartime co-operation was to lead the way for a postwar regional multilateral organisation, the South Pacific Commission, with its seat in Noumea, ironically in the former US headquarters.

2. France manages independence demands and nuclear testing 1945–1990s

The immediate postwar period saw growing demands for autonomy in the colonies and initially, signs of responsiveness in France. In the wave of postwar change, as its wartime allies shaped new international structures with the United Nations (UN) at its core, France acknowledged the need for more equality and evolution in the administration of its colonies. De Gaulle resigned in January 1946 because of differences over parliamentary powers in the new constitution, leading to a period of instability in French leadership. Steps to encourage more self-government and even independence for the colonies, particularly the African colonies, were initiated by the Fourth and Fifth Republics in the 1946 and 1958 constitutions. These steps were subsequently rolled back by successive statutory measures, to serve French national interests, in a pattern that was to characterise future treatment of the South Pacific overseas territories.

At a conference in Brazzaville (the Congo) in 1944, provision was made for more decentralised administration of the colonies and representation in bodies redrafting the French constitution. The conference called for local elected assemblies and representation of the overseas territories in the Paris parliament. The aim, however, was to contain nationalist aspirations and keep the colonies with France.

Some Melanesians and Polynesians (war veterans, pastors, customary chiefs) were accorded the right to vote in 1945. In 1945 and 1946 the French government decreed further rights for their overseas residents, including French citizenship, but not the universal right to vote. While the 1946 constitution affirmed that all residents of overseas territories were French citizens, it was only in 1951 that all French citizens in the colonies obtained the right to vote, and specifically only in 1956, with the Loi Defferre, that all native residents of the overseas territories were entitled to vote.

The 1946 constitution created a French Union and committed France to leading its people to administer themselves and to manage their own affairs democratically, '*écartant tout système de colonisation fondé sur l'arbitraire*' ('eschewing arbitrary colonisation', Preamble). The Établissements français d'Océanie (French Pacific establishments, EFO) and New Caledonia were henceforward able to elect their own *député* (member of parliament) to the French national assembly and senate in

Paris. The four oldest colonies (Guyana, Réunion, Guadeloupe and Martinique) became 'departments' of France while the others, including New Caledonia, French Polynesia and Wallis and Futuna remained external 'territories'.

France was not acting in a domestic vacuum. As postwar international structures evolved, the UN was founded in 1945 on a charter specifying the principle of equality of rights and self-determination of peoples (Article 1). It called for states administering non-self-governing territories to develop self-government and transmit technical information to the UN on them (Article 73). But in 1947 France decided unilaterally that it would not transmit to the UN information on New Caledonia and French Polynesia (and others of its colonies), arguing that they had a status similar to the French 'departments', but with the implication that they had administrative and political autonomy and were therefore no longer non-self-governing (see Mrgudovic in de Deckker and Faberon 2008, 178). France claimed that only New Hebrides was non-self-governing; it has resolutely maintained this position to the present, although it quietly began to report on New Caledonia from 2004 (see section on UN 'reinscription' below).

The 1956 Defferre *loi cadre* (framework law) aimed at more engagement by the *outre-mer* (Overseas France) peoples in their own administration (Law No 56-619 of 23 June 1956, Article 1). At the time, the French State was grappling with major challenges, particularly in Indochina and Algeria, and its own government was unstable. By 1954 France had withdrawn from Indochina. The Fourth Republic had seen 21 changes of government in 12 years. Echoing the interplay between developments in the overseas colonies and domestic politics in France, which obtained during the 19th century, mishandling of the rebellion in Algeria contributed largely to the demise of the Fourth Republic (see Dunmore 1997, 245; Ziller and Faberon 2007, 21; Bély 2001, 119), and de Gaulle again formed a government.

De Gaulle's Fifth Republic introduced a new constitution that enshrined the principle of free determination of its peoples and the possibility of new institutions for the overseas territories desirous of participating in them, with a view to their 'democratic evolution' (Preamble). De Gaulle turned the French Union into a Community, and referendums were held in 1958 throughout the empire on the new French constitution, which de Gaulle made clear was a vote for staying with France (Henningham 1992, 123). In his rhetoric, de Gaulle specified two things, first, that the contemporary world made it necessary to belong to large economic and political federations, and second, that a no vote would mean going it alone, with France not giving 'further moral or material help'. These are arguments that have been used by French leaders right up to the present. By voting yes, the colonies could choose either integration into France, to continue the status quo, or expanded autonomy as a self-governing member of the French Community, effectively laying the basis for independence. By

1960, all but one of France's African possessions had taken up the independence option. All three Pacific colonies voted to stay with France, New Caledonia with a vote of 98 per cent, and Wallis and Futuna 95 per cent. French Polynesia returned a far lower vote, 64 per cent, owing to the efforts of independence leader Pouvanaa who was promptly arrested (see French Polynesia below). But, as the years ahead were to show, political evolution was subsequently seen as taking place within an indivisible French Republic.

Strategic factors

De Gaulle's 'politics of *grandeur*' was based on the idea that France, befitting its status as one of the five Permanent Members of the UN Security Council, would restore its global position as a *puissance mondiale moyenne* (middle-sized world power), in the wake of the losses of World War II, Indochina and, in 1962, Algeria, not to mention the defeats of World War I and the 1870 Prussian War. Self-reliance was a key ingredient to this policy, based on the *force de frappe*, or independent French nuclear deterrent. In 1960, France acquired the atomic bomb, and established a testing program in Algeria. After 1962, nuclear testing that had been carried out in Algeria was to take place in the Pacific, at Moruroa and Fangataufa in French Polynesia. It would be essential to maintain the Pacific possessions in the French fold, lest a change in status in one encouraged independence moves in French Polynesia. De Gaulle told New Caledonians when he visited in 1966, 'You are *France australe* (France in the south). You have a French role to play in the world' (in Waddell 2008, 56), before landing in French Polynesia to witness one of the first nuclear tests there.

France's acquisition of nuclear capability and testing practices were not an isolated act by a pretentious European state in the Pacific. Its nuclear program formed part of a Western schema of similar activity there, by Britain, at Maralinga in Australia, and the United States, at Bikini Atoll in the Gilbert group. In the early days of the Cold War, the international reaction against nuclear testing was slow to gather momentum, but when it took hold criticism of France was strong, particularly in the neighbouring Pacific region, where a general distaste for nuclear testing by Western powers had been evident from as early as 1956 (see South Pacific Forum action below).

Another major international development in the strategic backdrop to France's changing approaches to autonomy demands in the postwar period was the 1982 Law of the Sea Convention (UNCLOS). After years of negotiation, the international community agreed to establish 200-mile Exclusive Economic Zones (EEZ), legally increasing dramatically the surface of global sovereignty to individual countries.

For France, as for many other governments still with overseas possessions, this was the most important single stroke for extending national sovereignty since the haphazard declarations of the eighteenth century. Although UNCLOS sets out the framework for, and records, nations' claims, consistent precise figures about each nation's rightful EEZ are difficult to establish. But the overall effect for France is clear. The French EEZ, i.e., its sea resources alone,[1] is now the second largest in the world after that of the United States. French territorial sovereignty including all of its departments and territories overseas (DOM TOM), now extended over 40 per cent of the total global maritime zones, or 8 per cent of the surface of the globe, while France's land area covered only .45 per cent of the globe. Compared to the EEZ of the French metropolitan 'hexagon' alone of just 340,290 square kilometers, France's total EEZ grew to 11.57 million square kilometres (m. sq. km.), of which 7.3 m. sq. km. arose from its Pacific possessions and just under 5 m. sq. km. of that, from French Polynesia alone (*Outre-mer* tables in Faberon and Ziller 2007, 8). While some French writers have claimed that France derives minimal economic return from its large EEZ (e.g. Leymarie 1985, 4) and it is true that much of the potential remains unknown, control over these resources boosted France's geopolitical prestige globally, and particularly at a time when it was under attack in the region, both for its handling of Kanak independence claims in New Caledonia, and for its nuclear testing in French Polynesia (see Mrgudovic 2008, 81 et seq).

Moreover, from the 1980s, the Pacific Ocean once again began to be described as the new centre of the world, with writers and thinkers heralding the twenty-first century as the Pacific century. In a sense, this was nothing new. There had been an earlier movement in France in the 1880s led by the Oceanic Lobby Group in Paris (Aldrich 1988). But this time, the new wave of attention to the Pacific was global, and arose from dynamic economic growth in the rapidly industrialising Asian tigers (South East Asia, Hong Kong, South Korea), with China poised in the background — all of these being littoral Pacific states. A European country with a direct stake in the region, even if it was simply in the southern hemisphere of the Pacific, where its Pacific naval presence was based, had a perceived advantageous foothold in an economically significant region (see Lacour 1987, 131). Europe's exclusion from the newly emerging Asian Pacific Economic Co-operation grouping in the late 1980s to early 1990s, and

---

1 Comparisons of EEZs are indicative only of a sovereign power's control over *sea resources beyond its territorial sea*. When comparing total land, territorial seas and EEZ areas, France ranks seventh after Russia, the United States, Australia, Canada, China and Brazil. It is worth noting that there is a minute difference between France's combined EEZ and territorial seas (11.57 million square kilometres (m. sq. km.)) and its EEZ, territorial seas and land (11.7 m. sq. km.) whereas for example with Russia there is a far larger difference (7.5 m. sq. km. to 24 .6 m. sq. km.), reflecting the larger land mass of the latter (Wikipedia EEZ accessed 1 July 2009). Thus the relative potential increase in resources by virtue of an EEZ is far greater for France.

British effective withdrawal from the South Pacific in the same period (although it had defined its 'east of Suez' policy much earlier), only served to strengthen French tenaciousness there.

Early postwar regional context

Within the South Pacific region, postwar France was increasingly working in a regional environment, joining up with the governments of the Netherlands, the United States and the United Kingdom, Australia and New Zealand to form the South Pacific Commission (known as the Secretariat of the Pacific Community from 1998) (SPC) in 1947, with its headquarters in Noumea. The genesis of the commission was one of consultations amongst those powers responsible for various Pacific islands on the basis of either colonial ties (France, the Netherlands, the United Kingdom) or UN mandates (the United States, Australia, New Zealand). After 1964, with the accession of the first independent Pacific island state, Western Samoa (which became independent in 1962), the organisation included independent states, and added a technical assistance role (see Foreign Affairs and Trade 1997; SPC 2007).

France from the beginning saw the SPC as a threat to its authority. Along with the Netherlands and the United Kingdom, France resisted proposals from Australia, New Zealand and the United States for elected delegates, and calls by island leaders from 1965 to have representation in Noumea (Bates 1990, 42). More critically for its own interests, France actively opposed *political* (as distinct from technical) discussion at SPC meetings. Frustrated by being unable to discuss in the SPC the issues of regional nuclear testing and New Caledonian independence demands, the new island governments formed the South Pacific Forum (SPF) in 1971 (renamed Pacific Islands Forum (PIF) in 2000; see Fry 1981; Henningham 1992, 197). The Forum was established specifically as a political forum, and its first political preoccupations targeted French policies (see Forum Communiqué 1971). France was to tread a rocky path with the Forum in the 1970s and 1980s, and bilaterally with some of its members (see New Caledonia and French Polynesia below). But, through it all, France was to retain the SPC headquarters in Noumea and its membership of the SPC, thereby retaining a privileged status and valuable asset when it finally sought to improve its standing in the region in the latter 1980s (see Chapter 3).

Institutional structures at home

The management of the colonies in metropolitan France changed little at this time. A ministry for colonies had been established in 1894. Before then, the office of colonies that Richelieu had established in 1710 had handled the overseas colonies for almost 200 years, attached to the marine secretariat, later ministry. The 1894 ministry was located at one end of the Louvre, which, Bélorgey (2002, 84) noted, justly reflected the poorly reduced empire after the Napoleonic losses that century. In 1910 it relocated to the *hôtel* at Rue Oudinot, where it remains today. The ministry was simply divided into economic and political directorates until after World War II.

During the war, both the Vichy and Free French governments had their colonial ministries, each seeing the 'Overseas France' as important elements of their power (despite their incapacity to defend them, see Thomas 1998, Chapters 1 and 2). Bélorgey noted the great hopes after the War that the colonial empire would contribute to maintaining France's global prestige in the wake of the ignominious wartime experience (2002, 85). In 1946 — with the *départementalisation* of the four 'old colonies' — Guyana, Réunion, Martinique and Guadeloupe came under the purview of the interior ministry. After 1958, the departments and the territories were reunited in the ministry of the DOM-TOM (*départements et territoires d'outre-mer*, or overseas departments and territories) under the prime minister, reflecting their importance as equal but different parts of France. The two remain so to this day, albeit under the simpler nomenclature of '*Outre-mer*' (Overseas France).

Autonomy demands in the Pacific collectivities

It is against this background that demands for increasing autonomy in the New Hebrides, New Caledonia, and French Polynesia emerged in the postwar period. Events in each exerted influence on the others and shaped current challenges.

As for tiny Wallis and Futuna, after it voted in 1959 to stay with France, it became a French Overseas Territory in legislation enacted in 1961 which governs the entity, essentially unchallenged, to this day (Loi No 61-814 of 19 July 1961) (de Deckker 2003a, 66; Faberon and Ziller 2007, 335). The islands' principal interconnection with the other French entities during this period has been the migration of a substantial part of its labour force to New Caledonia (see Chapter 4).

New Hebrides becomes Vanuatu

France did not want to lose its presence in the New Hebrides ('We're staying', said the French Resident in 1969 in Henningham 1992, 31), not least because of the example its loss might provide to its other Pacific entities. An independent Vanuatu represented a loss within the context of France's *grandeur* policy and its *puissance mondiale moyenne* status. But, despite French efforts to resist decolonisation, because France was sharing power in the New Hebrides with Britain, because Britain was on a path of relinquishing its presence east of Suez and granting independence to its Pacific colonies, and also because of France's own clumsy handling of demands for independence, the condominium of New Hebrides became the independent state of Vanuatu in July 1980. French interests in the Pacific were again usurped by Britain's interests, and local indigenous forces.

Again, the old French Catholic v. British Protestant fault line came into play. Calls for independence first came from mainly English-speaking Protestants, while those favouring autonomy of individual islands were primarily French-speaking and Catholic Melanesians. Each was suspicious of the other. As in New Caledonia during the war, the French attributed negative motives to Australia and New Zealand (Coutau-Bégarie 1987, 287; Dornoy-Vurobaravu 1994; Dunmore 1997, 268) and, indeed, Australia briefly considered taking over from Britain in a tutelage role for Vanuatu, but rejected the idea swiftly (Personal communication from former senior Australian official, 2009).

The key issues catalysing independence calls were land acquisition by settlers, and European legal systems, the latter challenging local custom. Such differences, together with a cargo cult mentality in a number of small groupings, provided an impetus to phenomena such as Jimmy Stephens' Nagriamel movement, which propounded independence. Moves made by French planters into cattle ranching in the 1960s, taking up interior land, also heightened differences. Although the numbers of French residents in the New Hebrides were small after the war (in 1949, 900 French citizens compared to 320 British citizens, and 1750 'protected French citizens', mainly Indochinese working on the plantations, Dunmore 1997, 253), France continued to invest extensively in infrastructure to support French planters there. In 1971 Stephens appealed to the UN for independence to be granted within a year. The same year, the former Anglican minister Walter Lini formed the Vanuatu Party. Numerous francophone parties were formed to counter it, one allying itself with Stephens' group. The French sought to discourage support for independence, using the familiar argument that resource-poor countries would collapse (Henningham 1992, 35). A representative assembly was formed in 1974. The Vanuatu Party won elections in 1975 and 1979, after forming and then disbanding a provisional government in 1977.

France, influenced by New Caledonian lobbyists with interests vested in trade and other links with their French New Hebrides compatriots, had been sympathetic to Stephens. French officials worked behind the scenes with parties opposing the Vanuatu Party before the 1979 elections. French Secretary of State for the Overseas, Paul Dijoud, played a role in securing a quasi-federal arrangement to allow for separate identities, and continued French influence, in Santo and

Tanna. This was probably motivated by the precedent set in the Indian Ocean territory of Mayotte in 1975, which had remained French while the Comoros in the same archipelago had become independent (described in Henningham 1992, 38–42). The victory of the Vanuatu Party was a surprise, especially in French-dominated Santo and Tanna. In response, Stephens' movement grew into a secessionist rebellion, proclaiming a Republic of Vemarana on Santo in 1979, which the French were suspected of having supported (Dunmore 1997, 269). Only a week before independence, the French Resident told French residents on Santo that France would intervene to protect it and give it special status. Since France vetoed sending a joint Anglo–French police force to restore order in the rebellious islands, the new independent government invited Papua New Guinea to send troops to assist it in dealing with the rebels, which it did — with Australian logistical support — within days.

Stephen Henningham's account of the 1979 elections leading to full self-government indicates that French policies may have suffered by the short-term rotation of its officials in the New Hebrides, in contrast to British officials who stayed for long periods and could develop deeper knowledge of the forces at play. In Paris, there were differences between the defence ministry and Overseas France department on the one hand, which were pro-settler, and the more pragmatic foreign affairs and political leadership. The bottom line was that the French Government had the power to control the policies of its officials but chose not to do so. A legacy of bitterness remained, despite customary ceremonies of reconciliation.

Vanuatu's first Prime Minister, Walter Lini, unsurprisingly, pursued anti-French policies. He expelled around 700 French residents including planters, missionaries, officials and security people, most of whom went to New Caledonia where they became ardent anti-independence supporters. Vanuatu joined the British Commonwealth. It supported independence groups in New Caledonia, promoting their cause in the UN, and criticised French nuclear testing at Moruroa. It became one of the founding members of the Melanesian Spearhead Group (MSG) in the 1980s, mainly to pursue these objectives. It was only after Lini left the political scene in 1991 that relations with France improved. Although French aid continued during Lini's tenure (about $A8 million in 1981 or one third of the budget, Henningham 1992, 44), it was controversial and heavy-handed, and centred on French cultural and education projects. France contributed financially to opposition parties on the eve of 1987 elections, resulting in the expulsion of the French ambassador (Chesneaux and Maclellan 1992, 197). And France threatened to withdraw its aid when Vanuatu agreed to host the dissident New Caledonian Kanaky government in 1987 (Mrgudovic 2008, 222–23). By 1990 things had improved to the point where Vanuatu had introduced a virtual diplomatic détente with France. Nonetheless, unease remains, represented, for example, in Vanuatu's continuing participation in the MSG; and in its claim, in competition with that of France, to Matthew and Hunter Islands, two islands 300-kilometres east of New Caledonia and south of Vanuatu.

One of the legacies of Vanuatu's colonial experience, and arguably its experience with the French, was the damaging effect on regional security, with implications for Australia and Western interests broadly. Vanuatu adopted anti-West policies, or, at the most generous interpretation, became skilled in playing off Western interests against those of external Cold War players like the Soviet Union and Libya. It entertained invitations by Libya for scholarships for its students in the 1980s, establishing diplomatic relations in 1987. It was one of only two island states (the other being Kiribati) to sign a fishing contract with the Soviet Union in 1986, and one of only a few states (New Zealand, Palau, Solomon Islands) to ban nuclear ships from visiting its ports. It was one of only two states (Tonga being the other) not to have ratified the South Pacific Nuclear Free Zone in 1986–1987. It is difficult to disagree with the judgement of Papua New Guinea's then Ambassador to the UN, Renagi Lohia, that France's policies were 'a direct threat to peace, security and stability in our region and they have serious implications for international peace and security' (cited in Bates 1990, 109).

The post-colonial experience of Vanuatu illustrated what may be in store for the other French entities seeking independence. Substantially reduced French aid forced Vanuatu to look for donors in new and less desirable places, and the composition of what France did provide, was perceived as political interference and therefore destabilising. Even today, French interlocutors will point to Vanuatu as the inevitable result should France leave its other Pacific entities (Personal communications 2001–2004). Vanuatu's leaders themselves warned New Caledonia leader Jean-Marie Tjibaou about not pressing too hard for independence, cautioning *'le risque est l'oubli'* (lest New Caledonia be forgotten), and mirroring de Gaulle's threats about withdrawing support from colonies voting to leave France (comments by Rollat in Regnault and Fayaud 2008, 57).

The Vanuatu experience hardened France's attitude to independence demands in New Caledonia and French Polynesia, and its anti 'Anglo-Saxon' prejudices. It stiffened French resolve to continue nuclear testing, and their resistance to regional criticism.

New Caledonia: Violent road to compromise and innovation

The story of New Caledonia's political development from World War II until the 1980s, reveals a pattern of French fitfulness and outright reneging over promised extensions of autonomy and self-government, which contributed substantially to the emotional eruption of protest in the 1980s, and which leaves continuing questions about the full implementation of agreements struck since then (more fully reviewed by Connell 1987, Dornoy-Vurobaravu1994, Henningham 1992, Faberon and Ziller 2007). There were 12 statutory changes from the 1950s to the present (summarised at Appendix 2).

As in Vanuatu, the first political groupings in New Caledonia directly reflected Catholic/Protestant demarcations. In 1946 two groupings were formed, the Catholic Union des Indigènes Calédoniens Amis de la Liberté dans l'Ordre (Union of Indigenous Caledonian Friends of Liberty in Order, UICALO) and the Protestant Association des Indigènes Calédoniens et Loyaltiens Français (Association of Indigenous Caledonians and French Loyalty Islanders, AICLF), which, when forged together by Maurice Lenormand in 1953, became the Union Calédonienne (Caledonian Union, UC), the first political party of New Caledonia, under the banner, 'two colours, one united people', and which persists today.

The UC was a remarkable combination of the interests of European and indigenous New Caledonians. Lenormand became the first vice-president, or head, of the small (7 member) Council of Government elected in 1957 in accordance with the Defferre laws (the 1957 Decree of 22 July 1957 implemented the 1956 Loi Defferre for New Caledonia). The 98 per cent support for staying with France in the 1959 referendum showed a certain unity of purpose of the peoples of New Caledonia, which could perhaps be explained by a feeling that their wishes for greater autonomy were in general being met by the French administration at the time. But, while at first the French State was committed to an evolving democratic system for its colonies, it was to rethink this position following local pressures for change from European settlers and residents concerned by the majority representation of the UC in the territorial assembly.

The Jacquinot Law of 21 December 1963 began a series of statutory changes to roll back the powers of the council. It relegated the council to a consultative role only, removed ministers, and increased the powers of the French State. It effectively returned to the *status quo ante* of 1957 (Bates 1990, 12). The 1969 Billotte Law (3 January), primarily focused on taxation exemptions for the mining industry, was designed to stop control of the mining sector being sought by the local political elite who were being lobbied by a major Canadian-based company, INCO, to allow competition against the French effective monopoly,

Société le Nickel (SLN) (Coutau-Bégarie and Seurin 1986, Chapter 2 and Maclellan 2005d). The law effectively gave the French State, already a major shareholder in SLN, power over any transaction relating to nickel, cobalt and chrome (Guillebaud 1976, 171). It also created communes under the control of the French State.

The nickel boom of 1969–1972 justified France's desire to hold the purse strings. Production of nickel virtually tripled from 1967 to 1971 and, for a time, some of New Caledonia's GDP indices outstripped those of metropolitan France (Waddell 2008, 74). The boom meant an influx of experts and service people related to the mining industry from metropolitan France (see Tables 4.1a and 4.2, Chapter 4). This influx of Europeans was not solely due to the nickel boom. Enunciating an overt French policy of encouraging external migration for political reasons, French Prime Minister and former DOM-TOM Minister Pierre Messmer wrote to his DOM-TOM secretary of state on 17 July 1972 that indigenous nationalist claims could only be avoided if residents coming from metropolitan France, or from elsewhere in Overseas France, became the demographic majority ('*À long terme, la revendication nationaliste autochtone ne sera évitée que si les communautés allogènes représentent une masse démographique majoritaire*' in Sanguinetti 1985, 26). From the late 1960s, the Melanesians were no longer the majority population, significantly changing the political complexion of the territory, and doubtless of the UC itself.

By 1969, Nidoish Naisseline of the Loyalty Islands, returning with many of his peers from studies in France with fresh experience of the 1968 student insurrections, formed the mainly Kanak Foulards Rouges (Red Scarves) calling for independence. In 1971, another Kanak, Elie Poigoune, formed the 1878 group, referring to the 1878 Kanak rebellion. This political activity, combined with the end of the nickel boom, meant that a number of Europeans left the territory from the mid 1970s. The UC continued to call for more autonomy, one of its Kanak leaders, Roch Pidjot, submitting proposals to France in 1971, 1975 and 1977. In 1975 Yann Céléné Urégei, having left the UC, formed the Union multiraciale (Multiracial Union) and went to Paris to seek more autonomy. His claims were rejected, and President Giscard d'Estaing declined to meet him. Stung, he transformed his objectives to independence demands, joining the Comité de coordination pour l'indépendance Kanak (Committee for the Coordination of Kanak Independence). Also in 1975, a rising political leader and former Marist priest, Jean-Marie Tjibaou, organised the Melanesia 2000 festival, an event funded by the French State and the local assembly, focused on Melanesian identity and culture which involved representatives from the wider Pacific region. Tjibaou travelled the islands of New Caledonia, consulting clans and unifying support behind the festival celebrating Kanak cultural identity (see Waddell 2008). And, in 1975, the Kanak parties joined to form the Parti de Libération Kanak (Kanak Liberation Party, Palika). Urégei's party became the Front Uni de Libération Kanak (United Kanak Liberation Front, FULK) in 1977.

While disaffected Kanaks left the UC fold, so did unhappy rightwing Europeans. When in 1977 the UC, now led by prominent Kanak leaders Tjibaou, Eloi Machoro and Yeiwene Yeiwene, began to push for independence, Jacques Lafleur formed the Rassemblement pour la Calédonie (Rally for [New] Caledonia, RPC), which became in 1978 the Rassemblement pour la Calédonie dans la République (Rally for [New] Caledonia within the Republic, RPCR). His party won the 1977 territorial elections, and he displaced Pidjot as elected *Député* in the French early in 1978, a position he retained until 2007. Lafleur's party, with an anti-independence coalition called the Front National pour une Nouvelle Société Calédonienne (National Front for a New Caledonian Society, FNSC) won the 1979 elections, although the independentists received 35 per cent of the vote (Faberon and Ziller 2007, 351). The RPCR was by no means solely European in complexion. Senior Melanesian loyalists Jean-Pierre Aifa and Dick Ukeiwé respectively became the RPCR government's president and vice-president.

French Government responses to demands for further autonomy from the moderates, and to growing support amongst Kanaks for independence and assertion of their cultural identity, were not seen as adequate. While the Stirn Statute (28 December 1976) claimed to deliver a path to autonomy, it comprised only small steps, including establishing a vice-president of the governing council and individual responsibilities for its members and withdrawing the right to vote from the French High Commissioner, who nonetheless continued to preside over the council. French actions were seen as manipulation of elections and surveillance of pro-autonomists (Guillebaud 1976, 121). The Dijoud Plan (1978) was focused on land reform, but only with the suspension of any consideration of independence for 10 years. The Loi Dijoud (Law no 79-407, 24 May 1979), which implemented an eligibility threshold of 7.5 per cent of the vote for parties to participate in the territorial assembly, to address the proliferation of small parties, was perceived as a tightening of the central government's control. These measures were rejected outright in the territory, the multiple Kanak parties forming themselves into the Front Indépendantiste (Independence Front, FI) to evade the Dijoud Plan's intentions. The FI included the LKS (Libération Kanak Socialiste, Socialist Kanak Liberation), FULK (Front Uni de la Libération Kanak, United Kanak Liberation Front), the UPM (Union Progressiste Mélanésienne, Popular Melanesian Union), and the PSC (Parti Socialiste Calédonie, [New] Caledonian Socialist Party). Its president was Tjibaou.

Les événements — violence erupts

Although there had been some violent incidents and tensions earlier (Naisseline and others were arrested for sedition in the 1970s, and a young Kanak was shot dead by a policeman in December 1975), it was in the early 1980s that violence and confrontation increased in what were referred to as the *événements* ('events' or 'disturbances').

By 1979 the polarisation of political interests had solidified into two camps, the primarily Kanak independentist group and the mainly European group loyal to France (loyalist), but with some Kanaks and Europeans in each. This has remained the basic dynamic of politics in the region. In 1981 the UC, which in August 1980 had announced it would declare independence on 24 September 1982, asked the French Government to recognise New Caledonia's right to independence, and the SPF sent a mission to Paris to argue the same cause. Here the role of French domestic politics must once again be recognised: a new socialist government headed by François Mitterrand had boosted the confidence of the pro-independence camp. Mitterrand responded favourably to the UC's demands, writing that *'nous demandons que le droit des peuples à disposer d'eux-mêmes … soit effectivement reconnu au peuple Kanak'* ('we ask that the right of peoples to decide for themselves should be recognised for the Kanak people' in Angleviel 2006, 139).

But, on 19 September 1981, the UC Secretary-General Pierre Declercq was killed; it is thought by rightwing extremists, though, somewhat incredibly, the culprit was never found. By June 1982 RPCR's former partner the FNSC, apparently with active French government backing (Henningham 1992, 72; Angleviel 2006, 140), moved over to join the FI in a new governing council headed by Tjibaou as vice-president (the president being the French High Commissioner). Rightwing demonstrators, disaffected by these arrangements (many Europeans from the FNSC shifted allegiance to the RPCR), turned out onto the streets that year, and assaulted FI and FNSC members in the assembly building. The FI mobilised its supporters and set up roadblocks. Tensions mounted. In early 1983, in separate incidents, a police station was bombarded with rocks by Melanesian youths at Touho; and, at Koindé, Melanesians protesting police action during a demonstration against sawmill pollution, shot at police, killing two gendarmes and wounding six others. In May 1983 a Kanak was killed by a settler at Koindé-Ouipoin after a quarrel, and Palika supporters destroyed a post office, houses and cars in retaliation. Numerous land occupations took place including an extensive one by Machoro in March 1984. Meanwhile the FNSC dissolved, its supporters returning to the RPCR.

In July 1983, representatives of the FI, the RPCR and others participated in a roundtable conference at Nainville-les-Roches in France chaired by DOM-

TOM Secretary of State, Georges Lemoine. This was the first meeting of all three parties (pro-France, pro-independence, and the French State) at the instigation of France and established a precedent of the French State taking at once the roles of arbiter, player, and enforcer of law and order, which persists until the present. It resulted in France's historic recognition of the Kanaks' 'innate and active right to independence' as well as Kanak agreement to the participation of the whole population of New Caledonia in determining the future — thus laying the seeds of the future Matignon and Noumea Accords. Although the RPCR refused to sign the resulting statement and the FI was obliged to denounce the outcome owing to its non-acceptance by the smaller parties, that the meeting itself took place was a watershed of sorts.

The French followed up the meeting with the Lemoine Statute (Lemoine Law, 6 September 1984) providing for elections in 1984, increased internal autonomy and a five-year transition period for a vote on independence in 1989. Despite the opposition of the territorial assembly, the statute was adopted by the French national assembly. The statute included some novel elements, such as seats for customary representatives, legislative powers and removal of the French High Commissioner from the ministerial council. But neither the pro-France nor independentists accepted it.

The essence of the differences centred on the effects of immigration, with the FI wanting a 'restricted' electorate confined to those with long-term connections to the territory, a concern that was to remain at the heart of future negotiations. They calculated that Kanaks formed close to 40 per cent of a general electorate, but outnumbered Europeans in a 'restricted' electorate defined by Kanaks and second-generation settlers.

In keeping up the pressure, the FI were also conscious that the election of a conservative French government in 1986 legislative elections would further set back their cause. On 24 September 1984, the anniversary of the 1853 annexation of New Caledonia by France, they transformed themselves into a more militant liberation front, the FLNKS (Front de Libération Nationale Kanak et Socialiste or Kanak Socialist National Liberation Front), which also included the UC, FULK, and UPM. Until 1986 it included the GFKEL or Groupe des Femmes Kanak et Exploitées, Group of Kanak and Exploited Women and, until 1989, the USTKE or Union Syndicale des Travailleurs Kanaks et des Exploités, the Federation of Unions of Kanak and Exploited Workers, a labour union federation. They declared the name of the future independent country would be Kanaky, with a green, red and blue flag overlaid with a *flèche faîtière*, or traditional hut-top totem finial. Two other, less hardline, pro-independence parties, also offshoots of the UC, remained outside FLNKS, Naisseline's LKS, and the PFK (Parti Fédéral Kanak, Kanak Federal Party). On the other side, an extremist rightwing party, the Front National (NF, National Front), emerged.

The FLNKS called for a boycott of the 18 November 1984 elections. On that day, Machoro wielded an axe against the ballot box at Canala, and burned the ballot papers, while others burnt town halls and disrupted polling, often violently. This act is commonly viewed as the beginning of the *événements*. The participation rate in the election was approximately 50 per cent, against the more usual 70 to 80 per cent. For weeks afterwards, militant Melanesians maintained roadblocks, sparking serious clashes, including killings. On 1 December 1984, the FLNKS formed a provisional government with Tjibaou at its head. The French State sent a new High Commissioner, Edgard Pisani, who secured agreement with Tjibaou, on 5 December, to lift the barricades. Later that day, however, at Hienghène in the north, 10 Kanaks were killed in an ambush, including two of Tjibaou's brothers. Tjibaou, who was expected to have been with the group, had unexpectedly stayed in Noumea. In a measure of his stature and leadership, Tjibaou overcame his personal loss and stuck to the dialogue process, and his agreement to lift the barricades. The assassins, local mixed-race farmers, were later acquitted.

The hastily concocted Pisani Plan (proposed only three days after Pisani's arrival in the territory on 4 January, elements of the plan were incorporated in the Fabius Pisani Law of 23 August 1985) essentially posited independence in association with France, consistent with Article 88 of the French constitution, an article which had never before been applied, providing for the Republic to conclude agreements with states 'which desire to associate themselves with it to develop their civilisations' (Christnacht 2004, 43). The plan provided for a vote within months, by July 1985, by those who were residents of three-years standing, with France retaining 'regalian', or core, sovereign responsibilities such as internal and external security in the event of independence. The plan appeared to have drawn on the US compacts-in-association with its Pacific possessions (Armand Hage in de Deckker 2006, 285). Pisani himself admitted that he saw the proposals as a shock tactic to oblige Europeans to understand the need for change (Henningham 1992, 86). The RPCR, while denouncing the plan, agreed to participate in the referendum if there were no change to the franchise, to demonstrate majority opinion against independence. Once again, the effects of immigration were at issue.

The Pisani Plan was the nearest that New Caledonia had come to a vote for independence since 1958. Paradoxically it was offered in the wake of almost intolerable tension and violence, and yet it was precisely these tensions that aborted it. In November, Eloi Machoro's supporters had attacked some hardline rightwing settlers and killed one of them, Yves Tual. Rightwing demonstrations and riots ensued, only ending on 12 January, when a military police sniper shot dead Machoro and an aide at a farm Machoro had been occupying near La Foa on the west coast. In a fleeting visit in January 1985, Mitterrand declared that

France would maintain its role and strategic presence and would reinforce the military base at Noumea (Leymarie 1985, 1). Sporadic incidents continued in 1985. Pisani left in May 1985, to be succeeded, perhaps aptly in view of the state of the territory, by the former ambassador in Beirut (Faberon and Ziller 2007, 354).

The next proposal, the Fabius Plan (Law of 23 August 1985), was a patch-up, window-dressing effort — against the background of the imminent and expected legislative victory of the conservatives in France in 1986, who would not be expected to implement it — to address the need for the Kanaks to have a measure of democratic control. The Fabius Statute provided for the break-up of New Caledonia into regions, in some of which, notably the north and the Loyalty Islands, the Kanaks would be in the majority and at least could exercise power there. The majority of the pro-France group in Noumea and overall would ensure a continuation of the status quo. This 'regionalisation' was a critical principle, which was retained in subsequent negotiations. But the Fabius Law returned executive power to the High Commissioner, tightening the power of the French State. The subsequent regional elections, in September 1985, saw strong participation and the return of Tjibaou in the north, and Lafleur in the south.

International and regional developments: UN reinscription of New Caledonia as a non-self-governing territory

The French disposition to broker some kind of compromise at this time was influenced by other developments in the surrounding region and in the UN. France had now become the focus of international attention and regional opprobrium, not only for its policies in New Caledonia but also for its nuclear testing in French Polynesia (see below). Its policies were contrary to the sense of political evolution in the surrounding region at the time, where decolonisation was under way (Western Samoa achieved independence in 1962, Nauru in 1968, Tonga and Fiji in 1970, Papua New Guinea in 1975, and Vanuatu in 1980).

France had persisted in its non-compliance with UN decolonisation principles, ignoring the 1960 UN Declaration on the Granting of Independence to Colonial Countries and Peoples and its associated Decolonisation Committee (also known as the Committee of 24) (UNGA Resolution 1514 (XV) and Resolution 1541 of 14 December 1960). FLNKS leaders had urged the SPF to support 'reinscription' of New Caledonia as a non-self governing territory with the UN Decolonisation Committee from the late 1970s and early 1980s. New Caledonia was the subject of close SPF attention. As the island states successively gained their own independence, they began to call on the UN for self-determination in the non-independent states. The FI presented a petition to the Forum in 1979. Although the SPF recorded its regret and concern at France's nuclear testing in its first communiqué (Forum Communiqué 1971), its first formal reference to decolonisation occurred in 1981, and in 1982 the SPF expressly referred to the need for New Caledonia's decolonisation (Communiqué 1982).

Melanesian countries neighbouring New Caledonia (Papua New Guinea, Solomon Islands and Vanuatu) united to form the MSG expressly to support Kanak independence in New Caledonia in the mid 1980s (including Fiji from 1988). The MSG acted as a ginger group within the SPF. It was Australia who had urged the Forum to exercise restraint on the New Caledonia, in order to give new French proposals a chance to work. Only in 1986, after France hardened its position with Chirac's reversal of reforms in his Pons I proposals, did Canberra's stance in the SPF change.

The Kanak independence issue had been gathering external momentum at the time. FLNKS sent 17 Kanaks to Libya, an international terrorist pariah, for training in 1985, sparking concern in Australia and amongst western allies. The Nonaligned Movement admitted the FLNKS as an official observer in 1986. Mounting international opprobrium against France over nuclear testing, particularly the bombing of Greenpeace's *Rainbow Warrior* (see below) added to the mix.

With Australia's change of position, in 1986, the SPF unanimously supported reinscription. Tjibaou went to New York to work with South Pacific delegations, culminating in the UN General Assembly (UNGA) affirming the inalienable right of the people of New Caledonia to self-determination in December 1986, and the reinscription of New Caledonia as a non-self-governing territory with the UN Decolonisation Committee (UNGA Resolution 40/41, 2 December 1986). Despite extensive French diplomatic lobbying and expenditure to reduce support, the UNGA reaffirmed this position in 1987 and to this day passes an annual resolution on New Caledonia, without a vote (see UNGA Resolutions Question of New Caledonia, 1987 to present). New Caledonia remains under consideration by the Decolonisation Committee, whose secretariat prepares annual working papers on New Caledonia (see for example A/AC.109/2012/15 Committee for Decolonisation Working Paper on New Caledonia). France declined to fulfill UN obligations to submit an annual report, as the administering authority, until well after the Noumea Accord was signed, from 2004 (see Chapter 4). The committee received submissions regularly from others, mainly various Kanak groups including, most often, FLNKS figure Roch Wamytan.

Despite the Australian government's restraining role within the SPF, civil society played a major role in mounting international pressure on France, fuelled by antipathy to French nuclear testing in the region. Non-governmental groups created direct links in New Caledonia and French Polynesia. Throughout the *événements*, Kanak students trained in Australia and had close contacts with Aboriginal, Church, student and union groups. Powerful unions, including of teachers and dockworkers, supported their case, with the New South Wales Teachers Federation contributing funds to a Kanak radio station in Noumea, Radio Djiido, which had been created by the Matignon Accords. These groups were key constituencies of the then Labor government led by Bob Hawke. Relations with France deteriorated as Hawke introduced a ban on uranium exports in 1985, and then on French ministerial and official visits in 1986 (although he reinstated uranium exports).

In 1987, France expelled John Dauth, Australia's Consul-General in Noumea. While the French did not give any public[2] or private background reason for the expulsion, they clearly were not happy with Australia's policies and, in particular, France's very public defeat on the floor of the UN General Assembly in New York at the hands of the SPF (Personal communication from former senior Australian official, 2009).

Institutional factors: *Cohabitation*

Unfolding events were to demonstrate once more the dominating influence of French national domestic politics on its Pacific entities. French national legislative elections took place in March 1986 and, as expected, returned a rightist government under Chirac as prime minister. This was the first period of *cohabitation*, when the president (then socialist Mitterrand) was of one political complexion, while the government, headed by Chirac, was of the other. This dynamic was to colour the handling of the New Caledonian situation at a critical time (see, especially, Cordonnier 1995b), the more so since it is the president who is responsible for defence and foreign affairs, and the prime minister who oversees the handling of internal policies. During a period when French policy in the South Pacific was constantly under international scrutiny, the effects of *cohabitation* were not constructive overall and arguably delayed resolution of New Caledonian internal tensions. The nature of the policy-making process, which engaged a broad range of agency interests only inadequately coordinated on a daily basis by the relatively junior Overseas France ministry, complicated these negative effects and led to policy mistakes. Moreover, there was a close relationship between Chirac and Lafleur, leader of the RPCR in New Caledonia, the latter supplying donations to Chirac's campaign funds and fuelling Chirac's criticism of Mitterrand's handling of New Caledonia.

---

2 It was put about as an ostensible reason that Dauth had given Australian Government aid to the Kanak Cultural Centre at Hienghiène, which the French construed as interference (Personal comments, O'Leary 2009), an idea which still had currency when the author served as Australian Consul-General as late as 2001–2004.

And so, the new French government once again set about rolling back the provisions of the previous statutes. It created a unified land agency, the ADRAF (Agence de développement rural et d'aménagement foncier — Rural Development and Land Management Agency) which effectively suspended the purchase of settler properties for redistribution and introduced redistribution to all communities, not just Melanesians (Henningham 1992, 100). Similarly, the Kanak Cultural Office was replaced by an organisation that represented all cultures, and Tjibaou was removed as director.

As early as July 1986 the Chirac government introduced the Pons I statute (Law of 17 July 1986) providing for a self-determination vote in 1987 on the basis of only three-years residence in New Caledonia, the latter which was patently unacceptable to the independentists. With a low 59 per cent turnout (compared to historically more normal turnouts of 70–80 per cent) following an FLNKS boycott, the July 1987 referendum unsurprisingly voted 98.3 per cent in favour of staying with France. France pulled out all the stops to secure support, setting up roadblocks to prevent agitators entering Noumea and pro-France rural supporters were bussed in (Personal communication, O'Leary 2009). Chirac flew by Concorde jet to New Caledonia to be there for the electoral victory, staying just three hours before heading back to Paris.

Meanwhile, violence continued, heightened by the acquittal, in October, of those who had killed Tjibaou's brothers and others at Hienghène. By now, over 6000 French military personnel were in New Caledonia, stationed under a policy of '*nomadisation*' near tribal villages, ostensibly to aid in rural development (a policy continued to the present), but also enabling close monitoring of Melanesian activists. In early January 1988, a further statute was enacted, Pons II (Law of 22 January 1988). It provided for implied abolition of Melanesians' special legal status, and a revised regional demarcation more sympathetic to pro-France views. But, although the pro-France group duly won in the newly created western region, and made gains in the other Kanak dominated regions owing to boycotts, this statute was never implemented, as dramatic events at the Gossanah cave intervened.

Gossanah cave crisis

The first Pons territorial elections were to be held 24 April 1988, the same day as the first round of the French presidential elections, in which conservative Chirac was competing with, and trailing far behind, the incumbent, socialist Mitterrand. On 22 April, the FLNKS attacked a police station at Fayaoué on the island of Ouvéa in the Loyalties group, killing four policemen and taking 27 others hostage at a cave at Gossanah (see Waddell 2008, Chapter 1, also Mathieu Kassovitz' 2011 movie, *L'ordre et la morale*, or *Rebellion*, reviewed by Fisher

2012b). On 5 May, just after the first round of the presidential national election and three days before the second round, the French military were ordered to attack the cave and free the hostages. This was done at the price of 21 dead, 19 Kanaks and two French soldiers. Both Chirac and Mitterrand had signed off on the order to attack so as not to be seen as weak on the eve of the second round of the presidential elections (see Legorjus 1990, cited in Angleviel 2006). The predominance of the defence ministry over the Overseas France ministry played a role, as did the apparent absence of consideration for issues of foreign affairs over domestic imperatives.

But the handling of the crisis backfired. Once again, domestic and international opinion focused on New Caledonia. Metropolitan human rights groups SOS-Racisme and the Ligue des droits de l'Homme (Human Rights League) sought an independent enquiry into the way in which the events had been handled.

Matignon/Oudinot Accords

In the event, Mitterrand was returned to the presidency (although in New Caledonia, with a very reduced voter turnout of 58.3 per cent, 92.3 per cent voted for Chirac) and appointed socialist Michel Rocard as prime minister. As Rocard himself described it (Colloque 2008 recorded in Regnault and Fayaud 2008, 13), one of his first jobs was to address the New Caledonian problem. This he did by sending a dialogue mission to New Caledonia, headed by DOM-TOM Prefect Christian Blanc, who had been Secretary-General for New Caledonia in 1984–1985; and including not only senior officials but, somewhat creatively, senior representatives of key religious affiliations (Catholic Monsignor Paul Gilberteau; the head of the Protestant Federation of France, pastor Jacques Stewart; and prominent Freemason Roger Leray). Once again, Tjibaou agreed to lead a process of dialogue rather than witness further violence. It is important to recognise here the role in the Kanak cultural context of the *parole*, or word. As elsewhere in Melanesia, the idea of extended discussion and consensus is important in the Kanak culture. And, as in Western culture, the idea of keeping one's word is of great importance. On the basis of the mission's consultations, negotiations were initiated at the prime minister's Matignon office in Paris. They were difficult negotiations with concessions extracted from both sides only at the eleventh hour, late on 25 June, with follow-up over the following three weeks at the Overseas France ministry in the rue Oudinot.

The resultant Matignon/Oudinot Accords,[3] marked by the symbolic handshake between Tjibaou and Lafleur on 25 June 1988, set aside the thorny independence issue for another 10 years, when a vote would be planned for a restricted electorate

---

3   The Accords included the Matignon Accords (a declaration and two texts) agreed on 25–26 June 1988, and the Oudinot Accord addressing legal provisions to be subject to a referendum in November 1988 (Christnacht 2004, 57–58 and *Textes fondamentaux*, New Caledonian Government and congress websites).

confined to those resident in New Caledonia in 1988 and their descendants. Only this restricted electorate would vote in provincial and congressional elections. The parties agreed in the meantime to work for the economic, social and cultural development of the territory, with a buffer one-year rule by Paris through the High Commissioner. Three provinces were created, with particular powers, and from their representatives, a congress was formed for the entire territory. A key underlying principle was to be '*ré-équilibrage*' or rebalancing of economic benefits — which were hitherto confined mainly to the European-dominated and wealthy Noumea — throughout the territory. With nickel as the key economic resource, part of the deal was that Lafleur would sell his shares in the South Pacific Mining Company (Société Minière du Sud Pacifique SMSP) to the Northern Province, with the necessary CFP1.8 billion ($A29.8 million, converted March 2009) financed by the French State. A formula of application of state financial credits to all provinces was devised, and a Kanak training program of 400 *cadres*, or 400 managers, was initiated.

The State, perceived as having been too allied with the independentists at one stage (Pisani) and the pro-France group at another (Pons), was to take the role of impartial arbiter, a virtually impossible undertaking, especially since executive power was returned to the French High Commissioner. Tjibaou, for his part, saw the inconsistencies in the role of the State, and warned, in a letter to the French Prime Minister at the time that, in the context of restoring sovereignty to the Kanak people, '… the State cannot hide behind the role of arbiter. It is not judge but actor' (cited in Waddell 2008, 176). Issues related to this dual role were to persist.

These undertakings were subject to a national referendum, both for political reasons, to reassure the Kanaks that the French people supported the agreement, but also for technical reasons, since such a referendum was not subject to constitutional council scrutiny, and it was not at all certain that the measures for a restricted electorate were consistent with the French constitution and its notions of indivisibility (see Christnacht 2004, 59). In the event, the national referendum endorsed it by 80 per cent, albeit with a low 37 per cent turnout (Waddell 2008, 181, noted that this was the lowest turnout in any French national referendum since World War II). In New Caledonia, with a 63 per cent turnout, only 57 per cent voted yes, with mainly pro-France Noumea voting 63 per cent against (and 54 per cent choosing not to vote in Ouvea, where the Gossanah events had occurred). Once again domestic French politics came into play, with the RPCR in New Caledonia campaigning for the yes vote, but its national ally, Chirac's RPR, campaigning for abstention to weaken Mitterrand. The pro-France RPCR's taking of this stance foreshadowed further situations where local imperatives surmounted metropolitan-based positions, ultimately leading to divisions within the pro-France coalition of interests in the early 2000s.

Ominously for the future, and for France's credibility with the pro-independence group, the only element not covered by the subsequent 'referendum law' was the application of the restricted electorate to the congressional and provincial elections, owing to the apparent constitutional obstacle. Touching as it did on the most sensitive issue for the independentists, the effect of immigration on the electorate, this issue was to resurface, unsurprisingly, 10 years later.

The difficulty in securing the Matignon Accords, and the continued volatility in the territory, were poignantly underlined a year later. In May 1989, attending a traditional ceremony to mark the lifting of the mourning period for those assassinated at Gossanah, Tjibaou and his deputy, Yéwéiné Yéwéiné, were assassinated by extremist militant, Djubély Wéa, who felt Tjibaou had sold out their cause. Wéa was subsequently shot dead and the person charged was subsequently released (uncertainties surrounding the assassination are set out in Wall 2009). The assassinations marked a turning point in New Caledonia's political development. They represented a stark reminder to the French of the intensity of continued hostility to their policies within the ranks of the Melanesians, many of whom felt that Tjibaou had sold out to pro-France forces. Together with the memory of the violence of the preceding years, the assassinations were a sobering reminder of what was at stake and arguably fortified all sides to implement the Matignon/Oudinot arrangements.

The next 10 years saw concerted growth and development. As envisaged by the French State, the Kanaks became more engaged in government, with their parties dominant in the Northern Province and Loyalty Islands Province following elections in 1989 and 1995; and the pro-France group becoming accustomed to engaging Kanaks politically, nominating senior Kanak pro-France supporters to prominent positions, such as Dick Ukeiwé to the European *Député* position in June 1988 (French overseas territories could vote for an overseas territory member of the European parliament); and Simon Loueckhote as president of the congress and then, in 1992, as the youngest senator for France. Roads, schools, clinics and hospitals and electricity lines were all established in the interior of Grande Terre and the islands. Land reform was accelerated. The ADRAF distributed 82,000 ha of land between 1989 and 1995, increasing by 36 per cent the land controlled by Melanesians (Angleviel 2006, 222). The 400 cadres program had a more mixed success, training numerous lawyers, some engineers and one pilot, but, as Christnacht admitted, resulting in inadequate numbers of mid-ranking Kanak managers (2004, 61 and see Chapter 4). The French State provided the bulk of the New Caledonia budget, spending $A470 million in New Caledonia in 1986. There were some limited cultural and economic contacts with Pacific island countries (Christnacht 2004, 61).

But the fragility of the arrangements, in the wake of such tension and bloodshed, was apparent to leaders. Both FLNKS and RPCR leaders were managing the dissatisfaction of extremists who were unhappy with the compromises they had made. On 27 April 1991, in the knowledge that any referendum was likely to result in a no-vote to independence given the demographics (an estimated 65 per cent of voters would have voted against, Angleviel 2006, 226), and that such a result risked re-opening old wounds and a return to violence, RPCR president Lafleur proposed a 'consensual solution' in order to head off a 1998 *référendum couperet* (literally 'cut-off' or 'guillotine-style' referendum). The UC took up this idea at its congress in 1993, designating such a solution as 'negotiated independence'. From 1995 onwards, negotiations began with both the RPCR and the UC preparing papers and ideas.

Meanwhile, there were changes at the edges of the two main political groupings. Pro-France supporters grouped in Lafleur's RPCR, were bookended by the rightwing National Front and a more leftwing party Une Nouvelle-Calédonie pour Tous (A New Caledonia for All, UNCT) formed in 1995 by Didier Leroux. The independentist FLNKS, now headed by Paul Néaoutyine of Palika (not headed by the UC, as when Tjibaou was leader) was riven by internal conflict. The LKS and the USTKE had left, leading to the creation in 1998 of the Fédération des Comités de Coordination des Indépendantistes (Federation of the Independentist Coordination Committees, FCCI), led by longstanding UC or Palika figures Léopold Jorédié, Cono Hamu, Raphaël Mapou, François Burck and Aymard Bouanaoué. Another party joined FLNKS in 1998, the Rassemblement Démocratique Océanien (Democratic Oceanic Party, RDO), formed in 1994 from the leftwing of the Oceanic Union, mainly representing Wallisians and Futunans, under Aloisio Sako.

The Noumea Accord

After a seven-year gestation, and drawing from the blueprint of the Matignon/Oudinot Accords, on 5 May 1998 the Noumea Accord (L'Accord de Nouméa 1998) was signed by representatives of the French State, the RPCR, and the FLNKS. The Accord had been hard-won. Lafleur (Colloque 2008) recalled that on the final day, as deadlines approached, the parties spent 10 hours at a stretch in discussion. It was endorsed by a vote by the people of New Caledonia, on 8 November 1998; 74 per cent of the people voted and, of these, 72 per cent supported the Accord: 87 per cent of voters in the north, 95 per cent in the islands, and 63 per cent in the south (Ziller and Faberon 2008, 369). While the support in the (pro-France dominated) south was in marked contrast to its rejection of the Matignon Accords, still over a third voted no, and 42 per cent of central Noumea also voted no.

In the background to the exchanges of ideas by the two principal parties over seven years, negotiations had been taking place on the distribution of the benefits of the nickel resource, which the independentists claimed as the *préalable minier*, or mining 'prerequisite'. As had been agreed at Matignon, Lafleur had duly sold his SMSP in 1990 to Sofinor (Société d'Économie Mixte de Développement Contrôlée par la Province Nord — Mixed Economy and Development Company of the Northern Province), thus facilitating Kanak access to the mining sector, with SMSP becoming the largest exporter of (raw) nickel in New Caledonia (see Christnacht 2004, 63).

But now the Northern Province wanted to move beyond extraction and export of the raw nickel product, to establish a processing plant with the Canadian company, Falconbridge. To do this, it proposed exchanging one of SMSP's mining sites with SLN-Eramet, to gain reserves for the Falconbridge project. The French State, itself a major shareholder in Eramet, negotiated the February 1998 Bercy Accord only over strong resistance by Eramet. The Accord allowed for the exchange of the rich Koniambo range to SMSP in return for mining titles formerly purchased from SLN by the Northern Province at Poum, provided that Falconbridge reached certain stages in the establishment of a nickel-processing plant by 2007 (the tortuous negotiations with SLN, amidst strikes and coercion by FLNKS-backed unions and the French State respectively, are set out in Chappell 1999, 383 and 384). The French State compensated SLN for the difference in value between the Koniambo and the Poum *massifs* (reserves). The Bercy Accord proved an indispensable element of the political negotiation process. While it signalled that greater control of, and return from, resources were an important part of pro-independence Kanak aspirations, it did not, however, mean that the resource issue would replace the continuing objective, that of independence.

The Noumea Accord is an innovative and groundbreaking agreement by all three partners, the French State, the mainly Kanak independentists, and the mainly European pro-France group. At its centre is a further deferral of any vote on independence, this time by 20 years, to a series of three votes between 2014 and 2018, to give more time for economic development and to postpone a potentially painful divisive vote. Its key features include an acknowledgement of the 'shock' of colonisation both to the identity of the Kanak people and those who had come either for religious reasons or against their will; a future for all groups within a common destiny; and a continued commitment to economic rebalancing. In a new concept of 'shared sovereignty', the French State would transfer all but the central, or *régalien*, sovereign competencies (defence, foreign affairs, justice, law and order, and the currency), progressively to local institutions in a defined schedule. New Caledonia is given a special status of '*pays*' or 'country'. Again, in an entirely new arrangement to the French republic, the congress is endowed with legislative powers to make '*lois du pays*' (laws of the country), subject only to French constitutional council review, and managed by a collegial executive elected by the congress on a basis of proportional representation. New Caledonia is empowered to conduct certain relations with regional countries.

Remarkably within the French unitary republic, the Accord recognises a New Caledonian citizenship, built on special definitions of those eligible to vote in the planned 2014–2018 referendum(s) and in territorial (as distinct from French national legislative and presidential) elections, and linked to special employment rights (Article 2). This step addresses Kanak concerns about the effects of immigration, and their core demand for a restricted electorate, which, it will be recalled, had met a constitutional stumbling block in 1988, thereby raising Kanak suspicions about the intent and word of the French State. Then, the ambiguity related to those who could vote in the planned final self-determination referendum. Under the Noumea Accord, whereas all French citizens are eligible to vote in French national legislative and presidential elections, the electorates for local elections and for the ultimate referendum are again especially defined. Those who could vote in local (provincial) elections are essentially those who had been resident for 10 years in 1998 (to reflect those who could have voted in 1988 as provided in the Matignon Accords). But, for the final referendum(s) of 2014–2018, it includes also newcomers, specifically those with 20 years residence by 2014 (i.e. continued residence from 1994, as opposed to residence from 1988 as for the local elections).

While the Accord is a considerable achievement, it is, nonetheless, ultimately an exercise by two parties to secure the acquiescence of the third in postponing the final resolution of fundamental differences. As further analysis will show, its subsequent implementation has revealed ambiguities in its drafting, precisely in those areas of difference, such as provisions restricting the electorate for the local elections.

On 21 March 1999, the Organic Law was gazetted, implementing the provisions of the Noumea Accord, marking a new stage in the statutory evolution of New Caledonia.

French Polynesia: Strategic pawn

French Polynesia has differed from New Caledonia in that its population has been more homogeneous, with far fewer long-term European, mainly metropolitan French, nationals, and more intermarriage between Europeans and locals.

Metropolitan French nationals numbered about nine per cent of the population in 1988 (Baudchon and Rallu in Cadéot 2003, 248) and they were relatively new arrivals, numbering around 30,000 in the 1980s as opposed to barely 1000 in the early 1960s, before nuclear testing began in the territory (Chesneaux and Maclellan 1992, 126). The majority of the people were of Polynesian descent (82.7 per cent in 1983 census), including large proportions of mixed race or *demis* peoples (14.2 per cent), reflecting a far greater degree of marriage between the Europeans and the indigenous peoples than in New Caledonia. Although there was a longstanding Chinese community, many of whom came in the mid nineteenth century as agricultural workers and then became urban business people (4.5 per cent of the population in the 1983 census), there was little immigration from outside France, unlike in New Caledonia.

This homogeneity of Polynesian ancestry underlay more broadly based support for greater autonomy and even independence. It has been the reason why there has been markedly less intercommunal conflict in French Polynesia than in New Caledonia. As Henningham has observed, without the 'ballast' of a large European/metropolitan French majority settler population as in New Caledonia, pro-independence pressures could grow rapidly (1992, 160). Therefore the hand of France has been all the firmer.

In the 1960s and early 1970s, the main political divisions were between pro-France groups, autonomists, and independentists, with the latter two groups in the ascendant. But, from 1980, all of the principal local parties have sought greater autonomy, the clearest division amongst them being between the pro-independence versus the autonomy-within-France groupings, the latter loosely described as autonomist. Because of the broad base of the shared autonomy goal, even more than in New Caledonia, politics in French Polynesia have consistently been characterised by changes of loyalty, divisions and bench-crossing.

As in New Caledonia, the French State has been a behind-the-scenes player supporting the pro-France groups. But, in French Polynesia, it has acted more overtly with the pro-France autonomist parties, owing to the central place of French Polynesia, until 1996, in maintaining France's position as a *puissance mondiale moyenne* (middle-sized world power) by providing the site for France's testing of nuclear bombs. Since then other motivations have come into play, which will be explored in later chapters. French Polynesian politics, like New Caledonia's, have also been marked by a succession of statutory change (summarised at Appendix 2).

Unsurprisingly, given the violent resistance to France in the nineteenth century in the EFO, local demands for autonomy and independence increased after World War II. Over 300 French Polynesians served with the Free French forces, 76 of whom died. The old warhorse Pouvanaa (see Chapter 1) wasted no time after the war, in 1947, in forming the Comité Pouvanaa (Pouvanaa Committee) to assert local Maohi (indigenous Polynesian) economic and cultural claims. Despite his arrest, and acquittal, that year for plotting against the French State, he was enormously popular. He founded the Rassemblement démocratique des populations tahitiennes (Democratic Assembly of the Tahitian Peoples, RDPT), and was elected *Député* or member of the French parliament in 1949 with 62 per cent of the vote, retaining the seat until 1957.

The 1957 decree (Decree of 22 July 1957) implementing the 1956 Defferre Law (Law of 23 June 1956) introduced new autonomy, but, at the same time, the EFO became more closely associated with France by becoming Polynésie française (French Polynesia). Pouvanaa was elected to the most senior local position, vice-president of the new governing council. His urging of autonomy increasingly became demands for independence, exploiting the dual meaning of the Tahitian word, *ti'amara'a*, (which means both autonomy and independence), a device to be used by later leaders. With his vocal demands, which included pushes for a tax on business to fund independence, he had alienated many powerful families and businesses, and the French. And his influence led to the relatively reduced support for staying with France in the 1958 September constitutional referendum (as indicated, only 64 per cent agreeing, as opposed to well over 90 per cent in the other Pacific entities), even though French officials were energetically promoting a yes vote, in the knowledge of the planned shift of the nuclear testing program from Algeria to French Polynesia (see Henningham 1992, 125).

On the heels of this vote, in December 1958 France issued new ordinances (*Ordonnance* No 58-1337 of 23 December 1958), winding back autonomy and reducing local freedoms. Immediately after the referendum, in October 1958, Pouvanaa was arrested, after arson incidents in Papeete were linked with him and his supporters, and weapons were found at his home. This time the French were thorough and he was exiled from Polynesia until 1968, and his party banned in 1963. But he remained popular despite his exile, and was elected as French *Sénateur* (senator, member of France's upper house) from 1971 until his death in 1977.

Nuclear testing begins

In 1962, the nuclear testing program was transferred from the Western Sahara to the French Polynesian islands of Moruroa and Fangataufa, with a support base on Hao in the Gambier archipelago, and headquarters in Papeete. To safeguard French interests, possession of the testing sites was ceded to the French State in 1964 by the Permanent Commission of the Territorial Government (see Henningham 1992, 164) and, in 1980, these areas were decreed national security zones. Atmospheric tests began in 1966, but were replaced by underground testing from 1975, after regional and international outcries, and only after a successful case was brought against France by Australia, New Zealand and Fiji in the International Court of Justice. But underground testing continued to 1992, and resumed from 1995 to 1996, despite mounting international opposition.

During the nuclear testing period, there was a massive inflow of funds, technology, jobs and infrastructure, including construction of the international airport at Faaa on Tahiti and airstrips and the Centre d'Expérimentation du Pacifique, (Pacific Experimentation Centre, CEP) on the island of Hao. This rapid social and economic change was as disruptive as it was artificial. Until 1960, the only airstrip was that constructed on Bora Bora during World War II. Papeete did not have an airport before then, although flying boats landed there. As the traditional copra and vanilla markets slumped, and phosphate reserves on the island of Makatea dried up in 1966, the islands became ever more dependent on French inflows. During the 1960s the budget of the army and the CEP increased 50 times (from 1961 to 1966) and the numbers of civil and military functionaries from 400 to 15,000 (1961 to 1968). GNP increased 75 times from 1962 to 1982, and the minimum wage 15 times. Consumption increased but much of what was consumed was imported holus bolus from metropolitan France including energy (99 per cent) and food (85 per cent) (Chesneaux and Maclellan 1992, 124–25).

Dependence on France increased dramatically. Before nuclear testing, French Polynesia did not rely heavily on metropolitan funding, with returns on exports averaging around 90 per cent of the cost of imports in the 1950s. By the early 1960s metropolitan transfers as a percentage of GDP averaged 16.1 per cent, and reached 39 per cent in the 1970s (Henningham 1992, 128). The public sector became the biggest employer with salaries artificially inflated and attracting no income tax. Metropolitan-based officials were posted with very large supplements to their salaries. Taxation was indirect and included import tax. All of this unnaturally elevated the cost of living. The windfalls were fitful, with the CEP employing 10,000 in the 1960s but only 3000 in the 1980s, and CEP contributing 37 per cent to GNP in 1970, but only 19 per cent in 1980.

Migration to Papeete increased substantially and rapidly. In 1951, 48.6 per cent of the population lived on Tahiti, reaching 70 per cent by the 1980s (Henningham 1992, 129–30). By 1995, the population of Tahiti and Moorea had tripled (49,800 in 1952 to 161,000 in 1995, Dunmore 1997, 265). From being mainly a subsistence economy up until 1960, French Polynesia rapidly increased its food imports to the point where 80 per cent of its food needs were imported by the 1980s. The self-employed peasant class rapidly became a worker class.

Pro-France versus pro-autonomy

With Pouvanaa out of the way, political divisions tended to coalesce between those wanting continued dependence on France, and those seeking increased autonomy. Overall, politics continued to be personal. Pouvanaa's supporters created political parties around their personal support bases. Francis Sanford and Daniel Millaud and their mainly mixed-descent *Demis* supporters created the Te E'a Api (New Way), and John Teariki and Jean Juventin and their more traditional Protestant Polynesian *Maohis*, the Te Here Ai'a (Love of Fatherland). The two parties became allies. Later, Émile Vernaudon split from Te E'a Api to form his Te Aia Api (New Fatherland). These autonomist parties joined to form the majority in the territorial assembly in the 1970s. Sanford was elected *Député* in the French national assembly from 1968 and 1973. Jean Chesneaux and Nic Maclellan note succinctly that, despite their generally autonomist disposition, these political groupings, sometimes allies, sometimes rivals, represented personal interests without a coherent political plan; and splits, defections, unexpected unions and changes of position were their political currency (1992, 131). France played a role in this, mainly by ignoring their political demands, as many French officials believed that autonomist demands were simply a means of squeezing more funding from France (see Aldrich 1993; Regnault 2005a; Henningham 1992, 135). The traditions of rapidly changing alliances and of playing the independence card to extract economic gain, persist until today.

For these local pro-autonomy political groups, the French nuclear testing issue became largely a pawn in the game of political power. Generally, the autonomist parties were critical of French nuclear testing. In 1974 Sanford and Teariki supported anti-test Mitterrand in the presidential campaign, but, in 1981, thought nothing of switching support to Giscard d'Estaing who supported nuclear testing, in return for various development promises (Chesneaux and Maclellan 1992, 131).

In the 1960s the territory became increasingly dependent on France, handing over to the French State responsibilities for posts and telegraphs, secondary and technical education, some public health programs, and aid and development of the outer islands. By the 1980s, France was spending over $A1 billion annually in the territory, twice as much as it was spending in New Caledonia.

Re-emergence of independence demands

Their demands ignored, the autonomist groups occupied the assembly building in June 1976 for almost a year, with no French reaction. Inevitably, pro-independence sentiment re-emerged. Jacqui Drollet formed the Ia Mana Te Nunaa (Power to the People) party in 1975, actively propounding independence from 1978, while acknowledging it would take a 10–15 year planning period. Also in 1975, Oscar Temaru formed a more militant pro-independence party, the Front de Libération de la Polynésie (Polynesian Liberation Front, FLP), which became the Tavini Huira'atira no Te Ao Maohi (Serviteur du Peuple or Polynesian People's Servant) in 1982. It argued for immediate transition to independence, and immediate cessation of the nuclear tests. A range of smaller independentist groupings were formed in the 1970s and 1980s.

It was not until the late 1970s that France responded to the sharper calls for autonomy. A 1977 statute (Law No 77-772 of 12 July 1977), described as an autonomy management statute, was passed recognising financial and administrative autonomy in the territory, restoring the governing council presided over by the High Commissioner, and reinstating a vice-president elected by the territorial assembly. The vice-president and the governing council had collegial control over specified portfolios and, while the High Commissioner had executive power, in practice he refrained from attending every council meeting. Sanford was elected vice-president and served from 1977 to 1982. But the changes were slight and fell short of the 1957 Loi Defferre provisions. In time Sanford began to demand further transfers of executive power from the French High Commissioner. At this point Gaston Flosse, who had led conservative, pro-France opinion, decided to change his position to favour autonomy.

Autonomy within France v. independence

From 1958 Flosse had been active in the Gaullist Union Tahitienne-Union pour la Nouvelle République (Tahitian Union — Union for the New Republic, UT–UNR), leading its 1971 iteration the Union Tahitienne — Union pour la Défense de la République (Tahitian Union — Union for the Defence of the Republic, UT-UDR) and leading the successor party, the Tahoeraa Huira'atira or People's Assembly, which he set up in May 1977. A gifted politician with an eye to the main chance, both for himself as much as French Polynesia, and stalwart of the French republic, Flosse began as a relatively poor *Demi* from Mangareva in the Gambiers. His skill in both Tahitian and French enabled him to relate easily to both worlds.

Until 1980 he and the conservative Gaullists staunchly favoured the nuclear testing program and its economic benefits, and opposed greater autonomy as inevitably leading to independence. But, by 1980, Flosse decided to support autonomy, doubtless recognising broad support for it, and hoping to head off independence. The switch paid off. His Tahoeraa won the 1982 elections, and he became vice-president. He was to stay at the head of the executive in various forms until 2004, except between 1987 and 1991. In 1986 Chirac appointed

Flosse the first French State secretary for the South Pacific, in which position he served until 1988. He was elected *Député* in the European parliament in 1984; to the French assembly in 1986; and as *Sénateur* from 1998.

The harnessing of the pro-autonomy sentiment from the broad Polynesian base saw a resurgence of interest in Polynesian and Tahitian cultural identity, reflected in the establishment of museums (Musée de Tahiti et des Îles, the Polynesian Centre for Human Sciences) and use of Tahitian language in schools from 1980 onwards. The new Internal Autonomy Statute of 1984 (Law No 84-820 of 6 September 1984) reflected these changes, allowing the use of Tahitian along with French as an official language, and the flying of the Tahitian flag alongside the French *tricolore*. The statute also considerably expanded self-government. While the French State retained responsibility for broad 'sovereign' matters such as foreign relations, defence, immigration, currency, public order, and economic areas, there were shared responsibilities and the territory was able to conduct some regional affairs. The statute established a local president of the territory, a position won by Flosse, which he held to 1987, when his party lost in the 1988 elections, but regained in 1991. The cultural symbols in the statute were tangible rewards for local support for the statute, in contrast to the New Caledonian nationalist opposition to a similar statute there. The symbolic autonomy changes also reflected the greater strategic significance of French Polynesia to France as a testing site at the time. It was around this time that Flosse began to speak of a 'free association' status for French Polynesia along the lines of the Cook Islands' relationship with New Zealand.[4]

In 1986 Flosse's Tahoeraa won the assembly elections outright, the first time a single party had done so since Pouvanaa's win in 1957. His party benefited from the electoral system's heavier weighting to the less populous outer islands, whose voters are more conservative and pro-France. This French manipulation of the system was a precursor to similar systemic change in the early 2000s.

At this time, international and especially regional pressure was reaching boiling point, at France's handling of the deteriorating situation in New Caledonia, and especially its bombing of Greenpeace's *Rainbow Warrior*, protesting against nuclear tests, in New Zealand (see *Rainbow Warrior* affair below). Chirac's appointment of Flosse as secretary of state for South Pacific affairs was part of a French regional diplomatic offensive (see Chapter 3). It meant that Flosse would be increasingly absent from Papeete. Already, his style and political decisions had alienated many supporters. He was authoritarian, and granted favours and

---

4   Under the Cook Islands arrangement, the Cook Islands has an independent international identity, full local self-government, and the right to proceed to full independence should it wish to do so, with New Zealand undertaking aid and defence commitments. Cook Islanders retain New Zealand citizenship and full immigration rights into New Zealand but control immigration by mainland New Zealanders. Cook Islands do not have a seat in the UN. See Henningham 1992, 161.

contracts to cronies while failing to address social problems and tensions in a timely way. The incompatibility of his national ministerial responsibilities with those of his presidency of the territory led him to relinquish the latter in January 1987. His absences from the territory and differences with key industry players led to a dockers' dispute erupting into a major riot in October 1987, which saw several businesses in Papeete damaged and looted.

Autonomy and independence alliance

In the end, defections from Flosse's party led to his loss of government and support for Alexandre Léontieff, a pro-France leader, heading a loose coalition of parties. This group was primarily united by their dislike of Flosse and included Tahoeraa dissidents (Te Tiarama), the Here Ai'a centre-left party and Ia Mana moderate leftwing, pro-independence party. This was not the last time such a disparate group would be gathered for electoral convenience, reflecting, as Sémir Al Wardi described it, 'political nomadism' where ideological distinctions took second place to securing resources for constituents by shifting alliances (Al Wardi 2009, 198). The coalition held together until the end of 1990. In achieving this, Léontieff had to tread a careful path promoting autonomist demands within France, advocating an advanced form of internal autonomy within the French republic, with all the advantages of independence without the disadvantages (*La Dépêche de Tahiti*, 10 June 1989).

The most important issue for autonomists remained French Polynesia's dependence on French funding arising from the nuclear testing site. Whereas formal opposition to nuclear testing was confined mainly to the Tavini and the Ia Mana, which in 1986 together only attracted around 15 per cent of the vote, general concern about testing was more widespread, but always tempered with concern that funding by France not be jeopardised. The Léontieff-led government encouraged long-term planning by France to prepare for when testing was wound down. The French State continued to pursue its strategic interests without regard for local sensitivities within French Polynesia or more widely in the region, with Mitterrand at one point, in late 1987, visiting the test sites via Hao and returning to France without even touching down in Papeete.

To answer some of the local concerns, France legislated amendments to the 1984 statute in July 1990 (Law No 90-612 of 12 July 1990). These granted to the territory further limited controls over foreign investment, the budget, exploration and exploitation of seabed, marine and subterranean resources, and set up a consultative committee over immigration. Local Conseils d'Archipels (island councils) were set up in the key island groups, Flosse's power base. Dissatisfaction continued, with unions organising disruptive and violent protests against rising fuel prices in July 1991.

Nuclear testing and beyond

Finally, in the face of world and regional criticism for its nuclear testing in the Pacific (see following section), Mitterrand imposed a moratorium in 1992. The decision immediately led to an economic slump. Mitterrand began consultations with French Polynesian leaders on the future without the economic boost of the nuclear testing apparatus. These talks led to the 1993 Pact for Progress, and the 1994 Economic and Social Development law for French Polynesia, with a development contract signed in May 1994, extended by another signed in October 2000 (Faberon and Ziller 2007, 316). Essentially, the French underwrote extensive ongoing financial support well beyond any cessation of the tests as compensation.

Much of the goodwill accrued in this process was eroded by Chirac's decision, when he was elected president, to resume nuclear testing in 1995. Protests resurged, leading to riots and burning of the international airport and numerous shops and offices. The territory's one remaining economic asset, tourism, suffered as a result. When he revised his decision, in 1996, ended the testing program and closing the CEP, Chirac promised just under 1 billion former French francs (around $A300 million) assistance over the succeeding 10 years. Ironically, France's major investment, through the CEP, in infrastructure, port installations, roads, hydro-electric and solar power schemes, and in providing jobs, had built the territory's standard of living and expectations to a high, possibly unrealistic, level. It would be costly to maintain.

France offered continued extensive financial support, in return for staying with France, along with continued self-government, albeit within constraints set by France and, it should be noted, with substantially fewer real powers than it accorded New Caledonia in 1998. French Polynesia's limited economic resources meant that the stakes were lower for France than in New Caledonia. Even Temaru acknowledged that independence would lower the standard of living in French Polynesia (on 13 April 2006 he told the *Nouvelles de Tahiti* that independence would only be possible 'when our country's economic development allows it to ensure sovereignty').

Regional concern

No doubt, with the bulk of testing requirements behind it, France was in any case ready to wind down its testing program by the early 1990s. The 1994 Defence white paper shifted emphasis from nuclear to conventional capability, and the focus of military research from nuclear to space technologies. While it remained committed to its continuing status as a nuclear power and the *force de frappe* (nuclear deterrent), France had already established its nuclear credentials. The Berlin Wall had fallen and the Cold War was in its final stages. But there is no doubt that international and regional criticism played a major role in forcing France to do without continued testing and to close the CEP. In this, France had necessarily to weigh its strategic influence in terms of its nuclear imperative on the one hand, and its international reputation on the other. Events showed once again that domestic political preoccupations in Paris, linked closely with France's international image, would determine outcomes, and that lack of coordination of agencies involved would lead to errors.

Rainbow Warrior affair

Just as civil society led Western government policy opposed to France's policies towards New Caledonia, so it was strongly ahead of Australian and New Zealand official policy against French Pacific nuclear testing. Greenpeace led the charge. But, on 10 July 1985, two French secret agents bombed the Greenpeace vessel, the *Rainbow Warrior*, in Auckland, killing a photographer, Fernando Pereira, just before the vessel was to head for French Polynesia to protest against nuclear testing there. New Zealand sentenced and jailed two of the agents responsible, Alain Mafart and Dominique Prieur, in November 1985. But, in retaliation, France impeded wool and offal imports from New Zealand, New Caledonia stopped importing New Zealand lamb, and France threatened European Economic Community (EEC) reductions in the EEC quota of butter imports from New Zealand.

UN Secretary General Javier Péres de Cuellar was called upon to negotiate a settlement, involving an apology and $US7 million compensation from France, as well as an instruction to France not to obstruct New Zealand imports, in return for New Zealand releasing the two agents into French custody for detention for three years on Hao atoll. But France did not respect this agreement, freeing the agents and returning them to metropolitan France within two years. An international tribunal ruled in 1990 that France had indeed breached its obligations and required a further payment of $US2 million into a French–New Zealand fund.

There were several consequences to this act of what some called state terrorism, which came on the heels of the most violent episodes of New Caledonia's *événements*. There were domestic repercussions. Until 1985, the nuclear testing and deterrent issue had broad-based French domestic support. But the *Rainbow Warrior* affair stimulated a change in public opinion within France (described in Dunmore 1997, 260, Chesneaux and Maclellan 1992, 116). France's disregard for its UN-brokered commitment and the legal case, protracted over five years, raised further questions in the minds of leaders of its own Pacific territories about its commitments to them, particularly in New Caledonia where France was negotiating the Matignon/Oudinot Accords based primarily on promises. The affair also underlined the role of the French defence ministry in dictating policy on the Pacific, over and above that of the foreign ministry. This did not result in good outcomes since defence planners were resentful of the activities of the anti-nuclear movement, had their own operational interests in prolonging the nuclear testing presence, and were not nuanced in foreign policy (see also Mrgudovic 2008, 185 and Dunmore 1997, 259).

The external effects were disastrous for France and its prestige. The clumsy nature of the attack, with France's role and agents so publicly revealed, followed by blatant disregard for UN mediation efforts, suggested more the action of a banana republic than a world leader. France's reputation was badly damaged and its behaviour, including showing blithe contempt for successive SPF resolutions condemning French testing, counteracted the efforts it was making in other areas to improve its image in the latter 1980s. The *Rainbow Warrior* affair enabled Pacific leaders to galvanise their efforts and to receive a sympathetic hearing on the international stage. France's argument against others interfering in their affairs had been cut dead by its own interference in a New Zealand port. Its action presented a golden opportunity for the islanders to demonise France, especially to portray it as an outsider creating instability (noted by Du Prel 1996, 9 and Maclellan and Chesneaux 1998, 190).

On a broader scale, the *Rainbow Warrior* incident hardened New Zealand's support for banning visits by nuclear ships, which was arguably against broad Western interests in the Pacific at the time, widening differences within ANZUS. Thus, just as French handling of issues in New Hebrides and New Caledonia had inadvertently opened the region to adverse strategic consequences, so did this aspect of its dealing with the French Polynesia testing issue undermine fundamental Western strategic interests.

Regional criticism

To understand the depth of feeling and intensity involved in regional opposition to French nuclear testing in the South Pacific, and France's seeming disregard of this opposition for many years, requires an acknowledgement of significant spatial, economic and cultural differences between France and the newly independent island countries, and between France on the one hand, and Australia and New Zealand on the other. Such differences remain to this day.

The spatial context of the issue for the Pacific countries is fundamental to their stance. In the first place, while to a well-entrenched European power, the South Pacific countries seemed thousands of kilometres removed from the 1945 Hiroshima experience of a nuclear explosion, those countries belong to the same hemisphere as Japan. For them, the recent lessons of Hiroshima, in their own neighbourhood, and the cost in human lives and suffering portrayed in local newsreels, were stunning in their immediacy and scope, and shaped attitudes to nuclear testing in the region itself.

Secondly, whereas France claimed the testing sites were on its sovereign territory, whatever the legalities, for Pacific island countries they were taking place in their immediate neighbourhood, in what they repeatedly referred to as their 'backyard'. The backyard is a concept of being at home and, therefore, the space for private family activity, to be respected by neighbours (France grew to appreciate this distinction: see comments made by David Camroux in Assemblée Nationale de France, 1996 report, 53). They felt affronted by violation of this space, so proximate to their homes. France might well claim that the Hao area was thousands of kilometres from neighbouring islands, but for island countries in the vast Pacific Ocean, the distances were perceived as relatively small. Moreover, they shared long-term historical, cultural and ethnic ties and a community of interests. For them, even if the claimed risks in testing were only moderate (which they did not believe), those risks should be taken on French metropolitan territory.

The concept of being a good neighbour was also different. France's approach to testing revealed much about its attitude to the region. Because of the lofty strategic significance of the testing program, France never ceased to conduct itself as a nuclear power even when ending its program. Even today, France would be unlikely to describe island countries of the Pacific as its neighbours (see Chapter 6 on France as 'in' versus 'of' the Pacific,). And so it has left a legacy that would take significant diplomatic and other resources to overcome.

There were other differences in perception. None of the Pacific countries, including Australia and New Zealand, had any experience of the positive uses of nuclear power in energy production, whereas in France, over 50 per cent of its energy needs were being met by nuclear power stations by the early 1980s. So, in the Pacific, there was no firsthand evidence of a successful use of nuclear energy and, by contrast, a vivid impression, from Hiroshima, of its most destructive impact. Furthermore, indigenous traditions are strongly disposed towards preserving and respecting natural forces. In contrast to secular France, Pacific island societies are religious, and operate within a more diffuse environment where the lines between religion and politics are blurred. Thus France tended to dismiss strong opposition region-wide by the regional interdenominational church group, the Pacific Conference of Churches, and Paris-based policymakers were too prepared to situate the conference's opposition in the context of the Anglo-Saxon Protestant v. French Catholic paradigm of the nineteenth century (although the conference included both Protestants and Catholics). Rather, given their traditions and religious background, many islanders saw nuclear testing as morally wrong.

And, for Pacific islanders, the nuclear issue was closely interrelated with the question of independence for both French Polynesia and New Caledonia.

South Pacific Forum action

Just as the Forum's strategy to urge self-determination in New Caledonia was based on broader, strongly held support for decolonisation, so its strategy to combat French nuclear testing was founded on a broader opposition to nuclear activity in the region. Forum member countries had opposed nuclear testing well before French testing and formation of the SPF. In 1956, both the Cook Islands and Western Samoan local assemblies, even before independence, protested against British and American atmospheric tests in the Pacific. Western Samoa's legislative assembly described the French plan to test in the Pacific as a serious threat to health and security in the South Pacific a full year before the tests began. New Zealand also protested against American testing at the time (Mrgudovic 2008, 113; Chesneaux and Maclellan 1992, 184).

Australia and New Zealand took France to the International Court of Justice (ICJ) in 1973, claiming the tests had negative radioactive fallout on the regional population. The ICJ found in favour of this proposition, at which point France withdrew from the judicial process, effectively nullifying it. But France did announce that it would switch to underground testing, which it did in 1975.

The islanders established, early, a link between independence and the nuclear testing issues, enunciated by Fijian prime minister and founding member of the SPF, Ratu Sir Kamisese Mara in 1973, when he said that by persuading the UN Decolonisation Committee to speed up the 'liberation' of the French territories, France would no longer have the right to undertake its tests there (quoted in Chesneaux and Maclellan 1992, 186). French writer Isabelle Cordonnier referred in 1996 to the South Pacific as a geopolitical region, and to its opposition to nuclear tests as opposition to something which was seen as one of the last incarnations of colonialism (*Assemblée Nationale* 1996, 54). The formation of a group for a Nuclear Free and Independent Pacific (NFIP) from 1975 reflected this thinking.

Such an approach was not shared by the governments of Australia and New Zealand who, in the early 1980s, exercised a moderating influence within the Forum on islander proposals targeting France and the United States, over and above their restraining role on Forum resolutions on New Caledonia.[5] This is not to say that civil society shared the official view: the colonialist–nuclear link

---

5 A role not unnoticed in France itself, see comments by French Minister for Foreign Affairs in 1985 to the French parliament noting Australia's moderation in its assessment of the situation in New Caledonia, and the moderating influence of Australia on the measured stance in the SPF, 29 July 1985, *Débats de l'Assemblée Nationale* 2 December 1985 (*Assemblée Nationale* 1985, 55549–50).

was made by interest groups and unions in each country. In Australia, these non-government groups conducted visceral campaigns against France including boycotts of French restaurants, interruption to French postal and maritime services, and protests and even bombing of French diplomatic and other premises. Many of these groups, particularly the unions, were constituents of the Australian Labor Party. In response to similar agitation, in 1983, the new Hawke Labor government banned uranium shipments to France, a ban which endured until 1986. Feeling in the Australian community was also running high against France's treatment of New Caledonia at this time (as France reversed autonomy provisions in the Pons Statutes). In retaliation France banned ministerial visits to Australia in 1986 and, as noted, expelled Australia's Consul-General from New Caledonia in 1987.

Islander anti-nuclear concerns were wide ranging. Many of the island countries not only opposed testing but wanted to control the disposal and movement of nuclear waste through the region, to limit missile testing, and restrict visits by nuclear ships.

To harness these strong feelings in the region within the context of the interests of the western alliance, Australia's Labor government proposed a South Pacific Nuclear Free Zone treaty in 1984. Australia exerted considerable diplomatic effort to refine the proposals, both with an eye to the needs of the major western ally, the United States, but also to protect the broad Western alliance, and therefore French, interests. The resultant 1985 Rarotonga Treaty prohibited Forum members from acquiring and stationing nuclear arms, nuclear testing, and depositing nuclear waste in territorial waters. Its annex exhorted the big nuclear powers not to conduct nuclear tests in the zone, not to use nuclear arms against Forum members and to apply the treaty in their territories. Individual members could make their own decisions on visits by nuclear vessels. But the definition of the zone, which included the French territories but not the US ones in Micronesia, gave rise to French grievances that they alone were being targeted.

Nuclear testing issues linger

There was considerable debate, which continues until today, about the environmental and health risks of nuclear testing. As time, and opposition, progressed, France became more skilled at mounting information and diplomatic offensives. France invited a succession of regional teams to visit French Polynesia and conduct tests (led by Haroun Tazieff in 1982; New Zealand scientist Hugh Atkinson, in 1984; their own world-renowned oceanographer Jacques Cousteau in 1987; and Dr Frank Feuilhade in 1990). None of these produced conclusive reports, largely because France did not allow free access to the sites. A US

Greenpeace team conducted its own tests on the reef without French support in 1990 and, before they were arrested and bundled off to Papeete by the French navy, they claimed to have found radioactive substances.

Civil society again played a role, lobby groups such as the NFIP keeping alive the question of negative impacts of the tests, ranging from damage to reefs and leaching of radioactivity into the sea, to direct health effects such as cancer or ciguatera fish poisoning. In April 2009 the French Labour Tribunal heard the first case by a group of eight plaintiffs seeking compensation for effects of the tests on their health. And, in December 2009, the French Government signed off on legislation providing for compensation for those assessed as having been affected by the tests, and set up a €10 million compensation fund (*Flash d'Océanie*, 23 December 2009). The matter remains controversial, with lobby groups saying the new legislation does not go far enough.

Infrastructure is another remnant of the nuclear testing era. Whereas much has been dismantled, empty buildings and airstrips remain, largely unused (Maclellan 2005e, 370). Whether and how this infrastructure is used in the future will reveal much about the safety of the atolls (and see Chapter 7 on US interest in using landing strips there). Also unresolved today is the question of the return to French Polynesia of Moruroa and Fangatufa, which were ceded to France in 1964 for the program.

Conclusion

France's presence in the Pacific in the postwar years to the mid 1990s was characterised by its strong need to re-establish its national prestige, based on the *force de frappe* (nuclear deterrent) which it tested in the region; but also on the value of an extended EEZ that its Pacific territories represented; and maintaining a foothold in a region widely proclaimed as the central player in the forthcoming century. It held fervently to the stated need to protect the interests of its nationals, which were most pronounced in New Caledonia. The ambiguities of its position were evident in the UN, where France claimed equal rights with the other four permanent members, but rejected reporting and other UN obligations towards its Pacific territories. It was France's attachment to the primacy of its national interests in the SPC, and its reluctance to accommodate growing islander confidence and independent participation, that lead to the formation of the political SPF, which opposed French policies. France initially responded with contempt, ignoring early Forum calls for change in its nuclear testing and decolonisation actions.

France's experience in New Hebrides/Vanuatu was seminal in shaping regional attitudes to France. Traditional rivalries with Britain, concerns to protect its nationals, an openness to innovation (in the Condominium arrangement) but duplicity in supporting rebellion and even secession, and leveraging of aid against economic support, undermining the fledgling independent state, along with institutional factors where officials answered to competing ministries in Paris, were all signals of what might come for a future independent New Caledonia or French Polynesia. And France's handling of Vanuatu's independence had strategic external repercussions, heightening regional anti-France sentiment, leading directly to the formation of another anti-France regional group, the MSG, with a strong Vanuatu base in support of New Caledonia. It also led the small Pacific states to efforts to look elsewhere, including Libya, or at least to be seen to be doing so, for support, which was contrary to the security interests of the Western alliance and Australia. The left-over issue of Matthew and Hunter Islands demonstrated both France's continuing wish to retain territory (and desirable EEZ) in the region and that it remained prepared to back up its claims with diplomacy underpinned by force.

These consequences constituted a critical message for France, and the region, as it managed its other collectivities, and remain relevant today.

In postwar New Caledonia, France has shown innovation and flexibility in its proposals to meet local demands while retaining sovereignty. But, as in earlier centuries in the Pacific, it also showed clumsiness and inconsistency. In its 12 statutes over five decades, France reneged on agreed autonomy and even independence measures. While this stop-start process finally resulted in an ingenious series of agreed, democratically based Accords drawing elements from many past proposals, it has also left questions about the veracity of the State's word and intentions not only within the territory, but more broadly in the region. The potential strategic consequences of doubts about France's commitment was seen when Kanak pro-independence groups began training and other activity with pariah state Libya, risking regional security at the time.

The 1998 Noumea Accord was devised as a transition arrangement to restore stability, based on promised rebalancing of economic development and political power, while remaining heavily dependent on the French State. The French State was both an actor and an arbiter in political and economic life, allied, by its predilection for New Caledonia to stay within the republic, to the pro-France parties. The basis of agreement to the Accord was a restricted electorate for local elections and the final future referendums and related immigration issues; and sharing between the main communities, the economic benefits arising from New Caledonia's main source of wealth, nickel. Handling these two issues, as Chapter 4 will show, would be critical to stability, and for the pro-independence group, a fundamental indicator of the perceived commitment of the French State.

2. France manages independence demands and nuclear testing 1945–1990s

The consistent lesson in postwar New Caledonian history was the French State's primary preoccupation with its own metropolitan political, electoral and constitutional priorities and timetables, which have complicated its administration of New Caledonia, even to the extent of provoking violence. As elsewhere in its Pacific territories, the French State linked economic support with fealty to France, and backed its presence by force, dealing firmly with protests, most notably during the *événements* and in its raid on the Gossanah cave. Institutional constraints included competing roles of the Overseas France, foreign affairs and defence ministries, with the latter predominating. As the postwar period progressed, France increasingly sent senior officials to the territory who had relevant experience (for example High Commissioner Alain Christnacht) but, as ever, they were rotated out within very short periods, continuing the early pattern of the '*valse des gouverneurs*'.

And in French Polynesia, where, as the site of its nuclear testing, the strategic stakes were the highest for France during this period, many of the same features were evident, with one or two important differences. The key difference was that, with a larger, more homogeneous indigenous population, demands for greater autonomy were always more broadly based. As in New Caledonia, French roll backs of initial provisions for independence resulted in strengthened support for autonomy and pro-independence political groups in the 1970s. But in French Polynesia, with the general dependence on the French nuclear testing program and in the absence of a substantial long-term French metropolitan settler population, the political dynamic shifted from pro-France v. independentist as in New Caledonia to, autonomist within France v. independentist in the 1980s. Prominent pro-France leader Flosse even advocated an independence-in-association formula as early as 1985.

Here too, with the added interest of its nuclear testing program, France flexed its military might to retain support, cracking down on protests and riots and, in 1985, fatally intervening even on a foreign vessel in a foreign port, to protect its interests. The dramatic economic windfall effect of its nuclear testing program heightened the nexus between economic support and political dependence. France's overt promise of ongoing funding for continued fealty encouraged the practice of local political groups threatening to change sides unless further financial support was forthcoming. Political allegiance became less ideological and more clientelistic focused and fluid than in New Caledonia, and the French State was a more direct player, overtly backing the interests of the pro-France autonomy group. And in French Polynesia, too, even more clearly than in New Caledonia, because of the nuclear testing program, the interests of one part of the metropolitan bureaucracy, the military in the defence ministry, regularly overrode the other ministries with an interest in the overseas territories. As an added overlay, in French Polynesia the close personal relationship between autonomist leader, Flosse, and French President Chirac, meant that administrative processes were circumvented and personal interests dictated policy, and even statutory change, a feature that was to intensify in the early 2000s.

Regional and international pressure played a role in shaping France's approach in both New Caledonia and French Polynesia in the postwar period, but did not succeed in forcing France to grant independence to either. But Forum efforts to engage the UN did succeed in securing French commitment to develop a roadmap to an independence referendum for New Caledonia through the Matignon/Noumea Accords.

By contrast, regional pressure over nuclear testing succeeded in changing French policy: in 1975, when France began underground tests and abandoned atmospheric testing, in response to the 1974 ICJ court decision brought by Australia and New Zealand against France; in 1989, following the 1985 Rarotonga Treaty, when France reduced the number of its annual tests and gave advance notice of them; and in March 1996, when France ceased testing and even signed the treaty itself.

And an important legacy of regional opposition to French policies was the change of heart by France towards the region itself, its efforts to engage with the region, and to implement statutory change within its Pacific collectivities with an eye to the broader regional context, which will be the subject of the next chapter.

3. Regional diplomatic offensive 1980s–1990s

While France introduced a suite of policies to improve its image and engagement in the broader region from the mid 1980s, these superficial changes initially met with mixed success. It was only after genuine French attention to independence demands in New Caledonia, and the nuclear testing issue, that regional attitudes began to change.

After the war, well into the 1970s, French policy was to keep its territories relatively isolated from the region. Chapter 2 described how France resisted efforts to draw new island states into the Secretariat of the Pacific Community (SPC), and the consequent formation of the South Pacific Forum (SPF), which excluded France and its territories. France had given some indication of a wish to be more involved in the Pacific region in the 1970s. Secretary of State for *Départements et Territoires d'Outre-Mer* (overseas departments and territories, DOM-TOMs), Olivier Stirn, claimed in 1975 that there was no wish for France to isolate itself or its territories, and affirmed its desire for its territories to establish relations with their neighbours (cited in Bates 1990, 94), and he travelled to some of the Forum island states. One of the first meetings of France's senior officials and representatives in the South Pacific region took place in 1978 to plan a strategy for greater regional co-operation, with little apparent result on the ground. Bates notes that a subsequent call, in 1980, for a new approach to explain its presence only occurred because some island states were stepping up the campaign for the decolonisation of New Caledonia. The idea languished in the early 1980s, although French Polynesia had lodged a request for observer status to the Forum by 1985.

It was only with the effect of the *Rainbow Warrior* affair on France's international and regional reputation in mid 1985, the re-inscription of New Caledonia in the United Nations (UN) Decolonisation Committee and the conclusion of the Treaty of Rarotonga, that President François Mitterrand and later Jacques Chirac (as prime minister) took action to repair the damage, always with a Gaullist eye to preserving France's national prestige.

But the exercise from the outset was one of damage limitation rather than genuine policy change. Chirac proceeded with the Pons statutes in New Caledonia throughout this period; and even later, when France declared a moratorium on nuclear testing in 1992, it resumed its nuclear testing program from 1995 to 1996. Bates wrote at the time that the exercise was ill founded in that it was designed to correct misperceptions that France believed Australia and New

Zealand were responsible for perpetrating, and therefore was competitive and presentation-focused rather than collaborating with these countries to clarify any differences (Bates 1990, 97).

The first step in this image-improving process was a pledge by Mitterrand to increase diplomatic involvement and spending in the region. He set up a South Pacific Council in Paris and proposed a French university in the region and numerous scientific and cultural projects with island states, but only after having visited Moruroa in late 1985 'to reaffirm France's commitment to its testing programme' (in Henningham 1992, 209). The council was composed of key cabinet ministers, the French High Commissioners and French senior diplomats from the South Pacific, attached to the office of the president.

Flosse as secretary of state for the South Pacific

Chirac, who became prime minister in March 1986, proceeded with regional co-operation projects to stave off criticism from increasingly disaffected island states. He appointed his personal friend, Gaston Flosse, then president of French Polynesia, as secretary of state for the South Pacific from early 1986, which post he retained until Chirac lost government in 1988. Flosse began a process of annual meetings on the South Pacific in which he engaged senior regional French officials. He visited island states and invited their leaders to visit Paris, French Polynesia and even Moruroa.

French regional multilateral activity increased. France increased its disbursements to the SPC. Links between its numerous research and scientific organisations and Forum countries, and regional organisations, improved. For the first time, French scientific and research activities were pitched to the development of regional island states (Bates 1990, 100). With the negative aspects of nuclear testing in the minds of island leaders, the French turned their attention to bolstering their environmental credentials, setting up an environment monitoring observatory to collect and disseminate data in coordination with similar laboratories in the region; and participated in conventions on the protection of natural resources in the South Pacific and on banning driftnet fishing in the region. France offered help in surveillance of Exclusive Economic Zones (EEZs) and set up emergency rescue and first aid supplies in its territories, for regional use (SPC Conference communiqué October 1990, Henningham 1992, 214). It set up a computer centre for the SP Geosciences Commission, later SOPAC, in Suva. France joined the Pacific Islands Development Program based in Honolulu, and established a consulate-general there in 1987, accredited to the Micronesian entities.

Flosse oversaw new bilateral aid to regional states, consisting of emergency and humanitarian aid in the wake of environmental disasters such as cyclones, and project aid and loans, including from his small ($US4 million per annum) South Pacific Co-operation Fund. Flosse's support to the Solomon Islands, in May 1986, which provided speedy and effective assistance in the wake of a devastating cyclone, set things off to a good start and was replicated in aid to the Cook Islands, Fiji and Vanuatu after similar natural disasters. Overall, France increased its bilateral aid expenditure to an average of $A12 million a year from 1987 to 1990, a modest amount given it was spending over one hundred times that in its own Pacific territories (Henningham 1992, 209).

In all of this, the French military took a high profile, the senior representative accompanying Flosse on visits, often in naval vessels. Naval courtesy calls to Fiji and Polynesian countries increased, sometimes delivering aid equipment. This was seen by many as designed to legitimise the presence of the French military in the region (Bates 1990, 99).

France encouraged French business and investment in the non-French Pacific. *Alliances françaises* were formed in Fiji and Tonga. At this time, reflecting shades of the old idea of France's *mission civilisatrice*, or civilising mission, there was prevalent reference to the concept of *rayonnement*, or dissemination of French culture, in the South Pacific region, including by President Giscard d'Estaing. This included the idea of the French territories there being seen as a means to spread French influence, just as the colonies had done in Africa (see, for example, Leymarie 1985, 2; Aldrich and Connell 1989, 5, Chapter 8 and 101; Cordonnier 1995a, 113; Henningham 1992, 194). This trend took place within the context of a revival of the idea of formalising the influence of French culture globally, and specifically in the French territories, as a source of spreading French influence. Mitterrand created a high council for *Francophonie* in 1981 and Chirac created a state secretary for *Francophonie* in 1986 (see Aldrich and Connell 1989, Chapter 8).

Flosse's leadership of the strategy proved a mixed blessing for many reasons. On the one hand, his Polynesian ancestry, ability to speak Tahitian — which facilitated communication with other Polynesian speakers, his flamboyant creativity, frenetic preparedness to travel widely, and obvious desire to help were all assets. Importantly, he was a strong regional personality working from Papeete, and not a metropolitan Paris-based functionary.

But his brief was problematic. It was based on chequebook diplomacy and corrective presentation rather than being collaborative. He was tasked to play a role in general policy and economic development in the French territories and improve relations in the South Pacific working with the DOM-TOM and foreign affairs ministries, but he was excluded from policy-making with regard to New Caledonia.

Apart from the confused messages inherent in Flosse's friendly overtures, while nuclear testing continued and policy tightened towards New Caledonia, he made some clumsy faux pas, reflecting a lack of understanding of island politics and a tendency to self-aggrandisement, which countered many of France's positive intentions. Financial payments were offered to the opposition in Vanuatu's elections in 1987, leading to the expulsion of the French ambassador there. In the Solomon Islands, even the generous and speedy French emergency response to the 1986 cyclone was undercut by Flosse's provision of aid to Prime Minister Peter Kenilorea's home village, which played into the hands of the opposition and resulted in Kenilorea having to resign (Bates 1990, 105). He also oversubscribed in the Cook Islands, where Prime Minister Sir Tom Davis, who had been well disposed towards French Polynesia despite opposing French testing there, also lost his job over the handling of aid from France. Flosse's personal manner stood out from generally modest island ways. For example, he arrived at the 1987 Apia Forum meeting with his own luxury armour-plated limousine, where all other Forum leaders, including the Australian and New Zealand prime ministers made do with the VIP cars provided by the Samoan Government (Chesneaux and Maclellan 1992, 197).

His regional impact was divisive, even to the point of threatening regional security. Already, France's New Caledonia policy had led elements there and in Vanuatu to consolidate ties with Libya, and Libya was glad to comply given its own problems with France over Chad (Henningham 1992, 222). This development undermined the overriding Western security strategy, led by regional powers Australia and New Zealand, and supported by France, of denial of the region to hostile powers. But Flosse's heavy hand added its own ingredient of insensitivity and counterproductivity. At one point, in 1986, he threatened that if France withdrew from New Caledonia, there would be civil war between the Kanaks and Caldoches and the resulting power vacuum would be filled by the Union of Soviet Socialist Republics (USSR) and Libya. In June 1987, he sought to galvanise Australia, New Zealand, the United States, France and Great Britain to define a policy for the South Pacific (Bates 1990, 109), seemingly unaware of the provocative nature of this suggestion to the independent island states, with its overtones of colonialism.

These lines of argument led to direct responses, especially by Melanesian leaders. In 1987, both Vanuatu's Prime Minister Ham Lini and then PNG ambassador to the UN, Renagi Lohia, referred to France's policies as 'a direct threat to peace, security and stability … in our region and they have serious implications for international peace and security' (*Islands Business* April 1987,19), and the Solomon Islands prime minister noted that 'the powers that perpetuate terrorism in the region do not include Libya' (*Post Courier* 21 May 1987, 2).

And, just as French policies in New Caledonia had proven divisive regionally by directly resulting in the formation of first, the Forum, and then, the Melanesian Spearhead Group (MSG), so now Flosse compounded the problem, by counter-proposing a Polynesian Community. Although Flosse credited Cook Islands Prime Minister Davis with the idea, it seems generally accepted that it was Flosse's (by Chesneaux and Maclellan 1992, 197; Bates 1990, 112). He organised meetings with Polynesian leaders to discuss it and raised it when he received regional leaders as his guests in Papeete. His actions were part of a deliberate policy of divide and rule, and were badly received.

France's relationship with Fiji was also regionally divisive. France sought to increase its influence, capitalising on the nuanced regional responses to the 1987 coups by military leader Colonel Sitiveni Rabuka. Australia and New Zealand, and the Commonwealth, instituted sanctions against Fiji, although some island leaders were more forgiving of Rabuka's actions. Although France publicly neither condemned nor condoned the coup, it conducted a joint naval exercise with Fiji shortly afterwards, and welcomed Prime Minister Sir Ratu Mara to Paris, providing much-needed international recognition in doing so (Henningham 1992, 216; Bates 1990, 101). France stepped up bilateral aid commitments to around $A16 million, which compared favourably to Australian annual aid of around $A14 million at the time. This aid included a helicopter and civil emergency equipment, which some saw as potentially usable by the rebellious army. France already had military links with Fiji arising from shared participation in the UN Interim Force in Lebanon. European Commission aid continued uninterrupted, no doubt influenced by French views. Meanwhile Flosse drew pointed comparisons between regional views criticising Rabuka's desire to reduce the influence of the Indian community while insisting the future of New Caledonia should be decided by the Kanaks; and questioning the Forum's view of New Caledonia as an international issue while maintaining its stance on Fiji was an internal matter (Bates 1990, 102).

The reaction of regional leaders was, understandably, mixed. The Forum, in its annual communiqués, continued to voice its strong opposition to France's nuclear testing, including its resumption in 1995; and to watch closely developments in New Caledonia. Some leaders, such as in Western Samoa and Cook Islands, favourably noted French efforts towards dialogue and to provide constructive aid, but continued to oppose France's nuclear testing and New Caledonia policies. Tonga's public position vacillated. Not surprisingly, Melanesian leaders were more resistant, with Papua New Guinea and Vanuatu not dissuaded from their efforts in the UN, attacking French nuclear and New Caledonia policies. As noted in Chapter 2, Vanuatu expelled the French ambassador and France reduced its aid there. Stephen Bates, in 1990, made the harsh assertion that the Flosse initiatives 'failed to reduce the hostility of the Melanesian countries towards France and ... there is no conclusive evidence that they had a moderating effect on the attitude of the Polynesian states' (113).

A policy shift from 1988

But, over time, with the nomination of socialist Michel Rocard in place of rightwing Chirac as prime minister amidst the Gossanah cave affair in May 1988, France bolstered its efforts with more concrete policy change. Rocard led the changed approach to New Caledonia with the Matignon Accords and, significantly, removed Flosse from his position in 1988. He revived France's South Pacific Council, which had been inoperative under Chirac, and established a regional roving ambassador for the South Pacific, a position that endures until today. Naval visits to island states increased. Rocard visited the Pacific in 1989, including stops in Australia, New Caledonia, Fiji and French Polynesia, but finished pointedly with Moruroa. During his visit he urged the French territories to integrate more in the cultural and economic life of the region. And, in 1992, his successor Pierre Bérégovoy announced a suspension of nuclear testing in French Polynesia.

The island governments at this time were certainly happy to accept more engagement from France in development co-operation. In 1992, Stephen Henningham, while noting continued opposition by island countries over New Caledonia and nuclear testing, pointed to France's diplomatic offensive having 'secured broader acceptance ... of the view that France has a legitimate role, and contributions to make to the region's economic welfare', particularly by Fiji, and countries of Polynesia and Micronesia, although he acknowledged some improvement even with Melanesian countries by 1990 (218–219). But these countries continued to oppose nuclear testing, and remained vigilant over New Caledonia. It took concrete policy change in both areas to improve regional acceptance. Even after cessation of nuclear testing in 1996, regional leaders did not see either the Matignon or Noumea Accords as sufficient in themselves to remove New Caledonia from the UN Committee of Decolonisation list. Thus, as noted in Chapter 2, every year, to this day, a New Caledonia resolution is passed without vote in the Decolonisation Committee, sponsored by Fiji and Papua New Guinea (see also Regional reactions, Chapter 6).

In Australia and New Zealand, grassroots sentiment was strongly anti nuclear testing (especially in New Zealand) and pro independence for New Caledonia. The two governments officially recorded these policy stances, but worked to moderate regional pushes for tough action against France. As described in Chapter 2, they had slowed down island leaders' moves for reinscription of New Caledonia with the UN Decolonisation Committee, only changing their stance when Chirac tightened policy with the Pons statutes. Differences with Chirac's approach had led to deterioration in relations, especially between Australia and France, culminating in the expulsion of Australia's Consul-General in Noumea, John Dauth, in 1987. No doubt relations were coloured by the complexion of governments in the respective countries, improving, for example, when both French and Australian governments were of the socialist left, as when Rocard became prime minister in France in 1988 while Bob Hawke led Australia's Labor Government. Throughout the difficult 1980s both the Australian and New Zealand governments had conducted private dialogue in Paris, to encourage change. Accordingly, both welcomed the Rocard reforms on New Caledonia, and strongly supported the Matignon Agreements. Australian Foreign Minister Gareth Evans, visited New Caledonia shortly after signature of the Agreements where, for the first time in many years, the Australian Consul-General at the time hosted a reception attended by both Rassemblement Pour la Calédonie dans la République (Rally for [New] Caledonia within the Republic, RPCR) and Front de Libération Nationale Kanak et Socialiste (Kanak Socialist National Liberation Front, FLNKS) members (Personal communication, O'Leary September 2009). Despite lingering strain in New Zealand over the *Rainbow Warrior* affair, New Zealand's foreign minister visited Noumea in 1989, offered technical assistance to support the success of the Matignon Accords, and spoke of France's important role and enduring legacy in the South Pacific. Both governments took a more measured approach to decolonisation than many other island governments, welcoming, for example, the Micronesian non-independent states into the Forum and regional structures in the 1980s (Henningham 1992, 222). This was to have the effect of paving the way for an accommodating view to the French entities in the 1990s.

By the end of the 1990s, France had begun to implement genuine policy change, ceasing its nuclear tests in the region by 1996, by which time it was well into implementing the Matignon/Oudinot Accords in New Caledonia, and adjusting its statutory provisions for French Polynesia to accommodate demands for change. These processes were not straightforward and involved extensive financial and administrative investment. France began advocating greater participation in the region by both collectivities in the 1990s and early 2000s. But, with a record of broken promises in the preceding decades, some of the difficulties France encountered in implementing changes in its entities, which will be explored in the next two chapters, left continued questions about its future role and acceptance in the region.

Part II — France in the Pacific: 1990s to present

4. New Caledonia: Implementation of the Noumea Accord and political evolution from 1998

Chapter 2 concluded that the fundamental political pillars, on which the compromise of the Noumea Accord was based, included defining restricted electorates in certain local elections and the final referendum(s) to meet Kanak concerns at the weakening effect on their vote by immigration inflows from elsewhere in France; and the fairer distribution of the benefits accruing from the nickel resource between the Kanak north and islands, and the mainly European south. Developments surrounding these two critical elements unfolded at the same time as the fledgling New Caledonian government began to test its wings, operating as a collegial executive, with resultant strains.

Restricted electorate and related issues, including immigration

Differences over defining the electorate in the Organic Law

Leaders of the different parties, both pro-France and pro-independence, and representatives of France signed the Noumea Accord on 5 May 1998. On 19 March 1999 the French national assembly gazetted its Organic Law, setting out the provisions by which the Noumea Accord would be implemented. Its wording (see below) led to strong disagreement about the definition of the electorates for local elections, known as the restricted electorate, a concept that was fundamental to the new notion of New Caledonian citizenship, specified in the Accord's Article 2 (as noted in Chapter 2). The wording was at best a gaffe or, at worst, a cynical effort to favour the pro-France political groups, given the centrality of the restricted electorate/citizenship issue to the negotiations.

It should be acknowledged that the very idea of defining different electorates for different elections, based on years of residency, was an innovative and flexible response to Kanak concerns, on the part of French authorities, within a constitutional system which claimed above all to be unitary and indivisible, in the sense of delivering one vote to one person (see Diémert in Tesoka and Ziller 2008, 234). Previously, the Matignon Accords had introduced the notion of a 10-year residence requirement for a vote in the independence referendum planned for 1998, however, the implementing law had been itself the subject of a referendum, to circumvent scrutiny by the constitutional council. The Noumea Accord, in contrast, introduced a new notion of New Caledonian citizenship linked with the 10-year residence requirement for local elections, and was subject to constitutional amendment, a device construed again to prevent consideration by the constitutional council (see Faberon and Ziller 2007, 390). It was a unique and difficult concept for the French legal draftsmen.

For the ultimate referendum(s) on the future of New Caledonia, Article 2.2.1 of the Accord, and Organic Law Article 218 (full text at Appendix I), defined the electorate as including those with 20-years residence to the referendum date no later than 31 December 2014 (i.e., those resident before December 1994); those eligible to vote in 1998; those having customary civil status or, if born in New Caledonia, having New Caledonia as the centre of their material and moral interests or having one parent born there with such material and moral interests; voting age persons born before 1 January 1989 who lived in New Caledonia from 1988 to 1998; and those born after 1 January 1989 having one parent who could vote in 1998. There was little difference between the meaning of what was enshrined in Article 2.2.1 of the Accord, and that which was subsequently spelled out in Article 218 of the Organic Law, although there was one obvious difference, the Accord referring to 20-years residence to 2013, and the Organic Law referring instead to 20-years residence to 31 December 2014. But, no complications arose (to the time of writing, mid 2012, at least) from the wording of these provisions.

For local elections, i.e., provincial assemblies and congress, it had been agreed that the electorate would be a narrower group, including those eligible to vote in 1998 as well as essentially those who had been resident for 10 years. But questions arose from the wording of the provisions applying to some voters as they appeared in the Organic Law, i.e., whether those on a particular annex list needed 10-years residence to the date of any particular congressional or provincial election being held during the Noumea Accord period (envisaged in 1999, 2004, 2009, 2014), or simply 10-years residence to 1998.

It was the wording of Article 2.2.1 of the Accord that gave rise to the ambiguity that led to a particular interpretation being enshrined in Article 188 of the Organic Law (see Appendix I). Article 2.2.1 of the Accord defined the electorate for the local provincial and congressional elections as including (a) those able to vote in 1998, (b) those on an annex list of those not normally able to vote in New Caledonia but who had 10-years residence *'at the date of the election'*, i.e., without specifying which election was referred to; and (c) those reaching voting age after 1998 who either had 10-years residence to 1998, or a parent either eligible to vote in 1998 or a parent on the annex list as having 10-years residence *'at the date of the election'* (again unspecified). Thus, this provision referred at one point (under (c)) to voters with 10-years residence *to 1998*, and in (b) and elsewhere in (c) to voters on an annex list, with 10-years residence *'at the date of the election'*. The inference, for pro-independence supporters, was that *'at the date of the election'* referred to the 1998 vote referred to in (a).

But, when it appeared in March, Article 188 of the Organic Law, as the implementing legislation, referred to (a) those able to vote in 1998, (b) those on an annex list and resident in New Caledonia for 10 years *'at the date of the election to the Congress and to the province assemblies'* and (c) those attaining majority age after 1998 either with 10-years residence in 1998, or having had one of their parents fulfilling the conditions to be a voter in the 8 November 1998 referendum, or having one of their parents registered on the annex and with 10- years residence in New Caledonia *'at the date of the election'* (i.e. unspecified election but with the implication that it would be the specific election to the congress and province assemblies referred to at (b)).

The wording of Article 188 referring to congress and provincial elections, and the confusion of meanings in the Noumea Accord article variously to 10-years residence *to 1998*, and to annex list voters with 10-years residence to an unspecified election, provided for ambiguities and ill feeling, which were to plague subsequent years.

The differences reflected fundamentally different ideological approaches. For the pro-independence groups, preserving the unique voting rights of the electorate as it stood in 1998 meant respecting the special place of the indigenous, Kanak, and for some, Caldoche, resident, amidst a fear of being outnumbered by continued influxes of newcomers. It was part of the agreed, 'rebalancing' process under the Accord, and the basis for the concept of New Caledonian citizenship and the objective of common destiny (see the position of the pro-independence party *Union Calédonienne*, *Nouvelles Calédoniennes* 7 February 2005; comments by Roch Wamytan, *Nouvelles Calédoniennes* 8 May 2003). The pro-independence groups argued for the 'frozen' (*gelé* or *figé*) interpretation, i.e., 10-years residence requirement to 1998, since this would freeze the electorate at the time of the Noumea agreement, and not include future immigrants from elsewhere in France who would distort the balance between pro-independence and pro-France support, in favour of the pro-France lobby. For this interpretation, the 'annex list' of those ineligible to vote remained that in operation in 1998.

The pro-France groups took as their starting point the defence of the fundamental right of each person to vote without exclusion (see, for example, the viewpoint of the Association of the Defence of the Right to Vote, *Nouvelles Calédoniennes* 17 March 2005; and the position of the pro-France *Rassemblement*, *Nouvelles Calédonienne*s 15 February 2005). They argued for the 'sliding' (*glissant*) interpretation, i.e., 10-years immediately preceding any provincial election, which, for the 1999, elections would mean people on the annex list resident for 10 years to 1998, but for subsequent elections held in 2004, 2009 and 2014, would include people who had ˌ10-years residency immediately before each of those elections — i.e., on subsequent annex lists that did not exist at the time the Noumea Accord was agreed. This would include French newcomers who could be relied upon to inflate the pro-France vote.

In the event, the French constitutional council ruled in favour of the 'sliding' interpretation, favouring the broader interpretation of the 'annex list', which favoured the pro-France groups (see Christnacht 2004 p. 65).

To remove any ambiguity and settle mounting concerns amongst the pro-independence group, the government of Prime Minister Lionel Jospin initiated a change to the constitution to re-establish its own interpretation of the frozen, restricted electorate. This involved a considerable procedural effort to make a creative compromise conceived in a particular local circumstance consistent with the fundamental one-person – one-vote principle of the French constitution. Presumably to hasten this unusual provision through the necessarily cumbersome processes (which involved convening the Versailles Congress, or joint session of both the national assembly and the senate), it was hooked for administrative purposes to another, unrelated, amendment on the independence of the French national superior magistrature. A statutory provision expanding the concept of citizenship and legislative powers for French Polynesia was also attached to this amendment (see Chapter 5). Both amendments failed, however, in 2000 when the magistrature amendment was abandoned having been judged not to have attracted sufficient support.

This device, whereby important New Caledonian and French Polynesian legislation was attached and randomly made hostage to a piece of unrelated national legislation, is a stark example of how the overseas collectivities' statutory needs are subordinated, often unnecessarily, to metropolitan political process. The issue reflected the paradox of reconciling indigenous rights with Republican constitutionalism. In New Caledonia, given the controversy about the restricted electorate issue, concerned local players could be forgiven for believing that the device was construed precisely to slow down the implementation of these pieces of legislation, and suspecting the commitment of the French State. In any case, that was the effect (see, for example, conclusions of the pro-independence group Palika's annual congress in 2004 questioning the French State's ambiguous positioning and its capacity to guarantee balanced Noumea Accord institutions, and calling for the immediate re-establishment of the fixed restricted electorate, *Nouvelles Calédoniennes* 17 November 2004).

Discontent amongst the pro-independence group, particularly the Kanaks, not surprisingly continued to simmer, so much so that when President Jacques Chirac visited Noumea in 2003 he promised to resolve the problem before the end of his mandate in 2007. In 2003 the Melanesian Spearhead Group (MSG) focused the attention of the Pacific Islands Forum (PIF) on the 'lack of implementation of certain provisions of the Noumea Accord, in particular the electoral process and issues relating to New Caledonia's referendum process' (MSG Attachment to 2003 Auckland Forum Communiqué), urging the Forum's ministerial committee to focus on the issues in a planned visit in 2004 (see also Chapter 6). In October 2005, Front de Libération Nationale Kanak et Socialiste (Kanak Socialist National Liberation Front, FLNKS) leader Roch Wamytan included concerns about the restricted electorate in a speech that he made to the United Nations (UN) Fourth Committee on Decolonisation (see UN Document A/C.4/60/SR.5, October 2005, 11), proving in the process that the UN procedures remain relevant to the New Caledonia situation.

Meanwhile, more recently arrived European residents of New Caledonia, with the backing of pro-French parties, had taken their case claiming that they had been deprived of a vote in local elections, to the French State Council, which, in 1998, rejected their claims, as did the Appeals Court (*Cour de cassation*) in response to similar claims in June 2000, and the Administrative Appeals Court in October 2003. Separately, aggrieved citizens took their cases to international courts. The European Human Rights Court decision on 11 January 2005, while indicating that the 10-year residence requirement seemed disproportionate to the goal pursued, recognised the validity of the statutory requirement taking into account the 'local necessities', which justified it. And the UN Human Rights Committee indicated on 15 July 2002 that the dispositions of the New Caledonia statute relating to voting rights were not contrary to the International Civil and Political Rights Convention (see Faberon and Ziller 2007, 393–94).

It was only in February 2007, almost nine years after the Accord was agreed, that the French legislative amendment was implemented, confirming the frozen electorate interpretation, and clarifying what had become for the independentists a continuing sore. To compound the ambiguous drafting in the first place, the procedural handling meant that France appeared to have redressed Kanak and independentist grievances only after three of its own courts and two international institutions had supported them. The word of the French State was thereby once again proven suspect.

Immigration: Removal of ethnic categories from the census

In a related development, Chirac further raised Kanak and pro-independence concerns. When he visited Noumea in July 2003, on the eve of a scheduled local census, he met a group of young New Caledonians and answered 'impromptu' questions. One young white New Caledonian referred to the forthcoming census and complained that she could not tick any of the 'ethnic membership' boxes on the form, not being Kanak, Wallisian, or Asian but 'just' being a French citizen. Professing outrage, Chirac described these questions in the census as irresponsible and illegal, saying 'There is only one reply to such a question, you are all French and there are French people of all ethnic origins' (RFO TV News 24 July 2003). He commanded that the New Caledonian census would thenceforward not seek information about ethnic origins. The census had to be deferred for a year while forms and procedures were reviewed.

This decision was troubling for Kanaks for two reasons. First, knowledge of their numbers and locations in the archipelago was an important instrument of rebalancing economic development, which was a fundamental element of the Noumea Accord. Second, ethnic figures revealed the extent of immigration from metropolitan France and other French overseas territories, and French encouragement of such immigration had historically been one of the Kanak and pro-independence group's prime concerns, and underpinned concerns about voting rights and calls for the restricted electorate. Jean-Pierre Doumenge, for example, noted that, to that point, France had specifically retained the ethnic classification for New Caledonia, given the evolutionary process arising from the Matignon and Noumea Accords (in Faberon and Gautier 1998); and that the ethnic statistic was relevant to the prediction that there would be a Kanak majority over time (Doumenge and Faberon 2000, 65). In response, some Kanak groups (Union Syndicale des Travailleurs Kanaks et des Exploités, Federation of Unions of Kanak and Exploited Workers, USTKE; Union Calédonienne (Caledonian Union, UC); Calédonie mon pays, (Caledonia my country) boycotted the 2004 census. The FLNKS agreed to participate only with the promise of a parallel 'cultural' survey of villages as a gesture to these concerns, even though such a survey was not comparable to a full census.

Concerns about the implementation of the restricted electorate, and ongoing immigration, were shared by some Caldoches (see Muckle 2009, 191). Shared local concerns over immigration-related issues contributed to a gradual coalescence of interests between some elements of the pro-independence and pro-France groups leading to a political realignment that incorporated both (elaborated below, Political transition and realignment).

More broadly, in the South Pacific context, the French State's doing away with ethnic indicators was anomalous. Other regional countries, including Australia, New Zealand, and Fiji, routinely counted ethnic numbers if only to assist in the economic development of disadvantaged groups. The decision to exclude those indicators from the census thus had important social and political ramifications, the more so because it was taken deliberately by the Chirac government.

In practice, the boycott rendered the 2004 census virtually useless on many counts and, up to early 2011, even official published statistics continued to draw upon 1996 figures as the most recent reliable figures (the two main sources are New Caledonia's Institut de la statistique et des études économiques, Institute for Statistics and Economic Studies (ISEE); and France's national Institut national de la statistique et des études économiques, National Institute for Statistics and Economic Studies (INSEE); see for example ISEE 2008 and Figure 4.1).

It was notable that there was no regional reaction to this change, reflecting the weakened impact of the MSG, and the tentative preliminary engagement in regional organisations by the new, pro-France-led New Caledonian Government. In its annual working paper on New Caledonia, preparatory to the annual UNGA resolution on New Caledonia, however, the UN Decolonisation Committee noted the removal of the ethnic category in the census and local indigenous opposition to it (UNGA Fourth Committee 2008, 2).

It was only in late 2008, perhaps conscious of the reference in the UN Working Paper, that France reversed the decision and announced that the ethnic categorisation question would be reinstated in the 2009 census. In the event, however, the New Caledonian Government questioned the manner of conducting the 2009 census and its result, claiming the outcome understated the population increase, an important indicator on which funding from France is based (Lepot 2010). The New Caledonian Government claimed that some households were not covered, and queried the coverage of the census, noting the numbers and efficacy of census agents had been affected by a flu outbreak at the time, and an unusually high turnover of agents. It queried the results for some suburbs and the census' migration figures. ISEE announced it would do a further study on immigration inflows in mid 2010 (Lepot 2010). Apart from the overall population figure and the three provincial figures, the publication of most figures from the 2009 census was delayed until April 2011, with the annotation initially that this was awaiting 'authentication by decree' (ISEE website 2009 census, accessed 13 May 2010) and, subsequently, that the figures were 'not available' (ISEE website 2009 census figures, accessed 3 December 2010 and 12 January 2011). By April 2011 the ethnic composition figures were included in ISEE's website, however they too were qualified, by the inclusion of extra categories which prevented direct comparison with previous census figures (see below).

Immigration inflows: Continuing increases from metropolitan France and *outre-mer* (Overseas France)

Despite the disruption to ethnic category numbers from 1996, the signs are that immigration from metropolitan France and other French overseas territories has increased since the 1998 Noumea Accord was agreed (see analysis below), and this has not gone unnoticed. New Caledonia's vice-president, the FLNKS' Déwé Gorodey, in her opening speech to a 2008 colloquium marking the 20-year anniversary of the Matignon Accords, referred early to the concerns of the drafters of the Matignon and Noumea Accords to legitimise the sharing by immigrants of a common destiny with the Kanak people, and concluded her speech by noting the fragility of the pact, which depended on trust (Regnault and Fayaud 2008, 25). FLNKS leader Wamytan, at the same colloquium, referred to the continued influx of metropolitan immigrants from 2000 to 2004 (Regnault and Fayaud 2008, 47). Palika leader Paul Néaoutyine at the December 2008 Noumea Accord Signatories Committee meeting flagged immigration as a continuing concern (*Relevé de conclusions* 2008, 7).

Table 4.1a shows the official breakdowns of Kanak[1] and European population percentages in various censuses since 1887. The graph in Figure 4.1, represents those figures from 1911 to 1996. Table 4.1a also includes figures reported by ISEE in April 2011 on the basis of the 2009 census, but these figures included extra ethnic categories and it is not possible to compare them with earlier years (see below). For analytic purposes, Table 4.1b includes the percentage breakdown of the communities in 1996 and the qualified, but not directly comparable, figures reported from the 2009 census in April 2011.

The increases in the 'Others' categories between 1911 and 1931, followed by the postwar dramatic fall from 1946 to 1956, can be attributed to the early development of the nickel industry, when workers were imported, many temporarily, from Indonesia and Vietnam. The number of 'Others' has increased dramatically and steadily with the nickel boom, and since, and has included Wallisians from Wallis and Futuna, Tahitians, Indonesians, Vietnamese and other Asians, Ni-Vanuatu, and others.

---

1 We use the term 'Kanak' in this population section to refer to New Caledonia's indigenous Kanak population. Official ISEE–INSEE statistics often refer to '*Mélanésiens*' (Melanesians) when referring specifically to New Caledonia's Kanaks, but do not include other Melanesians such as ni-Vanuatu who are reported separately as '*ni-Vanuatu*' or are included in their 'Others' category.

Table 4.1a New Caledonia — Population: Kanaks, Europeans and others 1887–2009

Year	Kanaks number	%	Europeans number	%	Others[a] number	%	Total
1887	42,500	68.0	18,800	30	1200	2.0	62,500
1901	29,100	53.5	22,750	41.8	2,550	4.7	54,400
1911	28,800	56.9	17,300	34.2	4,500	8.9	50,600
1931	28,600	50.0	15,200	26.6	13,400	23.4	57,200
1946	31,000	49.4	18,100	28.9	13,600	17.0	62,700
1956	34,969	51.1	25,260	36.7	8,351	12.2	68,580
1969	46,200	46.0	41,268	41.0	13,111	13.0	100,579
1976	55,598	41.7	50,757	38.1	26,878	20.2	133,233
1983	61,870	42.6	50,757	37.1	29,524	20.3	142,151
1996	86,788	44.1	67,151	34.1	42,897	21.8	196,836
2004[b]	n/a[b]	n/a[b]	n/a[b]	n/a[b]	n/a[b]	n/a[b]	230,789[b]
[2009[c]]	99,078[c]	40.3[c]	71,721[c]	29.2[c]	74,781[c]	30.5[c]]	245,580

a. Other: Includes Wallisians from Wallis and Futuna, Tahitians, Indonesians, Vietnamese, Ni-Vanuatu and others, except for 2009 (see note c)

b. There was no ethnic category in the 2004 census and it was subject to a boycott call by some parties

c. 'Others' in 2009 included new categories '*métis*' or mixed race, 'Caledonians', and more 'non-declared' and, for this reason, the figures are not comparable with 1996 or earlier years, see Table 4.1b

Source: Christnacht 2004, 29; ISEE-INSEE *Recensements de la population*, Population Census, 2008 and 2009

Table 4.1b New Caledonia — Ethnic composition of population, 1996 and 2009 (Limited comparability)

Community	1996%	[2009[a]]%	[2009]% main groups reallocated[b]
Kanak	44.1	40.3	44.3[b]
European	34.1	29.2	33.9[b]
Wallisian (Wallis and Futuna)	9.0	8.7	10.4[b]
Tahitian	2.6	2.0	
Indonesian	2.5	1.6	
Vietnamese	1.4	1.0	
ni-Vanuatu	1.1	.9	
Others	5.0	16.3	
Of whom[a]			
Other Asian		(.8)	
Mixed race, multiple		(8.3)	
Caledonian		(5.0)	
Other		(1.0)	
Non-declared		(1.2)	

a. Figures based on new census formulation with new categories under 'Others', shown

b. Figures calculated by ISEE reallocating some of the mixed race figures attached to the three main ethnic communities

Source: Pascal Rivoilan and David Broustet, *Synthèse — Recensement de la Population 2009* ISEE website, accessed 12 May 2011

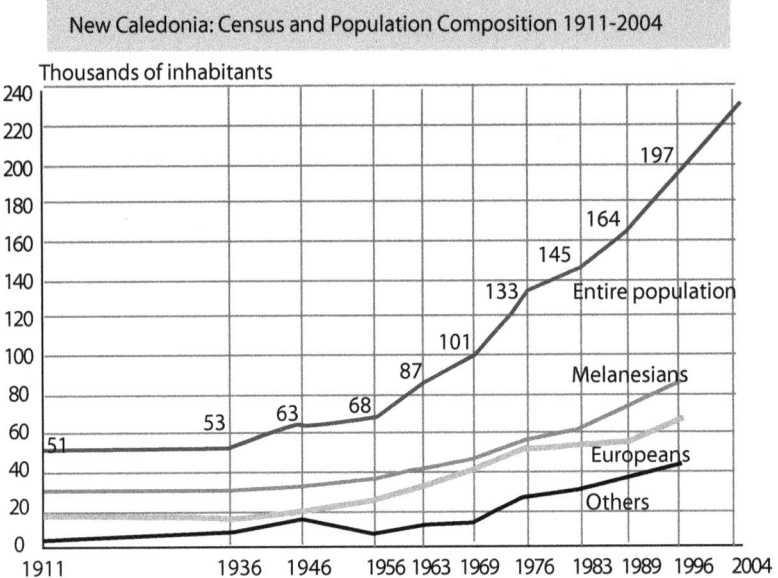

Figure 4.1 New Caledonia — Census and population composition 1911–2004

Note: 'Melanesian' refers to Kanaks, see footnote 1, this chapter

Source: ISEE website, accessed 16 February 2010

The ISEE noted that the large increase in the 'Others' category in the 2009 census (Table 4.1b) occurred in part because that census offered additional options under 'Others' for the citizen to nominate, including new categories of *'métis'* or 'mixed race', 'Caledonian', and 'non-declared' (Rivoilan and Boustet 2010). Why the 2009 census would do this when the ethnic category issue was so controversial was not explained. The ISEE not only set out the full breakdown (second column of Table 4.1b), which showed a marked decline in the Kanak and European populations and increase in the other categories, but went on to reallocate some of the 'mixed race' figures to the sensitive Kanak and European categories, resulting in a pattern similar to that in 1996, albeit with a slight increase in the Kanak community over 1996, and a slight decrease in the European category (columns 2 and 3 of Table 4.1b). How it was decided whether a person of mixed race was allocated to the European or Kanak group was not explained. The resultant uncertainties around these two key and sensitive indicators mean that they cannot reliably be used for comparative purposes. Still, they point to a continuation of the underlying general trends evident from Table 4.1a and Figure 4.1.

One trend maintains a steady and large increase in recent immigration from other parts of Overseas France, mainly from French Polynesia and Wallis and Futuna, which inevitably reduces the proportion of the population that is indigenous.

Overall, as Figure 4.1 shows, the numbers of Europeans and 'others' combined have increased steadily over time, rendering the Kanaks more of a minority over time (see Increasing European immigration, below).

According to Gérard Baudchon, then head of the ISEE, of the 34.1 per cent of the population in the 'European' category in 1996, more than half (or about 20 per cent of the population) were people of European ancestry who were born in the territory. Around a third (he estimated about 12 per cent of the population) had come from metropolitan France (Baudchon with Rallu in Cadéot 2003, 248). As a point of comparison, he noted that only around nine per cent of French Polynesia's population was born in metropolitan France (88 per cent being Polynesian), and four per cent of Wallis and Futuna's population (87 per cent being Polynesian).

Declining Kanak proportion of a more diverse population

While Kanak numbers dropped dramatically with the influx of European settlers late in the nineteenth until the early twentieth century, troughing in 1931, Table 4.1a and Figure 4.1 show that they increased thereafter, particularly after World War II and, again, after 1969. These changes are attributable to the early effect of disease and violence by the incoming settlers, and the return of confidence and prosperity after the world wars. The proportion of Kanaks in the total population was on a steadily decreasing trend from 68 per cent in 1887, down to about half by 1956, 46 per cent in 1969 and reaching a low of 41.7 per cent in 1976 (see Table 4.1a).

The relative decline in the 1970s underpinned Kanak independence claims and concerns about becoming a minority in their own country. There are some striking statistics. Alain Christnacht noted that the number of Europeans doubled from 1956 to 1976, with the number of Melanesians increasing by only two-thirds, and Asians, Polynesians and others by three times (2003, 3). Thus, Melanesians lost their majority position.[2] It is estimated that from 1970 to 1976 alone, 15,000 Europeans came into the territory, from metropolitan France or others of its overseas territories, bringing the European population to almost the same number as Melanesians (Chesneaux and Maclellan 1992, 147).

Since then, the Kanak proportion increased to about 44 per cent in 1996, the last clear comparable census, with the 2009 census indicating either a similar figure (44.3 per cent in column 3, Table 4.1b) or a decline to 40.3 per cent (column 2,

---

2   See also Table 4.1a and Figure 4.1; Barbançon in de Deckker and Faberon 2008, 124 notes that Melanesian population increased by 35 per cent or 14,408 from 1963 to 1976, while Europeans grew by 52 per cent or 17,402 and others by 124 per cent or 14,904; ISEE TEC 2008, 34 and 35.

Table 4.1b). This 2009 figure of 40.3 per cent for the Kanak population, before 'reallocation' increased it to 44.3 per cent as shown in Table 4.1b, shows a significant decline. Indeed it is lower than the 1976 all-time low of 41.7 per cent, and would be a serious concern to pro-independence Kanaks.

In both 1996 and the known 2009 results (i.e., both before and after 'reallocation' of the mixed race group), New Caledonia's largest population groups remain the Kanaks who represented 44.1 per cent in 1996 and 40.3 per cent (or 44.3 per cent 'reallocated') in 2009; then the Europeans: 34.1 per cent in 1996, 29.2 per cent (or 33.9 per cent 'reallocated') in 2009; followed by the Wallisians from Wallis and Futuna: nine per cent in 1996, 8.7 per cent (or 10 per cent 'reallocated') in 2009 (ISEE-INSEE TEC 2008 and 2009 published 2011). Kanaks also may be increasingly seen as one of a number of growing Pacific Islander communities relative to others. In 1996, Pacific Islanders represented 57 per cent of the population, compared to 43 per cent non-Islanders, mainly European and Asian. While exact comparison cannot be made with 2009 because of the 'Others' category issue, taking figures before reallocation of the 'mixed race' category (column 2 of Table 4.1b), the total of Kanak, Wallisian, Tahitian and ni-Vanuatu alone is 55.9 per cent and it could be assumed that most of the 8.3 per cent of 'mixed race' respondents would be of Pacific Islander origin. 'Post-reallocation' figures (column 3 of Table 4.1b) show Pacific Islanders as at least 57.6 per cent of the population (Kanak, Wallisian, Tahitian and ni-Vanuatu). Thus it seems that the Pacific Islander component is increasing while the non-Islander component (mainly Europeans and Asians) is declining.

Kanaks have traditionally lived primarily in the Northern and Islands provinces, whose populations are declining, as evident in Table 4.5. There has been increasing internal migration from those provinces to Southern Province (see analysis by Faberon and Ziller 2007, 357–58). Table 4.5 shows that in 2009, 74.5 per cent of the population was in Southern Province, 18.4 per cent in Northern Province (compared to 21 per cent in 1996), and a low 7.1 per cent in Loyalty Islands Province (compared to 10.6 per cent). In 2009, Kanaks formed 96.6 per cent of the population of Loyalty Islands Province, 73.8 per cent of Northern Province (Europeans 12.7 per cent and other communities 5.7 per cent), and 26.7 per cent of Southern Province (Europeans 35.9 per cent, Wallisians 11.4 per cent and other communities 9.7 per cent) (Rivoilan and Boustet 2011). Around 50 per cent of the Kanak community (whose numbers were qualified in the 2009 census, as indicated above) lived in Southern Province, whereas 90 per cent of all other communities lived there (Rivoilan and Boustet 2011).

In the past, Kanak fertility rates have been high relative to other residents, but they are declining. In 1997, the territory-wide average was 2.67 children per woman, while the rate was 3.3 in Loyalty Islands, and 2.9 in Northern Province, both provinces where Kanaks predominate (Baudchon and Rallu in Cadéot

2003, 248); compared to 2.5 in Southern Province. Figure 4.2 graphs the overall declining trend from 1981 to 2007. Internal migration by Kanaks from the Kanak provinces to Southern Province (see Table 4.5) limits the capacity to make assumptions about Kanak fertility rates on the basis of Province. However, in 2007, the territory-wide average dropped to 2.2, and all Provinces showed a drop from 1997, with the Loyalty Islands at 2.4, Northern Province 1.9, and Southern Province 2.2. Figure 4.2 shows that fertility rates for the predominantly Kanak provinces is declining more steeply than rates in the predominantly European Southern Province.

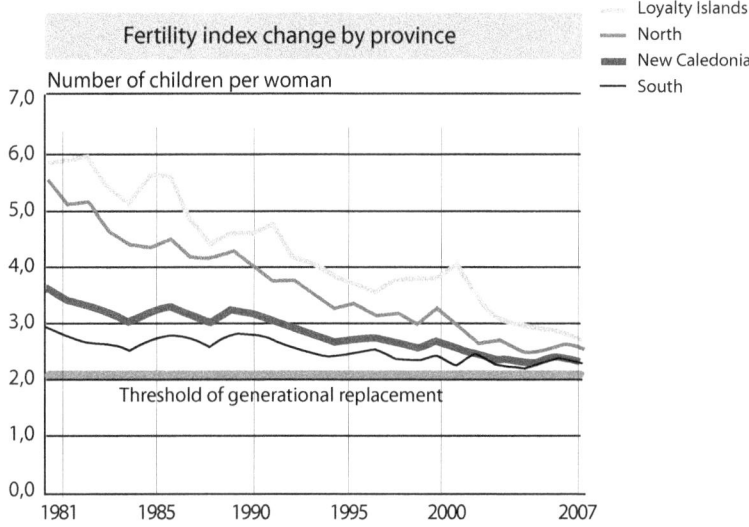

Figure 4.2 New Caledonia — Fertility index change by province 1981–2007

Source: ISEE-TEC, Éditions Abrégées, 2010, *Indice de fécondité par province*

Continuing immigration (see following sections) on a declining, minority Kanak base mean that Kanaks are unlikely to become the majority in New Caledonia for the foreseeable future. More importantly, as Table 4.1a and Figure 4.1 show, Kanaks were in the minority in 1994, which is the year of 20-year residence eligibility for the electorate voting in the final referendum(s) 2014 to 2018 (see Restricted electorate and related issues, including immigration, above).

As noted earlier, the influxes of outsiders in the past have consisted predominantly of Europeans from metropolitan and Overseas France; with some non-Kanak Islanders mainly from Wallis and Futuna, Vanuatu, and Tahiti; and Asians, principally from Indonesia, Vietnam and Japan who came as workers on the mines in the early twentieth century. All three inflows have occurred as a result of deliberate French policy that held sway for varying reasons at different times. The next sections concentrate on the two most sensitive inflows, those of Europeans (read French) and of Wallisians.

Increasing European immigration

France has encouraged the long-term presence of its metropolitan nationals. The size of the European population in Overseas France grew through the nineteenth century in response to the French State's establishment of convict and agricultural settlements (see Chapter 1). Table 4.1a and Figure 4.2 show that the numbers of Europeans increased at the turn of the century, declined until the mid 1930s, and rose, particularly after 1956, and again after 1969 and 1989. The decline early in the twentieth century coincided with the period of colonial torpor described in Chapter 1. The increases after 1956 can be attributed to Gaullist policies encouraging settlement of the territories, and an influx of French expatriates from Algeria (known as *pieds-noirs*). From 1969 the numbers reflect the influx of experts and administrators associated with the nickel boom, and those encouraged by Prime Minister Pierre Messmer's famously vaunted aim to head off independence claims of Kanaks by outnumbering them (see Chapter 2). The European population stabilised from 1976 to 1989 as the *événements* took hold. After the signature of the Matignon Accords in 1988, Figure 4.2 shows that the European population steadily increased, as did the Kanak ('Melanesian') population. This reflects inflows of expertise accompanying the development of the nickel projects and the relative stability secured by the Matignon and Noumea Accords. While figures after 1996 are less reliable, there is evidence that influxes from other parts of France occurred, partly because of development of the nickel resource, and partly as a result of French salary and retirement incentives (see below).

Public official statistics after 1996 are broken down unevenly, for example see Table 4.3, the columns of which were published in the ISEE-INSEE Censuses of 2004 and 2009, comparing periods of varying length, i.e., six, seven, eight and five years. ISEE-INSEE's *Situation Démographique* 2008 and 2009 offer annual population and migration figures and estimates, enabling a rough comparison of per annum migration at Table 4.4.

Although the figures set out in Table 4.1a show the European proportion of the population declining steadily from 41 per cent in 1969 to 34.1 per cent in 1996 (and 29.2 per cent, or, at most, 33.9 per cent in 2009, see tables 4.1a and 4.1b), they do not tell the full story. Many people of European origin tended to say in the censuses that they were New Caledonians of European origin (i.e., rather than born in metropolitan France) (see Faberon and Ziller 2007, 357–58 and Baudchon and Rallu in Cadéot 2003, 248), meaning they were not included in the European category and may have been registered in categories such as 'others' or 'undeclared'. In the 1996 census, a breakdown of the non-Kanak, non-European population (the broader 'others' category of 21.8 per cent in Table 4.1a) showed that figure included Wallisians (by then nine per cent of the total population), Tahitians (2.6 per cent), Indonesians (2.5 per cent), Vietnamese and other Asians (1.9 per cent), Ni-Vanuatu (1.9 per cent) *and 4.6 per cent of the population as either 'others'* (6829 or 3.5 per cent) or *'undeclared' (*2209 or 1.1 per cent) (ISEE statistics cited in Faberon and Ziller 2007, 359). Thus, as many as a further 4.6 per cent of the population represented in this 'others' or 'undeclared' group *may have been* European, which could bring the European proportion to as much as 38.7 per cent in 1996.

In 2009, when the 'others' group included many more categories, there were as many as 16.5 per cent who defined themselves as 'mixed race' (8.3 per cent), 'Caledonian' (five per cent), 'undeclared' (1.2 per cent), or 'other' (one per cent) (ISEE Census 2009). INSEE included some (4.7 per cent) of the 8.3 per cent 'mixed race' group in its 'reallocated European' figure of 33.9 per cent (column 3, Table 4.1b), but the criterion they used is unknown, so there may have been more who were European; and up to 7.2 per cent more (i.e., certainly many of the 'Caledonian' category, plus some from 'undeclared' and 'other') could conceivably be added to that figure.

Thus, the manner of presentation of ethnic breakdown figures, especially in 2009, can understate the European category.

Migration inflows 1989–1996

Table 4.3 fills out the picture from Figure 4.1 for the period from 1983 to 2009. Based on official ISEE-INSEE statistics, which vary in periods applied, and including figures from the boycotted 2004 census, it shows natural growth in the population of 2.6 per cent from 1989 to 1996, with migration inflows at .7 per cent, or over 9000 people in that period (compared to 2.1 per cent per annum from 1983–1989).

The 1989–1996 figure is similar to the extensive immigration of the nickel boom at the end of the 1960s and early 1970s (11,000 immigrants came to New Caledonia between 1969 and 1976, see Doumenge and Faberon 2000, 65). The official statistician, ISEE-INSEE, noted that, after the nickel boom around 1970, new arrivals had slowed by 1989, attributing the increase from 1989 to 1996 to the signature of the Matignon Accords in 1988 (ISEE-INSEE 2004 Census). Table 4.3 shows that per annum net migration significantly increased to 1996 (from 163 in 1983–1989, to 1298 1989–1996), and Table 4.4, too, shows relatively large increases in per annum inflows from 1990 to 1994 (an average of 1267 per year for that 5 year period). Most of these immigrants were French, as Table 4.2 shows that the number of people in New Caledonia born in France or its overseas departments increased from 17.2 per cent in 1983 to 17.5 per cent in 1996.

These figures are important as all of those arriving before 1994 will be eligible to vote in the 2014–2018 referendum(s) and, being mostly French, would be likely to vote pro-France in such a referendum.

Migration inflows 1996–2009

After 1996, figures are affected by the 2004 boycott, the non-inclusion of an ethnic category in the 2004 census, the qualification of the ethnic category figures from the 2009 census, and they continue to be reported and analysed by the French authorities over differing time periods. Moreover, figures on migration inflows for 2009 were only released in April 2011 and were unclear, applying two different methodologies (see Royer 2011).

Still, tables 4.2, 4.3 and 4.4 report overall population, natural and migration inflow increases, and country of birth figures and are less affected by the problems with the 2009 ethnic categories (albeit that all are affected by the 2004 boycott, and Table 4.3 by the presentation of different time periods and methodologies). They show an overall trend of continued steady migration mainly from France and the overseas French entities.

Table 4.2 New Caledonia — Place of birth 1983–2004

	(in %)				
	1983	1989	1996	[2004a]	2009
New Caledonia	76.8	78.0	76.7	76.8	75.6
France/other Overseas depts	11.6	10.8	12.4	13.9	15.0
French Pacific entities:					
Wallis and Futuna	3.5	3.6	3.4	2.9	2.9
French Polynesia	2.1	1.8	1.7	1.3	1.3
Total France/Overseas France	17.2	16.2	17.5	18.1	19.2
Foreigners	6.0	5.8	5.8	5.1	5.2
Total	**100.0**	**100.0**	**100.0**	**100.0**	**100.0**

a. Census subject to a boycott call by some pro-independence parties

Source: ISEE-INSEE *Recensement de la Population de la Nouvelle-Calédonie au 31 août 2004*; Recensement 2009 Tableau 1

Table 4.3 New Caledonia — Demographic summary 1983-2009

	1983-1989	1989-1996	1996-2004[a]	2004[a]-2009[d]
	(6 Years)	(7 Years)	(8 years)	(5 years)
Population (start of period)	145,368	164,173	196,835	230,789
Population (end of period)	164,173	196,836	230,789	245,580
Variation (start to end)	18,805	32,663	33,954	14,791
Net natural increase	17,826	23,552	27,817	14,134
Apparent net migration	979	9111	6137	657[a]
Natural increase (%) pa	2.0	1.9	1.5	N/A[d]
Net migration (%)[b] pa	0.1	0.7	0.4	N/A[d]
Total per annum change	**2.1**	**2.6**	**1.9**	**1.2 Est[a, d]**
				1.7[e]
Per annum apparent net migration[c]	163	1298	845	[2000-2007 1020 pa[f]]
According to Royer[g] analysis	N/A	1200	500	900

a. Census subject to a boycott call by some pro-independence parties

b. Difference between numbers of those entering and leaving, regardless of place of birth

c. Apparent net migration divided by number of years in the relevant period

d. Some figures not available, ISEE 2009 figures provisional

e. Figure presented by ISEE 2010 for 1996-2009 *Graphique complémentaire 1*

f. ISEE *Situation Démographique 2008* provided as basis of comparison in absence 2009 figures

g. Jean-François Royer, Les Fluxes migratoires externes de la Nouvelle-Calédonie 1989-2009, ISEE 2011

Source: ISEE-INSEE Recensement de la Population de la Nouvelle-Calédonie au 31 août 2004, ISEE Recensement 2009 (provisional figures), ISEE Recensement 2009, April 2011; Jean-François Royer, Les Fluxes migratoires externes de la Nouvelle-Calédonie 1989-2009, ISEE 2011

Table 4.4 New Caledonia — Estimated annual population and migration figures 1981-2007

Year	Population[a]	Migration	Year	Population[a]	Migration	Year	Population[a]	Migration
1981	141,136	331	1991	173,163	874	2001	215,260	932
1982	144,221	41	1992	177,560	1004	2002	219,387	1132
1983	147,178	25	1993	182,038	1532	2003	223,592	1305
1984	150,187	27	1994	186,953	1850	2004	227,878	1518
1985	153,072	28	1995	192,010	389	2005	232,258	1361
1986	155,828	21	1996	195,621	504	2006	236,528	751
1987	158,866	7	1997	199,506	350	2007	240,390	1134
1988	162,082	5	1998	203,330	528	2008	244,410	1760
1989	165,160	521	1999	207,228	751	2009	245,580	
1990	168,635	1078	2000	211,200	571	2010		

a. Estimates, at 1 January each year

Source: from Table P1 — Évolution générale de la situation démographique en Nouvelle-Calédonie, ISEE *Situation Démographique 2008 ; Recensement 2009*

Table 4.5 New Caledonia — Population by province 1976–2009

	(% of total)					
	1976	1983	1989	1996	2004[a]	2009
Loyalty Islands	10.9	10.7	10.9	10.6	9.6	7.1
Northern Province	24.0	21.5	21.0	21.0	19.2	18.4
Southern Province	65.1	67.8	68.1	68.4	71.2	74.5
Of which Noumea	55.8	58.5	59.4	60.4	63.4	66.7
New Caledonia	100.0	100.0	100.0	100.0	100.0	100.0

a. Census subject to a boycott call by some pro-independence parties

Source: ISEE-INSEE *Recensement de la Population de la Nouvelle-Calédonie au 31 août 2004*; ISEE Recensement 2009 Tableau 2

Table 4.4 shows that the large per annum inflows from 1990 to 1994 (an average of 1267 per year for that 5-year period), were followed by lower inflows from 1995 to 1999 (an average of 504 per year for that 5-year period), followed by similar inflows to those of the early 1990s from 2000 to 2009 (average of 1162 per year for the 9-year period). Jean-François Royer applies various methodologies to the 2009 census results and reports that, from 2004 to 2009, per annum net migration inflow was 900 people (mean of 5 years), compared with 500 from 1996 to 2004 (mean of 8 years) and 1200 from 1989 to1996 (mean of 7 years) (Royer 2011, 3). Despite qualifications, Table 4.3 shows a trend of increased migration inflows of 1.7 per cent per annum from 1996 to 2009, although at a lesser rate than the 2.6 per cent rate from 1989 to 1996 over seven years, with an apparently greater increase from 1996 to 2004 (1.9 per cent per annum over eight years) than thereafter (1.2 per cent 2004 to 2009 or five years, estimate). Royer postulates that the fluctuation and, according to some (for example, the New Caledonian Government who had questioned the results), surprising relative lack of growth in the population to 2009, had occurred because of young New Caledonians travelling to France and other places, including Australia, for higher studies, rather than reduced migration *flows per se* (Royer 2011, 3 and 4).

And, after 1996, even more of the newcomers came from France, either the hexagon or its overseas entities. ISEE reported that, from 2004 to 2009, 18,500 people born outside New Caledonia settled there, of which 75.5 per cent were from metropolitan France, 17.3 per cent from other countries, 4.9 per cent from Wallis and Futuna and 2.3 per cent from French Polynesia (Rivoilon and Broustet 2011, 2) (Differences between these numbers and the figures in tables 4.3 and 4.4 can be explained by different methodologies, including calculation of the net apparent migration inflow, which covers arrivals and departures, not simply arrivals).

In 2009, results reported in Table 4.2 show that, of 245,580 inhabitants, 75.6 per cent were born in New Caledonia, 19.2 per cent in metropolitan or other parts of *outre-mer* or Overseas France, and 5.2 per cent in foreign countries. The table shows that the number of people in New Caledonia who were born in France or its overseas departments increased from 17.5 per cent in 1996 to 19.2 per cent in 2009, exceeding the increase in the difficult 1980s period when French immigration was considered a problem. In 1996, the flawed 2004 census, and 2009, the percentage of French/Overseas France-born was 17.5 per cent, 18.1 per cent and 19.2 per cent respectively, each more than the 17.2 per cent in 1983.

Pierre Cadéot's analysis of the 1996 census shows that 23.3 per cent of residents of New Caledonia (see Table 4.2), and 35 per cent of those of the greater Noumea area, were born outside the collectivity. Of those born outside New Caledonia, 75 per cent were French, of whom 50 per cent were born in the metropole, the others from elsewhere, mainly the former French possessions in North Africa, Indochina, and New Hebrides (Cadéot 2003, 57).

Annual estimates for natural population increase show a declining trend from 2000 to 2007, averaging 3086 a year, standing at 2886 in 2007 (ISEE-INSEE 2008). However their figures for migration inflows slightly increased, averaging 1020 per year in that time, and standing at 1134 in 2007, increasing to 1760 in 2008 (see Table 4.4). Given earlier trends (Table 4.2) it can be assumed that most of the migration inflow was from metropolitan France or from other French overseas entities.

Even accepting the probable *underestimate* of the population increase of 1.9 per cent per annum from 1996 to 2004, owing to the census boycott by some locals, to a total increase of 33,953 over the five-year period (Table 4.3), official statistics note that this growth was far greater than in metropolitan France (.5 per cent), and French Polynesia (1.8 per cent) (ISEE-TSEE *Recensement 2004*).

Overall, these figures suggest a significant recent increase in numbers of migrants into New Caledonia from other parts of France. Added to the apparent understatement in statistics of the size of the 'European' (born in France) group, it is clear that the proportion of Kanaks relative to other communities is declining, in a generally more diverse population.

The development of three major nickel projects (see Nickel and rebalancing development, below) in the early 2000s has inevitably meant an increase in the number of French experts and companies to service them (Gérard Baudchon and Jean-Louis Rallu in Cadéot 2003, 250), just as the 1970s nickel boom saw similar inflows. This influx can be expected to continue and grow as the nickel projects develop.

Retirement incentives

Apart from the inflow of personnel relating to the production of nickel, a second factor underlying a large influx of immigrants from metropolitan and Overseas France has been the active encouragement by the French State of retirement by French officials to its overseas collectivities, including New Caledonia (and French Polynesia) (Chauchat 2006, 140).

From 1950, there have been special payments, or *surrémunérations* (extra remuneration) for French civil servants working in the overseas territories. As an example, when Mathias Chauchat was writing in 2006, the extra payments brought the normal salaries of working civil servants in New Caledonia to as high as 194 per cent of mainland French civil servants (in the more remote communes, a mere 173 per cent in Noumea, Chauchat, 143). In French Polynesia, the payments were even higher, going up to 204 per cent in some islands. Little by little, these special payments attached to retirement, and not only of Overseas France civil servants, but to any civil servant retiring to the French overseas entities, which was thereby expressly encouraged by the French State. In 2006 (and as of September 2008), retirees, not just former civil servants who had worked in the French Pacific territories, but any civil servant retiring from metropolitan France or other overseas territories, were paid 175 per cent of their normal retiring pensions if they retired to any of the French Pacific territories, with more if they had dependent children, and special extra entitlements for former military personnel (Chauchat, 147). Chauchat ascribes these payments to an active State policy encouraging movement of people to the overseas entities (140) and, clearly, such incentive payments are designed to encourage a strong presence of inhabitants from the hexagon, as opposed to local indigenous peoples.

From 2003 to 2006 there were three parliamentary efforts to curtail these payments, to address the soaring costs (which Chauchat 2006, 149, put at €2.2 billion in 2001, although Overseas France Minister Yves Jégo indicated that the sum was €295 million in 2007, perhaps measured differently, see *Flash d'Océanie*, 4 July 2008) given the relative attractiveness of the overseas entities to retirees, which removed the need for special incentive payments, but mainly to redress the situation where many beneficiaries had had no previous connection with the French overseas entities to which they were retiring. All three attempts met with opposition by the Overseas France minister at the time, who said such changes would need wide consultation, would profoundly impact the small economies, and could result in law and order problems (for example, Minister Girardin comments to senate review in 2005, Chauchat 2006, 176).

In April 2008, however, new President, Nicolas Sarkozy, said that the implementation of this system would be progressively curtailed, underlining that this was because it applied to people who had never worked in the particular overseas entity to which they were retiring (RFOFr website, April 2008, *Retraites : Menaces sur les fonctionnaires d'Outre-mer*, accessed 15 September 2008). In July 2008, Jégo, announced that the scheme was coming to an end (*Flash d'Océanie*, 4 July 2008). At that time, 83 per cent of civil servant retirees in New Caledonia (and 59 per cent of those benefitting in French Polynesia) had never served anywhere but metropolitan France. The French national assembly passed legislation by the end of 2008 that provided for a gradual phase-out of the provisions, to be completed by 2027.

The various (not necessarily consistent) figures quoted by French authorities show that such immigration had been increasing dramatically, particularly in recent years, from 2000 onwards. A French budget report showed that the scheme had experienced a 70 per cent increase in costs in 2005 over the payments in 2000 (*Flash d'Océanie* 4 July 2008). Jégo told *Les Nouvelles Calédoniennes* on 28 July 2008 that there had been a tripling of the numbers of such retirees in New Caledonia from 1658 in 1989 to 5198 in 2005. ISEE figures (TEC *Tableaux de l'Économie calédonienne*, Caledonian Economic Tables 2008, *Les fonctionnaires retraités en Nouvelle-Calédonie,* Retired Civil Servants in New Caledonia) showed there were 3927 retired French State officials receiving pensions in New Caledonia in 1990, and 3954 in 2001, after which there were big increases, almost doubling, to 5451 in 2007, receiving pensions worth a total of CFP20.3 million($A334 million, converted 16 March 2009). The daily newspaper *Les Nouvelles Calédoniennes* estimated that there were about 6000 recipients in 2008, on the basis of local statistics (*Nouvelles Calédoniennes* 28 July 2008, accessed 9 September 2008). Of New Caledonia's population, estimated to be just over 230,000 in 2008, 6000 French mainland or overseas retiree migrants is a significant figure, especially when the entire population grew at 1.9 per cent, around 4000 people, per annum in the five years to 2004 (Table 4.2, and see Faberon and Ziller, 358).

Those estimated 4000 retirees in residence by 1994 (on the basis of ISEE TEC 2008 figures, above) will be able to vote in the final referendum(s), having 20-years residence to 2014. These retirees, being newcomers from other parts of France, would be likely to vote pro-France. With the retirement incentives not fully cutting out until 2027, all of the 6000 or so retirees currently in New Caledonia would have a personal interest in the outcome of the Noumea Accord and their rights in a post-Accord New Caledonia.

Inflows from Wallis and Futuna and ethnic violence

The historic, relatively large and continuing influx of people from Wallis and Futuna is a sensitive issue in New Caledonia. The absence of the ethnic breakdown from the 2004 census is particularly relevant here. The qualifications of the 2009 census reporting on ethnic categories highlight these sensitivities, since the published figures show 'reallocations' from the new 'mixed race' category only for three communities: Kanak, European and Wallisian. Despite the apparent drop in numbers of people born in Wallis and Futuna in the flawed 2004 and 2009 censuses at Table 4.2 (from 3.4 per cent of the population in 1996 to 2.9 per cent in 2004 and 2009), and the apparent drop in proportion of Wallisians from 9.0 per cent in 1996 to 8.7 per cent in 2009, which shifts to an increase to 10 per cent in 2009 after 'reallocation' (Table 4.1a), other indicators are that their numbers are in fact increasing. A 2008 census of Wallis and Futuna showed that there were 13,445 Wallisians in Wallis and Futuna, representing a 10 per cent decline in population from 2003 (Hadj 2009), and the main destination of the emigrants is New Caledonia. There are more Wallisians in New Caledonia than in Wallis and Futuna. The 1996 census reported 17,763 Wallisians in New Caledonia then, while *Flash d'Océanie* of 27 August 2008 reported an estimated 20,000 Wallisians in New Caledonia at that time.

The inflows are set to continue. There is no source of income for Wallis and Futuna other than direct inflows from the French State and remittances from workers in New Caledonia (and to a lesser extent French Polynesia), and it is French policy to facilitate these remittances. Part of the Noumea Accord involved special commitments by New Caledonia towards Wallis and Futuna, specified in Article 225 of the 1999 Organic Law. An agreement was signed between the French State, New Caledonia and Wallis and Futuna in December 2003 providing working rights for Wallisians in New Caledonia, with the State undertaking to cover social services costs for Wallisians residing there for at least10 years. This unusual provision appears to have originated in the strong support Wallisians in New Caledonia have traditionally given to the pro-France political groups.

Violent disturbances

Wallisian immigration has been inflammatory. The only major outbreak of violence in New Caledonia since the *événements* of the 1980s has centred on ethnic differences with the Wallisians.

In 2001, ethnic violence erupted at the outlying mission township of Saint-Louis near Noumea, where local Melanesian Kanak communities uneasily lived side-by-side newcomers from Wallis and Futuna, who are Polynesians. Kanak tribes had been established in the area since the late nineteenth century. Wallisian workers began to be settled there from the 1960s (see Maclellan 2005a, 8–9). Ethnic differences were exacerbated by the fact that Wallisians, along with most newcomers from other French metropolitan and overseas collectivities, tended to support the pro-France group (Henningham 1992, 185). Problems were compounded by differences between two rival Kanak leaders, Robert Moyatea, who supported the pro-France Rassemblement–UMP group; and Kanak clan chief and FLNKS leader Wamytan. There were allegations that the pro-France Rassemblement Pour la Calédonie dans la République (Rally for [New] Caledonia within the Republic, RPCR) leader Jacques Lafleur had encouraged settlement of Wallisians in the Saint-Louis area to shore up electoral support in the Noumea outer area against the FLNKS.

Tensions mounted from 2001, and included a longstanding road blockade and violence engaging the local gendarmerie. At the height of the disturbances two Kanaks and a Futunan were killed, and a police officer and a French priest were shot. In July 2003, 250 French gendarmes intervened against Wallisian troublemakers. This attack occurred the same month that Chirac visited New Caledonia. It was followed by the removal of the Wallisian community from their homes, to be resettled in housing elsewhere in Noumea, in what could be described as an ethnic cleansing operation.

The unstable situation at Saint-Louis is a recent example of the fundamental volatility of New Caledonia, and shows how the French presence, even as a guarantor of law and order, continues to be based on military muscle. It also highlights the complexity of the political scene, where strong French action was taken to support the grievances of the Kanak, pro-independence peoples there.

Tension persists between the Kanaks and Wallisians, including occasional violent attacks on individuals.

Other immigration issues

To respond to Kanak concerns about immigration, the managers of the major nickel projects under construction have devised elaborate ways to limit the impact of imported labour. Inco used a prefabricated design for construction, largely outside New Caledonia, of the building element of the massive Goro project in the south. From 2006 to 2009, Inco imported close to 5000 workers from the Philippines for the construction phase of the project. The workers were flown in on charter aircraft, stayed for temporary rotations, usually six months, at campsites where they were housed without being allowed to circulate beyond the site. Xstrata are planning to do the same thing to meet labour demands when construction begins on a smelter in the north, at Koniambo. The arrangement resulted in industrial protests in late 2006 (see *Flash d'Océanie* 10 August 2007), arguably laying the basis for continuing strikes and the ultimate formation of the union-based Labour Party (see Political transition and realignment, below).

It remains to be seen how well a similar arrangement will work in the north, where the mining sites are located in the midst of Kanak settlements, and where the local Kanak people are keen to be employed. There are potential human rights issues relating to these workers.

Control over immigration

Another, related question is that of control over immigration. The Noumea Accord does not refer specifically to immigration, but does provide, under 'Shared Powers', at Article 3.2.2 that the New Caledonian executive will be 'associated with the implementation of rules relating to entry and stays of foreigners' (the implication being that it is the French State that has the principal power). And, under 'New responsibilities immediately transferred to New Caledonia' at Article 3.1.1, the Accord specifically indicates that local inhabitants' employment rights will be respected, and that regulation will be strengthened over people not settled in New Caledonia. But, in the Organic Law of 1999, the French Government's control over entry and stay of foreigners is stated explicitly (Article 21). Article 34 provides for the High Commissioner to 'consult' the local government on entry and stay and on visas for stays of more than three months, with the local government being 'informed' of decisions taken.

Currently, it is the French Government that has control over entry into New Caledonia, with the local government (the New Caledonian executive 'Government' or cabinet) approving work permits for foreigners. The executive considers every application by a foreigner to work in New Caledonia, on a case-by-case basis. The system is unwieldy, and foreign experts are in limbo while the bureaucracy churns through their applications, and many have no choice but to enter on tourist visas to do contracted work.

The New Caledonian Government has no power, however, to limit the entry or employment of French nationals from elsewhere in France or Overseas France, notwithstanding the protective provisions of Article 3.1.1 of the Accord.

It is significant that immigration is not mentioned in the five *régalien* or core, sovereign, powers to be the subject of the final referendums.

European Union immigration

Another potentially troublesome area for New Caledonia arises from the consequences of European citizenship of its inhabitants. All French nationals are citizens of the European Union (EU), including Melanesians, Caldoches, immigrants from other French entities such as French Polynesia and Wallis and Futuna, and French officials and their families on temporary posting in the collectivity. There is also a small number, difficult to quantify from official statistics, but apparently growing (see Faberon and Ziller 2007, 267, also discussion in Chapter 6 of the effects on the French collectivities), of non-French EU citizens (who would be included in the 'foreigner' category of Table 4.2, which in total was 5.8 per cent in the last comprehensive census, 1996, and 5.2 per cent in 2009).

Chapter 6 outlines in some detail the impact of EU membership on the French Pacific entities. France has negotiated special non-reciprocal rights for its citizens in New Caledonia relative to the EU. Thus New Caledonians can vote in EU elections, travel to and work in EU countries, and export goods to the EU at preferential rates, while there are restrictions on similar EU rights in the French collectivities.

Still, there is unease in New Caledonia (as in French Polynesia) about these provisions and their potential effects, particularly if EU immigration, especially from parts of Europe other than France, were to grow and add to the complexities of French inflows. This unease is reflected in low voter turnouts in elections for representatives to the EU parliament (21.82 per cent in June 2009, see background in Chapter 6).

In electoral arrangements negotiated by France, the EU has accepted that EU voters are not able to vote in New Caledonia's provincial and congressional elections, recognising the special reasons for which the restricted electorate was devised in New Caledonia. EU law provides, however, that any EU citizen may vote in *municipal* elections in any EU member country, including the EU overseas collectivities of member states, after a six-month residency period and registration with the local commune. The Noumea Accord does not specify a restricted electorate for municipal elections. Locals fear the effect of votes in municipal elections from newly arrived European residents, who lack understanding of the history of the restricted electorate and the sensitivities underlying it (Maclellan 2005b, 413). The broad number of EU residents includes French nationals who are otherwise ineligible to vote locally, such as French and European newcomers, and newcomers from other French collectivities, arriving since 1998; and French officials posted temporarily in New Caledonia and their families; who could be expected to support pro-France political groups. The dimensions of the potential impact of the European vote is evident in New Caledonia, where the eligible voting population was 154,228 in the June 2009 EU election, compared to 135,000 who were eligible to vote in the May 2009 provincial elections. In 2009 the winning Pacific candidate was Maurice Ponga, a longstanding Kanak UMP (pro-France) representative who had retired from the congress.

Immigration: Summary

Managing the effect on Noumea Accord commitments of immigration inflows from metropolitan and Overseas France, and potentially the EU, is a continuing concern for the Kanaks, the Caldoches, and the French State. The way in which the French State handled the definition of the restricted electorate, Chirac's decision to remove ethnicity from the census, which has been belatedly but only incompletely rectified, and the inclusion of non-comparable ethnic categories in the 2009 census, renewed local concerns about France's commitment to its word, particularly given continued increases in numbers of newcomers from the rest of France. Local concern consolidated into new political alignments (discussed below).

Sarkozy's early attention to curtailing retirement provisions designed to encourage French migration into the Pacific entities was a positive development for Kanaks and other long-term residents, although the phase-out will not take full effect until 2027, well beyond the Noumea Accord deadlines.

Population inflows from the other French entities, particularly Wallisians, has created different and more serious concerns. The only significant recurrence of violence since the *événements* occurred in 2001–2003 over ethnic and political issues arising from the presence of Wallisians in a Kanak tribal area. The import of thousands of temporary immigrants from the Philippines to work on the major nickel projects also presents potential problems, including human rights issues. And EU citizenship has created obligations which complicate implementation of the Noumea Accord.

The French State's handling of these issues will be a critical determinant of trust and stability for the future. Concern has been noted earlier by pro-independence leaders Néaoutyine, Gorodey and Wamytan. UN Special Rapporteur James Anaya, in his 2011 report on New Caledonia, is highly critical of the handling of ethnic data collection by French authorities, saying that the 'formal equality' underlying it 'mask (sic) ongoing discrimination' (Anaya 2011).

Nickel and rebalancing development

The second core issue that is critical for the success of the Noumea Accord, is the more balanced distribution of economic returns to the collectivity between indigenous and non-indigenous interests. This principle had been established by Michel Rocard in the Oudinot Accord, hammered out after signature of the Matignon Accord, i.e., to restore economic, social and cultural balance, which was dubbed the 'bet on intelligence' by Rocard (see Angleviel 2003). By far the most valuable resource at this stage is nickel, and this has been the principal focus of the rebalancing effort.

New Caledonia has over a quarter (possibly up to 40 per cent) of world nickel reserves, is the third-largest nickel producer in the world and the largest producer of ferro-nickel (Horowitz 2004, 299, Maclellan 2005c). Folklore amongst old mining hands has it that, in an ancient geological upheaval, what is now New Caledonia broke away from the vast Gondawanaland (the major part of which now forms Australia), turned upside down and exposed massive reserves of red iron along the whole of Grande Terre. Wilfred Burchett in 1941 wrote of the expanses of the red ore so dense that lakes formed because water simply sat on top of soil so iron-rich it prevented absorption (161). New Caledonia's nickel reserves are the more valuable at a time when world demand for nickel is increasing, and as China and India industrialise and consume more stainless steel, of which nickel forms the principal component, in household and other products, although the 2008–2009 global financial crisis has impacted on these trends.

The French State is the largest contributor to New Caledonia's budget, contributing CFP121.5 billion or $A2 billion in 2007, about a sixth of its GDP of an estimated CFP768.1 billion ($A13 billion, converted 7 July 2009) that year (ISEE TEC 2008 p. 96; ISEE website <http://www.itsee.nc>, accessed 28 October 2008). But nickel is by far the largest single source of income: nickel mineral and matte exports were worth an estimated CFP177 billion ($A3 billion) in 2007, when prices were high, contributing around a quarter of New Caledonia's economic growth between 1998 and 2006 (ISEE TEC 2008 p. 91, *Bilan économique* 2009, 5). (Raw nickel is currently exported to Australia (worth around $A85 million in the financial year 2007–2008, DFAT website <http://www.dfat.gov.au>, accessed 7 July 2009).) The vast bulk of these profits, however, accrue to French interests (see below, Greater returns of profits, for breakdown of SLN ownership).

While the principal funding and investment effort in New Caledonia is directed towards expanding the nickel sector, to date (mid 2012) the single nickel producing unit remains SLN's 150-year-old Doniambo plant in the south; and the only completed new processing plant, the enormous Goro nickel complex, is also in the south, albeit not yet producing, after substantial financial setbacks (see below). While much planning and groundwork has been achieved in the north, completion of these projects is still a long way off, in part a consequence of the global financial crisis.

Ambiguity in the responsibility for mineral resources

Under the Noumea Accord, the New Caledonian government was given responsibility over the exploration, exploitation, management and conservation of natural resources in the Exclusive Economic Zone (EEZ) (Article 3.1.1), a significant concession. But there are ambiguities. The transfer or responsibility for hydrocarbons, potash, nickel, chrome and cobalt is under the heading of 'Shared Powers' (between the French State and New Caledonia) (Article 3.2.5), without specifying when or how these powers will be fully transferred. The New Caledonian Government was given responsibility for drafting mining regulations (but see paragraph below), and the provinces the power to enforce them. The State participates in a mining council.

But, in the 1999 Organic Law implementing the Accord, the State is described (Article 21, point 7), as being responsible for regulation in matters mentioned in Article 19, point 1, of Decree No. 54-1110 of 13 November 1954 reforming the regime of mineral substances in the overseas territories, and installations which use them. That decree covers substances that are useful in research and activities relating to strategic substances linked to national defence (including related to atomic energy, see Faberon and Ziller 2007, 380). In Article 22 of the Organic Law, New Caledonia is given (at point 10) responsibility for the regulation *and exercise of rights of exploration, exploitation, management and conservation* of natural, biological and non-biological resources *in the exclusive economic zone*; and (point 11), for *regulation relating* to hydrocarbons, nickel, chrome and cobalt (my italics) (Organic Law 1999 points 10° *Réglementation et exercice des droits d'exploration, d'exploitation, de gestion et de conservation des ressources naturelles, biologiques et non-biologiques de la zone économique exclusive*; and 11° *Réglementation relative aux hydrocarbures, au nickel, au chrome et au cobalt*). The lack of specification of the exploration and other rights on the latter resources lying other than in the EEZ is an effective qualifier.

The ambiguity is related to earlier qualifiers of the mineral responsibility in the Matignon Accords and its Referendum Law of 1988. According to a senate report at the time, any strategic primary resource linked to national defence and mentioned in the referendum law of 9 November 1988 endorsing the Matignon Accord remained the responsibility of the French State. Article 8 point 7 of that law referred to 'any strategic primary substances as defined for the entire territory of the Republic' (see Referendum Law 88-1028 of 9 November 1988; and French Senate Document No. 180 p. 68, report by M. Jean-Jacques Heist on the draft Organic Law).

The ambiguity, at the least, gives rise to confusion. Thus, Frederic Angleviel noted that there is an overriding stipulation, defined by the French Council of State, relating to strategic ore (uranium) and oil, which could enable the predominance of national interests over local or international ones (*New Pacific Review* 2003, 157). Lafleur maintained (Personal communication March 2009) that the French State continued to hold power over the subsoil of the EEZs, regardless of the provisions of the Accord. Australian companies interested in exploration offshore have had difficulty clarifying which State or New Caledonian authority was responsible for what. The ambiguity over responsibility for such an important resource has the effect of limiting external interest in investment during the Noumea Accord period, which may well be the intent, and raises the question of whether France intends to retain control over the development of minerals-related industry. Indeed, in a major speech in New Caledonia in August 2011, Sarkozy clearly stated that the French Government would retain control of Eramet, a major participant in nickel development in New Caledonia 'today and tomorrow' (Sarkozy 2011).

Greater returns of profits from SLN France to New Caledonia

Still, France has ensured that more of the returns from nickel production return to New Caledonia than in the past, although French interests retain the largest shares.

Until the time of writing (mid 2012), the only productive nickel processing unit is the 150-year-old Doniambo plant just out of Noumea, in the mainly European Southern Province. The plant is run by Société Le Nickel (Nickel Company, SLN). The French State acquired a 50 per cent share and exclusive ownership in 1947 (see Horowitz 2004, 292) and it has retained a large ownership since. The 1969 Billotte Laws shored up French control over mining during the 1960s/1970s nickel boom and, indeed, were designed to head off Canadian interests in the industry at the time (see Chapter 2). In 1983, the French State owned 70 per cent of SLN by way of its public company, ERAP (Entreprise de recherches et d'activités petrolières), the remaining 30 per cent being equally divided between Elf Aquitaine and Imétal, two other French companies; by the late 1990s the French State share had increased to 85 per cent in a new conglomerate, Eramet (Entreprise de recherches et d'activités métallurgiques).

These days, while the French State's share in SLN has been reduced, the largest share of SLN's revenues continues to return to France (see also Horowitz 2004, 300 and Henningham 1992, 78). This predominance is an issue for the pro-independence groups. The FLNKS sought a 51 per cent share for New Caledonia in SLN (Néaoutyine 2006, 164). Today, French company Eramet remains the largest shareholder in SLN (56 per cent), and Nishin Steel Japan owns another 10 per cent. In a deal struck in 1999, however, as background to the Noumea Accord, New Caledonia now has a 34 per cent share in SLN through the New Caledonian company STCPI (Société Territoriale Calédonienne de Participations Industrielles, [New] Caledonian Territorial Company for Industrial Participation). When STCPI was created in 1999, it acquired 30 per cent of SLN and 5.1 per cent of SLN's parent company Eramet. This was substantially less than the 51 per cent sought by the FLNKS. Under an option arrangement established in

July 2007, STCPI's share of SLN was revised upward to 34 per cent of SLN along with a downward revision of its share of Eramet to 4.1 per cent (see <http://www.euroinvestor.co.uk>, accessed 20 October 2008; and <http://www.sln.nc>, accessed 21 October 2008).

Apart from New Caledonia's (STCPI) 4.1 per cent share of SLN's parent company Eramet, the other major shareholders in Eramet are French. They include the French Duval family (37 per cent); Areva (26 per cent), a strategic nuclear power-related company that is 93 per cent owned by the French State (but with negotiations at the time of writing for outright purchase of Areva by the French State's Fonds stratégique d'investissement); a private French investor Romain Zaleski (13 per cent); a US company Northern Trust (three per cent); and remaining shares, of which the ownership is unknown (see <http://www.transnationale.org/companies/eramet.php> and <http://www.eramet.com>). There is an agreement between the Duvals and Areva that they will vote and act together (see <http://www.pressreleasepoint.com/eramet-sorameceir-and-areva-renew-their-shareholders039-agreement>).

STCPI continues to seek to increase its holdings in both SLN and Eramet. As indicated above, Sarkozy has publicly stated the French State's intention of retaining control of Eramet (Sarkozy 2011).

With these changes in shareholdings in favour of New Caledonia, through STCPI, New Caledonia has benefitted substantially. Through the nickel boom years of 2007 and 2008, SLN paid over CFP20 billion (€167 million or $A300 million, converted 7 July 2009) in taxes and CFP2.3 billion (€19.2 million or $A33 million) in dividends to the New Caledonian government. SLN claims it spent another CFP25 billion or €209 million ($A366 million) in local purchases, and CFP663 million or €5.55 million ($A9.7 million) in training and working conditions in New Caledonia. In addition SLN spent CFP35 billion or €293 million ($A513 million) on expanding Doniambo's capacity to 75,000 tonnes (see Doniambo expansion, below) (<http://www.sln.nc>, accessed 17 March 2009).

Extended production of nickel in the south and new production in the north

At the same time, plans were set in place to develop mining outside of the European-dominated south. Chapter 2 describes how, as a background prerequisite to the signature of the Noumea Accord, the mainly Kanak Northern Province was endowed with the Koniambo mountain range, and with a share in the establishment by a multinational company (initially Falconbridge, and subsequently taken over by Anglo–Swiss company XStrata) of a processing plant at Koniambo. The development of a third processing unit at Goro in the mainly European Southern Province by Canadian company Inco was a further arm of this agreement to achieve balanced development, along with expansion of production to 75,000 tonnes a year of the Doniambo plant in the south.

The success of this rebalancing strategy will be integral to the continued peaceful presence of the French in New Caledonia and, more broadly, in the South Pacific. Leah Horowitz (2004), in a perceptive review of nickel politics, notes that the balanced development of projects in the north and the south will reflect the expectations under the Noumea Accord itself, i.e., the expectations of the Kanaks that economic independence will lead to the possibility of political independence, and the expectations of the pro-France groups in the south (and the French State itself) that rebalanced economic development will, by its very prosperity, head off independence demands. She wrote that 'The Koniambo Project is thus viewed either as representing the possibility of greater political and economic autonomy for Kanak as a precursor to independence or, in contrast, as yet another in a series of actions that have used economic gains to deter pro-independence aspirations' (2004, 309).

Challenges affecting rebalancing success of the mining projects

At the outset it must be recognised that development of even one major nickel plant in an island economy is a massive undertaking, involving billions of dollars, complex technological and metallurgical challenges, labour concerns, social and environmental factors. Such projects challenge any government. For France, the development of the three nickel projects in New Caledonia represents the largest French mining interest ever on its soil. Indeed the Goro project alone is the largest French mining venture within sovereign French territory (see Newman 2001). Undertaking this multi-strand project thousands of miles from the capital in an island environment adds further dimensions of complexity. And the fact that it is being done at the same time as it is developing the statutory framework for the entity of New Caledonia, within its Noumea Accord commitments, adds another complication. Even for the French State, the projects are enormous (as Noumea's Mayor Jean Lèques, charmingly put it, even the most beautiful woman can only give what she has, Personal communication March 2009).

Added to that is the fact that the relatively inexperienced New Caledonian Government, and provincial administrations, under their new-found powers from the 1998 Noumea Accord, are tackling these large projects in their first years of existence, while developing legislative frameworks along the way.

A second consideration is that, accepting that producing the annual existing 50,000–60,000 tonnes of nickel from the Doniambo plant adjacent to the relatively sophisticated infrastructure of Noumea has never been simple or straightforward throughout the 150 years of its existence, it is even more complicated to envisage establishing a further plant in the south, which is still relatively near to Noumea. Factors include the far greater volume of ore to be processed, the new technology involved (acid leaching), the extensive infrastructure in terms of port facilities and power generation required, and the extremely fragile nature of the environment at Goro and Prony Bay.

But, development of a similar plant in the northern tip of Grande Terre, where Koniambo is located, multiplies the demands by several degrees. While there has been a Northern Province Government which has run the province effectively since it was created by the Matignon Accords in 1988, particularly under the current province president, the respected and capable Néaoutyine, local government there is a relatively new phenomenon. Because most economic development has taken place around Noumea, there is far less infrastructure and support in the north, even in the small provincial capital Koné, 200 kilometres north of Noumea, let alone at nearby Koniambo. The logistical requirements for development are enormous. The initial investment in establishing housing, shops, schools and transport within the area to service the new plant is considerable.

Added to all these elements are the normal vagaries of the international market and multinational business activity. The biggest single threat to the success of the rebalancing plan in the nickel sector is, as in the past, the volatility of the market. The global financial crisis of 2008–2009 has had devastating effects on the rebalancing effort. For example, the all-time high price for a tonne of nickel in early 2007 was $US54,000. With the effects of the global financial crisis, the price dropped to below $US10,500 by early 2009. By November 2012 the price centred at approximately $US16,000. Moreover, in October 2008, two major bankers who proposed backing the critical northern Koniambo project (the failed Lehman Brothers, and the Hong Kong Shanghai Bank) withdrew from the project (*Flash d'Océanie*, 20 October 2008).

The French State's support for the nickel projects, financial, administrative, and especially in law and order and the framework of judicial and legislative backing, on a daily basis, led by its successive high commissioners there, is its most important indicator of good faith and commitment to its word under the Matignon and Noumea Accords. At the same time, this commitment by the French State is a strong indicator of its will to keep New Caledonia French. There is no doubt that the running of the major nickel projects favour French interests, businesses and personalities.

Southern Province — Doniambo expansion

Investment:	$US380 million
Projected production:	75,000 tonnes p.a. (from 62,000 tonnes in 2007)
Projected employment:	2200 (from current 2000)

In 2001, SLN initiated a program to expand its capacity at the existing Doniambo plant from around 60,000 tonnes of nickel per annum, to 75,000 tonnes per annum after establishing an enrichment plant at Tiébaghie in late 2008. With the dramatically lowered nickel prices consequent to the global financial crisis, these plans were revised.

Doniambo's production reached 62,000 tonnes in 2007 as nickel prices rose, but with the effects of the global crisis, production dropped to 51,000 tonnes in 2008. Profits dropped from CFP70 billion ($A1.1 billion, converted March 2009) in 2007, to CFP8 billion ($A130 million) in 2008. (See above, Greater returns of profits, for details of SLN's ownership.)

By late February 2009, when the company was losing CFP100 million a day ($A1.6 million, converted March 2009), SLN Managing Director Pierre Alla announced a series of measures, including reduced working hours, to meet revised production needs without retrenching staff (*Nouvelles Calédoniennes* 21 February 2009). As the largest employer in New Caledonia, these measures met stiff union opposition, including by the prominent militant, mainly Kanak union the USTKE, which had just formed a political party, thereby exacerbating divisions on the pro-independence side of politics in the lead-up to the May 2009 provincial elections (see Political transition and realignment, below). Despite work on expanding production capacity at Doniambo, effective increases will depend on world markets.

Southern Province — Goro

Investment:	$US4.3 billion
Projected production:	60,000 tonnes p.a. (possibly 2013) nickel
	5000 tonnes p.a. (possibly 2013) chrome
Projected employment:	2000 (construction)
	(plus 4000–5000 temporary imported workers)
	800 (production)
	2,000 (indirect at production)

The massive Goro project has been a hard-won effort on the part of Inco (which became Vale Inco in 2006 when the Canadian company was taken over by Brazil's Companhia Vale do Rio Doa, or CVRD, later Vale). Inco had had interests in New Caledonia since 1902. In 1969, it undertook exploration in the Goro area, a large stretch of bright red land, rich with ore. The Billotte Laws, described in Chapter 2, were expressly designed to prevent local authorities from dealing with Inco and to keep control of negotiations in French hands. Inco's work in New Caledonia has been long and has required considerable patience.

In 1999 Inco constructed a pilot project to test the new hydrometallurgical process, itself an impressive refinery. Construction of the huge Goro plant, which is 100 times bigger than the pilot project, began in 2002. As the first of the planned projects, the start of construction threw up a range of difficulties, which needed to be tackled by the relatively inexperienced New Caledonian Government under its new powers. Getting it right was fundamental, not only to the success of the Goro project itself, but for the other planned New Caledonian projects in the south (Prony) and north (Koniambo).

Problems emerged as soon as the bulldozers reached the ground, and massively increased the cost of investment. Despite dramatically increasing nickel prices at the time, driven by growing demand in China, barely a year after they began, Inco had to suspend operations, from late 2002 until 2005, to re-cast the project, in the wake of local concerns and demands impacting on costs. The revised project boosted the investment cost from $US1.4 billion to $US2 billion, but this was to rise to $US3.2 billion by 2008, and $US4.3 billion by 2011. Concerns focused on local employment and workers rights, environmental issues, and cultural issues arising both from the neighbouring Kanak communities and the Caldoches.

A shared concern was that the Kanaks and Caldoches would be bypassed in the project. The Kanaks were concerned that their status as indigenous residents and their relationship to the land at Goro would not be respected. They wanted assurances that their communities would receive some of the financial benefits and employment opportunities. They were concerned about environmental issues, and particularly opposed a plan to dump manganese wastes into the ocean. They established a committee, *Rheebu Nhuu* ('eye of the land') under the leadership of Raphaël Mapou, and staged protests, strikes and blockades. This grouping represented a further fragmentation of the FLNKS parties (see Political transition and realignment, below). Separately, the customary senate established a resource management council (see Waddell 2008, 206). In 2003, sponsored by Inco, Mapou and others travelled to Canada where they met Inuit leaders from whom they took further cues on ways to secure assurances and make claims for compensation.

For their part, established Caldoche small business and contractors were concerned about being sidelined by large foreign firms and personnel including from Canada and neighbouring Australia, in providing goods and services to the mining project. Not surprisingly the scale of the project was unfamiliar and overwhelming for many of them. Cultural issues, of a different nature than for the Kanaks, also emerged. After decades of protection and isolation from the region, the Caldoches were unused to the manner and ways of foreign company representatives who came to set up local offices. Small matters such as the kind of electric plugs used (the regional Australian standard or the French European one which had prevailed till then) set off accusations of foreign takeover.

What followed was an example of practical cooperation and teamship in a tense and fractious environment. The French State, through the office of the then High Commissioner, Daniel Constantin, played a key advisory role. Constantin's input was underrated at the time, mainly because of his low-key approach and discretion.

In consultation with senior French and province officials, Goro's management, led by Inco's Brisbane headquarters and its local CEO at the time, Alla, undertook a thorough review of the project and developed mechanisms to deal with local concerns. A brief consultation of Goro's website reveals the result: a pilot committee of the Southern Province; a local community involvement program to ensure the provision of opportunities to local contractors; a community participation program for the employment and training of local communities, including Kanak communities; a business participation alliance; a community relations office; and, a worksite accord that was concluded with project workers. The company also took groups of Kanak leaders to Toronto to meet senior company representatives and see how Inco operated in its Canadian projects.

Share participation by the three provinces of New Caledonia was also devised. Vale Inco has a 69 per cent interest in the project. The three provinces of New Caledonia together hold a 10 per cent equity interest. This was increased from an initial five per cent following FLNKS opposition to the Southern Province grant outright, in 2002, of an exploration permit to Inco relating to the neighbouring Prony site (see below). The New Caledonian share is paid to the Société de Participation Minière du Sud Calédonien (SPMSC, South [New] Caledonian Mining Participation Company), of which 50 per cent is owned by the Southern Province and 25 per cent each by the other two provinces (see Faberon and Ziller 2007, 361; and <http://www.inco.com/global/goro>). Through a jointly owned company called Sumic, Nickel Netherlands, Japan's Sumitomo Metal Mining Co. Ltd. and Mitsui Co. Ltd. own the remaining 21 per cent interest in the project.

Apart from its business and community consultation, Inco complied with the environment code set up by France's INERIS (Institut National de l'Environnement Industriel et des Risques, National Institute for Industrial Environment and

Risk). For its part, the French State enabled the inclusion of the neighbouring Southern Coral Reef on the UNESCO Common Heritage list, while negotiating arrangements allowing for the Goro project activities in Prony Bay.

Inco also established extensive training facilities and, to deal with concerns about imported labour, devised a method of prefabrication for the construction phase, whereby 400 modules making up the plant were to be constructed in the Philippines. The company brought in close to 5000 workers from the Philippines during the construction phase (2006 to 2008), chartering planes from the Philippines, immediately bussing the workers to campsites where they were confined for the duration of their contracts (generally up to six months), and returning them to the Philippines in the same way. Given the extreme sensitivity of the local population to immigration issues, French immigration and security personnel were engaged to ensure quiet movement in and out of the small island, with minimal social disruption or media attention.

The plant will process low-grade ore using hydrometallurgical technology. It is estimated that there are 50 years of reserves remaining. At capacity, the site will produce 60,000 metric tonnes of nickel per annum and 4300 to 5000 metric tonnes of cobalt. It will generate around 800 local jobs directly, and 2000 indirectly and during the construction phase.

Construction was due for completion in 2008, with production to begin in phases from 2009. The global financial crisis, however, declining nickel prices, and technical problems delayed production, which was suspended at the time of writing (mid 2012). One report referred to a production date of 2013 (*Voila encylopedie* website 'Vale Inco Nouvelle-Calédonie' accessed 13 June 2011).

Southern Province — Prony

Investment:	$US1.5 billion
Projected production:	60,000 tonnes p.a. (2023) nickel
	6000 tonnes p.a. (2023) chrome
Projected employment:	n/a

In 2002, Lafleur, then president of Southern Province, granted an exploration permit to Inco for the Prony mining resource, contiguous to Goro. The grant potentially allowed Inco to double its production capacity at Goro, at a time when Inco was re-examining the viability of the Goro project in the face of cost overruns and local opposition. The decision was controversial at the time. Lafleur's own supporters in the provincial assembly resented his lack of consultation, and the Kanaks believed that Inco was granted the licence free of charge (Néaoutyine 2006, 169). News of the permit was not well received in

New Caledonia and, arguably, contributed to the defeat of Lafleur's party by a more broad coalition of pro-France and pro-independence supporters in 2004 provincial elections, in which Lafleur lost the Southern Province presidency (see Political realignment and transition, below).

The grant was challenged in the administrative tribunal, and taken to the Paris appeal courts. In June 2008, a judgement was pronounced against the allocation of the licence to Inco. The new Southern Province president, Philippe Gomes, called for tenders. Vale Inco, SMSP and SLN all tendered and the rights were granted to the French company SLN. This bolstered the longstanding French State and private French interests that were already vested in New Caledonia. It is worth noting that, in the meantime, Inco's former CEO Alla, who had overseen the construction of the Goro project, had taken up the position as director-general of SLN. In this way, French-dominated interests once again held sway over the beleaguered Inco. It is ironic that the original concerns that one company, Inco, should not dominate both Goro and Prony projects did not prevent the single, major French company SLN being accorded Prony rights, notwithstanding its dominance of the nickel industry through the only working unit, Doniambo.

Few believe that the Prony development will proceed speedily. Alla believed in 2009 that it would be 15 years (i.e., 2023) before production would begin. In proceeding with the project, SLN will necessarily conduct negotiations with Vale Inco, who manage the neighbouring Goro project, over joint infrastructure issues — including energy requirements and other inputs — efficiencies that were at the heart of the earlier decision to grant the Prony licence to the operators of the Goro project in the first place. The granting of the licence to SLN gave power to the dominant French company with its own interests at Doniambo, to dictate the pace of production.

Northern Province — Koniambo

Investment:	$US3.8 billion
Projected production:	54,000 tonnes p.a. (mid 2012 to 2014)
Projected employment:	2000 (construction)
	750 (production)
	2000 (indirect at production)

The Koniambo nickel project in the mainly Kanak Northern Province is a critical element of rebalancing efforts. The Koniambo deposit is a rich resource. It is estimated that it holds reserves sufficient for 100 years of production (Néaoutyine 2006, 170). Under the terms of the Bercy Agreement (see Chapter 2), which granted the Koniambo massif to the Northern Province company Société Minière du Sud Pacifique (SMSP), the Canadian multinational Falconbridge was obliged to complete a feasibility study, make the decision to construct a refinery, and establish an investment program by 1 January 2006 to forestall the return of the Koniambo massif to its original owners, Eramet and SLN. In 1996 the Northern Province company and Falconbridge submitted a plan for construction of the plant to the French Government, which was approved. As the deadline approached, Falconbridge was subjected to a takeover bid by Inco, which would have meant an effective monopoly of the two major planned nickel projects by the one multinational. Behind the scenes, French officials sought alternative investors to stave off domination of all of the new major New Caledonian projects by Inco. There was also interest by Chinese companies, which was of concern to senior French officials.

In the event, Falconbridge was taken over by the Anglo–Swiss company Xstrata (which already had a 20 per cent stake in the company) in 2005. Xstrata holds 49 per cent interest in the Koniambo Nickel SAS company, with SMSP holding 51 per cent. The project involves refining ore through established pyrometallurgical processes, and producing 54,000 tonnes of nickel a year, equal to the annual production at Doniambo. The deadlines for the project feasibility study were duly met, and construction of infrastructure providing access to the site, roads, a port and townships, began in early 2007. Earthworks for the refinery site were concluded by early 2009.

With the withdrawal of two major backers of SMSP's share in the wake of the global financial crisis (Hong Kong and Shanghai Banking Corporation and Lehman Brothers), two New Caledonia-based French companies, Caisse d'Epargne and the Bank of New Caledonia extended credit lines, but for amounts that were far short of what was needed by SMSP ($US212 million over 20 years, with SMSP Chairman Andre Dang noting that further amounts would be needed, *Oceania Flash* 6 January 2009). This arrangement was a less satisfactory solution for the Northern Province than external backers, as it restored a degree of French control.

Inevitably, the global financial crisis has meant delays in the construction phase of the refinery itself. The project involves investment of $US3.8 billion, with tax exemptions by the French State worth $US150 million. The project will also require an electric power station and dam to provide electricity and cooling for the refinery. It should create 2000 jobs in the construction phase, 750 jobs when up and running and a further 2000 indirect jobs in the area (Horowitz 2004, 307). It will also require the importation of foreign labour, which may be more difficult in the Kanak heartland than it was at Goro in the south (see Other immigration issues, below). At the seventh meeting of the Noumea Accord committee of signatories in December 2008, caution was registered about the need to 'carefully prepare' for the necessary use of foreign workers (*Relevé de conclusions* 2008).

Horowitz concluded in 2004 that the development of the Koniambo project suggested that the French State and the pro-France forces had succeeded 'in their attempts to convince independence-minded Kanak — through financial assistance that increases political dependency — to focus their efforts on economic development while postponing the push for independence to a point in the indeterminately distant future'. She believed that pro-independence Kanaks 'have used political pressure to negotiate a very favourable deal for their mining company' (309).

In the immediate aftermath of the global financial crisis, the pro-independence parties generally understood that the pace of the project was certain to be affected, and were not unduly concerned by that fact (Personal communication 2009). Should the crisis, and delays, persist closer to the 2014–2018 Noumea Accord deadlines, however, their position could change, particularly if other projects in the south manage to increase their production, or if their own northern project should stall, again skewing production and benefits towards the south at the expense of the Kanak north.

To put the exogenous difficulties in context, Xstrata was expected to proceed with construction at a time when three nickel mines closed in Western Australia (BHP's Ravensthorpe, Norilsk's Cawse mine, and Xstrata's own Sinclair mine) owing to the effects of the global financial crisis.

Northern Province — Gwangyang

The Northern Province investment arm, SMSP, has entered into a 30-year agreement with the Korean company Posco. Two joint subsidiaries have been created, the Nickel Mining Company (NMC) and the Société du Nickel de la Nouvelle-Calédonie, New Caledonian Nickel Company (SNNC). SMSP owns 51 per cent of the venture, and Posco 49 per cent. Using raw ore imported from three companies based in the Northern Province (1.8 billion tonnes over the next 30 years), the smelter in Gwangyang, Korea hoped to produce 30,000 tonnes of matte in 2010, up from 4000 tonnes of matte in 2008 (from exports of 1.8 billion tonnes of raw ore from New Caledonia). The first shipment left New Caledonia in June 2008. The Northern Province hopes to use the revenue from the venture to offset costs of the Koniambo project.

Northern Province — Poum

Consistent with the Bercy Agreement (see Chapter 2), as Xstrata's proceeded with the Koniambo project as scheduled, SLN duly took over the Poum massif in January 2006, but, to date, there is no indication as to how this resource will be used (<http://www.sln.nc>, accessed 21 October 2008).

In summary, whereas very solid progress has been made towards increasing New Caledonian shareholdings in existing projects, and in establishing a Northern Province nickel plant, progress has fallen short of Kanak and FLNKS expectations. FLNKS and other New Caledonian groups are seeking a bigger share for New Caledonia in SLN and Eramet, the French companies controlling existing nickel production. Progress on the big projects (Doniambo expansion and Goro) in the south has been more rapid, and potentially more lucrative, than the northern Koniambo project. This has not gone unnoticed by the Kanaks. FLNKS spokesman Victor Tutugoro warned in 2002 that it would be disastrous if the Southern Province were to have two projects and the Northern Province none (in Horowitz 2004, 308).

The sleight-of-hand of southern pro-France leaders in allocating a third project to the south through the Prony permit, the subsequent legal redress and open tender which resulted in increased control by the existing dominant French company SLN, was also a blow to the confidence of the FLNKS in the context of rebalancing development. The stepping-in of two French companies to replace substantial foreign investors in the Northern Province Koniambo project similarly strengthened French control. Local concerns over job protection and the environment aggravated divisions within the pro-independence and the pro-France political groupings, to be reflected in the political developments outlined below. The huge drop in the international price of nickel with the international financial crisis in late 2008, to less than a quarter of what it was in 2007, inevitably affected the pace of the projects. While there is time for a recovery in world prices, questions about the viability of the projects and the real effect on economic rebalancing efforts are likely to remain in the critical 2014–2018 decision-making period.

Hydrocarbons

Another major source of potential revenue for New Caledonia, rarely spoken about publicly, is evidence of the presence of hydrocarbons offshore, within its EEZ.

The presence of oil and gas in the west of Grande Terre has been known since early in the twentieth century, although it was not believed to be of commercial quality (Vialley et al 2003). From 1994, Australia and France (via Institut français de pétrole, the French Petroleum Institute, IFP, in collaboration with the Mining Service of New Caledonia) participated jointly in the FAUST (French Australian Seismic Transect) within the framework of Zonéco (the program of resource assessment of New Caledonia's EEZ) to assess the likelihood of hydrocarbon resources within the contiguous EEZ.

The 2001 FAUST Zonéco survey found likely petroleum potential, both oil and gas and gas hydrate, in the northern part of the New Caledonian Basin and at the Fairway Ridge Basin (see Vialley et al 2003), although later research (Nouzé et al 2009) disproved the gas hydrate possibilities. French and Australian scientists have conducted numerous prospectivity assessment surveys and studies in French and Australian waters, respectively, on either side of the EEZ/Australian continental shelf line during the last 10 years, in areas shown at Map 3 (Location of hydrocarbons off New Caledonia). These areas are being studied closely on the basis of indicators of the presence of hydrocarbons (mainly sedimentary thickness, for early background see Symonds and Willcox 1989 and Bernardel et al 1999).

While the potential resource reserve in New Caledonian waters may be comparatively large, there is some question about the viability of exploitation using existing technology. The increasing price of petroleum, and its expected scarcity in decades to come, suggest that, at some point, New Caledonia's offshore resources are likely to become exploitable. Some oil companies (Total and Hardman Resources) have shown interest in exploration rights.

The hydrocarbon potential represents a strategic asset for France into the future, and thus would bring into play the clauses placing a caveat over New Caledonia's responsibilities for its resources, cited earlier in this chapter (see Ambiguity in the responsibility for mineral resources, above). Clarifying who has control over the hydrocarbon potential offshore is likely to come into play in the lead up to the 2014–2018 Noumea Accord deadlines.

Progress in implementation of the Accord

Against the background of the complex tasks of managing the immigration/electorate issue and rebalancing the benefits of the mineral resource, other aspects of Noumea Accord implementation have proceeded, with mixed results.

Institutions and symbols

Generally, the structures introduced by the Accord have been established and work well. These include the provincial governments and congress, along with a parallel Paris-organised Committee of Signatories to discuss and monitor the implementation of the Accord schedules.

New institutions, such as a customary senate, have been established, and are regularly consulted by legislators. A committee was formed in 2007 to consider New Caledonian symbols and, by 2008, the government had endorsed a New Caledonian anthem and motto, although issues such as a name and flag remain under discussion. Debate on the flag has exposed divisions (see The flag issue, below).

Despite the provision in the Accord for New Caledonia's special status as a 'country', the French State and pro-France groups actively avoid using the term. Instead, references are made to *'la Nouvelle-Calédonie'*, *'la Calédonie'*, the *'collectivité'* or, even, the outmoded and incorrect *'territoire'*. Pro-independence leaders use *'pays'* (see, for example, Sarkozy 2007b; Frogier in *Nouvelles Calédoniennes* 8 March 2010; Néaoutyine 2009), but Australian representatives in Noumea are regularly reminded by French authorities not to use the term..

The land issue has receded in the public eye, with a conference on land held in Noumea in 2001, and ADRAF (*Agence de développement rural et d'aménagement foncier* or Rural Development and Land Management Agency) carrying out its acquisition and distribution with generally very little publicity. In 2008, in the context of development of the northern mine at Koniambo, agreement with customary leaders was secured for a housing estate to be built on customary land. FLNKS leaders, however, continue to monitor the land issue and claim few resources have been given to ADRAF in recent years to allow it to continue its work. The current schedule of transfers show the handover of ADRAF as being one of the last, projected to take place by January 2014 (*Flash d'Océanie* 21 September 2010). UN Special Rapporteur Anaya, reported in October 2011 that there was continuing frustration amongst Kanaks over land issues, and that a promised land survey and registry had not been set up. He also urged further expansion of customary rights in law (Anaya 2011).

The three provincial governments are responsible for the administration of their regions, effectively with the Kanaks governing the Northern and Island provinces, and the pro-France groups governing the Southern Province. This federal provincial system was devised to provide a means whereby the Kanaks could govern themselves within a united New Caledonia. But some think that, in the implementation, too little power has been exercised by the provinces relative to the collectivity-wide congress (Colloque 2008, Bretegnier in Regnault and Fayaud 2008, 49 and 91), which dilutes the power of the pro-independence groups (since, while they are in charge of two of the three provinces, it is the pro-France groups that dominate in the collectivity-wide (collegial) government). It could be argued, however, that the jury is still out on the issue. Certainly the provinces wield some key powers relating to development of resources, including mineral resources, despite ambiguities in the Noumea Accord and Organic Law (see Ambiguity in the responsibility for natural resources, above).

Education, employment and training

The '*400 cadres*' (400 managers) training program (later called '*Cadres avenir*' — future managers program) was set up in 1988 to redress the chronic underrepresentation of Kanaks in the professions (at that time, fewer than six per cent, see *Nouvelles Calédoniennes* 10 August 2009; see Haut Commissariat, 1999; and Guiart 1999, 131). At the time, a senior Kanak leader cautioned that the training program, over 10 years, would lead to the emergence of a Kanak bourgeoisie, and was part of a strategy of integration, to silence nationalist demands (Waddell 2008, 205). This may well have been the intention.

The French high commission issued a 10-year review of progress in 1999. It noted that 444 people had concluded some kind of training, 70 per cent of them Melanesian (generally meaning Kanak) (this proportion, it claimed, was consistent with rebalancing objectives), with a 70 per cent success rate defined as having an employment placement (Haut Commissariat 1999, 8). By June 2010, the committee of signatories noted the High Commissioner's report that, by 31 December 2009, there were 1058 trainees, of whom 69 per cent were Melanesian; of the 700 of these who had returned to the collectivity, 490 were Kanaks who had been employed (*Relevé de conclusions* 2010, 5). This means that over 30 per cent of the intake was non-Melanesian. The inclusion of non-Melanesians itself is a shift from the original aims of the program, which was to focus on providing opportunity for Kanaks. It is not clear where the returning trainees have been placed for employment. These former trainees are not evident in the upper echelons of government or industry. A newspaper report in mid 2009 suggested that to that point the program had trained 41 engineers, four pilots, three doctors and two architects (*Nouvelles Calédoniennes* 10 August 2009) — a low return for the investment in the program. Anaya reported in 2011 that 'There are no Kanak lawyers, judges, university lecturers, police chiefs or doctors, and there are only six Kanak midwives registered with the State health system, out of a total of 300 midwives in New Caledonia' (Anaya 2011).

It is true that Kanaks are heavily engaged in government in the Northern and Islands provinces. But, in 2009, the administration of these provinces still included large numbers of French and Caldoche officials, teachers and advisers (one Kanak leader illustrated this by referring to the Northern Province official directory, where just three of the 10 directors of departments were Kanak, and the remainder were European, Personal communication, March 2009). Anaya reported that only 57 Kanaks were represented in the middle or upper levels of the administration, of a civil service of 3660 (Anaya 2011).

Progress on efforts to enshrine protection of local employment in local law, a critical element in the concept of New Caledonian citizenship under the Accord, has been slow. A draft law prepared by the Avenir Ensemble (Future Together, AE) led government, relating to preferential employment in the local civil service, was rejected by the French Council of State, and a subsequent draft before the congress, aiming at protecting access to local jobs by local residents of 10-years' residence was hampered by an abstention by the FLNKS in December 2009 (Muckle 2009, 190–91; *Nouvelles Calédoniennes* 14 January 2010). A text was agreed and voted on by July 2010, with some reservations on the criteria applying to the locals, who the law was intended to protect (*Nouvelles Calédoniennes* 28 July 2010). The committee of signatories, in December 2010, foreshadowed further consideration of this issue by the congress in the future (*Relevé de conclusions* 2010, 5). Congress' handling of this issue was vexed, but a revised law was to come into effect in 2012.

The French State has respected its commitments to 'accompany' the collectivity by providing the requisite funding transfers as various responsibilities have been devolved. There remain, however, issues over the phased handover of some powers to the New Caledonian Government by the French State, particularly the responsibility for education. The Noumea Accord provided for transfer of primary school responsibility in the first term of the newly created New Caledonian Government (i.e., 1999 to 2004), which was duly completed; and secondary schooling in the second and third terms (2004–2009 and 2009–2014 respectively). Little had been done by the end of the second mandate (2009), to transfer secondary education to New Caledonia, amidst concerns by some pro-France forces that changing the French national system carried the risk of undermining standards. While this opposition came mainly from the Caldoches, French transients (posted in the collectivity) and mainly European urban population of Noumea, some FLNKS elements shared the concerns. It was only well behind schedule, in November 2009, that the New Caledonian congress passed legislation providing for the handover of the secondary education function by January 2012.

The education issue is delicate, as the French education system was a major issue in the *événements* period, with FLNKS supporters establishing Kanak people's schools in the rural areas in the early 1980s. There has been some progress in responding to Kanak concerns. The primary school curriculum has been altered to cover local history, and an Académie des langues kanak, Academy of Kanak

Languages, was established in 2007. But, whereas the local French system is one with universal access, in practice it remains two-tier in New Caledonia. Kanak children attend local primary schools in the provinces, but only by travelling long distances or by boarding at very young ages, or both. Schooling is also conducted in French, a handicap for the indigenous people, particularly when it is considered that there are 28 indigenous languages in use in New Caledonia (Tryon in Faberon and Hage 2010, 399; also Mokkadem et al 1999). When important exams occur at the end of middle school, the '*brevet*', many Kanaks are funnelled into technical streams, while academic streams tend to be dominated by non-Kanaks. Most of the 30 per cent of students who drop out of the school system are Kanaks (Maclellan 2009c). Kanaks represented only 23 per cent of candidates for the baccalauréat exam in 2009, compared to 69 per cent Europeans (*De l'école coloniale à l'école d'émancipation, Nouvelles Calédoniennes* 22 March 2010). The 2009 Census showed that in 2009, 54.1 per cent of Europeans had the baccalauréat, compared to only 12.5 per cent of Kanaks and 14.2 per cent of Wallisians. Tertiary degrees were held by 20,233 Europeans, but only 2214 Kanaks and 470 Wallisians had the same level of education.

Slippage in other transitional arrangements

Implementation of the main follow-up process, convening the Noumea Accord Committee of Signatories, was fitful. After the seventh meeting in December 2008, the committee did not meet until June 2010, with Paris twice deferring scheduled meetings (from 2009 to early 2010 *Nouvelles Calédoniennes* 29 March 2010), citing pressing domestic preoccupations, but, perhaps, also responding to emerging differences within each of the pro-France and pro-independence groupings. The Conclusions of the Meetings reveal a hesitation and slippage in implementation, particularly on the key issues.

The seventh meeting of the committee, in December 2008, agreed that transfers in the key areas provided for in the Noumea Accord (secondary public education, and responsibility for the Agence de développement de la culture kanak (ADCK or Agency for Kanak Cultural Development) and ADRAF) should proceed. While it underlined that no transfer should be partial, it did agree that transfers could be 'progressive', i.e., that the pace of transfer could be negotiated. The French State agreed to provide accompanying funding. The meeting decided that certain other powers, specifically civil security, and civil and commercial law, should be treated with 'flexibility'. In mid 2009, the transfer of these powers was deferred from 2009 to 2011 (*Relevé de conclusions* 2008).

In May 2010, following scheduling of the June 2010 meeting, the New Caledonian congress sought, in preparation, to endorse a convention on the transfer of responsibilities to be signed by Gomès, then president of New

Caledonia, when the committee of signatories met. UC members, however, absented themselves from the vote and instead sought a review of progress under the Accord (*Nouvelles Calédoniennes* 20 and 24 May 2010). The eighth meeting essentially established a number of subcommittees to handle ongoing issues: a pilot committee on the transfers of responsibilities, to assess progress; a strategic industry committee to continue the work of a mining assessment team; and, a committee to prepare for the post-2014 vote, as provided for in the Accord *(Relevé de conclusions* 2010).

Gomès duly signed a framework agreement with French High Commissioner Yves Dassonville, on 24 September 2010, but it simply listed some responsibilities that had already been transferred (public service training, public telecommunications and post office functions), and provided for the transfer of secondary and other forms of education by 1 January 2013. The New Caledonian Government announced at the same time that working groups were looking at transfers in further areas, including civil and commercial law, civil status, civil security, all three levels of education, lands and cultural institutions. Transfer of the ADCK was envisaged to take place by January 2012, of the ADRAF by January 2014. The New Caledonian congress agreed, in November 2009, that it would take over control of maritime affairs in its territorial waters on 1 January 2011 and control of domestic air transport and airport police in January 2013, although the international airport at Tontouta would remain under French control (*Flash d'Océanie* 1 December 2009; *Oceanie Flash* 21 September 2010 and Maclellan 2009c).

The ninth committee of signatories confirmed the composition and focus of the three pilot groups, and foreshadowed New Caledonian legislation on civil law and security by the end of 2011. By the time of writing (mid 2012) this legislation had not been concluded. The committee reminded all participants of the complexity, scale and scope of change to be achieved before 2014, and urged all parties to maintain the best conditions possible for these changes to be effected (*Relevé de conclusions* 2011). Palika leader Néaoutyine publicly expressed frustration after the meeting, emphasising the need to progress the transfer of responsibilities (Néaoutyine 2011).

External affairs responsibility

The Noumea Accord provides for New Caledonia to take over some aspects of external trade, air and maritime services (Article 3.1.1), the French State specifically retaining responsibility for foreign affairs, but with New Caledonia able to have its own representation in South Pacific countries, and certain South Pacific, EU and UN organisations, and to negotiate agreements with these countries in its areas of responsibility under the Accord (Article 3.2.1). The Accord specifically states that training will be provided to prepare New Caledonians for their new responsibilities in international relations (Article 3.2.1).

In practice, however, as in the other two Pacific entities, there has been little substantive investment in preparing New Caledonian local officials for such responsibilities. Although a unit for international cooperation exists under the office of the president, it is poorly staffed and resourced. Bernard Deladrière, an experienced advisor to the New Caledonian Government under Pierre Frogier, handled foreign affairs virtually single-handedly until the 2004 elections, after which the government of Marie-Noëlle Thémereau engaged a New Zealander to head its external affairs unit. From 2008 to 2009, however, the government of Harold Martin attached no priority to the external affairs unit, did not appoint a director for it and moved the unit to a different building from that occupied by the government. Staff had received little or no training in English, or in international relations and diplomacy. The 2011 committee of signatories agreed that local personnel would be attached to French embassies in the Pacific (*Relevé de Conclusions* 2011), the beginning of a training process — but firmly under the French umbrella. Without a solid and well trained secretariat of their own, strong English-language skills, and an identity separate to that of France, it is difficult for senior New Caledonian Government officials to participate meaningfully in the many specialised regional meetings that they ideally should attend each year.

France's claim over Matthew and Hunter Islands

The potential complexities thrown up by New Caledonia taking on regional affairs responsibilities are illustrated by competing French and Vanuatu claims on the Matthew and Hunter Islands.

Notwithstanding the transitional nature of the Noumea Accord, France has continued to assert its claim over the islands of Matthew and Hunter, a claim that has been contested by elements of the FLNKS.

Although originally discovered by British vessels in the late eighteenth century, both France and Britain claimed the islands relatively recently (France in 1929 and Britain in 1965). France retained its claims after Vanuatu's independence in 1980, when Vanuatu asserted its own claim. To make a point, France established a weather station on one of the islands in 1981. In November 2004, France detained a Taiwanese fishing boat for illegally fishing in Matthew and Hunter waters, but allowed the vessel to leave when the fishermen flashed a fishing authorisation issued by Vanuatu authorities. Subsequently, both France and Vanuatu agreed to negotiate an agreement on the sharing of resources in the area and France proposed further cooperation with Vanuatu in policing the maritime zone. In May 2005, Vanuatu threatened to take the matter up with the UN (*Flash d'Océanie* 25 May 2005), but did not subsequently do so.

In May 2007, as part of Law of the Sea procedures enabling members to extend their continental shelves, France lodged a submission on behalf of New Caledonia, relating, inter alia, to the area encompassing the Matthew and Hunter group. In July 2007 Vanuatu's Prime Minister wrote to the President of France objecting to UN consideration of the submission, and subsequently registered its objection with the UN. In a letter from the office of the French Prime Minister to the Secretary-General, France wrote that it 'takes notice of this objection' (Gorce 2007).

In recent years, France has sent annual *'missions de souveraineté'* (sovereignty missions) to the island groups, often with scientists aboard (see for example *Nouvelles Calédoniennes* 3 February 2009).

Vanuatu has called upon Melanesian solidarity in advancing its claim. In July 2009, on the eve of France's hosting its Oceanic Summit with regional leaders, the MSG, which has its secretariat in Vanuatu, and includes Papua New Guinea, Solomon Islands, Vanuatu, Fiji and the FLNKS from New Caledonia, signed the Kéamu Declaration, stating that the Matthew and Hunter group traditionally belonged to Vanuatu. The FLNKS signatory, Tutugoro, had secured the agreement of New Caledonia's customary senate (*Flash d' Océanie* 28 and 29 July 2009).

Action on post-Noumea Accord sovereign or *régalien* powers

The Noumea Accord provides that votes will be held after 2014 on the transfer of responsibility for the final sovereign powers: foreign affairs, defence, justice, law and order, and currency (Article 3.3). But France has acted in two of these areas, defence and the currency, in ways that would bear on the future, post-Accord characteristics of New Caledonia.

Defence commitments

In 2008 France constructed a large military complex in Noumea, for the first time bringing together the headquarters of all of its Pacific military forces under one roof, strategically sited at the naval dock situated not far from central Noumea. In the same year, the French installed a listening post facility near Tontouta, the international airport in New Caledonia (*Nouvelles Calédoniennes* 6 September 2009). And, in its defence white paper that year, the Sarkozy government announced that New Caledonia would form the base for France's Pacific military presence (see Chapter 7). Also in 2008, France announced a Mutual Logistical Support Arrangement with Australia, under which New Caledonia would give ongoing logistical support to Australia (see Chapter 6).

Since the defence function is one of the five *régalien* or sovereign responsibilities that are specifically mentioned in the Noumea Accord as being subject to a vote after 2014, the timing of France's consolidation of its defence presence raises questions about its commitments to the Accord. Indeed, this French action is reminiscent of the declaration made by François Mitterrand about reinforcing Noumea as a military base in the troubled mid 1980s, which was designed to underline French military power to potential troublemakers (see Chapter 2).

The inconsistency with Noumea Accord principles has not gone unnoticed. Kanak leader Wamytan opposed the defence measures (*Islands Business* November 2009), declaring that such steps were inconsistent for 'a country on the path to emancipation'. Acknowledging that defence was currently a French sovereign responsibility, Wamytan noted that the French State was making decisions lasting five to 20 years into the future, without involving the pro-independence signatories of the Noumea Accord.

Question of the Euro

One further inconsistency in the implementation of the Noumea Accord has been on another of the five sovereign powers to be addressed after 2014, the currency. New Caledonia's currency is rooted in the colonial past. The three French Pacific territories have used the CFP from 1945, when it referred to '*colonies françaises du Pacifique*' or French Pacific colonies, but was known as '*Change français du Pacifique*' from 1947, although it has been defined variously as '*cours*' or '*comptoir français pacifique*' (all loosely meaning 'French Pacific Currency'). France negotiated a special exception in the EU Maastricht Treaty when it adopted the Euro and stipulated 'France will retain the right to issue currency in its overseas territories … and will be the only authority to determine parity of the cfp' (Special Protocol Number 13, Maastricht Treaty. From 1 January 1999, with France's adoption of the Euro, the CFP was linked with the Euro at a specified rate (EUR 1:120 CFP). Until then, it had been linked with the US dollar for a number of years through the US:French franc rate.

With France's switch from its own franc to the Euro in 2002, the French State's position on the CFP has been that it can be replaced by the Euro if all three French Pacific collectivities agreed to do so. Despite initial opposition, French Polynesia has agreed to the change, and the question is not an issue in Wallis and Futuna. But, for the pro-independence parties in New Caledonia, the question is a sensitive one. They see the CFP as a symbol of the past. For FLNKS leaders, resorting to the currency of the *métropole*, let alone that of Europe, would be a backward step in the move to independence. Some even believe that, if a change were to be made, it would be preferable to move to the Australian dollar, given the economic realities of the region, a position which is unacceptable to the French State (Personal communication to author 2004; see also Maclellan 2005b, 413, on local concerns that a move to the Euro would be inconsistent with linkages to the Pacific region).

Most importantly, pro-independence leaders see discussion of this issue as premature. They point out that the currency is one of the five *régalien* issues that are to be looked at within any new political organisation resulting from the 2014–2018 consultations following a referendum (see Néaoutyine 2006, 78 and Personal communication Tutugoro 2009). They wonder why France has raised this issue and see it as divisive.

The seventh meeting of the committee of signatories in December 2008 diffused the issue by providing for working groups to 'study' a possible move to replace the CFP with the Euro (*Relevé de conclusions* 2008).

Social and cultural factors

It is difficult to assess the social effect of the implementation of the Noumea Accord to date. As in other regional island countries, urban drift is a fact of life (see Table 4.5). But, a two-tier society is particularly evident in the city. Chirac's decision to excise the ethnic category from the 2004 census, questioning by the New Caledonian Government of official 2009 census results, and the inclusion of non-comparable ethnic categories in 2009, make it difficult to quantify the ethnic characteristics of Noumea. The 1996 census showed that of Greater Noumea's population of 118,823, Melanesians (Kanaks) totalled 25,613 (21 per cent), Europeans 54,323 (45.7 per cent), and others 38,887 (32 per cent, including Wallisians, Tahitians, Indonesians, Vietnamese, ni-Vanuatu and others) (ISEE TEC 2008, 35). So, Kanaks were far outnumbered by Europeans and other islanders and ethnic groups.

The 2009 census showed that the population of Noumea itself (i.e., not Greater Noumea, as cited above) had increased from 76,293 in 1996 to 97,579 in 2009; and the population of the Southern Province as a whole from 134,546 to 183,007 in the same period. The populations of the two Kanak-dominated provinces showed an annual decline of 1.38 per cent and small increase of .66 per cent respectively, whereas the white dominated Southern Province grew by 2.4 per cent per annum in that period, suggesting that much of the inflow to the south consisted of Kanaks from the Northern and Islands Provinces.

Noumea has remained clearly a European city. The council housing blocks on the outskirts of Noumea, while pleasant and of a high quality, but nonetheless council housing, were fully occupied by Kanaks, and the miserable squats in certain outlying areas solely Kanak, and growing. A 2009 survey showed that the middle classes were deserting Noumea (15 per cent decline from 1996 to 2002), which revealed a widening gap between the very well-off (who are generally European) and the squatters (mainly Kanaks) (*Les classes moyennes désertent Nouméa, Nouvelles Calédoniennes* 22 March 2010). The new, small and efficient public buses that service the capital were almost exclusively used by Kanaks and, occasionally, foreign tourists, rarely if ever by Caldoche or French residents

In central Noumea, Kanaks are notable by their absence from meaningful employment in government, shops or business. They occupy low-level service jobs, such as in garbage collection and domestic cleaning. The only other visible Kanaks are the aimless groups, mainly of young Kanaks, sitting and strolling around the Place des Cocotiers.

According to Gorodey, a senior Kanak leader, many young people take refuge in music and drugs (mainly light hashish), and by returning to their villages periodically, rather than participating in modern life. Drug and alcohol use is of real concern when set in the context of Jean-Marie Tjibaou's concerns about the reasons for, and effect of, alcohol consumption by Kanaks, which were important underpinnings for his leadership of the independence movement (Waddell 2008).

The creation of the impressive Tjibaou Cultural Centre on the Tina peninsula on the outskirts of Noumea, and of the ADCK, also reflect the society's dichotomies. These institutions certainly represent the financial commitment of the French State to encourage the evolution of Kanak culture. But it is ironic that Renzo Piano, a European architect, designed the Tjibaou Centre's main buildings. Although inspired by the concept of a *case*, or Melanesian house, in the process of construction and evolution, the construction became essentially a European one. Kanak-sponsored performances in this elegant structure have been overshadowed by large-scale rock concerts which Kanak groups organise regularly in fields and stadiums elsewhere, featuring international and local indigenous artists. Young Kanaks flock to these rock concerts in large numbers.

Anaya, while recognising the programs France has put in place, concluded in 2011 that the Kanak people

> are experiencing poor levels of educational attainment, employment, health, over-representation in government-subsidised housing, urban poverty, ... and at least 90 per cent of the detainees in New Caledonian prison are Kanak, half of them below the age of 25.

He noted that the situation of Kanak children and youth was a particular concern, and recommended affirmative action to address this (2011).

Mwâ Kâ and cultural symbolism

The continuing role of Kanak cultural symbolism, and the ambiguous views of the French and local Caldoches towards it, were evident in the effort by the Conseil National des Droits du Peuple Autochtone (National Council for Indigenous Peoples Rights, CNDPA) to give a totemic monument, the *Mwâ Kâ* (literally, 'big house') to the city of Noumea (see Maclellan 2005a for a full discussion of this). The monument, 12-metres high and carved by representatives of the eight traditional Kanak areas, was designed to represent the unity of the people of New Caledonia. The organisers had planned to erect it on 24 September 2003, the day when France's taking possession of New Caledonia is traditionally marked, and specifically for the 150th anniversary.

The organisers had hoped to erect the monument in the central Place des Cocotiers, in between the statues of two governors, Jean Olry (described by one organiser as a symbol of military repression) and Paul Feillet (referred to as representing economic development for profit alone).

Not surprisingly, the event was fraught with tensions and differences. Senior FLNKS leaders were at pains to emphasise that the initiative had not been an FLNKS one, but rather one introduced by a small group of Kanaks (Personal communication, 2009). On the pro-France side, Mayor of Noumea Jean Lèques declined to situate the monument in the central Place des Cocotiers as requested, with veteran Southern Province president Lafleur stepping into the breach and inviting its temporary location in a square not far from the New Caledonian Government and Southern Province offices. For different reasons, this offer displeased some Kanak activists and pro-France supporters alike. Differences over this issue highlighted, and reflected, divisions that were emerging at the time within both the pro-independence and pro-France groupings (see discussion in Political transition and realignment, below).

It was only on 24 September 2005, when a new AE government agreed to the monument's permanent placement, that a handover ceremony took place, at a site near the Museum of New Caledonia. Some senior pro-France New Caledonian leaders did not attend the ceremony. Tensions re-emerged on 24 September 2012 when the Mwâ Kâ activists constructed local huts, or *cases*, at the Mwâ Kâ, with permission, but then declined to remove them. By mid November 2012 the mayor sent in bulldozers to remove them by force.

Family reconciliation: Tjibaou meets Wéa

More encouragingly, the easing of tensions and stable climate engendered by the Noumea Accord did allow for a rapprochement of sorts between the Kanak clans affected by the 1989 assassination of Tjibaou at Gossanah.

In 2004 Marie-Claude Tjibaou led a ritual reconciliation ceremony between the Tjibaou family at Hienghène and the Wéa family of Ouvea. This gesture, however, designed to signify not only forgiveness by the wronged family, but a unity of common cultural purpose, was itself fraught with tension. One of Tjibaou's sons did not participate, and customary leaders in Hienghène were reserved about the ceremony. Strong emotions continue to surround not only the assassination, but the path represented by Tjibaou, leaving question marks for the future, particularly should a new young Kanak pro-independence leader emerge (for a sympathetic elaboration of the dynamics in Ouvea as opposed to elsewhere in the Kanak communities, see Waddell 2008).

Political transition and realignment

The Noumea Accord is based on an inclusive, collegial government, albeit one which votes on issues and passes local legislation, necessarily strengthening the power of a majority. The Accord, continuing measures established in the Matignon Accords, provided for three provinces, each of which elect representatives to provincial assemblies, some of which serve in New Caledonia's congress (see Table 4.6). Southern Province elects 40 members (of whom 32 are in the congress), Northern Province 22 (15) and Loyalty Islands Province 14 (7). Elections operate on a party list system, and only parties securing more than 5 per cent of the vote can earn representation. The congress in turn elects a collegial 'government', or executive made up of members (similar to ministers) who hold assigned portfolios. This government may include from five to 11 members, elected on the basis of a formula reflecting the proportion of party strength in the congress. The congress has legislative powers in specified areas within its competence.

Table 4.6 New Caledonia — Political institutions

Provincial elections →	Congressional seats →	New Caledonian Government
(Elections based on restricted electorate)		
Southern Province 40 seats of which	32	from 5 to 11
Northern Province 22 seats of which	15	
Southern Province 14 seats of which	7	

Source: ISEE TEC 2008 p. 3.2

The Noumea Accord envisaged elections to the provincial assemblies and Congress every 5 years, i.e., four sets of elections (1999, 2004, 2009, 2014), after which the issue of proceeding to a series of up to three referendums would be addressed.

As the following sections will show, despite, or perhaps because of, the violent differences which led to the Matignon and Noumea Accord provisions, the collegial province-based system has shown itself to be generally resilient in its first decade, surviving political division. Not unnaturally in this transition period for taking over the levers of government in a new collegial format, both major groupings have undergone significant change and fragmentation. The first three elections to the congress in the post-Noumea Accord period have reflected a number of these political changes (see Table 4.7 on Political representation 1999 and 2009), and are a good measure of the success of the Noumea Accord system.

Pro-France fragmentation

The most significant political change in New Caledonia from 1999 to 2009 was realignment within the pro-France groups. This change represented in part generational change. The old pro-France guard, led by the authoritarian and energetic, albeit ageing, Lafleur in the RPCR, renamed the Rassemblement-UMP (R–UMP) after its conservative counterpart in France, the UMP (Popular Movement Union), was challenged by a younger group, the AE led by Martin, Thémereau, Gomès, and Didier Leroux. This new party was formed just months before the 2004 elections, but managed to win 16 of the 54 congress seats in that election.

Apart from concern over the centralised style of Lafleur and related personality differences (for example, Lafleur and Leroux participated in a heated televised debate leading up to the election), the formation of the AE was driven by a feeling that Lafleur's Rassemblement–UMP was running the congress and executive more as a majority government than as a collegial group, as was explicitly intended in the wording of the Accord. These concerns were not without foundation. At the outset, in the first years of the first term, the executive had been scrupulous to observe the externalities of a collegial government. The (RPCR) president was never seen at public functions without the (FLNKS) vice-president at his side, with amusing cartoons showing the ubiquitous image of the tall Frogier with the diminutive bespectacled Gorodey in her flowered oceanic dress. The image was a powerful symbol of the new arrangements.

But, within that first five-year term, the RPCR's inclusiveness and patience with the FLNKS cooled. Increasingly, the exigencies of government demanded that the executive vote on key government decisions, inevitably leading to a pattern of dominance by the majority over the FLNKS minority. By 2003 Gorodey no longer appeared with Frogier, and physically distanced herself from the RPCR/R–UMP. She declined to move into new congress headquarters, across the road from the grander Southern Province waterside offices, on the basis that the congress would be literally overlooked by Lafleur (president of Southern Province) (*Nouvelles Calédoniennes* 4 December 2002). (Reviving the 1980s tendency to blame Australia for problems with the Kanaks, the satirical *Chien Bleu*, reported an RPCR view that asserted Gorodey's preference for the company of the Australians, a reference to the location of the Australian consulate-general in the same building as the former government offices, where Gorodey had chosen to remain, January 2003.)

Meanwhile, there were many developments, apart from concerns at how collegiality was working, which established and reinforced a commonality of interests among some pro-independence and pro-France supporters. These common concerns resulted from the French State's handling of definition of the restricted electorate, the removal of the ethnic category from the census, and over employment protection and environment concerns highlighted by the rapidly developing nickel projects. As discussed below, the FLNKS was also experiencing further fragmentation and disaffection, partly as a result of the old divide-and-rule habits of the RPCR/R–UMP. For example, the RPCR had been instrumental in husbanding the support of immigrant Wallisians, and stirred the pot at Saint-Louis between Wallisians and Wamytan, who was chief of the local Kanak tribe there. These moves backfired when some disaffected Kanaks gravitated towards the new AE. The AE thus came to unify many Caldoches and Kanaks around common concerns. In a way it reflected a new pro-New Caledonian ideal, which eclipsed for a time other fealties, and led it to win as many seats in the 2004 congress as did the RPCR/R–UMP (Table 4.7). This development led to a shake up in the R–UMP itself, with Frogier replacing Lafleur as president, followed by the resignation of Lafleur who formed a further party, the Rassemblement pour la Calédonie (RPC) in 2006 along with Senator Simon Loueckhote. But, by 2008, Loueckhote had formed yet another pro-France party, the Mouvement de la Diversité (Diversity Movement, MDD).

The split in the pro-France camp, especially around these New Caledonian-centred issues, concerned the French State. The government of newly elected UMP candidate Sarkozy called for the AE and R–UMP to unite, which, while resulting in a short-term reshuffle, instead led to further splits in the pro-France ranks into a number of small parties. In July 2007, AE leader Martin agreed on a cooperation pact with Frogier of the R–UMP, which was opposed by other AE founders Gomès and Leroux. Thémereau and Leroux resigned from the executive. Frogier became congress president and Martin, president of the executive. By the end of 2008, just months before the 2009 provincial/congress elections, the AE had split into numerous parties, including those led by Gomès (Calédonie Ensemble, Caledonia Together, CT), Thémereau (Union pour un avenir ensemble, Union for a Future Together) and Martin and Leroux (AE). The ultra right wing Front National split when its former leader Guy George formed the Mouvement Calédonien français (French Caledonian Movement, MCF). Moreover, a number of small lobby groups emerged (on environment, local employment protection), some neither pro-France nor pro-independence, but all hoping to be courted by either side for representation in electoral lists.

In the end, the pro-France side paid a high price for disunity. In provincial elections held in May 2009 it returned with a reduced majority, winning 31 of the 54 seats, five fewer than in 2004. The overarching role of the RPCR had been replaced by three major groups, the R–UMP headed by Frogier (13 seats), the CT headed by Gomès (10 seats) and the AE by Martin (six seats), together with Lafleur's new party, the RPC (2 seats). The most nationalist group, the National Front/MCF), won no seats at all. And no pro-France group won any representation in the Loyalty Islands, which was an unprecedented result.

Pro-independence disunity

The FLNKS, too, were divided. Leaders could not agree even on who should be president from 2001 onwards, although in the consensus-centred Kanak culture, this was less a problem than in the non-Kanak political parties. Whereas the FLNKS ran on a relatively united ticket in 1999, by 2004 the UC and a new UC Renouveau could not agree to run on the FLNKS ticket, dividing the vote and considerably damaging their chances in the Southern Province. In 2004 the FLNKS did not win any seats in Southern Province. This was a new and worrying trend for collegiality, especially when there was pro-France representation, however small, in the Northern and Island Provinces (see Table 4.7). The real concern was that, with no representation in the Southern Province, where the vast Goro project was proceeding relatively swiftly compared to the Koniambo project in the north, the Kanak polity would feel further marginalised and isolated from centres of power and money.

The FLNKS appeared to have learned the political lesson of its losses in the Southern Province. Together with the Libération Kanak Socialiste (Socialist Kanak Liberation, LKS), it secured four cabinet ministries in the executive elected in 2007 following the R–UMP/AE accommodation, as opposed to the three positions it had held before then. Its efforts to agree on a united ticket in the south, in order to win back representation there, were frustrated, however, by the formation of a new, more vocal and potentially disruptive, pro-independence force.

In November 2007, the USTKE formed a new political party, the Parti travailliste (Labour Party, PT). The USTKE, although not the largest or most powerful Kanak union, was highly visible, and had been behind numerous strikes, protests and blockades for decades, including in the years following the signature of the Noumea Accord, stirring up general strikes and airport blockades over local employment protection issues. As a union, it had also been manipulated in the past by pro-France groupings in order to undermine Kanak unity.

The PT platform included an undertaking to protect Kanak employment rights and ensure implementation of the Noumea Accord. At its first congress in November 2008, it refined its objective to seeking full sovereignty and independence in 2014, noting the non-implementation of the Noumea Accord, particularly in local employment protection and economic rebalancing. In March 2009 it staged a blockade at the international airport on employment rights (opposing SLN measures to reduce working hours in the wake of plummeting nickel prices) to which the French State responded with police force and tear gas (see Fisher 2009a). In the lead up to the May 2009 provincial elections, the PT supported the idea of proceeding immediately to a referendum on independence in 2014 (see Referendum issue, below).

Although the formal membership of the PT is small (just over 500 people attended its 2008 congress), its potential to mobilise has been proven, not only to rally supporters to demonstrate, as in the early 2009 airport blockade, but also in the USTKE's sponsoring large music festivals which have attracted tens of thousands of young New Caledonians (see, for example, Maclellan 2005a, 11).

So the new PT presented a problem for the unity of the pro-independence group. It ran its own lists in all three provinces, drawing away votes from the mainstream FLNKS groups.

Still, in the provincial elections of May 2009, the mainstream pro-independence groups were able to increase their support in both the Loyalty Islands and the Southern Province, enabling them to restore representation that they had lost in the latter province in 2004 (although it is arguable that FLNKS could have won more than the four out of 40 Southern Province seats if the PT had not run its own list). They increased their total representation from 18 to 20 seats in the 54-member congress, with the UC and Union Nationale pour l'Indépendance (National Union for Independence, UNI) winning eight seats each; FLNKS, three; LKS, one; see Table 4.7). The PT won three seats, bringing total pro-independence representation to 23 seats.

The PT also managed to secure representation in both the Northern and Loyalty Islands provinces. It was not, however, satisfied with its win of two seats in Loyalty Islands, and called for a re-run of the election there owing to electoral anomalies (principally the disproportionately high number of proxy votes for those islanders residing on the main island). The French Council of State voided the province's election and, in a re-run in November 2009, the PT doubled its representation, to four. This meant a further increase in its representation in the congress, from three to four seats.

Meanwhile divisions within the FLNKS mainstream groups persist (for example, in the election of the vice-president, the former incumbent and expected winner, Palika's Gorodey, was displaced by UC's Pierre Ngaihoni).[3] How the mainstream FLNKS groups manage their own divisions, and more extreme PT demands, will be a challenge as the 2009 congress prepares for the transition to a post-Noumea Accord New Caledonia.

Evolving views on what comes after the Noumea Accord

Referendum issue during the 2009 campaign

The campaign for the 2009 provincial elections saw the emergence of preliminary positions on both sides relating to the holding of one to three final referendums as provided for under the Noumea Accord.

The Accord provides that from the beginning of the fourth term (2014), with the approval of three-fifths of congress, a date will be set for a referendum on the transfer of the *régalien*, or five sovereign, responsibilities to New Caledonia (i.e., justice, law and order, defence, currency and foreign affairs); on its access to 'an international status of full responsibility'; and on the organisation of citizenship and nationality (Article 5). The electoral body for such a referendum is broader than that for provincial elections, including all voters in those elections but also those establishing 20 years' residence to December 2014; that is, those establishing residence before 31 December 1994 (see Appendix 1). If voters vote against the proposals in the first referendum, and if one third of the congress decides so, a second referendum will be held, and if the vote is again negative, a third will go ahead on the same basis. If the response is still negative, then 'political partners' will meet to examine the position. If congress has not fixed a date for a vote before the end of the penultimate year of the mandate (2017), the French State will do so in the final year (2018). This provision, together with the successive three-vote option, led senior French adviser to suggest, in early 2011, that technically a vote could slip to 2023 (Christnacht 2011). Whatever the case, the 'political organisation', set in place by the 1998 Noumea Accord, will remain, at its latest stage, without any regression to the *status quo ante*.

---

[3] The post-2009 elected New Caledonian 'Government' or cabinet consisted of seven members from pro-French parties (for Rassemblement-UMP: Bernard Deladrière, Jean-Claude Briault, Sonia Backes, for Calédonie Ensemble: Philippe Gomès, Philippe Germain, Philippe Dunoyer and for Le Mouvement pour la Diversité (LMD), which had entered into an alliance with Rassemblement-UMP: Louekhote) and four from the pro-independence side (UC: Ngaihoni, Yann Devillers, Palika: Gorodey, FLNKS: Jean-Louis d'Anglebermes).

Table 4.7 New Caledonia — Post-Noumea Accord election results

	1999	2004	2009 (May)	2009 (Dec)[a]
Turnout	74%	76.42%	72%	
NEW CALEDONIAN CONGRESS				
RPCR (pro-France)	24			
RPC (Lafleur)			2	2
Rassemblement-UMP (Frogier)		16	13	13
Front National	4	4		
Alliance (pro-France)	3			
Avenir Ensemble (pro-France)		16	6	6
Calédonie ensemble (Gomès)			10	10
Total pro-France	31	36	31	31
UNI-FLNKS (independentist)		8		
FLNKS	12		3	3
UNI (Palika)	6		8	6
Union Calédonienne		7	8	8
Fédération de Coordination des Indépendantistes (FCCI)	4	1		
UC Renouveau		1		
LKS	1	1	1	1
Parti Travailliste			3	4
Union nationale pour le renouveau				1
Total pro-independence	23	18	23	23
Total pro-France + pro-independence	54			
EXECUTIVE				
AE		4		
RPCR/Rass UMP	8	4	3	
M'mt pour la Diversité			1	
Calédonie Ensemble			3	
Total pro-France	8	8	7	
UNI-FLNKS	3	2		
UC		1	2	
Palika			1	
FLNKS			1	
Total pro-independence	3	3	4	
Total pro-France + pro-independence	11			
SOUTHERN PROVINCE				
AE (pro-France)		19	8	
Calédonie Ensemble			11	
RPCR (pro- France)	25	16		
RPC			2	

	1999	2004	2009 (May)	2009 (Dec)[a]
Rassemblement–UMP			15	
Alliance Pour la Calédonie (pro-France)	4			
Front National (pro-France)	5	5		
Total pro-France	**34**	**40**	**36**	
FLNKS	6		4	
Total pro-independence	**6**	**0**	**4**	
Total pro-France + pro-independence	40 (of which 32 in Congress)			
NORTHERN PROVINCE				
UNI-FLNKS (ind)		11	9	
FLNKS-UC			8	
Parti Travailliste			3	
FLNKS	6			
UNI	8			
UC (independentist)		7		
FCCI	4			
Total pro-independence	**18**	**18**	**20**	
RPCR	4	3		
AE		1		
Rassemblement-UMP			1	
Une Province pour tous			1	
Total pro-France	**4**	**4**	**2**	
Total pro-France + pro-independence	22 (of which 15 are in Congress)			
ISLANDS PROVINCE				
FLNKS	6			
FLNKS/UC			6	
Palika	2			
UC		4		6
UNI		2		
UNI/FLNKS			4	
LKS	2	2	2	2
Parti Travailliste			2	4
UC Renouveau		2		
FCCI	2	2		
Union nationale pour le renouveau				2
Total pro-independence	**12**	**12**	**14**	**14**
RPCR	2	2		
Total pro-France	**2**	**2**	**0**	**0**
Total pro-France + pro-independence	14 (of which 7 are in Congress)			

a. December 2009 figures reflect a re-run of the Islands elections in December 2009

Source: Author's compilation from official results, see <http://www.nouvelle-caledonie.gouv.fr>

Well before the May 2009 provincial elections, the pro-France side planted the seed of an alternative to the provisions of the Noumea Accord. They claimed that proceeding to the referendum(s) envisaged in the Accord would result in the predictable outcome of a vote to stay with France, since, in all elections held since the Noumea Accord, the pro-France side has won the most seats. They warned that proceeding to a doomed vote would, therefore, needlessly arouse sensitivities and probably violence (see for example 'L'Interview: Jacques Lafleur mêlera sa voix à la campagne', Les Nouvelles Calédoniennes 27 February 2009). The caution is probably justified. The demographics discussed earlier in this chapter show an increasing predominance of newcomer immigrants from France, and other French entities, who support staying with France; and a decline in the percentage of Kanaks, who form the bulk of those supporting independence. It was concerns such as these that led to the proposal by Lafleur to renegotiate and extend the Matignon Accords well before they expired in 1998. At that time, he envisaged an extension of an independence vote by 30 years, although compromised on the 15 years provided for in the Accord (i.e., from 1999 to 2014) (according to Frogier, Lafleur made the concession in the pressured final hours of the negotiations, Personal communication, March 2009).

On 4 January 2008, echoing Lafleur's earlier moves in 1998, AE's Martin, in his inaugural speech as president of the congress, referred to the Noumea Accord provision for the post-2014 congress referendum process. He noted that the result of any such vote would be predictable (i.e., not in favour of the independence camp) and proposed devising 'a new accord for New Caledonians', without waiting for the referendums (see *Flash d'Océanie* 8 January 2008). His suggestion was met with silence from the pro-independence FLNKS side, whom he had evidently not consulted.

Separately, from early 2009, Lafleur persistently floated the idea of a 50-year further delay in moves to any vote for independence in a *'pacte cinquantenaire'* (50-year agreement) (for example, *Nouvelles Calédoniennes* 26 February, 27 April, 5 March, 25 September, 27 October 2009; 13 January 2010).

During the 2009 provincial election campaign, there were mixed views amongst the parties on the idea of delaying a vote. Interestingly, the most strident views came from elements of each opposing camp, both favouring the idea of proceeding as early as possible to a *'référendum couperet'* (cut-off referendum), but for different reasons. Frogier, R–UMP leader, spoke volubly and publicly about the need to proceed immediately in 2014 to a referendum, i.e., not to wait until later in the agreed period to 2018 to vote. He described holding an early referendum openly, and provocatively, so as to *'déclencher'* or *'purger'* (to 'activate' or 'purge') discussions of a new future sooner, rather than to delay inevitable decisions any longer, probably with the aim of thereby forestalling independence indefinitely.

Ironically, the only other proponent of an earlier rather than later referendum was the PT, situated at the extreme end of the pro-independence spectrum (*'Le Parti travailliste pour l'indépendance en 2014'* Nouvelles Calédoniennes 18 November 2008). Its support was potentially troublesome given the tendency of its backbone, the USTKE, to initiate strikes and even violence to progress its causes.

Other parties were more cautious. On the pro-France side, the views of Martin's AE were already known, i.e., favouring talks to circumvent the need for the referendums (see above). Gomès, leading the CE, supported this view (*Nouvelles Calédoniennes* 20 April 2009). In a rare public comment from the mainstream FLNKS, Néaoutyine disagreed with Frogier's idea of a 'purging referendum', saying it was based on a disrespectful view of independence. Independence, he said, was a right to be respected, not something to be feared. He favoured a consensual approach, one which was yet to be explored (*'un résultat qui doit se rechercher'*), but one in which all the options were on the table, i.e., independence as well as staying with France (*Nouvelles Calédoniennes* 20 April 2009).

For its part, the French State maintained a public distance on the question during the election campaign, with President Sarkozy having said, addressing the December 2008 Noumea Accord signatories meeting, that it would be for New Caledonians to decide on a referendum 'pro-independence or otherwise … there is a rendezvous and you will decide, but without violence' (*Nouvelles Calédoniennes* 10 December 2008). Preserving the role of an impartial state, representatives of the French State were privately unequivocal in claiming its commitment to proceed to referendums strictly consistent with statutory requirements under the Accord and the 1999 Organic Law (Personal communications February 2009 and May 2008).

In the event, in the 2009 election, both parties that publicly had supported an early referendum did very well, the R–UMP winning the most seats of any single party, and PT winning four seats after its establishment only 18 months earlier.

L'après-Accord: Independence and sovereignty

Pro-France groups

The fact that the most conservative pro-France party had shared a strong position in favour of an early referendum with the most extreme, pro-independence party, galvanised the mainstream pro-France parties around a position advocating caution about holding an early referendum, which may well have been the intent behind Frogier's position. Indeed, the R–UMP stance seemed to have been simple posturing: by October 2009, Frogier was no longer speaking of 'purging' independence by the earliest possible 'yes or no' vote, but rather of a vote proposing a choice between independence and an option of substantial autonomy (*Nouvelles Calédoniennes* 26 October 2009). He proposed an option of a form of free association where New Caledonia would remain French and allow France to continue to be in charge of the more expensive powers (which he defined as the five *régalien* powers), while New Caledonia took on the remaining powers (*Flash d'Océanie* 27 October 2009). In his proposal, Frogier was reflecting the recently evolved positions of other pro-France parties, in an effort to respond favourably to Sarkozy's desire for the pro-France parties to work together.

On the pro-France side, Martin and the AE, who had long supported discussions to circumvent a referendum, endorsed Frogier's October proposals. Martin saw any definitive '*solution de sortie*', or post-Noumea Accord scenario, as having to be shared with the pro-independence groupings and the French State. It was thus 'necessary to negotiate these sovereign responsibilities'. He linked the idea with Sarkozy's support, expressed in 2007, for the most innovative solutions for New Caledonia, in order to guarantee the personality and powers of New Caledonia within France (Sarkozy 2007a, Martin in *Nouvelles Calédoniennes* 29 October 2009). Separately, Martin proposed engaging former High Commissioner and Noumea Accord negotiator Christnacht in preparing for *l'après-Accord* (*Nouvelles Calédoniennes* 12 September 2009).

Gomès' CE adopted a more nuanced position. Before the 2009 provincial elections, he had warned about the risks of an early 2014 referendum, raising the spectre of a resurgence of political tensions concealing ethnic cleavages (*Nouvelles Calédoniennes* 20 April 2009). He had also supported a referendum affirming a Caledonian identity providing for enlarged responsibilities and possibly even 'shared sovereignty' with the French State; for example, joint exercise of *régalien* responsibilities in the region, an idea which Frogier appeared to subsequently take up. By February 2010, after Frogier had spelled out his association-style proposal, Gomès noted his continuing opposition to a 'useless' referendum, and said he favoured early discussions with pro-independence groups to outline what was to come after the Noumea Accord. But he underlined that it would be for the representatives elected in 2014 to finalise arrangements. No doubt mindful of the damaging effect of the 1988 presidential election campaign on New Caledonia's history (see Chapter 2), he also cautioned lest the discussions be influenced by the French presidential election campaign in 2012 (*Nouvelles Calédoniennes* 22 February 2010).

Pro-independence groups

The thinking of the pro-independence groups was also evolving.

Néaoutyine, of Palika, had elaborated on his ideas of independence in a comprehensive interview published in 2006. At that time, he had referred to *'décolonisation en douceur'* ('soft decolonisation') whereby a New Caledonia which had been accompanied by France in its emancipation, rather than left on its own, would be able to establish links with France, as with any other country (Néaoutyine 2006, 68). Tutugoro, official spokesman for FLNKS, spoke in similar terms in 2008, agreeing with his interviewer that independence was a dead concept in a globalised world. He argued that independence and sovereignty meant the capacity to choose one's own interdependencies, to choose with whom one wanted to work and exchange (*Nouvelles Calédoniennes* interview, 17 June 2008). In a personal interview with the author, Tutugoro was more precise, saying the FLNKS wanted the right for New Caledonia to decide who it concluded treaties with, and that France was one of a number of possibilities (Personal communication April 2009).

In their emphasis on the post-Accord New Caledonia having the capacity to decide with whom it would deal, both Néaoutyine and Tutugoro were building on the foundation established by Tjibaou when he said that

> Sovereignty is the right to choose partners; independence is the power to manage all the needs that colonisation, the present system, has created ... Sovereignty gives us the right and the power to negotiate interdependencies. For a small country like ours, independence is choosing our interdependencies skillfully (Tjibaou 2005 p. 152).

In his 2006 interview, Néaoutyine also emphasised that, while independence was a right, the ways and means to it could be negotiated. On the currency (Euro) issue and defence relationship with France, as for the three other *régalien* areas (justice, law and order and foreign relations),

> we can be included in a more global disposition and keep our independence ...We have already entered into independence ... [and with the planned transfer of responsibilities] we can never go back ... What we decide over the last five [*régalien*] responsibilities, will only concern areas which we will share with others. *At that stage we will be practically already independent.* I think most citizens understand that'

Néaoutyine also said that by the end of the Noumea Accord the country would be *'virtually independent'*:

In other words, we are on the way to acceding to sovereignty. The Noumea Accord is a concrete process, at the end of which the responsibilities will be transferred from the governing colonial power to a country on the way to emancipation … (my italics, Néaoutyine 2006, 61 and 82).

In May 2009, on the eve of the provincial elections, Néaoutyine told the *Nouvelles Calédoniennes* that independence was written into the Accord, and that, after 2014, when the transfer of the last responsibilities would be effected, 'our country Kanaky-New Caledonia would be independent' (6 May 2009). A few days later, he elaborated that the final referendum would focus on the future of the five remaining *régalien* responsibilities, which he noted independent states in the world exercised in varied formulas, even in 'shared ways' such as was the case for France in its currency and defence:

I consider then that our country will be in the situation of quasi-independence; and it is possible to resolve this question and the future of the five sovereign responsibilities by discussion (*Nouvelles Calédoniennes*, 8 May 2009).

By September 2009, Néaoutyine was supporting Gomès' ideas of 'shared sovereignty' as contributing to accelerating the implementation of the Noumea Accord. He underlined Palika's support for the continued transfer of responsibilities, adoption of identity signs (for example, a flag), and equitable social and economic reforms. He indicated once again that the objective of decolonisation as proposed by the Noumea Accord was reached by transferring responsibilities and preparing for the final referendum, and defining a clear political framework for Caledonia's exercise of regional and international responsibilities.

At the same time, in a reference to the activities of the PT, Néaoutyine denounced any strategy of destabilisation, saying the new social contract would be through social dialogue, not through street movements resulting in imprisonment of the young in the name of an industrial union that they did not understand. Despite statistics showing widening social gaps, Néaoutyine said the new institutions of New Caledonia, including the provinces, had resulted in many improvements in the distribution of public monies. He said he had no sense of an impoverishment of the people in the bush or tribes, although there was a problem of access to employment (*Nouvelles Calédoniennes* 24 September 2009).

Participating in a visit to Australia in March 2010, as part of the collegial government, Néaoutyine said that as the pro-independence group was a minority, majority government would exclude them (Personal communication Néaoutyine 2010). As such, a collegial, proportional representation system was important to give the *indépendantistes* access to power via the provinces. He underlined that the pro-independence group were *'acteurs'*, i.e., they had an active role, in the 'emancipation' process.

Also early in 2010, as some previously agreed legislation on the protection of employment was returned to the congress after Council of State approval, only to meet further discussion, Néaoutyine flagged a 'destabilisation' that was occurring. He warned that

> If the non-sovereign responsibilities are not transferred, constitutionally, the referendum [foreseen by the Noumea Accord] cannot be organised … If this is the aim of the manoeuvre [i.e. questioning agreed legislation], to delay things, to find ourselves again in a new situation, this must be clearly said (*Nouvelles Calédoniennes* 29 April 2010).

Palika's Charles Washetine shared Gomès caution about what was strictly *required* under the Noumea Accord in 2014. He spoke of respecting the calendar and modalities of the Accord, which stipulated only that provincial elections must be held in 2014, i.e., with greater flexibility on the timing of a referendum (*Nouvelles Calédoniennes* 30 November 2009). In other comments he said that the FLNKS were prepared to 'play the game' of the Noumea Accord to its full completion (Personal communication 24 February 2009). Palika's Gorodey added, in October 2009, that her priority was not independence at any cost, but rather, successful decolonisation, with access by the Melanesian world to every place it was legitimately able to claim. The essence was not a referendum, with winners and losers on different sides; what counted was an outcome of the Accord, through which those who had nothing today 'feel they are winners' (*Nouvelles Calédoniennes* 7 October 2009).

For their part, the broad FLNKS coalition was more cautious, and suspicious about the motives and actions of the French State. In September 2009, the FLNKS met to review political developments. In comments reported by the *Nouvelles Calédoniennes*, the FLNKS ascribed nefarious motives to the French State, specifically in its dealings with social conflict (i.e., a heavy-handed approach to USTKE action), the evolution of the Organic Law (i.e., amendment to allow for slower implementation of some transfers of responsibilities) and on the international stage (a possible reference to efforts to have New Caledonia displace the FLNKS in the MSG). By all this, the FLNKS saw the French State as aggressively preparing the way for a new negotiated solution in place of a referendum on full sovereignty. The FLNKS described the recent agreement between the R–UMP, CE and AE as 'a deviation from democracy dictated by the French State'. 'What the State is not able to say in view of its international engagements, it tries to impose by a strategy aiming to suggest that the Noumea Accord has broken down … But the FLNKS will not be duped in this, and would remain vigilant' (*Nouvelles Calédoniennes* 4 September 2009). Nonetheless the FLNKS leaders singled out Gomès, namely his policies aimed at tackling inequality in wealth distribution, for positive comment.

The FLNKS remained mute on Frogier's October 2009 'in association' proposal, despite holding a further scheduled meeting shortly after his announcement (*Nouvelles Calédoniennes* 30 October 2009). In a private comment, the FLNKS spokesman Tutogoro noted that the final referendum would pose a choice between remaining under guardianship ('*tutelle*') with considerable autonomy, or acceding to 'full sovereignty' (which would not seem so very different from the 'association' v. 'independence' choice Frogier was proposing). But he specifically rejected leaders 'slicing up' the Noumea Accord by deciding not to apply certain aspects of the Accord, which had been ratified by the people (Personal communication 30 October 2009).

Elements of the FLNKS added their own comment in subsequent months, marking further areas of concern. Jacques Lalie (Union national pour le renouveau — National Union for Renewal, UNR) declared that his party shared the FLNKS position, noting that in view of what the 'colonised people' had already given up, 'it was difficult to say that we had still more to offer'. It was necessary, however, to work on a democratic outcome, and proceed to an initial referendum, one or two years after 2014 (*Nouvelles Calédoniennes* 2 December 2009). The UC's Charles Pidjot said his party aimed at the transfer of all responsibilities, except the sovereign responsibilities, before 2014, followed by a referendum (*Nouvelles Calédoniennes* 6 November 2009).

French State

When the Secretary of State for Overseas France, Marie-Luce Penchard, visited New Caledonia in November 2009, she reportedly supported Frogier's 'free association' idea, provided it was endorsed by a consensus in New Caledonia (*Nouvelles Calédoniennes* 6 November 2009).

In his New Year speech to the Overseas France in January 2010, Sarkozy said discussion was required amongst Caledonians so that the vote foreshadowed in the Accord 'would translate into a result approved by a very large majority' (Sarkozy 2010a). Since he had ruled out independence for the Overseas France as a whole, earlier in his speech, he clearly hoped for the people of New Caledonia to agree on an alternative option (see Chapters 7 and 8).

The flag issue

Discussion and decision around the issue of a flag or flags for New Caledonia have sharpened divisions and tested the provisions applying to the workings of the congress.

The R–UMP's Frogier proposed, in February 2010, that the Kanak and French flags be flown together as a gesture of recognition in the context of talks about future institutions (*Nouvelles Calédoniennes* 9 February 2010). Gomès of the pro-France CE, and Néaoutyine of the pro-independence Palika, alike rejected the idea as contrary to the Noumea Accord, which, Néaoutyine pointed out, called for 'one' identity sign (*Nouvelles Calédoniennes* 15 and 29 April 2010). Article 1.5 of the Accord provides for common discussion of identity signs, including of 'a flag' in the singular, whereas Article 5 of the Organic Law provides for New Caledonia to 'mark its personality alongside the national Emblem and signs of the Republic' under certain conditions, including the agreement by three-fifths of the congress.

The committee of signatories agreed on 24 June 2010 that both flags would be flown together in view of the 2011 Pacific Games to be held in New Caledonia the following year (*Relevé de conclusions* 2010). On the same day, Sarkozy endorsed flying both flags above the French high commission building in Noumea, provided the New Caledonian congress endorsed the idea by passing a pertinent resolution. He recognised that the recommendation had not been easy for the parties, and that it was one preliminary step in a longer process that would result in the choice of one flag that would be accepted by all (Sarkozy 2010b). On 13 July the congress voted by a strong majority (42 of the 54 members) in favour of flying the two flags (*Voeu* No 1, 13 July 2010). The resolution occurred days before French Prime Minister François Fillon arrived in Noumea to witness the flying of both flags over the French high commission building.

Despite congress' resolution on the issue, some municipalities declined to fly both flags. The UC took exception to this, and resigned from the government on 17 February 2011, precipitating a vote for a new government by the congress. Article 121 of the Organic Law provided that, if one member of the collegial government resigned, all resigned, and a new government should be elected by the congress within 15 days. On 3 March, following the election of a new government, Gomès authorised one of his CE members to resign, triggering another election on 17 March, following which another CE member resigned, with another election on 1 April. In all three elections Martin was elected president with his R–UMP/AE grouping winning the most seats. Gomès claimed that the initial UC action had been taken in concert with Frogier's R–UMP in order to oust him, and pushed for province-wide elections so the people could have a voice over the flag issue. He also appealed to the French Council of

State against the High Commissioner's decision to allow the election of a new government on 3 March once his party representative had resigned (*Le Figaro* 8 April 2011). This appeal was not upheld by the Council.

The UC called for a public demonstration by its supporters on the issue on 3 April, and the CE likewise called out its supporters for the same day, leading the High Commissioner to ban such demonstrations on that day. Meanwhile, Penchard visited the collectivity on 17 April and negotiated an agreement to suspend further resignations and elections, and to endorse the continuation of the Martin government in caretaker mode, until Article 121 of the Organic Law could be amended, in the interests of stability and the continued working of the government (*Flash d'Océanie* 18 April 2011). This occurred, with the amendment providing for an 18-month period after a resignation before a subsequent resignation could occur (*Nouvelles Calédoniennes* 28 May 2011).

These developments were important as they showed the underlying emotion surrounding the issue of the flag, and the risks associated with precipitating action outside of the congress (i.e., through the committee of signatories) without adequate consultation and under pressure from external and French domestic events such as the visit by the French Prime Minister, the French President and the hosting of the Pacific Games (the latter two events were planned for August 2011). The developments also showed that, even when the majority of the congress voted for a particular action, if underlying concerns were unresolved, progress would not occur, an important lesson for addressing key questions for the future.

Metropolitan and other institutional factors

Despite the French State's financial and political commitment to implement the letter and the spirit of the Noumea Accord, there has been a tendency for the French State, as the Noumea Accord signature recedes in time, increasingly to treat New Caledonia (and the more so French Polynesia and Wallis and Futuna) as just another administrative unit. Institutional changes suggest diminished attention to Overseas France and the Pacific entities, particularly over the first years of Sarkozy's leadership.

Ministerial level

From 1999 to 2010, there were eight ministers or secretaries of state for Overseas France (see Table 4.8), all of them relatively junior in the ministerial pecking order, and with progressively less experience or background in the Pacific. Early appointees had some close engagement with the region and issues

(Secretaries of State Jean-Jack Queyranne and Christiane Paul, by virtue of their direct engagement in the Noumea Accord and Matignon processes respectively). Brigitte Girardin, a former senior bureaucrat, had at least worked closely with Australia on issues relating to Antarctica. But, after Girardin, appointees had little or no familiarity with the Pacific.

Table 4.8 List of French ministers/secretaries of state for Overseas France 1999–present

All working under the minister for the interior

M. Jean-Jack QUEYRANNE Secretary of State for Overseas France 4 June 1997
M. Christian PAUL Secretary of State for Overseas France 29 August 2000
Mme Brigitte GIRARDIN Minister for Overseas France 7 May 2002
M. François BAROIN Minister for Overseas France 2 June 2005
M. Hervé MARITON Minister for Overseas France 27 March 2007
M. Christian ESTROSI Secretary of State for Overseas France 19 June 2007
M. Yves JEGO Secretary of State for Overseas France 18 March 2008
Mme Marie-Luce PENCHARD Secretary of State for Overseas France from June 2009 Minister for Overseas France from November 2009
M. Victorin LUREL Minister for Overseas France from May 2012

Source: Ministry of Overseas France website <http://www.outre-mer.gouv.fr>

There was also a pattern of appointing political figures to what became very short stints (notably the terms of Mariton and Estrosi, less than a year each), with incumbents using the position for their own domestic political ambitions (for example, Estrosi took up the position of mayor of Nice following his short stint as secretary of state).

The pattern has not gone unnoticed. One of the clearest messages from the New Caledonian participants at the 2008 commemorative colloquium on the Accords was the loss of knowledge and understanding of their concerns, in Paris (see for example comments by Wallis Kotra noting the worry that younger generations of officials belonged to a culture at odds with the Overseas France and with New Caledonia in particular, in Regnault and Fayaud 2008, 55).

From the time of de Gaulle, all French presidents, Georges Pompidou, Valéry d'Estaing, Mitterrand, and Chirac, shared the Gaullist view that Overseas France *was* France, and contributed to the *grandeur* of France. On his election in May 2007, Sarkozy's views on France's possessions overseas were little known. Sarkozy departed from the usual cast of French presidents, coming from a younger immigrant generation and with a foreign wife. He did see Overseas France as important in his presidential candidature, sending his advisers on information gathering missions there during his campaign. In New Caledonia's case, he also set out his views in writing, portraying himself as overly sympathetic to the pro-France view, and was obliged to correct this impression in later contacts (see Chapter 7). While his priorities clearly lay with Europe and economic reform, this in itself was not new for French presidents.

Early in his presidency, however, Sarkozy did not give a high priority to the overseas possessions. What little clues he gave about his policy seemed to stem from his own background as a tough interior minister who cracked down firmly on crime and local disturbances. He initially relegated the Overseas France portfolio, which had been held under Chirac by a full minister (albeit one working to the interior minister), to a secretary of state. His ministers for the interior, to whom the secretary for Overseas France worked, have consistently been individuals with strong metropolitan political ambition but no familiarity with the Overseas, or French Pacific (Michèle Alliot-Marie to 2009, succeeded by Brice Hortefeux in mid 2009 and Claude Guéant in February 2011).

Estrosi, a close supporter, was Sarkozy's first appointment. At first the administration glossed over Estrosi's disastrous handling of his inaugural visit to New Caledonia, in October 2007. The visit occurred after a long period of industrial unrest, strikes and blockades. No doubt taking his cue from Sarkozy's firm domestic security policy, Estrosi directed the High Commissioner to control a protesting crowd assembled outside the commissariat. Experienced High Commissioner Michel Mathieu, who had served a full term in French Polynesia before arriving in Noumea two years before, resigned over the incident. Estrosi used the incident to underline the Sarkozy government's intolerance of industrial disruption and social unrest (*Flash d'Océanie* 15 October 2007). The FLNKS reacted badly, accusing Estrosi of precipitating a political crisis (Radio New Zealand International, 15 October 2007). In Tahiti, Estrosi also announced reforms to deal with ongoing political instability in French Polynesia. Although close to Sarkozy, Estrosi had no prior background in the Pacific. He was essentially a domestic political animal with his eye on the mayorship of Nice, a position he subsequently assumed, resigning from the Overseas France portfolio to do so in March 2008. Sarkozy replaced him with Yves Jégo, one of his own advisers who also had no background in either Overseas France or the South Pacific.

Jégo, likewise, created difficulties. As Overseas France permanent secretary from 2007 to 2009, he supported the trend of *ad hoc* attention to the *outré-mer*, and of treating the latter as more or less another domestic part of France. He even publicly posited a reorganisation whereby the Overseas France secretariat could be abolished, with matters relating to the overseas entities being handled within each relevant ministry (*France 24* interview 19 February 2009). Handling matters in this way would mean that the special challenges and characteristics of the overseas entities, and certainly the particular regional settings in which they operated, could be lost in bureaucratic processes. This presented particular risks for New Caledonia in the Pacific, as the last phase of the Noumea Accord processes began.

The new administration's relative disregard for the particularities of Overseas France changed in early 2009, after violent strikes and protests about the high costs of living in Guadeloupe, speedily spread to Martinique, Guyana and Réunion. After a failed visit to Guadeloupe by Jégo to deal with the protests (when he speedily retreated to Paris despite having promised to stay in that territory until the matter was resolved, see, for example, *Le Figaro* 10 February 2009), Sarkozy was forced to address the issues himself. By June 2009 he had called a general review of the state of Overseas France; created an interministerial council; and, replaced Jégo with Marie-Luce Penchard, a Guadeloupe bureaucrat, the first Overseas France local resident to be appointed to lead the portfolio. In November 2009 he announced a number of measures principally to address economic concerns in Overseas France arising from the review. He also upgraded Penchard to full minister status, albeit continuing the long tradition of serving under the more senior minister of the interior. He continued with his overall firm approach to security issues.

So, Sarkozy learned about managing Overseas France essentially by trial and error. But whether his reformed general approach translated to better handling of the Pacific entities, particularly New Caledonia, was arguable (chapters 7 and 8 analyse Sarkozy's approach to New Caledonia). Penchard, while coming from Guadeloupe, had no experience of the French Pacific. So Sarkozy's presidency pointed to a continuation of the relative institutional relegation of the management of the Overseas France of recent years, which, as the experience of Estrosi and Jégo showed, had negative consequences in terms of stability of both the French Pacific and the Caribbean.

François Hollande made a slightly better start, appointing a full minister for Overseas. Victorin Lurel, like Penchard, was from Guadaloupe, but similarly had no Pacific experience.

Officials level

Generally, however, many of the most senior officials posted to the Pacific entities, i.e., as high commissioners, have had some previous experience of the region. Since the conclusion of the Noumea Accord, French High Commissioners in Noumea Thierry Lataste, Constantin, Mathieu, and Dassonville all had previous experience in the region and South Pacific issues. They also had in common long years of experience as prefects, the internal mainland counterpart of the high commissioner designation in overseas collectivities. But, as Mathieu's fate has shown, their experience can be overlooked by zealous political appointees to the position of secretary/minister for Overseas France.

In February 2011, Sarkozy interrupted the trend by appointing as high commissioner in Noumea Albert Dupuy, a senior and experienced prefect who lacked any experience in the South Pacific. Many of the other French officials posted to support the high commissioners routinely do not have previous experience of the Pacific. They are officials of the interior or other domestic ministries such as education, posted for two-year terms. They may have extensive experience in administering densely populated, complex and sometimes ethnically charged situations within metropolitan France. They may sometimes have experience in other overseas territories (in announcing his Caribbean-focused reforms on 6 November 2009, Sarkozy provided for the nomination and consideration of at least one Overseas France resident applicant when posts in the Overseas France were being filled, on a trial basis, Sarkozy 2009). But they often have little knowledge of the South Pacific region and, as interior ministry officials, they are not versed in foreign policy. Their primary interest is domestic. Thus, they use the same mechanisms to address local concerns as they might in mainland France when handling urban racial violence, i.e., a heavy-handed police force armed with batons, tear gas and shields.

One worrying and continuing trend in terms of the effectiveness of the Overseas France secretariat, in working with a clear understanding of the regional context, is its position in Paris that is largely in isolation from other ministries, even the defence and foreign affairs ministries. Coordination is *ad hoc*, with different ministries becoming involved in the work of the secretariat only as issues relating to them arise (Personal communication, senior French official, Paris, May 2008).

Sarkozy's new interministerial council for Overseas France, formed in 2009, did not fulfill a possible promise to redress this situation, concentrating mainly on a review of Overseas France policy after problems in the Caribbean. Announcing Overseas France reforms after the problems in Guadeloupe and Martinique, on 6 November 2009, Sarkozy said that he wanted all ministries to feel that they had a role, not just the Overseas France portfolio (Sarkozy 2009). But the council did not have an ongoing role.

While Sarkozy at the time upgraded the relevant senior politician to minister as opposed to secretary of state for Overseas France, the incumbent was still to work to the more senior interior minister. As in the past (see Chapter 2), the relatively junior place of the Overseas France permanent secretary in the hierarchy of ministries means that the critical tasks of inter-ministerial consultation and coordination cannot be carried out effectively. This provides a particular weakness in respect of co-operating with such senior ministries as foreign affairs and defence, whose inputs are particularly important in successful implementation of policies in the South Pacific. History has shown the strong role naval personnel have played in France's evolving presence in the Pacific.

French analyst Gérard Bélorgey noted in 2002 that not only did the relatively low level in the ministerial pecking order hamper the Overseas France minister or secretary in the coordination and arbitration of other ministries' activities in the overseas entities, he emphasised that dealing with Overseas France often involved issues which, by their very nature, were not conducive to easy ministerial partnerships. He noted that the coordination function involved sophisticated political activity, not only because it meant ensuring toeing a certain line of conduct, but because Overseas France inherently involved power stakes (Bélorgey 2002 p. 92). As is evident in earlier chapters, these coordination difficulties have been an ongoing issue since early colonial times.

In practice, when there are differences of view, the arbitrating function falls to the political advisors in the offices of the president and the prime minister, officials who are versed in domestic politics and rarely, if ever, have even visited the South Pacific or the French overseas entities. Whereas in the Pacific region itself, there are annual meetings of senior French functionaries, including the resident ambassadors, high commissioners and senior military representatives (see below), in Paris, such regular structured consultation on an ongoing basis does not occur. There is no overarching political eye, or steering inter-agency Overseas France committee that meets regularly. In practical, day-to-day matters, each functional ministry operates on their usual (domestic) policy basis, guided mainly by an objective that the political masters not be bothered by problems from the overseas entities. When a serious problem does arise, the political advisors step in (Personal communications Paris 2008).

Within the secretariat, the interests of the Pacific entities with their individual statutes are not helped by the fact that the secretariat also manages the French overseas *départements*, entities with an entirely different status and set of needs, being juridically integral parts of France itself. Sarkozy's interministerial council for Overseas France similarly handled the affairs of the entire Overseas France, which diluted attention to the peculiarities of the French Pacific (indeed most of the resultant 137 reforms announced in November 2009 applied primarily to the French Caribbean entities Guadeloupe, Martinique, and Guyana).

For its part, the ministry for foreign affairs has three ambassadors, one for the Pacific, one for the Indian Ocean, and one for the Caribbean overseas entities. They are nominally assigned to the prime minister's office, not the Overseas France secretariat, mainly because they are more senior to most of the personnel in the secretariat, an arrangement which is unlikely to endear itself to secretariat personnel and thus is likely to impede close cooperation. The ambassadors are, however, physically located within the Overseas France permanent secretariat at Rue Oudinot.

The main job of the ambassador for the South Pacific is the representation of France to the SPC, and guiding the expenditure of the Special Fund for the South Pacific, the latter role itself having been diluted in recent years with the establishment in 2003 of a steering committee for the fund, which includes representatives from the entities themselves who take turns in chairing meetings. The ambassador has a role in France's relationship with the Pacific Islands Forum, but tends to focus on technical rather than political issues. As diplomatic professionals, they carry out their tasks discreetly and without fanfare, and for relatively short appointments (around three years). The occupant also needs to take care not to step on the toes of the bilateral resident ambassadors. Moreover, the position is based in Paris, not in the region. The ambassador has an assistant, a diplomat from the foreign affairs ministry, based in Noumea. The main role of this position is to provide ongoing liaison with the SPC, and to advise the High Commissioner on foreign policy issues. The value of these arrangements in providing a well-informed decision-making apparatus in Paris and in the Pacific entities themselves depends mainly on the personalities involved, and on the willingness of the neighbouring bilateral French ambassadors to copy their reporting and analysis to Noumea and Papeete.

There are annual meetings of officials in the region, including France's regional ambassadors (from Australia New Zealand, Papua New Guinea, Vanuatu and Fiji), the ambassador for the South Pacific, its resident High Commissioners from Noumea and Papeete and the delegate from Wallis and Futuna, and senior Paris-based officials. In 2008, at France's invitation, Australian Parliamentary Secretary for Foreign Affairs responsible for the South Pacific, Duncan Kerr, attended one of these meetings. Although the meetings generally focus on technical issues, there is potential for them to address broader strategic questions. The extent to which their discussions influence decision-making in Paris is limited, without a similarly regular Paris-based interagency mechanism.

New Caledonia, and the other two French Pacific entities, all have a presence, of sorts, in Paris. The main function of the three offices for the Pacific collectivities, however, has been to provide support for visiting residents of the entities, directing them to social services and other functional support. The offices are not staffed with trained diplomats or functionaries and do not carry out a role of advocacy for the entities with the French State. French Polynesia has had a delegation in Paris since 1971, long occupying, with the Tahitian Tourist Office, fashionable premises in the Boulevard Saint Germain. Until recently, New Caledonia's presence was modest, having been established in 1989. In 2008 the Maison de Calédonie moved to more impressive premises near the Place de l'Opéra. Wallis and Futuna, in contrast, has a very small office within the Overseas France secretariat at Rue Oudinot.

None of this is conducive to regular, informed policy review, definition of an overarching strategy, or even coherent policy implementation in relating to the South Pacific entities, particularly New Caledonia in this sensitive period. Furthermore, the administrative structures and the relative infrequency of strategic policy statements do not ensure accurate public or media understanding in metropolitan France, of the issues in the overseas collectivities, which is already at a low level (Bélorgey 2002, 88). The risk here is that, should the situation change suddenly, as occurs often in the Pacific, and as is increasingly likely with approaching New Caledonian deadlines, the media and public opinion can react in an uninformed way, and become an aggravating factor.

Conclusion

A fundamental question for the future of New Caledonia remains the credibility of the word of the French State, ultimately defined by its full implementation of the spirit and letter of the Matignon/Noumea Accords. In the conclusion of his 'intellectual biography' of Tjibaou, Eric Waddell underlined Tjibaou's understanding of the importance of the *parole*, or word for the Kanak people:

> He knew full well that the *parole* is at the origin of and determines the *geste* — the act. It is binding, with one having no sense or meaning without the other. France's unfulfilled words and shallow memory have been a constant source of frustration and bitterness for the Kanak people (Waddell 2008, 208).

At the 2008 colloquium marking the 20th anniversary of the Matignon Accords, the idea of France keeping its word was a recurring theme, with then Overseas France Secretary Jégo underlining the importance of France delivering on its *parole donnée* (having given its word) (see Regnault and Fayaud 2008, 23 and 167). The French State and the pro-independence and pro-France sides have all put considerable energy, effort and resources into sustaining a stable political situation for the first 10 years of the Noumea Accord. The political system established under the Accord has generally proven resilient in its first decade.

Cracks have emerged, however, which need ongoing attention.

In the first instance, the 'word' of the Accord has meant different things to different sides, as evident in the disagreement over the fundamental definition of the restricted electorate. Similarly, the Accord itself represents different things to each side, as Horowitz has argued. For the pro-independence groups, the Noumea Accord means a step forward in the acquisition of more autonomy on a path ultimately leading to independence. For the French State, it provides more time during which France may, through generous financing and judicious control of the handover of elements of more autonomy, and by keeping its promises, secure the support of the pro-independence groups to relinquishing their goal of independence. Indeed, nowhere in the Noumea Accord are the words 'independence' or 'self-determination' used. Instead, there are references to 'emancipation' and 'a common destiny' (see Berman 2001, for an elaboration of what these omissions may mean for the future). But, the question of whether this rules out full independence per se, cannot yet be answered. The public comment by 'mainstream' (FLNKS) pro-independence leaders has so far been ambiguous, as they wait for the interim terms of the Noumea Accord to be fulfilled; and the influence of the more definitively independence-oriented PT is yet to be fully tested.

France's dilatory approach to fulfilling the restricted electorate promise, its longstanding encouragement of immigration, its delayed and ambiguous handling of the critical ethnic category in the census, and the relatively slow transfer of important responsibilities such as education, have all strained Kanak, and some Caldoche, credulity. Even as Noumea Accord deadlines approach, with defence and the currency among one of the five powers yet to be decided, France has built up its defence infrastructure near Noumea, and urged replacement of the CFP by the Euro. Despite rhetoric about implementing Noumea Accord provisions for New Caledonia to engage directly in regional relations, little preparation of a working regional relations capacity is evident.

Similarly, despite significant financial support by France, the economic rebalancing and redistribution of the benefits of exploiting nickel have, to date, been demonstrably and quantifiably more successful in the European-dominated south than in the mainly Kanak north. World economic conditions have had an effect, slowing the pace of investment and production schedules, and leading to withdrawal of external investors to be replaced by French interests, in the Kanak north. To the time of writing, despite all the planning and expenditure, the only working processing of nickel remains in the ageing, French-dominated SLN unit at Doniambo in the south. There remain as yet untested statutory ambiguities about responsibility for minerals pertaining to the exploitation of the nickel resource, and the potential for hydrocarbons. And Sarkozy has underlined the intention of the French State to maintain the majority share and control of SLN.

Kanaks remain generally isolated and alienated in society and politics in the wealthy, more populous and predominantly European south. They have so far shown patience with this situation. As global demand for nickel waxes and wanes, and if ongoing global constraints on nickel exploitation continue as Noumea Accord deadlines draw near, their patience will be tested.

Financial shares that have been granted to New Caledonia in the major nickel companies SLN and Eramet, as well as Inco's Goro project, which have been used to buy off support for independence, have been the subject of bargaining, and are seen to be inadequate, especially by the pro-independence group. There has been considerable local concern about job protection and environmental issues. The overall result is shared anxiety, by Kanaks and some Caldoche alike, about the French State's intent and impartiality, which has underpinned the fracturing and realignment of parties within the pro-France group.

For its part, the pro-independence group has sought to participate constructively within the Noumea Accord structures, but is dealing with divisions of its own, including the emergence of a radical new political force in the PT. One writer has described French efforts to redress the economic gap as divisive of the Kanaks, precisely by focusing on economic development as distinct from political emancipation (Waddell 2008, 206; see also his reference to writer Thomas Ferenczi's description of Michel Rocard, the architect of Matignon Accord, as a 'virtuous Machiavelli', footnote 11, 214). Outside of the agreed political institutions, Kanak activism finds expression through ethnic disharmony, primarily but not solely at Saint-Louis, with a potential for further violence remaining so long as Wallisian ethnic issues are not fully resolved; assertion of environmental protection principles, through the *Rheebu Nuu*; and of indigenous rights, for example through the CNDPA efforts to establish the *Mwâ Kâ*, with mixed responses from the Caldoche and the French. Kanak leaders have used and will continue to use international forums to raise their concerns.

In the context of the importance of keeping the *parole*, feelers by the pro-France groups about opening negotiations on the future, circumventing the proposed Noumea Accord referendums, have been met with a mixed reaction from the mainstream independence group. In the May 2009 elections, it was the group at either end of the political spectrum (Frogier's pro-France R–UMP and the pro-independence PT), that supported an early referendum under the Accord, i.e., 2014, which fared well (R–UMP winning the most pro-France seats, PT making inroads in the new Congress). But, since then, conscious that holding a referendum, which is most likely to result in a vote against independence, risks a return to violence by the pro-independence groups, even R–UMP's Frogier has advocated a more moderate consultative approach to manage the referendum process.

Handling of the dual-flag proposition, which was raised by the pro-France R–UMP — apparently influenced by external events such as visits by French dignitaries — has highlighted deep-seated divisions, which go beyond agreements reached within institutions such as the committee of signatories and even the congress. The strength of divisions has tested the viability of these institutions. These developments raise cautions about the future handling of sensitive, core Noumea Accord issues.

Pro-independence groups are cautious and insistent on the full implementation of the Noumea Accord, including full transfer of responsibilities as promised, before a referendum can pose the choice between remaining with France with a high degree of autonomy, and independence. So future negotiations are likely to centre on the subject of a referendum (see Chapter 8). But the demographics, and electoral patterns so far, suggest that the majority of eligible voters will not support the independence option. Thus, there is potential for violence and disruption.

Overlaying all of these issues, senior French officials in Paris are increasingly less directly experienced and without first-hand knowledge, of either the transitional issues or of the region, and work only in stop-start contact with other related ministries including defence and foreign affairs.

Finally, implementation of the Accord so far has shown the continued relevance of the UN, the PIF, the MSG, and even the EU, in enabling a Kanak dissenting voice to be heard. The Kanak voice will be listened to in the UN Decolonisation Committee, and UN human rights and indigenous rights organisations such as the relatively new UN Rights of Indigenous Peoples Forum, as evident in Anaya's 2011 report. The UN Decolonisation Committee has heard Kanak concerns, particularly on the restricted electorate, protection of employment, the ethnic census category, and Matthew and Hunter issues. The MSG has been the vehicle for Melanesian agreement on Vanuatu's claim to Matthew and Hunter. And the PIF and EU Human Rights Court have been engaged on electoral process issues.

All of these factors operating together, in a transition period as new government systems are settling into place, mean there are fundamental vulnerabilities and instabilities which could yet surface in a way prejudicial to smooth negotiations for a durable, stable future in New Caledonia beyond 2018.

5. French Polynesia: Autonomy or independence?

With the cessation of nuclear testing in 1996, and the French commitment to the 20-year Noumea Accord process in New Caledonia underpinned by massive investment in developing nickel at a time of rising global, especially Chinese, demand, New Caledonia displaced French Polynesia as France's primary strategic asset in the South Pacific. There was accordingly less attention paid by Paris to responding to demands from French Polynesia, leading to instability and hasty measures to address resultant problems.

In this period, from the end of the 1990s, as in New Caledonia, French Polynesian politics have also been characterised by the fragmentation of principal parties, loyalist and pro-independence alike, and surprising alliances, but, unlike New Caledonia after 1999, this has taken place against a background of constant statutory change without broad consultation. Local corruption and overt French intervention have been characteristic of French Polynesian politics in the last decade.

Elections in 1996 saw the return of Gaston Flosse's Tahoeraa Huira'atira (People's Assembly) but also an increase in support for Oscar Temaru's pro-independence Tavini Huira'atira no Te Ao Maohi (Serviteur du Peuple or Polynesian People's Servant). Flosse closely followed developments in New Caledonia, especially its Organic Law of 1999 giving it special status (where it was assigned sui generis status and referred to as a '*pays*', or country). He sought similar provisions for French Polynesia. While he did not claim a self-determination referendum or restricted electorate, as applied to New Caledonia, he did seek legislative powers and special citizenship provisions linked with protecting local labor and property rights. Despite the difficulties of *cohabitation* (the coexistence of a presidency of one complexion and a government led by a prime minister of another) conservative President Jacques Chirac and socialist Prime Minister Lionel Jospin endorsed Flosse's proposals, as did a constitutional review. The final step, however, adoption by a joint sitting of the French assembly and senate in a Versailles Congress, was frustrated by linking the measure with a separate and unrelated amendment on the independence of France's Superior Magistrature, which was judged in the end unlikely to attract support and was thus withdrawn, the same provision that held up the restrained electorate amendment for New Caledonia (see Chapter 4). As indicated, this reflected the familiar old pattern of other domestic metropolitan priorities dictating policy change in the South Pacific entities.

After Flosse's Tahoeraa won local elections in 2001, and Chirac was re-elected as president in 2002, a renewed constitutional review process judged, in March 2003, that the proposals could not go as far as Flosse had sought. French Polynesia would have to remain as an overseas 'collectivity' (not 'country' like New Caledonia, as proposed), albeit a collectivity with considerable autonomy. It would also not take on legislative powers of its own, as the New Caledonian government had done. Without the full support of the local assembly, the resulting Organic Law of February 2004 (Law No 2004-193 of 27 February 2004) was passed by the French national assembly. While not delivering everything Flosse had sought, it was a monument to Flosse and his majority, pro-autonomy within France, party. It strengthened the presidency (Flosse was to be titled President of French Polynesia) and included a measure allocating a bonus of one third of the seats, in each electorate, for the winning party, presumed to be Flosse's Tahoeraa, in local elections. But in subsequent elections in May 2004, the provision backfired. Despite winning eight per cent more votes in the collectivity as a whole, Tahoeraa was defeated by just 400 votes in the most populous electorate, the Iles du Vent (Windward Island), in Papeete and Faaa. Thus the bonus 13 seats went to Temaru's Tavini-led coalition Union pour la Démocratie (UPLD, Union for Democracy). Of the 57-seat assembly, UPLD won 26 seats, anti-Flosse autonomist parties a further three, and Flosse's Tahoeraa 28. Temaru's alliances, and winning over one Tahoeraa member, enabled him to take government with 30 votes. Aside from the procedural aspects, the election of and support for Temaru reflected increasing dissatisfaction with Flosse's personal style and government of patronage. The phenomena of change was called the '*taui*'.

Pro-independence ascendance

For the first time, the government was led by avowedly pro-independence parties. At the time, Temaru was measured and conciliatory, announcing that the goal of independence was a long-term one, to be achieved perhaps over 15 to 20 years (see Chappell 2005b, Regnault 2005a, 43). He spoke about shared sovereignty along the lines of the Cook Islands/New Zealand model (Mrgudovic 2008, 360, Nichols 2007). For some years, he was relatively silent on the concept of independence in the domestic arena, as opposed to regionally. In June 2009, in stocktaking discussions with French officials as part of a French program of consultations after the violent May 2009 protests in Guadeloupe, Temaru made a distinction between 'sovereignty' and 'independence', expressing his support for sovereignty for French Polynesia while noting that independence would not mean a 'full break' (Radio New Zealand 17 June 2009).

Immediately after his election Temaru also made no reference to his earlier reiteration, since 1990, of a demand for the United Nations (UN) Decolonisation Committee to re-inscribe French Polynesia as a non-self-governing territory. But, by the end of 2004, with his leadership frustrated by the efforts of the pro-France group, Temaru raised the question of independence in regional forums, with a predictable French response (see Regional Issues below). And, again, reflecting his frustration after years of leadership challenges, by 2011 he secured a resolution by the French Polynesian assembly to call for reinscription with the UN.

On Temaru's surprise election, there began an ongoing game of musical chairs, with various members and elements of the coalition switching sides in votes of no-confidence in successive presidents. Flosse thus regained the presidency in October 2004. But, in a move that looked like French collusion with Flosse, the French Council of State annulled the 2004 election in the Windward Islands electorate a month later, requiring a re-run. At the same time, in a move reminiscent of France's resistance to Vanuatu's independence (see Chapter 2) Minister for Overseas France, Brigitte Girardin, threatened to turn off the economic aid tap if Temaru won the election (Chappell 2005b, 199). Again France's efforts backfired: a re-run election delivered a slightly increased vote to Temaru, this time he won by 600 rather than 400 votes, leading to his reinstatement as president in March 2005 (29 seats to 26). Destabilising activity by Flosse (backed by his French supporters) continued. By the following year, the UPLD majority lost the presidency of the assembly in April 2006 but regained it the same month, only to lose it again in December 2006. This time, aware of mounting feeling against Flosse personally, the Tahoeraa did not put forward Flosse as president, but, rather, one of his supporters, Gaston Tong Sang.

The French Government, dismayed by the chronic instability inherent in French Polynesia, and no doubt the loss of support for the pro-France faction — seemingly as a result of its 2004 electoral changes — sought to stabilise the situation with two pieces of legislation, provisions in an Organic Law for Overseas France in February 2007 (Organic Law No 2007-223 of 21 February 2007) with the effect, for French Polynesia, of abolishing the one-third bonus for the majority in each electorate, and a revision of French Polynesia's 2004 Organic Law in December 2007 (Law No 2007-1720 of 7 December 2007) which Paris again pushed through the national assembly, despite the local assembly's vote against it (in 44 of 57 votes). To limit the proliferation of new parties, the new law provided for proportional voting in two rounds, with only those receiving a minimum of 12.5 per cent of the vote in the first round proceeding to the second. To curb the constant change of presidents and speakers, the president could henceforth only be replaced by a motion, which included the simultaneous election of a successor; and the speaker could only be elected once for a full five-year term. Various parties in the assembly, including the Tahoeera and UPLD, were united in their opposition to the legislation, which they saw as France tampering with local issues (*Flash d'Océanie* 11 October 2008). As succinctly described by Lorenz Gonschor,

> This episode proved once more that the statute of autonomy does not guarantee real local self-government, as France remains able to make arbitrary modifications to its political system against the explicit will of the local assembly (Gonschor 2009, 154).

As in New Caledonia, French efforts to rally the pro-France parties backfired by inadvertently promoting a coalescence of interests between the local parties around their own French Polynesian interests. Partly, too, developments were influenced by Sarkozy's election as President in May 2007, meaning that Flosse had lost the close political support in Paris of his friend Jacques Chirac. But then Flosse's supporters became disenchanted with Tong Sang when they were left out of a delegation visiting Paris in mid 2007 (see Gonschor 2009 p. 152). Tong Sang's government also proved to be short-lived, to be replaced in August 2007 by the unlikely coalition of Flosse and Temaru, with Temaru as president. Flosse's chameleon politics operated once more, as they had when he changed from pro-France advocate to pro-autonomy champion in the 1980s. By agreeing to share power with his former archenemy, pro-independence Temaru, he was preserving his own position and role, but also working to represent local interests.

Regnault, in 2005, noted the increasing similarities between the Flosse and Temaru camps, their shared view of an evolving autonomy along the New Caledonian model, a desire to distance French Polynesia from links with the metropolitan power, but with a strong awareness of the need for cooperation for development and aid (Regnault 2005a, 38). As Flosse lost personal support and Temaru gained experience in government, their objectives merged sufficiently to allow for an alliance that was convenient to both. Nonetheless, some of Flosse's supporters deserted to Tong Sang at this time (Gonschor 2009, 152).

In February 2008 elections, Tong Sang became president. He had formed a new party, O Porinetia to Tatou Ai'a (Polynesia is our country), leading an alliance called the To Tatou Ai'a (Our Land) with Tahoeraa dissidents including Jean-Christophe Bouissou's Rautahi (Unity) party; former Temaru ally Emile Vernaudon's Ai'a Api (New Homeland); the former centrist *Fetia Api* (New Star of Philip Schyle); and some small pro-France parties. Tong Sang's alliance won 27 of the 57 seats, Temaru's UPLD 20, and Flosse's Tahoeraa 10. This suited the French State, which had envisaged a coalition of pro-autonomy Tong Sang–Flosse supporters (as opposed to pro-independence supporters). Indeed, Secretary of State for Overseas France, Christian Estrosi, had visited the collectivity during the months before the election, showing support for Tong Sang and reportedly telephoning Flosse and another party leader Nicole Bouteau, in between rounds, to urge them to join with Tong Sang (Gonschor 2009, 155); and again after the second round, when Tong Sang's coalition fell short of a majority, phoning Flosse to urge him to support Tong Sang.

But Flosse found it intolerable for Tong Sang to take the presidency, notwithstanding his strong showing. To the chagrin of the French State, a few days later, on 23 February, Flosse, having pledged during the election campaign that he would never again work with Temaru, struck a last-minute alliance with him, cobbling together further support from other dissidents, and became president, with Temaru as speaker of parliament. Unlike his treatment of Tong Sang, Estrosi did not congratulate Flosse, but rather 'took note' of his presidency (Gonschor 2009, 157). To show their concern, Nicolas Sarkozy's UMP government in Paris expelled Flosse from the metropolitan party (*Flash d'Océanie* April 16 2008).

In his analysis of the results, Gonschor points to Temaru's loss of support through the departure of his key ally, Émile Vernaudon, to Tong Sang, and disappointment with Temaru's performance. At the same time, Tong Sang had proved skilful in consolidating a relative majority after a short time because of the desire of many for a co-operative relationship with France, particularly amongst the growing number of French settlers and the Chinese community from which Tong Sang came (Gonschor 2009, 157) and who, in the past, had supported Flosse. Flosse's Tahoeraa indeed appeared to have retained mainly the support of rural and working class Polynesians, who tended to be critical of France and who, therefore, had more in common with Temaru, thus explaining the odd working relationship between Flosse and Temaru.

But the situation did not end there. In April 2008 Tong Sang was once again elected president with the support of bench-crossers. Secretary for Overseas France, Yves Jégo, again congratulated Tong Sang, noting that as president he reflected truly the will of the people expressed in the February elections; stating, or perhaps warning, that this time stability would prevail; and, pledging support for large-scale projects in French Polynesia.

Instability and divisions, however, continued to prevail. On 12 February 2009, following Tong Sang's resignation as president, the assembly elected Temaru, with 37 votes of the 57 members, including support by his own Tavini but also that of Flosse's Tahoeraa, and of a Tong Sang breakaway group Iorea Te Fenua headed by Jean-Christophe Bouissou. Tong Sang received 20 votes. The change was the tenth since 2004 elections, and the fourth time that Temaru was elected president since 2004, which suggested majority support lay with him, whatever the divisions. This time Temaru proclaimed he would govern in a form of national unity government, to bring stability for the remainder of the term, to 2013. He consolidated his support in succeeding months to 40 of the 57 seats. In April 2009, Temaru reshuffled his cabinet to reflect differences with Flosse, retaining two Tahoeraa members who were considered to be serving in their personal capacities. By November 2009 instabilities emerged again, as the collectivity's budget appropriation was being debated, with Tong Sang once more winning a parliamentary vote on the presidency.

In the meantime, Flosse was under personal pressure. His murky past included corruption charges, which he evaded resulting in, at most, minor charges and penalties. Amongst other charges that he faced, Flosse had been given a three-month suspended sentence in June 2006 after having been convicted of abuse of political office related to a preferential investment in a hotel by his son (see *Radio New Zealand International* 21 June 2006). A journalist mysteriously disappeared while investigating Flosse's alleged involvement in the Clearstream secret accounts allegations by then Prime Minister Dominique Villepin against Sarkozy. In November 2009, however, Flosse's immunity from prosecution, deriving from his status as French senator, was removed at the request of judges investigating irregularities in the office of posts and telecommunications. He was charged with passive corruption, embezzlement of public funds and complicity in destruction of evidence, involving alleged financial kickbacks via an advertising company that was once in charge of the French Pacific territory's phonebook and related advertising revenues (*Flash d'Océanie* 24 December 2009). He was imprisoned temporarily, securing a release on bail of just under $US1 million in December, when he again took up his assembly and French senate seats. Separately, in early December, Flosse was found guilty in a 'fictitious jobs' scam (involving numerous jobs for friends and allies which were not seen as serving any public purpose and which were not advertised) while he was president and required to repay over $US2 million, and a hefty fine (*Flash d'Océanie* 24 December 2009). Gonschor (2009) enumerates many examples of the political nepotism that was rife under Flosse's leadership.

In January 2010, in a message to Overseas France, Sarkozy foreshadowed further reforms of the electoral system and institutional mechanisms in French Polynesia, 'in order to guarantee more stability to elected majorities and therefore to give more capacity to envisage political and public actions in the long-term' (Sarkozy 2010a). The promise did not put an end to instability: in April 2010 Temaru was elected as speaker of the assembly, with 30 votes of the 57 members, prompting President Tong Sang to appeal to Sarkozy to dissolve the assembly given the untenable political situation.

When released in March 2011, the draft electoral reforms limited the number of cabinet members, specified a minimum five-year term for the president of the assembly, increased to two-thirds of the assembly the number of votes required for a no-confidence motion to succeed, and increased the minimum percentage of votes required for a party to proceed to the second round of votes in an election. The reforms, however, specifically included an electoral 'bonus' of 33 per cent (or 19 seats) to the majority in the first-past-the-post system, when it had been a similar bonus that had caused problems in 2004. Tong Sang was the only party leader to support the reforms. After another no-confidence vote, in April 2011, Temaru was once again elected president, for the fifth time in seven years. The change of government was the 13th in the same period.

In the context of division and partiality by the French State, Temaru has managed time and again to maintain leadership and a certain dignity.

Regional issues and UN reinscription demands

In a regional context, Temaru's leadership is significant. He has maintained longstanding links with regional leaders, to whom he is well known, unlike Tong Sang, and well liked, unlike Flosse. He understands regional history and is able to play the regional and Pacific Islands Forum (PIF) cards when possible. For example, in September 2007, under threat from Tong Sang's new coalition, and being obliged to work with Flosse, Temaru used his regional contacts to dissuade some regional Polynesian island leaders from participating in a royal Polynesian gathering sponsored by a descendant of the Tahitian royal family, Joinville Pomare, with the support of Tong Sang. While representatives from New Zealand, Cook Islands, Wallis and Futuna and Hawaii attended, Temaru and Flosse successfully discouraged representatives from Western Samoa and Tonga from attending. (Pomare, like Temaru, is a pro-independence supporter, but sees a greater role for traditional leaders than Temaru, and has allied himself with Tong Sang, see Gonscher 2008, 153.)

Temaru is skilful in using his regional influence, via public calls in the region for independence and reinscription of French Polynesia with the UN, to consolidate his position in the archipelago particularly on those many occasions when the French State and others resist his electoral pull. After France's tinkering with the electoral system and the electoral re-run of 2004, Temaru has continued to raise independence issues in the PIF. When he attended the Forum summit, following French Polynesia's admission as an observer in 2004, he said he wanted reinscription with the UN Decolonisation Committee to be on the Forum agenda (*Radio New Zealand* 5 August 2004). He raised the issue at the 2006 Forum summit, where the French were quick to react, a French official saying that French Polynesia already had the capacity for self-determination and did not need external support for what was essentially an internal matter (Nichols 2007, 118). This was redolent of the French rationale for non-cooperation with the UN in 1947.

After the passage of French unilateral legislation to change the political system yet again in 2007, at the 2007 Tonga PIF summit, Temaru called again for Forum support for reinscription, and called for an autonomy solution for French Polynesia, a 'Tahiti Nui' Accord, along the lines of the Noumea Accord of New Caledonia. He warned about French efforts to change statutory provisions relating to elections, and to seek further elections in early 2008 (TV New Zealand 17 October 2007). No doubt this influenced French support for other contenders in the local leadership stakes at the time (for regional reactions, see Chapter 6).

At, home Temaru and his followers did not let independence issues rest either. In January 2008, his Tavini party sought signatures on a petition favouring UN reinscription. And, in June 2009, after he once again acceded to the presidency following Tong Sang's resignation, in the context of discussions with French officials in the wake of violent protests in Guadeloupe, Temaru said that the issue of sovereignty (as distinct from a complete break with France) needed to be discussed, and proposed discussions of an alternative name for French Polynesia, such as Tahiti Nui (the Greater Tahiti) or Maohi Nui (the Greater Indigenous people) (Radio New Zealand website <http://www.radionz.co.nz> 16 and 17 June 2009 accessed 19 June 2009).

When Noumea hosted the UN Decolonisation Committee's 2010 Pacific regional seminar, Temaru visited Noumea and staged a protest outside the Secretariat of the Pacific Community (SPC) headquarters, where the meeting was being held. While claiming that he was not speaking as the French Polynesian speaker, but in the name of the *Maohi* or indigenous people (*Flash d'Océanie* 18 May 2010), he asserted that, if they won the next election, they would declare the country independent and sovereign. He again called for reinscription of French Polynesia with the UN (*La Depêche de Tahiti* 21 May 2010). By July 2011, his party began to lobby regional governments (Personal communication, Tuheiava 2011).

The PIF leaders' response to Temaru's calls for support has been measured. They have not to take a position on the question of reinscription of French Polynesia with the UN Decolonisation Committee, but have instead used their communiqués to consistently urge France and French Polynesia to work together for French Polynesia's self-determination. Once again, in 2011, the Forum leaders

> recalled their 2004 decision to support the principle of French Polynesia's right to self-determination. They reiterated their encouragement to

French Polynesia and France to seek an agreed approach on how to realise French Polynesia's right to self-determination (PIF Communiqué 2011).

There are signs, however, that regional support for Temaru is growing. On the eve of the 2011 PIF meeting, a number of leaders met (from Fiji, Solomon Islands, Papua New Guinea, Vanuatu, Tuvalu, Nauru, Tonga, Timor Leste, Kiribati, Federated States of Micronesia, Republic of Marshall Islands and French Polynesia), and signed their own communiqué indicating that

> Leaders supported the re-inscription of French Polynesia/Tahiti Nui on the UN Decolonisation Committee's list as the first step in the process of self-determination, at international level (Nadi Communiqué 2011).

As always in the Pacific, the role of civil society with a reach into the region has been important. The Pacific Conference of Churches and the World Council of Churches have supported French Polynesia's inscription, the latter calling for self-determination for the people of 'Maohi Nui', *maohi* referring to the ancestral French Polynesian people (see World Council 2012).

French Polynesia increasingly looks to New Caledonia as a model for its own political development. French Polynesia signed an agreement to work more closely with the other French Pacific entities in February 2010. At the time, then assembly speaker and pro-France leader, Philip Schyle, said that he was interested in how aspects of New Caledonia's congress and the institutional arrangements under the Noumea Accord might apply to French Polynesia (*Nouvelles Calédoniennes* 26 February 2010). But encouraging closer consultative relations between the three French Pacific entities enables France to provide a regional alternative for French Polynesia to Temaru's support within the PIF. In time, depending on how the grouping evolves, and on whether or not the French entities become full members of the PIF, it could represent a pro-France ginger group, or sub-group, within the PIF. As such, it will be encouraged by France.

Economy

Unlike New Caledonia, French Polynesia's economy offers no single valuable resource to fuel its economy. For most of the second half of the twentieth century, its mainstay has been income derived from France's nuclear testing, directly, until cessation of the tests in 1996; and, since then, from massive compensation payouts over periods that have successively been extended. This means that the French budgetary contribution is far higher than in New Caledonia, around a third (of the total GDP of CFP536.3 billion ($A6.8 billion, converted 24 February

2010) in 2006). France contributed around CFP190 billion ($A2.4 billion) in 2007, CFP159 billion ($A2.0 billion) in 2006, and CFP148.6 billion ($A1.8 billion) in 2005 (*Haut-Commissariat, Direction des Actions de l'État, Bureau des affaires économiques et des entreprises* in ISPF website accessed 24 February 2010). Its expenditure includes EUR150 million ($A307 million) per year (*Sénat* 2006) in its ongoing nuclear compensation commitment.

All political players understand this dependence. Thus, when Temaru talks about independence, he also speaks of a continuing role for France, for example as noted in his favouring a formula of association with France. No one doubts that any form of independence would require continuing aid from France. And France, by constant reference to its largesse, has made it clear that independence would mean French Polynesia going it alone.

Local resources are minimal and based mainly on tourism and pearl exports. The high cost structure makes it an expensive place to visit, so the number of tourists is unlikely to increase and indeed has hovered around 210,000 per year since 2004. In 2007, 218,000 tourists visited, mainly from the United States, metropolitan France, Europe, and Japan. Global conditions resulted in a drop to 196,496 in 2008, and 160,000 in 2009, with large decreases from all destinations other than metropolitan France. This has led the major hotels to re-think their presence and, by early 2010, the Tahiti Hilton was set to close *(La Depêche de Tahiti* 11 March 2010). Although Flosse secured the identification of French Polynesia as a target tourist destination by the People's Republic of China, so far his efforts have not been rewarded by an influx of Chinese tourists. Services, mainly tourist-related, dominate the economy, employing 54,000 of 69,000 total salaried workers in 2007.

Pearl exports are valuable but a modest and declining proportion of total exports (Table 5.1).

Table 5.1 French Polynesia — Contribution of pearl exports to total exports 2006–2008

	In millions of CFP[a]		
	2006	2007	2008
Total exports	22,380 ($A284.4 million)	17,135 ($A217.7 million)	22,239 ($A282.6 million)
Pearl exports	11,098 ($A141.0 million)	10,681 ($A135.7 million)	8,473 ($A107.6 million)

a. $A converted 24 February 2010

Source: IPSF website <http://www.ispf.pf/ISPF/Chiffres/bref.aspx> accessed 24 February 2010

Although successive governments have nominated fisheries as a development priority, for various reasons, including migration of fishing stocks, inadequate infrastructure, high local costs, and the increasing habit of importing frozen fish from France, fisheries have not taken off and sales from local production have declined from 683 tonnes in 2004 to 539 tonnes in 2007, rising to 612 tonnes in 2008 (ISPF 2008 <http://www.ispf.pf> accessed 28 October 2008 and 24 February 2010).

Metropolitan handling and institutional factors

As in New Caledonia, the French State has continued to play a behind-the-scenes role to push the local leadership in a pro-France direction, notwithstanding the democratically expressed sentiments of the local people. Its failed early support for Flosse, including by introducing statutory measures specifically designed to bolster his majority, were followed by a distinct public preference for Tong Sang over Temaru. No supportive public statements were made by French officials when Temaru was elected in 2004; instead a re-election was held in which, once again, he won without comment from the French State. And the French State was again quiet following Temaru's subsequent election in early 2009.

As for New Caledonia, senior officials in Paris dealing with French Polynesia have generally been individuals with little experience of the Pacific region (see Chapter 4). It may be unsurprising that the period of instability from 2004 coincided with a period of resident French High Commissioners (after the departure of High Commissioner Michel Mathieu for Noumea in 2005) who, although highly trained professionals from the interior ministry, were not particularly experienced in regional affairs or even with previous experience in French Polynesia itself. This changed with the arrival in early 2011 of Richard Didier, who at least had spent two years in Wallis and Futuna.

Conclusion

The recent history of French Polynesia demonstrates the mixed legacy of France's presence in the Pacific. Because of the dominance of personality-driven politics, with the small-time corruption and nepotism that that implies, the dynamics have evolved around the French State's preference for the archipelago to be led by a pro-France big man, rather than an avowed pro-independence indigenous leader. Thus, France has taken a partisan, interventionist position, with constant reminders of the archipelago's dependence on French largesse, which has encouraged a venal coalescence of interests between the local pro-France and autonomist supporters who switch allegiance for personal gain, defying French efforts to consolidate the pro-French grouping. Frequent statutory change has been imposed without full consultation and assent by the local assembly. The fact that the economy of French Polynesia offers no dominant resource such as New Caledonia's nickel, and that its principal resources — tourism, pearls, and fisheries — offer limited scope for development, means that the collectivity would be less likely than New Caledonia to survive as an independent entity without substantial French aid. It is arguable that the instability arising from local, personality driven politics, corruption, and French interference, which ensures a weak economy dependent on France, serves French interest in remaining in French Polynesia. But as such, these elements of the political scene create ongoing uncertainty and instability, which is ripe for exploitation, particularly should a sufficiently motivated and powerful leader emerge.

In French Polynesia, as in New Caledonia, the UN and PIF remain relevant venting points for dissatisfied pro-independentists, Temaru having raised the issue of reinscription of French Polynesia with the UN Committee of Decolonisation in the Forum, making himself visible at the committee's regional seminar in Noumea in May 2010, and lobbying regional governments in July 2011. In contrast to the second half of the last century, when French Polynesia was France's most important strategic asset in the Pacific, with the cessation of nuclear testing, it has now been displaced by New Caledonia in strategic significance for France. Nonetheless, serious problems or questions about French Polynesia's status, particularly on the international and regional stage, will have flow-on effects for France's status relative to New Caledonia. There are signs of regional support for Temaru's call for reinscription, potentially raising difficulties for France, reminiscent of regional opposition in the 1980s.

The French State has reacted to Temaru's periodic efforts to draw regional attention to French Polynesia's dependent status, by seeking to dislodge him from power over the last five years. This raises questions about respect for democratic principles in French Polynesia, and also reflects France's determination to retain control over French Polynesia, and its other Pacific collectivities.

6. France's engagement in the region from the 1990s: France, its collectivities, the European Union and the region

As memories of the aberrations of the 1980s receded, and as France finetuned its approaches in New Caledonia and French Polynesia while mounting its regional diplomatic offensive in the 1990s, it became a more familiar and accepted regional participant into the 2000s, albeit as an outside player. It built its image as a regional partner, particularly as a partner of the major regional power, Australia. While the French State continued to invest heavily both financially and politically in managing aspirations in its Pacific entities for more autonomy, it encouraged greater contact by all three with the region, within limits.

France develops its regional links

Diplomatic representation

France continued to deepen and broaden its own links with the region, particularly Australia. The foreign affairs ministry maintains resident diplomatic representation in the largest Pacific countries, Australia, New Zealand, Papua New Guinea, Fiji and, for historical reasons, in Vanuatu; and continues to have a Paris-based ambassador for the South Pacific, supported by a diplomat based in Noumea. The interior ministry sends high level representatives to each of its collectivities, known as high commissioners and delegates of the French Republic in Noumea and Papeete, and known as prefects in Wallis and Futuna. In April 2009, announcing a global reorganisation of priorities in its foreign representation, which was based on a 2008 white paper, Paris indicated that its embassy in Canberra would carry the highest diplomatic responsibility in the region ('*mission élargie*', i.e., with the broadest range of responsibilities); that Wellington and Port Vila would be secondary missions ('*missions prioritaires*', with a secondary set of responsibilities) and Suva and Port Moresby would be considered as posts with a simple diplomatic presence (*Flash d'Océanie* 30 March 2009). The mission at Suva covers Fiji, Tonga, Kiribati, Tuvalu and Nauru.

Since the 1980s France has conducted annual meetings of its Pacific-based high-level officials, including its regional ambassadors and ambassador to the South Pacific, its high commissioners and prefect from its three entities, and Paris-based Overseas France ministry or secretariat officials. In 2008, for the first time, it invited Australian Parliamentary Secretary for the Pacific, Duncan Kerr, to participate in one of these meetings in Noumea.

Oceanic Summits

France has been a dialogue partner with the Pacific Islands Forum (PIF) from 1989, participating in post-Forum summit meetings with island leaders each year. These contacts at the highest level were boosted when President Jacques Chirac launched an initiative for regular consultations with regional leaders, called France–Oceanic Summits, the first of which was held in Papeete in 2003. France hosted a second summit in Paris in 2006, and a third in Noumea in 2009. At these summits, France has expressed support for the Pacific region, reinforced its desire to see its own collectivities participate more in the life of the region, and pledged co-operation principally in environment, climate change and fisheries surveillance, and through its South Pacific Fund (see South Pacific Fund below). Each successive summit has represented a demonstrable effort to address issues of significance to the island states, in the context of objectives defined in the PIF and other organisations, and to integrate European Union (EU) activity as well. The third summit in Noumea, however, which was the first to be held during the presidency of Nicolas Sarkozy, lost momentum when he decided not to attend, relegating French representation to his foreign minister, Bernard Kouchner, with concomitant lower level representation by Pacific leaders (only the presidents of Micronesia, Marshall Islands, and the prime ministers of Samoa, the Cook Islands, and Niue attended themselves, all other delegations were headed by ministers, MFA spokesman, 28 July 2009, website of French Embassy Fiji accessed 24 February 2010). No summit was held in the French presidential election year of 2012.

In its second and third meetings, France sought to engage Australia. But there were mixed messages from France and Flosse at the first meeting. Australia was absent from the 2003 Papeete summit, owing to an apparent diplomatic hiccup. Then, French Polynesian President Gaston Flosse, long disaffected with Australia, omitted to invite the Australian Government. When Paris-based French officials belatedly extended an invitation, just weeks before the event, the Australian prime minister and foreign minister were unable to attend, and France did not accept the Australian proposal to send a special envoy, maintaining at the time that it was a senior leaders meeting. (Interestingly, at the same time Australia had extended an invitation to France to participate in a regional counterterrorism ministerial summit in Indonesia and yet accepted a designated ambassadorial level representative when French ministers were unavailable.) At the same summit, Chirac, in his opening statement, pointedly contrasted France's, and the EU's, global leadership on climate change with those 'neighbours' in the Pacific (Australia, the United States) who had not then ratified the Kyoto Protocol (Chirac 2003 and see Mrgudovic 2008, 318–20). Nonetheless, the Australian Government has been supportive of France strengthening its links with regional leaders in such meetings. Foreign Minister Alexander Downer participated in the second Oceanic summit in June 2006 in Paris, and Parliamentary Secretary for the Pacific, Duncan Kerr, in June 2009 in Noumea.

Co-operation within the United Nations

At the same time as it was initiating its Oceanic Summits, France was reviewing its approach to the United Nations Decolonisation Committee, or Committee of 24. As noted in Chapter 2, it had removed its Pacific colonies from the UN Decolonisation list of non-self-governing territories in 1947, arguing that its entities were self-governing, and declining to transmit reports to the UN as the Charter required (Art. 73(e)).

France did not alter its approach when the UN Decolonisation Committee was established in 1960. The committee prepares working papers on non-self-governing territories on the basis of reports by the respective administering authorities. UN General Assembly (UNGA) Resolution 1541(XV) of that year set out the principles that should guide members as to whether or not an obligation exists to transmit information called for under Article 73e of the charter. It refers to non-self-governing territories as 'those in a dynamic state of evolution and progress towards a full measure of self-government'. France bitterly opposed New Caledonia's re-inscription on the UN List of Non-Self-Governing Territories, after intense lobbying by the Pacific island countries, in 1986. Even after it had concluded the Matignon Accords in 1988, France declined to transmit reports on New Caledonia to the UN.

But from January 2004, without any public fanfare and for the first time, France, as administering authority, began to submit (confidential) annual reports on the situation in New Caledonia to the committee, (Personal communication from Committee Secretariat 2008). Against the background of the history of France's noncompliance with the committee, this was an extraordinary step, undoubtedly reflecting France's renewed confidence in its position, and a belief that the international community would endorse its unfolding plan for New Caledonia. Several of the current 29 members of the committee come from the region: Papua New Guinea, Fiji, East Timor and Indonesia are all on the committee. Moreover, in the post-Cold War world, committee members Indonesia (with an eye to its troubles in West Papua and Acheh), Papua New Guinea (concerned about Bougainville), Russia and China amongst others, for domestic reasons, are disposed to resist active decolonisation moves that might bolster separatist claims. France calculates that its Noumea Accord framework for an outcome in New Caledonia will receive widespread support in the very committee that regional Pacific and Kanak independentist leaders used, by re-inscription, to further their claims.

In the same spirit, in October 2009, the New Caledonian government, with France's blessing, sent a delegation to make a presentation to the UN Decolonisation Committee for the first time. The delegation was led by pro-France leader Philipe Gomès and included representatives of the collegial government, including Front de Libération Nationale Kanak et Socialiste (Kanak Socialist National Liberation Front, FLNKS). Gomès referred to his government's participation as providing a more balanced input to the committee, which, until 2004, had received petitions and presentations from non-government sources in New Caledonia, mainly the FLNKS.

France and the delegation extended an invitation for the Decolonisation Committee to hold its regular Pacific regional seminar in Noumea in May 2010. The committee agreed, and duly held its seminar in the Secretariat of the Pacific Community (SPC) headquarters in Noumea, 17–18 May. The regional impact of France's efforts to court the committee was undercut by France's treatment of Kanak customary leaders and visiting French Polynesian Speaker and intermittent President Oscar Temaru, all of whom protested outside the building at their non-inclusion. French authorities sent them on their way (*Nouvelles Calédoniennes* 21 May 2010, *Flash d'Océanie* 17 May 2010), although they were given an opportunity to meet committee representatives at a dinner hosted by Kanak customary leaders.

There are signs that France is picking and choosing those elements of the decolonisation process that it will support. The suggestion by at least one member of the Decolonisation Committee, that a quid pro quo for holding the committee's seminar in Noumea should be requiring a UN investigatory mission there, was not implemented. France has never accepted a visit by such a UN mission to New Caledonia, despite the record of co-operation by other administering authorities (for example, New Zealand has accepted five visiting UN missions to Tokelau since the 1970s, UN Paper A/AC.109/2006/20), and despite strong exhortations by the committee that administering authorities do so (see UN Paper A/AC.109/2009/L.6). The ministerial PIF missions to New Caledonia have sent their reports to the UN committee (PIF Communiqué 1991, paragraph 34), although there has not been a visiting PIF mission since 2004 (see Pacific Islands Forum watching brief, below).

There have been occasional moves to overhaul the core wording of the annual UNGA Resolution on the Question of New Caledonia, which has been a thorn in the side of France each year from 1986. A general review of the text would provide an opportunity for France to modify its longstanding critical references.

Implicit in France's taking on its UN responsibilities as administering authority, is an acknowledgement that New Caledonia is a non-self-governing territory, the future of which would therefore be bound by UN decolonisation principles. These principles provide a pointer to the possible future status of New Caledonia. The principles are laid out in two linked UNGA resolutions (1541 and 1514). UNGA Resolution 1541 of December 1960 provides for three options by which a territory 'can be said to have reached a full measure of self-government: (a) Emergence as a sovereign independent State; (b) Free association with an independent State; or (c) Integration with an independent State' (Annex). The principles include a commitment to an outcome based on 'the free and voluntary choice by the peoples concerned' (Principle VII (a)). In the case of the integration option, the outcome is to be based on 'equal status and rights of citizenship between the peoples of the erstwhile territory and the independent territory to which it is to become integrated' (Principle VIII), begging questions about the special citizenship rights France provided under the Noumea Accord (i.e., the restricted electorate for the final referendum on New Caledonia's future status).

In the recurring UNGA Resolutions on the Question of New Caledonia, the UNGA has invited 'all the parties involved to continue promoting a framework for the peaceful progress of the Territory towards *an act of self-determination in which all options are open* and which would safeguard the rights of all sectors of the population, according to the spirit and letter of the Noumea Accord' (UNGA A/Res/66/87 operative clause 13).

France's taking on its administering authority responsibilities also reasonably means that France should comply with injunctions such as that in UNGA Resolution 35/118, which in its Annex calls for member states to ' adopt the necessary measures to discourage or prevent the systematic influx of outside immigrants and settlers into Territories under colonial domination, which disrupts the demographic composition of those Territories and may constitute a major obstacle to the genuine exercise of the right to self-determination and independence by the people of those Territories' (UNGA 35/118 Plan of Action for the Full Implementation of the Declaration on the Granting of Independence to Colonial Countries and Peoples, 11December 1980). UNGA resolutions on New Caledonia have variously referred to the problem of immigration, noting 'the concerns expressed by representatives of the indigenous people regarding incessant migratory inflows' (A/RES/66/87, 12 January 2012, operative para 7).

Separately, France has been steadfast in ignoring calls by Temaru (referred to in Chapter 5) for re-inscription of French Polynesia with the Decolonisation Committee.

France no doubt calculates that its objective to retain its Pacific entities will be enhanced by complying with some UN decolonisation procedures. But UN mechanisms, with the history of non-compliance by France, remain a vehicle for any dissenting pro-independence voices in the French Pacific entities, particularly New Caledonia, to make themselves heard, should their aspirations not be met. The relatively new UN instrument protecting indigenous people's rights (such as the 2007 Declaration on Indigenous Rights, see Chapter 8), provides a further avenue of redress for disaffected Kanak peoples in implementing the Noumea Accord and its aftermath. An example has been the 2011 visit to New Caledonia by the Special Rapporteur for the Rights of Indigenous Peoples, James Anaya, and his report which identified areas of concern relating to Kanak rights in the implementation of the Accord so far.

Aid to region

France contributes aid to the region through its participation in the SPC and the South Pacific Regional Environment Program (SPREP), and support for Forum activities. France contributes to emergency disaster management and fisheries surveillance through a trilateral FRANZ (France Australia New Zealand) arrangement (see below), and defence training and exercises engaging regional countries and its armed forces in New Caledonia and French Polynesia. Its main aid delivery arm, the Agence Française de Développement (French Development Agency, AFD), has only one bilateral aid program in the region, for Vanuatu, which it operates from Noumea after closing its Vanuatu office in 2002. France is a major contributor to the European Development Fund (EDF) activities in the region and participates in the Asian Development Bank (ADB). And its ambassador to the South Pacific administers a small South Pacific Fund.

Inconsistent statistics

Statistics about French contributions through these various mechanisms are opaque and inconsistent. Depending on sources, there is clearly some overlap in stated expenditures, creating a confused picture (for example, overlaps in reported French bilateral aid and EU aid, see below; also some program assistance, as distinct from core budget support, to SPC comes from the South Pacific Fund; and some emergency assistance under the FRANZ arrangements is included in expenditure by the New Caledonian army (FANC, Forces Armées de la Nouvelle-Calédonie)).

The French Ministry of Foreign Affairs shows variable and not necessarily comparable figures over time. Whereas figures were available in past years, by 2012 the ministry's website gave only the broadest aid figures, and did not break expenditure down by countries. It indicated that of EUR9.751 billion (approximately $A12.5 billion, converted May 2012) total aid in 2010, 60 per cent was directed at Africa, 20 per cent to Mediterranean countries, 10 per cent to countries in crisis, and the remaining 10 per cent to 'emerging countries' (website <http://www.diplomatie.gouv.fr/fr/enjeux-internationaux/aide-au-developpement> accessed 7 May 2012). South Pacific island countries can be assumed to be within the latter, modest amount.

Earlier access to the website was more productive as an indicator of French aid to the Pacific region, and for this reason figures to 2009 are used. But figures are variable and unclear. An item on the website dated June 2006 (accessed 27 February 2010), entitled 'France and the Pacific Region', showed that in 2006, France's total bilateral aid budget to the region was around EUR15 million per year, and specified a further EUR12. 8 million that year through EU channels, a total of EUR27.8 million (approximately $A40 million, converted 19 May 2010). An item on the same ministry website, dated October 2009, showed France's bilateral aid disbursement to the Pacific totalled EUR103 million ($A146 million) in 2008 and EUR98 million ($A140 million) in 2007, and was not clear whether that included funds through the EU. These figures are a leap from the EUR27.8 million in 2006, but may include French contributions through the EU (French foreign affairs website <http://www.diplomatie.gouv.fr/fr/pays-zones-geo_833/oceanie_14692/index.html> accessed 14 May 2009 and 25 February 2010 and superseded by May 2010; and bilateral aid section accessed 25 February and 19 May 2010).

If these figures do include contributions by way of the EU, then the situation is further muddied by the caveats to EU aid (see EU representation and aid to the region, below) such as the pattern of underspending allocations; and the occasional lumping together of EU funding to the independent Pacific countries along with EU overseas collectivities (such as the French Pacific ones there) (see for example EU website overview on EU and the Pacific, <http://www.europa.com>).

France also sometimes includes in its aid figures expenditure in its own entities. A figure provided by the French Government to the Organisation for Economic Co-operation and Development (OECD) in 2006 and cited by OECD as gross French bilateral aid to '*Océanie*' or the Pacific (undefined), amounted to $US110 million ($A128 million, converted 19 May 2010), but this included some items to its own three collectivities (OECD 2008a, Tables B.3 and B.4, 86 and 87). Some other analyses (see for example Mrgudovic 2008, 326 footnote 1012; Hughes 2003, 20) also include in aid figures France's financial support for its own three Pacific entities.

This practice is distorting, since this amount is very large, totaling over $A4.6 billion in 2008 alone (EUR2.65 billion for the three Pacific entities, communication from Senate Finance Commission 2008; in 2007 the figure was $A4.2 billion comprising $A1.8 billion or CFP121.5 billion to New Caledonia, ISEE TEC 2008, 960; $A2.4 billion or CFP159.1 billion to French Polynesia in 2006 from French High Commission press release 7 August 2007; and $A8.3 million or CFP562 million to Wallis and Futuna in 2006, IEOM website, all figures converted 28 May 2009).[1] While there is no doubt that much of this expenditure in the French collectivities benefits economic development there, and therefore the region, since it is expenditure on sovereign soil of a developed country, it is difficult to describe this as development assistance to the region.

Table 6.1 Indicative figures on France's assistance to the region

	In millions of Euro ($A)		
	2006[a]	2007[b]	2008[b]
Aid to region[a]	27.8 ($A40)	98 ($A140)	103 ($A146)
Of which, bilateral[a]	15.0 ($A21)		
Of which, through EU (just under 20% EDF)	12.8 ($A19)		
Some indicative programs funded (not complete):			
South Pacific Fund	2.4 ($A3.4) average p.a. 2007–2009		
SPC[c]	3.0 ($A4.2) average p.a. 1999–2009		
Plus French share/EU	1.0 ($A1.4) average p.a. 2002–2007		
Coral Reefs Initiative 2004–2009	2.0 ($A2.8) average p.a. 2004–2009		
Activities through FRANZ (emergency aid, logistic support)[d]	1.0 ($A1.4)		

Sources:

a. French Ministry of Foreign Affairs website <http://www.diplomatie.gouv.fr/fr/pays-zones-geo_833/oceanie_14692/index.html> accessed 14 May 2009

b. French Ministry of Foreign Affairs website accessed 26 February 2010; may include allocations through EU programs

c. SPC Annual Reports and Financial Statements, France and EU support to SPC 1993 to 2009

d. Estimate from FANC

---

1 With the effects of the Euro crisis, figures available to time of writing show that although France had increased its disbursements in 2010 to CFP147 billion for New Caledonia, CFP179 billion for French Polynesia, and CFP12.4 billion for Wallis and Futuna (ISEE, BIEP, and IEOM websites accessed 22 November 2012), the total translated to a combined *lower* total in Australian dollars, at $A3.5 billion (converted 22 November 2012), owing to a far weaker Euro. To facilitate comparison with latest regional statistics available (2009, 2010), the figure of $A4.6 billion, converted in 2009, is used.

While there are apparent discrepancies, the conclusion to be made is that France, on its own account and through contributions to the EU effort, spent EUR27.8 million in 2006, EUR98 million in 2007 and EUR103 million in 2008, on aid to the Pacific region, over and above its expenditure in its own Pacific collectivities (Table 6.1). France's 2006 expenditure of EUR27.8 million in the Pacific included assistance in governance (against drug trafficking and money laundering), sustainable development and climate change (through SPREP and SPC projects including on coral reefs), health (including a joint Australian project on AIDS through the SPC, and a New Zealand project on public health monitoring), education (university co-operation and professional and technical training), broadcasting (co-operation with Radio France Outre-Mer and other French broadcasters), infrastructure (modernisation of secondary airports and renovation of Vanuatu's hospital) and natural disaster assistance (including implementation of the FRANZ arrangement). France has been a member of the ADB from 1970 with 2.322 per cent of shares (fewer than Australia's 5.773 per cent but much more than New Zealand's 1.532 per cent). It is described as a non-regional member. The ADB supported projects in the South Pacific through loans and financing to a value of $A684 million in 2007 (ADB 2008, 16).

Considering it is a country resident in the region, France's aid to the region is relatively modest, given the contributions of other Pacific region donors and given its own contributions to other regions.

Australia's 2009–2010 budget for the region totalled $A1.092 billion (Australian Minister for Foreign Affairs Press Release 12 May 2009). New Zealand spent $NZ 205.5 million in the Pacific in 2007–2008 and allocated $NZ756 million, or $NZ278 million per annum, for the three years from 2009–2010 (NZ AID website <http://www.nzaid.govt.nz/programmes/c-pac-countries.html> accessed 19 May 2009 and 6 July 2010).

As a point of comparison, the OECD Official Development Assistance (ODA) figures are useful. ODA only includes specially defined assistance (essentially official government aid with the main aim of economic development of developing countries and containing a certain percentage of grant aid, see OECD 2008b). The OECD ODA statistics used by Australia's Ausaid in its 2009 publication, *Tracking Development and Governance in the Pacific*, showed that France provided $US16.7 million ($A19.4 million, converted 19 May 2010) or 1.4 per cent of total ODA contributed to PIF countries in 2007, with the EU contributing $US71.2 million ($A83 million) or 6.1 per cent (and France contributes around 19 per cent of EU funding to the Pacific). In the same comparison, Australia provided $US649.3 million ($A757 million) or 55.7 per cent of ODA, and New Zealand $US120.9 million ($A141 million) or 10.4 per cent. France was also outshone by the United States (14.7 per cent) and Japan (six per cent) (Ausaid 2009, 42).

Compared to its own expenditure in other regions, France's aid to its immediate neighbours in the Pacific region seems meager. The French Foreign Ministry site's table of global disbursements (Table 6.2) showed that the 2008 and 2007 figures for the Pacific represented just two per cent of total French bilateral aid disbursements, well behind Africa (which received 53 per cent in 2008), the Middle East (12 per cent), Asia (only three per cent) and South America (three per cent). In 2005, the tiny state of Mauritania alone received EUR36 million ($A64 million), more than the entire Pacific region at the time (French bilateral aid, French Foreign Ministry website <http://www.diplomatie.gouv.fr/fr/pays-zones-geo_833/oceanie_14692/index.html> accessed 14 May 2009). These figures suggest that, despite its sovereign presence, France does not see the Pacific as its own immediate region, with special aid contribution responsibilities.

Table 6.2 French global bilateral public development assistance disbursements 2007 and 2008

	In millions of Euro			
	2008	% total	2007	% total
Europe	295	7%	180	4%
North Africa	436	10%	459	10%
Sub-Sahara Africa	1886	43%	2140	47%
South America	141	3%	263	6%
Middle East	531	12%	724	16%
Central and southern Asia	120	3%	135	3%
Far East	372	8%	218	5%
Pacific	103	2%	98	2%
Non-zone assistance	550	12%	356	8%
Total bilateral assistance	4435	100%	4572	100%

Source: French Ministry of Foreign Affairs website <http://www.diplomatie.gouv.fr> accessed 19 May and 8 December 2010, posted 12 October 2009

Moreover, the relative disproportion of France's expenditure in its own entities relative to the rest of the region underlines the paucity of its aid to the region. France contributed $A1.8 billion or CFP121.5 billion to New Caledonia alone in 2007 (not including its metropolitan based expenditure such as payment of military personnel see ISEE 2008, 96), more than the GDPs of each of the Forum island members except Papua New Guinea, Guam and Fiji. Its total contribution to its three territories in 2008 ($A4.6 billion, converted 28 May 2009) was worth more than any individual Forum member's GDP except Papua New Guinea and Guam (SPC statistics translated into CFP, Table, ISEE TEC 2008 p. 12). France's expenditure in its own Pacific collectivities compared with Australia's total global aid program of $A3.8 b. in 2009–2010 (Ausaid's website <http://www.ausaid.gov.au> accessed 5 October 2009).

South Pacific Fund

At the same time that France talks of improved political dialogue and hosts its Oceanic Summits, its assistance to the region through its own South Pacific Fund is declining. The fund is the same one originally established by Flosse when he was minister for the South Pacific (see Chapter 3). It has fluctuated in value, from close to EUR3 million per year in the 1990s, but has declined in recent years, from EUR2.7 million in 2007, to EUR2.5 million in 2008 and EUR2 million in 2009 (see *Flash d' Océanie* 13 March 2009, 14 November 2008 and 2 April 2008). Moreover, the focus in the last few years has shifted from Flosse's idea of supporting local Pacific island projects, to funding projects primarily and overtly to assist the French Pacific entities' involvement in the region (see the list of priority areas under the program, article 'Le Fonds Pacifique', website of the French Embassy in Papua New Guinea, <http://www.ambafrance-pg.org/article.php3?id_article=427> accessed 8 March 2010). This means that the fund serves France's regional objectives, more than the priorities of the independent Pacific island countries themselves.

France and the Secretariat of the Pacific Community

From 1947, France has hosted the headquarters of the SPC in Noumea, including throughout the regional difficulties of the 1980s. Originally housed in the former US military headquarters from World War II, the French State facilitated the construction of an impressive new headquarters at a valuable nearby beachfront site, completed in 1995. It provided 75 million francs ($A20 million), the largest single component, towards construction costs (*Journal Officiel du Sénat*, response to question 10070, 15 October 1998). The main conference room, designed by a Fijian architect, takes the form of an upturned boat with oceanic details such as a reflective pool mirroring the ocean against its internal walls, and finishes of ropework over the glossy wooden panels. The organisation has operated in both French and English since its inception, a significant symbolic achievement for France given the cost and limited capacity of most of the members to draw on the French translations. Despite France's modest ongoing financial contributions to the SPC, French nationals have held prominent positions in the organisation. New Caledonia's Jacques Iékawé was appointed secretary-general in 1992, but passed away before assuming office. The office of deputy director-general to the

SPC has recently been occupied by French nationals (the former cultural attaché to the French embassy in Sydney, Yves Corbel, served as deputy from 1997 to 2006; and his successor, Richard Mann, is a French national).

Since it is the largest international conference facility in Noumea, the French State and New Caledonia have benefitted from their investment. The SPC has been amenable to the conference facility being used for a range of domestic political meetings, including a New Caledonian land issues conference in 2001, and a satellite video hook-up between the New Caledonian Government and the then Overseas France Minister, Brigitte Girardin, in 2003.

Mrgudovic (2008, 139) argues that the SPC had been a strong force for the integration of France and its entities into the Pacific. If so, this is more because of the institutional presence of the SPC in Noumea and the political effect of Pacific island experts and officials travelling to Noumea regularly, than because of French engagement in the work, and funding, of the SPC. The technical focus of the SPC has set it apart from political differences over the years, and is a testimony to the maturity of the Pacific island countries, supported by large regional donors, Australia, New Zealand, France, to a lesser degree the United States and, in the past, the United Kingdom.

France's contribution to the SPC has averaged just over EUR3 million in each of the last 10 years although, according to one senior SPC official, the amounts expended in any year fluctuate owing to the nature of program assistance (SPC 2009). For example, SPC figures show that it contributed $US7.1 million in 2007, about half of what Australia and New Zealand respectively contributed (Australia: $US14.7 million, New Zealand: $US14.5 million) (SPC 2007). But in 2010, France had increased its contribution to $US3.7 million (SPC 2010). France also contributed to the region through its contributions to the EU, which also, by their nature (going to programs rather than the core budget), are variable and averaged close to EUR5 million per year from 2005 to 2007, SPC 2007).

France, Australia, New Zealand and regional defence and other links

While France's 2008 defence white paper said very little about the Pacific per se (see Ministère de la Défense 2008; Fisher 2008c), it did highlight the importance of regional partnerships, specifically mentioning Australia in this context. The paper sought to focus France's domestic priorities on better intelligence and technology, while rationalising and reducing overall numbers of personnel and bases. In this context, the paper announced that Noumea would host the pre-eminent French defence presence in the region, with personnel in French

Polynesia to be reduced by half between 2011 and 2015 to 1100. New Caledonia's defence personnel would be reduced slightly from 3000, but its police and civil security personnel would increase. France had already built a consolidated headquarters that brought together all arms of the defence presence at a new $A13 million structure in Noumea.

Co-operative defence relations between France and Australia, often with New Zealand, have grown. The tripartite FRANZ arrangement, based on an exchange of letters in 1992, provides for disaster relief coordination engaging aid and defence elements from all three countries. There have been numerous examples of FRANZ co-operation to assist regional countries after natural catastrophes (for example, the Solomon Islands in 2007 following a tsunami). Aid officials from each FRANZ country meet regularly for planning purposes. In recent years the Arrangement has been extended to cover maritime fisheries surveillance, which was formalised in a joint declaration signed in Canberra in March 2006. Overflights by French military aircraft provide feedback to Pacific island countries on illegal fishing identified in vast areas contiguous with its territory. It is a complementary mechanism to similar activity by Australia and New Zealand in other areas of the South Pacific, with regular day-to-day engagement by France with regional countries providing useful, economically valuable regional intelligence.

FRANZ countries, along with the United States, participate in annual quadrilateral discussions on maritime security, including fisheries and Pacific traffic issues. France has participated from 1998 through its military forces based in French Polynesia and New Caledonia. The French force contribution to FRANZ is estimated to be worth around EUR1 million per year ($A1.75 million, converted 7 July 2009, Personal communication, senior French military official, 2009).

Australian and French defence co-operation in the Pacific operates within the context of close bilateral defence relations, outlined in the 2006 Defence Co-operation Agreement, which came into force in July 2009. Co-operation includes regular political/military consultations from 2001, defence supply compatibility programs, and commercial Australian defence contracts involving French companies, particularly EADS. France is the world's fourth-largest defence materiel exporter, and Australia is one of its biggest customers (see Maclellan 2009b, 13). In September 2008, after meeting the new Australian Labor Minister for Defence, Joel Fitzgibbon, the French Defence Minister Hervé Morin announced that New Caledonia would be available to give military logistical support to Australia in a Mutual Logistical Support Arrangement (Joint press conference Australian and French defence ministers 17 September 2008). This arrangement formalised the kind of military support the French had provided from New Caledonia on various occasions. For example, New

Caledonia provided an evacuation point for injured Australian personnel when an Australian military Blackhawk helicopter crashed on an Australian vessel, HMAS *Kanimbla*, during an evacuation operation offshore from Fiji during the 2006 Fiji coup, and served as a staging point for Australian ships preparing for the eventuality of consular evacuations from Fiji (see Fisher 2008c).

An important bilateral gesture to Australia and New Zealand respectively is made every year by France in its commemorations of Anzac Day in New Caledonia. The event is commemorated over three days in three different locations. On the first day, usually Anzac Day itself, a ceremony is held in the centre of Noumea, in the presence of the High Commissioner, New Caledonian President and other dignitaries, and war veterans. On the second day, officials travel en masse to participate in similar ceremonies at the Commonwealth cemetery at Bourail; and, on the third day, to a hilltop overlooking the Plaine des Gaiacs in the north, the site where US Seabees had laid an airstrip, now overgrown, to Australian design early in World War II. These pilgrimages engage the local communities as much as the French representatives, and mark their great affection and respect for the ANZACS who fell in metropolitan France and in the region during the two world wars.

France participates in regular military exercises with Australia and New Zealand from its base in New Caledonia, many of which include other Pacific island countries. These include the annual Equator naval exercise off the coast of Queensland; the biennial Southern Cross exercises in New Caledonia, and Australian regional exercises including Pitch Black and Kakadu (DFAT Country brief on France accessed 28 October 2008; French Embassy in Australia website, <http://www.ambafrance-au.org>, accessed 11 November 2008). Many training exercises routinely involve Tonga, Vanuatu and Papua New Guinea often alongside French, Australian and New Zealand troops. French senior military officials visit Papua New Guinea regularly.

Ship visits and visits by respective senior military leaders cross frequently between New Caledonia and Australia and have increased in number in recent years (for example from around four per year to more than eight from 2001 to 2005). This form of co-operation draws France in to the normal defence activity of the region, enhancing interoperability, and facilitating close co-operation in times of need. The official French approach has been positive, with local French forces who undertake joint exercises on French soil communicating in English. This is an important symbolic effort that illustrates the willingness of the French defence forces to adapt to the region.

Beyond formal agreements and exercises, France has taken great care to support Australian regional defence objectives. France was the first regional country to respond when Australia called for participants in the UN-backed International

Force for East Timor in 1999, arriving there even before New Zealand. This is a significant reminder of the potential strategic benefits for Australia and the region deriving from France's physical presence in the Pacific. France let Australia know that it would be interested in participating in the Regional Assistance Mission to the Solomon Islands (RAMSI), deployed in July 2003, although it did not in the end participate given regional sensitivities (see Regional reactions to French efforts, below). And, as indicated above, France provided important logistical support for Australian activity at the time of the 2006 Fiji coup.

Mixed reaction in New Caledonia

Whereas these formal defence links are a positive indication of Australian–French co-operation, local feeling in New Caledonia is mixed. Roch Wamytan has commented on the incompatibility of France's recent restructuring of its Pacific bases and building a new headquarters in New Caledonia with New Caledonia's decolonisation process (Maclellan 2009b, 13). An FLNKS leader has commented privately that it was disappointing for the first sign of the then new Australian Labor, under Kevin Rudd, government's interest in New Caledonia was the military pact (status of forces arrangements).

Reforms flowing from France's 2008 defence white paper will lead to New Caledonia becoming a major French defence logistical base from 2011, literally on the eve of the final five-year stage (2013–2018) of the Noumea Accord. Reflecting Kanak sensitivities, in a submission to the UN Decolonisation Committee in November 2008, FLNKS leader Wamytan noted the French decision to regroup its military forces to New Caledonia violated the obligation of administering authorities not to use non-self-governing territories for military bases or installations (see UNGA 2008 A/C.4/63/SR.5) .

French–Australian scientific co-operation

The French Pacific collectivities, particularly New Caledonia, also provide a venue for French–Australian scientific and cultural co-operation.

France and Australia have signed a number of bilateral scientific agreements. These include the Scientific and Technological Agreement, October 1988; the Scientific and Technological Marine Agreement, May 1991; the Industrial Research Program Agreement, May 1991; the French Australian Science and Technology program (FEAST), November 2003; and a scholarship program benefitting Australian students in France (Fisher 2004).

Co-operation also flows from France's presence in New Caledonia. There is significant contact between Australian research institutions and the many French research institutions based in New Caledonia. Australian scientific co-operation is handled by Australian tertiary institutions individually, not the government, as is the case with France. It is therefore difficult to identify the full range of co-operation. As an indicator, in 2004, the New Caledonia-based Institut de Recherche pour le Développement (Institute for Development Research, IRD), co-operated with more than 10 Australian institutions in a number of scientific areas. These included the Commonwealth Scientific and Industrial Research Organisation (CSIRO) on oceanography, biology and entomology; Geoscience Australia on geology and coastal modeling; Australian Nuclear Science and Technology Organisation (ANSTO) on radio-chemical applications to the marine environment; the Queensland Museum on marine natural substances in Vanuatu; the Sydney Botanical Gardens on algae; the Sydney and Victorian museums on crustaceans; the universities of Canberra and Queensland on climatology; James Cook University and ANSTO on metals in soils; and, Monash University on botany (Personal communications Colin 2004).

In the area of educational exchanges, since the Noumea Accord was signed, Australia has provided about $A1 million per annum to fund scholarships to enable students from all three French Pacific collectivities to study in Australia. The take-up has been excellent. Despite ongoing problems with the recognition of Australian qualifications in the French entities, New Caledonia has made an effort by allowing case-by-case consideration of Australian-qualified applicants to its civil service. As the mining sector grows, companies are less likely to be concerned about where training occurred and employment prospects for Australian-trained New Caledonians will increase. There is little or no exchange in the other direction. Indeed, from 2008, New Caledonia began to send many young people to train in francophone Canada, suggesting that it would prefer French language institutions rather than the regional Anglophone ones (see *Partir pour mieux revenir, Nouvelles Calédoniennes* 7 August 2008).

France and Australia co-funded a house of residence for Vanuatu students at the University of New Caledonia in Noumea in 2001.

Trilateral development co-operation

Other forms of regional co-operation with Australia and New Zealand have included a tripartite declaration on the surveillance and combating of illegal fisheries (April 2006), the Pacific Regional Endeavour for an Appropriate Response to Epidemics (PREPARE) program with New Zealand and the World Health Organisation (WHO) on treatment of epidemics, the prevention of sexually transmissible diseases and HIVAIDS, the Santo 2006 project on marine and land-based biodiversity in Vanuatu, and the Coral Reef Initiative for the South Pacific Program (CRISP) from 2002 (see Gazsi 2009).

Regional participation by the three French collectivities

Regional institutions

Statutory provisions reserve responsibility for foreign affairs to the French State, but enable both New Caledonia and French Polynesia to establish regional relationships in their own right. The Noumea Accord, Article 3.2.1, provides essentially for New Caledonia to be a member, or associate, in international bodies including specifically Pacific regional organisations, the UN, UNESCO, International Telecommunications Union (ITU) and a broad 'et cetera'; to have representatives in the Pacific zone and EU organisations, and to negotiate agreements with these countries in areas of its responsibility, which are defined at 3.1.1 to cover external trade, rights of foreigners to work, some specified air services, and maritime services. The February 2004 Organic Law for French Polynesia provides for it to have its own representation in any State (although the Constitutional Council has specified that this is not full diplomatic representation); for the president to negotiate administrative arrangements with any Pacific state or territory to advance its social and economic development; and to sign co-operation agreements in any area within French Polynesia's responsibility (Articles 15 to 17). With the agreement of the Republic's authorities, French Polynesia can be a member, associate or observer of international organisations, or its president can be associated with work undertaken by regional Pacific organisations in the areas of its responsibility (article 42). The Law defines French Polynesia as having all responsibilities other than those (*régalien*, or sovereign) functions of the French State which are specified (and include foreign policy, defence, entry of foreigners (not their access to work), and air services within the Republic (see Faberon and Ziller 2007, 323–25).

All three French Pacific entities have participated in the SPC since 1983, although they functioned for many years as part of the French delegation and have not been active in their own right.

Membership of the PIF has been more problematic, since the organisation is political in nature and was created as a vehicle of opposition to French policies in the Pacific. The Forum allowed only entities on the way to self-government to become observers. With the signature of the Noumea Accord, New Caledonia was seen as having qualified and became an observer in 1999, and French Polynesia in 2004 after changes to its Organic Law. But, in acknowledgement of significant efforts by France to develop relations, including by the Chirac government hosting a meeting of the France Oceania Summit for Pacific leaders in Papeete in 2003 and in Paris in June 2006, the PIF welcomed both in a new category of associate member in 2006, when Wallis and Futuna became an observer. Since then, New Caledonia's President Gomès has indicated that he wants full membership status for New Caledonia (see *Flash d'Océanie* 19 January 2010, and Regional reaction, below).

All three French entities are members of the Pacific Islands Telecommunications Association and the Pacific Power Association (PPA) and the Secretariat of the Pacific Regional Environment Program (SPREP). New Caledonia and French Polynesia are members of the South Pacific Tourism Organisation (SPTO), known as South-Pacific Travel; the Pacific Islands Development Program (PIDP); and associate members of the Secretariat of the Pacific Applied Geoscience and Technology Division (SOPAC). French Polynesia is an observer at the Forum Fisheries Agency (FFA). (Department of Foreign Affairs and Trade website, at South Pacific regional organisations, <http://www.dfat.gov.au> accessed 9 March 2010).

Table 6.3 Participation of French Pacific collectivities in Pacific regional organisations

	New Caledonia	French Polynesia	Wallis & Futuna
SPC (Secretariat for the Pacific Community)	M	M	M
PIF (Pacific Islands Forum)	A/M	A/M	O
SOPAC (Secretariat of the Pacific Applied Geoscience and Technology Division)	A/M	A/M	
FFA (Forum Fisheries Agency)		O	
PECC (Pacific Economic Co-operation Council)	A/M*	A/M*	A/M*
SPTO (South Pacific Tourism Organisation)	M	M	
PIDP (Pacific Islands Development Program)	M	M	
SPREP (Secretariat of the Pacific Regional Environment Program)	M	M	M
PPA (Pacific Power Association)	M	M	M
OCO (Oceanic Customs Organisation (non-CROP, Council of Regional Organisations of Pacific))	M	M	M

Note: M Member, A/M Associate Member, O Observer, A/M* combined Associate Member with France

Source: ISEE TEC 2008 p. 13

Thus, as Table 6.3 shows, the French collectivities are represented, in some way, on seven of the 10 inter-governmental members of the Council of Regional Organisations of the Pacific (CROP), i.e., in the SPC, SPREP, SOPAC, PIDP, SPTO, FFA, and the PPA. There are only three CROP bodies in which the French Pacific collectivities are not represented: the University of the South Pacific, the Fiji School of Medicine, and the South Pacific Board for Education Assessment. The Universities of New Caledonia and of French Polynesia (which split apart from the united French University of the Pacific in 1999) are not members of CROP. The universities operate in the French language, which limits the potential for co-operation. Still, there would be a good argument for closer collaboration between France, its regional universities and CROP's education members.

France and its collectivities together participate as an associate member of the tripartite (government, business, academic) Pacific Economic Co-operation Council (PECC) through the Paris-based France Pacific Territories National Committee for Pacific Economic Co-operation. The collectivities are members of the Oceanic Customs Organisation, which was headquartered in Noumea in 1999, but which subsequently moved to Suva.

Much of the promising breadth of participation by the French collectivities is limited by the cultural divide between their senior officials and those of the regional groupings. The Noumea Accord specifically states that training will be provided to prepare the collectivities for foreign affairs activities (Noumea Accord 3.2.1). Whereas France has been active in overtly campaigning for full participation of its collectivities in the PIF, and allowing for their participation in their own right in Forum activities and those of other regional organisations, it has been less energetic in ensuring that local officials are equipped to participate fully in this Anglophone organisation. Senior New Caledonian leaders have privately expressed their expectation that the Forum, made up of the poorest island states that happen to be English-speaking, should fund parallel French language interpretation services, an unrealistic hope given the dominance of Anglophone countries and the cost of translation services. Lacking an adequately resourced local secretariat for external affairs, New Caledonian leaders and officials are also not conversant with key Forum and CROP issues.

For their own part, the collectivities have displayed a mixed attitude to regional participation. The government of Pierre Frogier (2000–2004) was distinctly unenthusiastic, senior leaders complaining privately about the fact that proceedings were conducted in English about issues on which they had not been fully briefed, either from their local viewpoints or certainly in the regional context. Chapter 5 noted the limited development of an external affairs unit in New Caledonia.

French President Sarkozy underlined his wish that France's overseas entities integrate more closely in their regions, and he exhorted the French territories to be economically open to the countries surrounding them (Sarkozy 2009 and 2010a). To assist the French Pacific collectivities to participate effectively and genuinely in their own right, training in English and regional affairs, perhaps through exchanges, will be essential. A greater effort needs to be made by France, and regional donor countries, Australia and New Zealand, in this area.

Melanesian Spearhead Group

As seen in Chapter 2, the Melanesian Spearhead Group (MSG) was formed to show solidarity with New Caledonia's Kanaks and press for their independence. Since the signature of the Matignon/Noumea Accords, the grouping altered focus to economic co-operation, but maintains an interest in the New Caledonian decolonisation issue, along with support for the autonomist aspirations of West Papuans. The MSG is now made up of the independent governments of Papua New Guinea, Fiji, Vanuatu and Solomon Islands, and the FLNKS. New Caledonia as an entity is not a member. The MSG put in place a Free Trade Agreement in 1993, and established a Free Trade Zone in 2006, with limited effectiveness.

France has shown some flexibility towards the MSG. Perhaps with a concerned eye on China's funding of a new secretariat building for the body in Vila, which was inaugurated in 2007, the French State allowed Noumea to host an MSG meeting in 2001, and French High Commissioner Yves Dassonville met MSG representatives in late 2008 to discuss technical issues (address to Colloquium on Melanesian Integration, de Deckker and Faberon 2008, 10).

In October 2009 Gomès, then President of the New Caledonian Government, told the UN Committee on Decolonisation in New York that his government wanted New Caledonia to become a full member of the MSG (see *Flash D'Océanie* 19 January 2010). Although such participation would possibly strengthen the effectiveness of the MSG as an economic subgrouping, the idea was not welcomed by some of New Caledonia's Kanak leaders. FLNKS spokesman Victor Tutugoro commented that the idea of the MSG, formed as part of the Kanak fight for liberation, was that a fully independent New Caledonia would eventually become a member in its own right. He also noted that New Caledonia, or Kanaky, was not yet fully emancipated (*Nouvelles Calédoniennes*, 19 February 2010). His comments came after a debate at the annual FLNKS congress at which Palika (Parti de Libération Kanak/Kanak Liberation Party) generally supported developing regional links for New Caledonia, while the more ascendant Union Calédonienne (Caledonian Union, UC), defended the traditional objectives of the FLNKS within the MSG. In June 2010, an MSG delegation visited New

Caledonia in order to assess Noumea Accord implementation, and expressed continuing concern at the slow rate of implementation of Accord commitments (May 2011, 6 and see Regional reaction, below).

'Franconésie' unity

France has encouraged its three Pacific entities to consult and work together in recent years. France's intention for the three collectivities to work together has been referred to as a kind of 'Franconesia', designed to 'reinvigorate a French regional role' (Rumley et al. 2006, 244).

From 2003, the three have taken turns to chair meetings on the allocation of the South Pacific Fund. In 2009, they agreed to meet and work together on a regular basis. In February 2010, the heads of the assemblies of the entities signed a partnership agreement under which they agreed to consult and formulate common approaches to French State policy announcements. While this grouping is embryonic, when set against long-term objectives of the French entities of fuller participation in the PIF and other regional groups, it can be seen, potentially at least, as operating as a subgroup of interests within regional bodies.

Trade engagements

New Caledonia has used its capability to negotiate, and even sign (on behalf of the French State), bilateral agreements in the region in areas of its responsibility (Noumea Accord Articles 3.1.1 and 3.2.1). The first country to sign an agreement with New Caledonia was Australia (Trade and Economic Relations Arrangement in March 2002); followed by Vanuatu (in co-operative agreements in 2002 and 2006). The Australian Arrangement provided for regular bilateral talks between economic officials. In practice these have been infrequent. By mid 2009 only two had been held, the first in Canberra in September 2002, the second in Noumea in November 2005. There has been other high-level contact, with visits by senior New Caledonian leaders (2010 and 2012), and visits to New Caledonia by the Australian Parliamentary Secretary for Pacific Island Affairs Richard Marles in 2010, and again in April 2012, accompanied by Australia's Governor-General.

Bilateral economic links between the collectivities and the region are few. The big two, Australia and New Zealand, are unsurprisingly more important for the collectivities than the collectivities are for them. New Caledonia, the most economically significant of the three collectivities, ranks as Australia's 51st trading partner, with two-way trade equal to .1 per cent of Australia's total. It is, however, Australia's fourth-largest trade destination in the South Pacific. Australia's exports there (mainly coal, and civil engineering equipment and parts) amounted to $A379 million in 2010–2011, and this is trending upward. Imports largely consisted of nickel ore, and were worth $A174 million. Australia was New Caledonia's fourth-largest export destination in 2010 (after France, Japan, and Korea), taking just nine per cent of New Caledonia's exports. Australia was New Caledonia's fourth-largest source of imports that year, after France, China and Singapore (from where New Caledonia imports its petroleum), providing 9.7 per cent of its imports. French Polynesia's links with Australia are even slimmer, with Australian exports there worth approximately $A50 million in 2010–2011 (mainly processed and other food) and Australian imports valued at close to $A4 million (pearls and measuring instruments). Australia was French Polynesia's ninth-largest export destination and seventh-largest import source in 2010 (Department of Foreign Affairs and Trade, Fact Sheet, New Caledonia, French Polynesia <http://www.dfat.gov.au> accessed 27 May 2012).

French Polynesia represents New Zealand's second-largest Pacific island market, and New Caledonia its third. In 2010, New Zealand exports to French Polynesia totalled $NZ231 million (yachts, meat, dairy and other food and ore products) and to New Caledonia $NZ174 million (milk powder, wood, iron and food). Its imports were negligible, at approximately $NZ3 million from each collectivity (New Zealand's Ministry of Foreign Affairs and Trade Country Brief, <http://www.nzmfat.govt.nz> accessed 7 May 2012).

Economic links with the Pacific islands are even more limited and tend to be focused on Melanesia. In 2010, New Caledonia imported some products from Fiji (worth CFP368 million or $A3.9 million, converted 7 May 2012) and Vanuatu (CFP314 million or $A3.3 million) (ISEE website accessed 7 May 2012) but no longer exported to Papua New Guinea and Solomon Islands, as it had in 2007 (ISEE TEC 2008). Further growth in economic links is affected by the French collectivities' restrictive trade barriers and reliance on the French and European markets, apart from the relatively limited range of imports from other island economies.

It is therefore unsurprising that there is much to be done to engage the French collectivities in regional economic activity. Although the French entities have been invited to participate in regional free trade programs — the PACER (Pacific Agreement on Closer Economic Relations) and the PICTA (Pacific Island Countries Trade Agreement) — they have responded cautiously. There is a strong awareness of the differences between the well-off, heavily subsidised economies of the French collectivities and the majority of Pacific island states, and of the corresponding economic responsibilities that a regional economic agreement would impose on the better-off economies. The French collectivities have made much of the need to protect local business in order to develop economic activity. So, while New Caledonia is studying the two agreements, and has officially indicated its willingness to enter into negotiations for its eventual participation, it is unlikely to move quickly to do so (for an indication of the protectionist approach in New Caledonia, see a contribution by the then head of its regional co-operation and external relations unit, Laurent Sémavoine, in de Deckker and Faberon 2008, 241).

France, the European Union and the region

Beyond France's specific bilateral and regional engagement, and that of its collectivities in the Pacific, France has led the way for greater EU activity in the region. It has done this in two ways, first, by leading European support for the overseas territories of EU members, including those of France in the Pacific; and second, by pioneering the ACP (African–Caribbean–Pacific) program whereby Europe assists developing countries in Africa and the Pacific, with France providing a significant contribution to funding for this EU development co-operation, including in the Pacific.

Because many aspects of EU handling of the French overseas collectivities highlight specific regional concerns and departures from overall EU practice, and because their treatment under EU provisions differs to those that the EU applies to the island Pacific countries, the dispositions of EU treatment of the French Pacific collectivities and the Pacific island states will be considered (a fuller analysis is in Fisher 2012c).

EU and the French Pacific collectivities as European overseas countries and territories (OCT)

From the beginning of the creation of the EU, with its origin in the European Economic Community (EEC), France led the way for some form of association with European members' overseas possessions. This meant that the French Pacific entities have represented a slice of Europe in the Pacific from the late 1950s.[2]

Overseas countries and territories

The first European treaty, the 1949 Statute of the Council of Europe, did not refer specifically to overseas territories of member states. The 1951 Treaty of Paris on coal and steel made only cursory mention of extra-European territories of member states, guaranteeing that any preferential measures in those territories

---

2 For ease of reading, EU is used to refer to the various iterations of the European Community.

would be extended to other member states (Article 79). The 1952 Paris Treaty on a European Defence Community made oblique mentions of Algeria and Saint-Pierre et Miquelon.

But, from the 1957 Treaty of Rome, provision has been made for 'overseas countries and territories' (OCT) to be associated with the EU, which at the time essentially meant the French overseas possessions, Belgian and Italian African territories and Dutch territories in the Americas. And French influence was the decisive factor ensuring that these provisions were included (see European Commission 1998, 11; Faberon and Ziller 2007, 249; Jorda in Tesoka and Ziller 2008, 343). The OCT arrangements have remained broadly unchanged since then. The provisions stop short of seeing the OCTs as legally part of Europe. They aimed at advancing economic and social development of the OCT and the establishment of close economic relations between them and the whole community (Article 131). The French OCTs include New Caledonia, French Polynesia, and Wallis and Futuna, the French Southern and Antarctic Territories, Mayotte, and Saint-Pierre et Miquelon.

The treaty included the creation of the EDF, from which the French overseas possessions have derived considerable financial benefits. France has consistently contributed around 20 per cent of the fund, a larger amount than other European countries with overseas possessions. For the 10th EDF (2008–2013), France will become the second largest contributor (19.55 per cent) after Germany, but in advance of Britain, Netherlands and Denmark (Tesoka and Ziller 2008, 347).

Africa–Caribbean–Pacific

With the decolonisation of many overseas European, including some French, possessions in the 1960s and 1970s, the EU developed links with the newly independent African states and Madagascar in the 1963 Yaoundé Convention; and preferential trading measures with the countries of the new ACP under the 1975 Lomé Convention. The ACP arrangements were agreed at regular intervals, most recently in the Cotonou Agreement of June 2000, and are applicable for 10 years. Parallel arrangements for the OCTs include periodic renewal, initially by an agreement of application, then by decisions of association taken by the European Council.

Preferential treatment of OCTs relative to ACPs

Under these agreements, the preferential access to European members markets was the same for ACPs and OCTs until 1991, when the OCTs were accorded free and unlimited access to the European market, while the ACPs had to comply with rules of origin and transborder requirements.

Further benefits were accorded to the OCTs in 1997, following the establishment of the EU in 1993, in an annex to the Treaty of Amsterdam. No EU customs duties or other charges were payable by OCTs. The arrangements are not reciprocal, and OCTs can make their own customs legislation, for example to protect sensitive sectors of their economies. By this time, overseas territories of other European members had been added to the OCTs (those of the United Kingdom in 1973, Denmark in 1986). But the special nature of the French OCTs was accentuated here by two further protocols to the Treaty of Amsterdam, one called the 'Protocol on France' preserving the privilege of issuing currency in its overseas entities, the other a declaration reserving the right of each member state to act separately from other member states in the interest of an OCT (European Commission 1998, 30).

Both French Polynesia and New Caledonia have provisions in their respective Organic Laws for their governments' executives to be involved in relations and negotiations with the EU, and for consultation with their assemblies on proposed acts of the EU (Articles 30 and 89 of the 1999 Organic Law for New Caledonia, and Articles 41 and 135 of the 2004 Organic Law for French Polynesia). In practice, the collectivities themselves have not been directly engaged with the EU, without the presence of a representative of France, although French Polynesia has had a representative in Brussels from 1994.

In the Pacific, the French Pacific entities as OCTs have thus held a privileged position over other Pacific island states, who are ACPs, in relation to their treatment by Europe.

French Pacific entities: Implications for citizenship

The way in which EU provisions apply to the populations in the OCTs is variable, and still being worked out. Recent reforms are moving in the direction of treating them increasingly as normal EU members, thus bringing them increasingly into the EU family and in doing so giving the EU a stake in French sovereignty in the Pacific (see Fisher 2012c). But the French OCTs retain particular privileges relating to citizenship, which impact on local sensitivities there.

Because of their French citizenship, and its 'indivisibility' or supposed non-discriminatory application to all citizens (Faberon and Ziller 2007, 253, and Gohin 2002, point 4), inhabitants of the French Pacific entities who are French can vote for special overseas seats in European elections and are entitled to European passports (European Commission 1998, 15); they enjoy non-reciprocal rights of mobility and settlement in EU member countries; and they can protect sensitive sectors of their economies from EU imports and can issue their own currency. It is ironic that these benefits derive from the 'indivisibility' of French citizenship, given the unique status of New Caledonian citizenship, the restricted electorate and protective local employment conditions provided under the Noumea Accord, which seem incompatible with the notion of indivisibility and equality of all French citizens (Gohin 2002, points 32 and 33). The arrangement is yet another example of the creativity of the French State in supporting their collectivities even against the background of monolithic Europe.

Voting rights

In view of the controversies surrounding New Caledonian citizenship issues, and to some extent French Polynesian employment-protection citizenship issues, the association of the French Pacific collectivities with the EU, and its generally reciprocal arrangements, not surprisingly touch sensitive nerves (see Chapter 4).

Jean-Yves Faberon and Jacques Ziller note that the EC treaty applied fully to all EU citizens, and therefore to all French citizens wherever they resided, in metropolitan France, in its overseas departments, in its overseas collectivities enumerated in Article 74 of the French Constitution, or in New Caledonia, despite its sui generis status (2007, 240). All French citizens, including all those French citizens in the French Pacific collectivities, have the right to vote in EU elections. They are the only member state nationals living outside the EU who may do so (Muller 1999, 43; *Commission Européenne* 1998, 15). Three special *Députés* (members of Parliament) positions were created specifically to represent the French overseas collectivities.

But, for the locals in the three Pacific collectivities, this right to vote is seen as a mixed blessing, reflected in the low voter turnouts (around 20 per cent, compared to around 70 per cent turnout in other elections, see for example Table 4.7) and general lack of appreciation of the benefits, or potential benefits, of European membership. In French Polynesia, most parties boycotted or did not actively become engaged in European elections in July 1989 because of concerns about French Polynesia's status and the potential for immigration inflows from Europe. France was dismissive of these concerns, referring to controls held by the French State since 1932 over entry and residence, supplemented by French Polynesia's1984 statute which provided for consultation with the territory on immigration and the control of expatriate residents. But local leaders at the time warned that the EU vote risked fuelling independentist sentiment and Flosse suggested that the EU identity could erode local culture and identity (Muller 1999, 44). It is possible that the changed status of the OCTs relative to the ACPs from 1991, according more privileges to the OCTs from their association with the EU, may well have resulted from an effort to allay such sensitivities.

In New Caledonia, the pro-independence Palika has traditionally opposed participation in EU elections on the basis that it would imply integration into a system that condoned colonialism in Kanaky (Chappell 1998, 443). As Chapter 4 described, after the Noumea Accord was signed, France secured special non-reciprocal rights by which EU members resident in New Caledonia could not vote in congressional or provincial elections. They remained able to vote in municipal elections, however, which aroused particular concern amongst the pro-independence groups.

These efforts by France failed to reduce the sense of concern and isolation in its entities: in the June 2004 EU parliamentary elections, voter turnout was a low 25.43 per cent in New Caledonia, and 39.85 per cent in French Polynesia. In May 2005 Palika, a leading constituent of FLNKS, called for a boycott of the French vote on the EU constitution (Maclellan 2005b, 413). This was consistent with its anti-EU election stance noted above, and occurred when Palika was challenging the pro-France group's interpretation of the restricted electorate for provincial elections in New Caledonia.

A further effort was made to encourage more active participation in EU elections. Until 2009, the three French overseas positions in the EU parliament were contested on a basis of one electorate and list of candidates on a proportional basis. This meant that candidates from the more populous Réunion invariably won all three seats. Again, at the instigation of France, for the 2009 election, this procedure was changed, with the creation of three electorates, enabling the election of one representative from each of the Caribbean, Indian Ocean and Pacific collectivities. During the lead-up to the election, newspapers reported extensively on the substantial funding the OCT received from Europe, to remind the voter of the benefits of EU association. But this effort too failed. Voter turnout in New Caledonia and French Polynesia was even lower than in 2004 (21.82 per cent in New Caledonia in 2009, and in French Polynesia, 22.59 per cent) (see also Muller 2010, 6). These turnouts are low when compared with the local turnout for local elections (above 70 per cent in New Caledonia in 2009 and French Polynesia in 2004) and also compared to overall turnout for France in EU parliamentary elections (46.76 per cent in 1999, 42.76 per cent in 2004, and 40.63 per cent in 2009).

Non-reciprocal rights of travel and settlement

Again, by virtue of their French citizenship, the French Pacific originating populations are able to settle in each of the other 26 EU member states on the same terms as residents of other EU member states. In so far as the reciprocal right is concerned, the 1957 treaty provided for regulation of this right by agreements requiring the unanimity of the members of individual states, which have never been adopted (Faberon and Ziller 2007, 254–55; European Commission 1998, 27). Therefore the OCTs benefit from the non-reciprocity of the right to travel and settle in other EU states.

In 1985, some countries of the EU, including France, agreed to create the Schengen area of free movement of peoples, abolishing border checks at internal borders. By 2008, most EU countries participated. At France's request, the French OCTS are not part of the Schengen group and, unlike Schengen member countries, they maintain their own police border controls (see Faberon and Ziller 2007, 256).

The special employment protection provisions of New Caledonia and French Polynesia are also permitted. Thus, the French OCT can take protective measures on employment, so long as incoming workers from EU members are treated no differently to those from third countries (European Commission 1998, 27, Faberon and Ziller 2007, 267). Interestingly, in theory this would provide a means for local French collectivities to treat incoming French citizens, as EU citizens, seeking employment, just as rigorously as those from third countries, although so far the local governments have not taken up this option. Senior French officials acknowledged in personal communication in early 2009 that local political parties in New Caledonia were pressing for greater controls on French immigrants. The sensitivity of the immigration issue means that all applications by foreigners for employment visas are individually seen and decided upon in the executive (or cabinet) of New Caledonia. This is bureaucratically demanding. The criteria for endorsement are opaque. Faberon and Ziller (2007, 267) have noted that, while statistics are difficult to come by, judicial experience indicates that the EU provisions have resulted in a greater influx of EU workers into the French OCTs, particularly French Polynesia.

Economic benefits

The French OCTS are given full access to the internal market of the EU, which is a meaningful privilege given that virtually all of the OCT's economic activity is geared towards the European community (European Commission 1998, 30). Moreover, the French OCTs can make their own customs legislation protecting sensitive sectors of their economies, and issue their own currency (which has been a controversial issue, see Chapter 4). In these respects, it is worth noting that the four French overseas *départements*, Guadeloupe, Guyana, Martinique and Réunion, are not OCTs as they are considered an integral part of the EU by virtue of their status as departments of France. As such, they cannot make their own customs legislation, must apply European customs arrangements to imports and are given support from the Structural Fund rather than the EDF (European Commission 1998, 18).

While the French Pacific collectivities enjoy, and exercise, their right to make their own protective customs legislation even against European imports, the reality is that their economies are dependent on France and on Europe, particularly given the habits and tastes of the inhabitants and this, together with strong vested local interests, acts as a brake on the exercise of this privilege. As a result, duties and import taxes are more likely to be directed against regional imports, for example from Australia, New Zealand, and the neighbouring Pacific states, than against European imports. The net result is that the economies of the French Pacific collectivities remain inexorably linked to France and Europe, which impedes their integration within their own region, even given the dramatically higher costs such as those associated with freight.

Thus, in 2011, exports from New Caledonia, the largest economy of the French Pacific entities, went principally to the EU (of which over half went to France), and then to Japan, Australia and Taiwan, while imports came primarily from the EU (of which half came from France), followed by Singapore, Australia, Japan, New Zealand and the United States. Its trade with the regional Pacific island countries was so negligible that it did not warrant a line report in official statistics (ISEE website accessed 16 February 2012). Australia holds only 10 per cent of market share in New Caledonia (after France, China and Singapore) and in 2010–2011, Australian exports there totalled only $A348 million, and imports $A174 million (Country Brief, Department of Foreign Affairs and Trade website accessed 16 February 2012).

The ambiguities of OCT status for the fledgling participation of the French Pacific entities within their own region have led to some misunderstandings. In the early 2000s, senior New Caledonian leaders would argue publicly that New Caledonia would provide a door for Pacific economies (including the large Australian and New Zealand economies) to European markets. In practice, this is not the case, as the EU maintains local content rules and rules of origin which preclude processing of essentially foreign imports in an OCT, for example, New Caledonia, for subsequent preferential entry to its markets.

Development benefits

The French Pacific collectivities as OCTs benefit from aid flows and projects under the EDF. These benefits are not as favourable to them as the Structural Fund available to EU member states. The EDF applies not only to OCTs but also to ACPs. Because New Caledonia and French Polynesia are large and enjoy a higher standard of living than many other OCTs and ACPs, and because they fall outside some of the specific recent EDF programs, they do not receive as much as others. This has become a motivation for France to make the OCTs eligible for other EU programs (Personal communication by senior French officials 2012). They nonetheless have had access to considerable support.

Under the current 10th EDF (2008–2013), projected expenditure in New Caledonia is EUR19.81 million; French Polynesia EUR19.79 million; and Wallis and Futuna EUR16.5 million (Europa website accessed 8 November 2011). But, problems arising from time-consuming bureaucratic processes, the isolation and distance from Brussels of the French OCTs (despite the presence of a resident EU representative in Noumea and Suva), means that the often impressive notional allocations are rarely fully spent (this problem is one shared by the ACP Pacific countries, see EU aid to the region, below). Thus, although the 9th EDF (2000–2007) allocated support to New Caledonia totalling EUR21.5 million, to cover a number of projects including a new aquarium, roadworks and professional training, this figure included as much as EUR7.8 million that was unspent from the previous period (see ISEE website, accessed 25 November 2008). Wallis and Futuna, defined as a least-developed OCT, was allocated EUR16.7 million in the 9th EDF, of which EUR5.2 million was carried over from the previous period.

The OCTs also benefit, as do the ACP countries, from the EU's STABEX and SYSMIN systems for supporting agricultural exports and financing mining products respectively. They also have access to the European Investment Bank. Given the level of economic development, however, French Polynesia and New Caledonia do not generally qualify over other OCTs, although New Caledonia has received some training and mining rehabilitation funding from SYSMIN.

With French support, the OCTs are increasingly being granted access to other mainstream EU programs funded by the EU budget (i.e., outside the EDF funding arrangement) such as education, training, competitiveness and innovation framework and cultural and audiovisual programs (see Custos in Kochenov 2011, 110).

Currency: The Euro

France would like its three Pacific collectivities to adopt the Euro instead of the special French Pacific franc that is currently in circulation, but has indicated that it will introduce the Euro only if all three collectivities agree to do so. Wallis and Futuna has indicated it will fall in with such a decision taken by the other two collectivities; French Polynesia voted in 2006 to introduce the Euro. Chapter 4 refers to the reasons why New Caledonia has so far been disinclined to accept the Euro as its currency, essentially seeing such a move as stepping back from the Noumea Accord's stipulation that currency would be dealt with as one of the final sovereign matters to be voted on between 2014 and 2018.

Political benefits

Importantly too, the OCTs have the right of petition before the European parliament mediator, introducing a new area of influence over what happens in their (OCTs) territory (European Commission 1998, 30). It is notable that New Caledonian pro-French interests had recourse to the European Court of Human Rights over the restricted electorate issue, with that court judging in favour of local interests given the special sensitivities of the New Caledonian situation (see Chapter 4). Thus, the political association with Europe provides a potential check to French administration practices and a new pressure point to which the French Pacific collectivities can have recourse, not only on local issues but also on issues of interest to the wider Pacific region.

Review of EU–OCT relationship

The EU is reconsidering its approach to the OCTs, and France has been instrumental in driving change. A 2008 green paper was followed by a 2009 European Commission Communication and a joint EU/OCT position paper in February 2011, the latter being an outcome of a meeting hosted by France in Noumea.

The 2008 green paper set the pace, noting that the emphasis to date on development co-operation, and the relatively high expenditure on the OCTs relative to the ACPs was outmoded (the average per capita level of EU financial assistance to the OCTs was approximately six times higher than the average per capita level of its assistance to the ACP states). The paper notes that the approach had been formed when most OCTs had been African colonies, and is no longer consistent with the contemporary realities of the OCTs. Aspects under consideration, and taken up by the subsequent communication and joint position paper, include whether or not the development co-operation approach was the most relevant, given the relatively high standards of living in the OCTs; whether and how the OCTs could play a key role as strategic outposts for the EU; whether better means could be found for their integration into their geographic regions; and how they could better engage in environmental protection of their unique biodiversity. The green paper also raises the special role and influence of other countries in respect of the OCTs, in the case of the Pacific, the role of the United States, Japan, China, Australia and New Zealand was raised (European Commission 2008, 13). The directions of these changes, notably the view of the EU's OCTs as strategic outposts, and the trend towards their integration in their own region, are clearly inspired by French policy approaches to its own OCTs, enunciated by the French President and other leaders in recent years (see Chapter 7).

EU representation and aid to the region

The OCTs themselves form an important part of the EU's presence in the Pacific region, and are seen as such by the EU. The 2008 green paper on the OCTs states that 'Indeed, while the OCTs do not form an integral part of the EU, they are a part of or at least closely related to an EU Member State, which means that they cannot be uncoupled from the EU and, in a sense, are "part of its ultimate frontiers"' (European Commission 2008, 7). But apart from the EU's engagement with France's three OCTs in the Pacific (and Britain's minuscule Pitcairn Island), the EU is formally represented in the region, contributes to some regional organisations and has been involved in assisting the independent Pacific countries through the ACP relationship. France has been a major contributor to this process, and to funding.

The EU has residential diplomatic representation in Australia and New Zealand, a regional delegation office in Fiji and a delegation office in Papua New Guinea, technical offices in East Timor, Samoa and Kiribati, and offices in Solomon Islands and Vanuatu. It also has an office for the French OCTs in Noumea. The European Investment Bank has an office in Sydney. The EU participates in dialogue discussions that are held immediately after PIF summit meetings.

The EU launched a new strategy for the Pacific in 2006 (European Commission 2006). It noted that its support for regional governments dated from the 1975 Lomé Convention, revised in 2000 as the Cotonou Agreement, and totalled EUR1.8 billion to 2006. It described itself as the second-largest aid contributor to the region, but included in its calculations the separate aid contributions by some of its members (France, United Kingdom and Portugal) (European Commission 2006, 25 and 26). Its assistance focused on governance and regionalism, and sustainable development of natural resources and climate change, elements that corresponded to the Forum priorities of economic growth of sustainable development, good governance and security. The strategy noted France's regional and military presence in its three OCTs, along with the desirability of promoting integration of these entities (as well as Pitcairn Island) into the region (European Commission 2006, 4 and 5).

The 10th EDF 2008–2013 allocated to Pacific programs an overall envelope of EUR293 million ($A441 million, converted 2 March 2010, or just under $A90 million per year) with a possible 25 per cent increase if countries demonstrate clear commitments to good governance (European Commission 2007, Preface, 7). There are regional and bilateral (i.e., EU/individual Pacific island states) programs. The regional program allocates EUR105 million over the five-year period ($A157 million, converted 9 March 2010), within the broad objectives of the Forum's Pacific Plan, which is focused on sustainable energy and preservation and exploitation of natural resources. Of this amount EUR45 million ($A67.4 million) has been earmarked for regional economic integration, EUR40 million ($A60 million) for sustainable management of natural resources and the environment and climate change, and EUR10 million ($A15 million) for non-state actors and the Forum (EU website <http://www.http//ec.europa.eu/development/geographical/regionscountries/eupacific_en.cfm> accessed 6 April 2009).

Until 2009, little of this funding had been channelled through the SPC. The EU does not contribute to the core budget of the SPC , but it does provide funding for programs, and therefore the annual amounts fluctuate widely depending on the timing and pace of expenditure in the programs that it supports. It averaged contributions of just under EUR5 million ($A7.4 million) per annum in the five years to 2007 (SPC 2009). In 2007, the EU contributed EUR1.8 million ($US2.8 million or $A3.1 million), or 5.16 per cent of SPC income (SPC 2007 Income by Source, SPC Annual Report 2007, Part 2 Annual Accounts). France contributed $US7.1 million in that year, or 12.97 per cent of total income. Since France contributes just under 20 per cent of EU EDF funds, it can be assumed it contributed an estimated EUR1 m. ($A1.5 million) per year to the SPC, via the EU contribution, in the five years to 2007.

By 2010, the situation had reversed, with Europe contributing 11.17 per cent of total SPC income, or $US9.4 million, and France 4.4 per cent or $US3.7 million (SPC Annual Report 2010 Part II, 46–47). This suggests a French policy objective of channeling more of its support through the EU prism than in the past. By 2011, the SPC itself was claiming that the EU was expected to become the second largest contributor to SPC programs after Australia, having allocated 23 per cent of the SPC's projected funding for 2011 (SPC Annual Report 2010 Part 1, 9).

As for the OCTs, EU funding to independent Pacific island governments is limited by the capacity of the bureaucratic processes in Brussels to deliver, in a timely way, appropriately tailored projects to remote micro states. The capacity for these small states to provide the necessary documentation required by EU procedures is also an issue, as is the propensity for the Europeans to prefer region-wide programs, which are often unsuited to the diverse needs of the Pacific states. Together, these factors account for the past underspending of generous European allocations. There was a 36 per cent underspend for the 6th EDF 1985–1990 and 49 per cent for the 7th 1990–1995, which led to an emphasis in the 9th EDF 2000–2007 on redressing this situation (Mrgudovic 2008, 332). By 2011, the EU website claimed that, for the first time, the 10th EDF (2008–2013) began with the resources from past EDFs already committed to programs (Aid Funding, Developing Efficiency, entry dated 31 December 2010, Europa website accessed 22 November 2011). As noted, however, an estimated 20 per cent of these funds are committed to implementing programs that are hangovers from the previous EDF.

Other EU links

Trade between the region and the EU is minuscule. Both-ways trade was worth just over EUR1 billion in 2008, of which EU exports comprised just under EUR700 million. The EU's main exports to the Pacific region are machinery and transport equipment (about 60 per cent of its exports in 2008). It imports consist mainly of palm oil (49 per cent of its imports in 2008) and sugar (14 per cent) (Europa website accessed 6 December 2011). Although the EU takes 10 per cent of Pacific ACP exports, over 90 per cent of these come from Papua New Guinea and Fiji (European Commission 2006, 24). The importance of the EU to Fiji is reflected in its taking half of Fiji's major commodity, sugar, at guaranteed prices, until the phase-out of the program in 2010, although this preferential treatment has been suspended on occasion to sanction Fiji's undemocratic practices (most recently, on 18 May 2009, the EU cancelled $A31 million aid to Fiji's sugar industry in response to the establishment of its military dictatorship). It has signed fishery agreements with the Solomons, Kiribati and the Federated States of Micronesia, covering fishing licenses for Spanish and French fishing vessels. The EU has acceded to the Western Central Pacific Fisheries Convention.

From September 2004 the EU has been negotiating Economic Partnership Agreements (EPAs), to replace the preferential Cotonou arrangements. Although Australia and New Zealand have not insisted on prior consultation, as provided for in the PACER, negotiations have been slow and have extended well beyond the original deadline of 2008. No doubt this reflects the limited interest for Europe in the Pacific island states as sources of trade or investment. By 2011 Pacific EPAs had only been signed between the EU and Papua New Guinea and Fiji (both in 2009) granting them duty- and quota-free exports to the EU from 1 January 2008. In the interim, the other Pacific island countries benefit from the EU's generalised system of preferences, which does not have a major impact given their weak trade links with Europe.

Regional reactions to French efforts

As with its efforts to improve its image in the region in the 1980s, the reaction in the region to French overtures in recent years has been mixed.

On the one hand, regional leaders have responded to France positively. They have participated in the France Oceanic Summits. Many (Papua New Guinea, Tonga, Vanuatu, Fiji) participate in defence exercises and exchanges with France, and welcome French naval visits. Just as some Melanesians were uneasy with the Rudd government's conclusion of a defence agreement with France over the use of French defence facilities (see Co-operation with the United Nations), however, so are some island leaders cautious about engaging France in regional defence activity. When Australian Foreign Minister Alexander Downer was putting together RAMSI, in 2003, in response to a request to Prime Minister John Howard from the Solomon Islands Prime Minister Sir Allan Kemakeza, he had in mind French participation. In the event, regional island leaders, sounded out informally in the corridors of a meeting hosted by the Australian Government in Sydney to plan the mission, were not responsive to the idea of French participation, and the idea was dropped.[3]

The same hesitation was evident at the time Australia was encouraging Indonesia to develop a long-term democratic solution in East Timor. Indonesian President B. J. Habibie strongly rejected Howard's proposal to apply a Matignon Accords-type solution to East Timor. Then Australian Ambassador to Indonesia John McCarthy reported at the time 'that he (Habibie) found the choice of a colonial example unpalatable' (McPhail 2007, 116 and 117). Alison McPhail attributed the rejection to 'the bitter legacy of Dutch colonisation of Indonesia which made any suggestion that Indonesia was acting as a neo-colonial power highly offensive to the President'.

The MSG, despite holding one of its meetings in Noumea, has stopped well short of full endorsement of France and its presence in the region. An example of its reticence towards France is its support for Vanuatu's claim to the Matthew and Hunter Island group, drawing on traditional Melanesian links and history, in the face of France's continued assertion of its own claim by virtue of its New Caledonian presence (see Chapter 4). Gomès, New Caledonia's pro-France President, has flagged his wish for full membership of the MSG by the government of New Caledonia, as a replacement for the FLNKS (*Flash d'Océanie* 19 January 2010). This would mean that the collegial, albeit pro-France dominated, government, would replace and therefore significantly weaken, the voice of the Melanesian grouping which first mobilised the MSG. The idea has been met with a studied silence from the MSG. Instead, the MSG sent a visiting mission to New Caledonia in June 2010, which in its private report expressed some criticism of progress in the implementation of the Noumea Accord so far (Personal communication by senior Pacific island country official, 2010 and May 2011 p. 6). While the MSG has been preoccupied with economic issues in recent years, it has not forgotten its core concerns about New Caledonia's status.

Pacific Islands Forum stance: A watching brief on New Caledonia

A certain reserve about France is also evident within the PIF, particularly in responding to the French entities' desire for full membership in 2010.

---

3   Downer mentioned the idea to the French Ambassador, at a lunch he was hosting for European ambassadors. Preliminary indications were that the French would have responded positively (Personal comments Downer 2003 and 2009).

Forum membership is confined to 'independent and self-governing states' (PIF website accessed 27 September 2010). Nonetheless, the Forum made special provisions to accommodate the three French entities. At the time, in 1999, the Forum specifically defined observers as 'A Pacific island territory on a clear path to achieving self-government or independence' (Pacific Islands Forum Koror, Palau, Communiqué 1999), yet it created a special category of associate member (not defined and subject to leaders' discretion, Article 1, Agreement Establishing the Pacific Islands Forum (revised), 27 October 2005) for French Polynesia and New Caledonia. The Forum has so far held the line at these forms of association, with Wallis and Futuna as observer, while retaining a separate mechanism for engagement of France in the post-Forum summit dialogues.

This creation of a special category for New Caledonia and French Polynesia was ambiguous. On the one hand, Forum action suggests that the two collectivities had transcended the category of observer in some way. The granting of observer status to Wallis and Futuna seemingly overlooked the fact that that entity was not on a path to self-determination or independence (although other observers include entities as various as Tokelau, the Commonwealth, and the ADB, with East Timor as a special observer). Meanwhile applications to be observers by the US dependencies, American Samoa and Guam, have simply remained under consideration.

On the other hand, assigning a special unique category to these two French entities is not inconsistent with ongoing monitoring of the as yet unfolding process of self-determination. The evolution of New Caledonia's status has remained on the Forum agenda since the PIF welcomed the Noumea Accord in 1998, but its support for the Accord was not unqualified. The Forum at the time specifically recognised New Caledonia's right to self-determination (which it has reiterated in subsequent Communiqués). The 1998 Pohn Pei Forum communiqué expressed support for continuing contact between the Forum and all communities in New Caledonia, and established a mechanism for monitoring implementation of the Accord. 'Leaders agreed to a continuing future monitoring role for the Forum Ministerial Committee on New Caledonia *during the period* of the Noumea Accord, *particularly with respect to the referenda that will be conducted pursuant to the Accords*' (my emphasis) (1998 Pohn Pei Forum Communiqué). As noted above, when it admitted New Caledonia as an observer to the PIF in 1999, the Forum took care to define observer explicitly as a territory on a clear path to achieving self-government or independence. At the same time, Forum leaders agreed 'to continue to bring to the attention of the UN the question of New Caledonia's political future' and called on members to consider making available training awards for the Kanak people (1999 Koror, Palau, Forum Communiqué).

The Forum sent a ministerial committee to visit New Caledonia in 1999, 2001 and 2004. The 2002 Fiji Communiqué noted that the report of the committee

(2001), welcomed the establishment of institutions under the Noumea Accord, and encouraged all communities to support and implement the Accord, and supported self-determination in New Caledonia. Once again, 'The Forum also agreed to continue to bring to the attention of the UN the question of New Caledonia's political future', and agreed to support more Kanak training through a Kanak training fund. Forum leaders encouraged greater integration and participation of New Caledonia in the Forum region and endorsed the continuing monitoring role of the ministerial committee.

The Forum also acts as a conduit for what is effectively a subgroup, the MSG. Wamytan, the MSG representative at the time, secured the inclusion in the 2001 Nauru Forum Communiqué of a reference to Noumea's hosting of a summit meeting of the MSG in July that year. In an attachment to the 2003 Auckland Communiqué, the MSG leaders, 'noted with concern the lack of implementation of certain provisions of the Noumea Accord, in particular the electoral process and issues relating to New Caledonia's referendum process'. They noted the planned visit by the Forum Ministerial Committee the following year, and urged it to focus on these two issues.

In 2005, after the 2004 Forum Ministerial Committee's visit to New Caledonia, the Madang Forum Commúniqué welcomed the high degree of political will from all stakeholders in the implementation of the Noumea Accord. But it also endorsed the committee's 'continuing role in monitoring the affairs of the territory' and in encouraging closer regional engagement (Madang Forum Communiqué 2005). A Forum visit has not taken place since 2004.

The MSG sent its own visiting mission to Noumea in 2010, a mission that was critical of some aspects of implementation of the Accord (see Melanesian Spearhead Group, above).

More recently, Forum leaders have made clear their ongoing concern about resolving the status of New Caledonia. At the same time as he was seeking New Caledonia's full membership of the MSG in late 2009 and early 2010, Gomès also pressed for its full membership of the PIF (*Flash d'Océanie* 19 January 2010). In response, at their August 2010 summit, Forum leaders, specifically referring to New Caledonia's wish for full membership, noted that the Noumea Accord 'self-determination' process itself would resolve the question of New Caledonia's international standing, and pointedly referred to further engagement, including by a visiting Forum mission, which as noted, had not taken place since 2004. The Forum 'welcomed the continuing interest of French Polynesia and Wallis and Futuna to deepen their engagement with the Forum' (Pacific Islands Forum Communiqué 5 August 2010). The 2011 and 2012 Forum Communiqués made no mention of New Caledonia's interest in full membership, notwithstanding the French State having expressed its support publicly only a few weeks before the

2011 Forum. Minister for Overseas France, Marie-Luce Penchard had supported the formal request by New Caledonian President Harold Martin at a meeting of ambassadors to countries adjoining the French Overseas collectivities (*Flash D'Océanie* 8 September 2011).

For its part, Australia has distinguished itself from Pacific island members of the Forum by supporting the full membership of New Caledonia in the Forum (Rudd–Juppé press statement 11 September 2011 and DFAT Media Release 13 October 2010). But for the Forum, the real test of French intentions, and the long-term status of the French entities, will be the post-Noumea Accord outcome in New Caledonia.

Pacific Islands Forum advocates self-determination in French Polynesia

As the date of the last French nuclear test recedes, the 2004 election of pro-independence leader Temaru as president of French Polynesia, and perceived French efforts to frustrate his leadership since, keep alive a regional focus on developments in that collectivity. Temaru has shown a willingness to exploit his longstanding personal links with Forum leaders to maintain pressure on the French State (see Chapter 5).

The PIF has underlined the importance of self-determination in its consideration of French Polynesia. French Polynesia's admission as an observer had to await its constitutional review, and only occurred in 2004 once statutory change had been put in place (see the 2003 Auckland Forum Communiqué, in which leaders noted constitutional developments in French Polynesia and agreed to pursue a visit there the following year). After Temaru's election in May 2004, and the ensuing uncertainty and then outright frustration at the result, the Forum's response was careful. The August 2004 Forum Communiqué expressed leaders' welcome to French Polynesia as an observer 'in its own right', and their support for French Polynesia's right to self-determination; and pointedly encouraged it and France to seek 'an agreed approach on how to realise French Polynesia's right to self-determination'. Moreover, leaders asked the chair to convey their views to French Polynesia and France, and called for the secretary-general to report on 'developments in respect of French Polynesia's progress towards self-determination'. In 2005, the Forum noted the secretariat's report on French Polynesia, again in the context of the entity's 'progress to self-determination' (Madang Communiqué 2005), i.e., at no time did the Forum judge that French Polynesia had attained self-determination.

At the 2006 Forum summit, Temaru raised the issue of re-inscription of French Polynesia on the UN's list of non-self governing territories, to which the French responded by publicly saying French Polynesia already had the potential for self-determination (see Chapter 5). It was at this summit that the Forum gave associate status to French Polynesia (along with New Caledonia). Temaru once again called for Forum support for re-inscription of French Polynesia at the 2007 Forum summit, also calling for a 'Tahiti Nui' Accord, along the lines of the Noumea Accord of New Caledonia. Doubtless because of the constantly alternating leadership between pro-France groups and the pro-independence Temaru, the 2007, 2008 and 2009 Forum Communiqués make no mention of French Polynesia's political issues. The 2010 Communiqué welcomed French Polynesia's continuing interest in deepening its engagement with the Forum, after referring to New Caledonia's self-determination process under the Noumea Accord. Once again, in 2011, the Forum leaders 'recalled their 2004 decision to support the principle of French Polynesia's right to self-determination. They reiterated their encouragement to French Polynesia and France to seek an agreed approach on how to realise French Polynesia's right to self-determination' (Auckland Communiqué 2011). The 2012 Communiqué repeated this language, noting that the election of a new French government 'opened fresh opportunities for a positive dialogue between French Polynesia and France on how best to realise French Polynesia's right to self-determination' (Rarotonga Communiqué 2012).

Australia was silent on the issue until very recently, when it enunciated a public position, again, like that on New Caledonia's membership of the Forum which was slightly different to that of Forum members. Marles made a rare comment on the question of French Polynesian independence on 17 April 2012, interestingly on the eve of French presidential elections. Responding to a call by Temaru for Australia's support for French Polynesia's independence, Marles referred to Australian support for the Forum's position that French Polynesia had a right to self-determination. But he said Australia 'very much' supported France's role in the South Pacific and would 'follow France's lead about how the process should play out best in French Polynesia'. He said that French Polynesia was not ready for self-determination yet (Marles 2012).

The PIF's approach to the French collectivities is therefore ambiguous, and indications are that its hesitations arise from the inconclusive state of self-determination in the French entities, and discomfort with what it sees as France's continued colonial presence. Just as Forum leaders were not swayed by the simple Flosse-led public relations program of the 1980s, but awaited concrete policy change (cessation of nuclear tests in 1996 and the conclusion of the Noumea Accord in 1998) before they responded to French overtures, so they are waiting for resolution of the long-term status of the French entities before welcoming them as full-fledged equals in relevant regional political bodies (PIF, MSG) (argued in Fisher 2010b). The Forums treatment of the French entities, separately to the dialogue arrangement with France, suggests that the Forum would not want to see a situation develop where the French Pacific entities' participation becomes a guise for French participation. The Forum is kept informed about the statutory evolution in French Polynesia, and has recognised, by keeping Wallis and Futuna at a different observer level, that the latter is in a category of its own

This suggests that the PIF, the MSG, and the UN Decolonisation Committee, while relatively dormant in recent years on the French collectivities, maintain ongoing monitoring processes which could be activated if necessary to defend particular collectivity interests and focus international attention on any issues.

France 'in' or 'of' the Pacific: Ongoing ambiguity

A strand of debate amongst academics, related to France's desire as a global power to be present in the Pacific, has been that of whether France is simply 'in' the Pacific, or whether it is also, or should be, 'of' the Pacific (a debate more fully explored in Fisher 2012a). The distinction is not merely semantic, but goes to the heart of how France wants to be seen in the region, and in the world. While there is little doubt that, by virtue of its sovereign collectivities, France is 'in' the region, academic discussion has focused on whether it, or even its collectivities, can or should be more 'of' or 'from' (the French *de* means both) the region.

Jean-Marie Tjibaou gave France the benefit of the doubt. He told Jacques Lafleur, pro-France leader, in a televised panel discussion in 1983 that a big difference between Lafleur's people and the Kanaks was that 'We are from here and nowhere else, you are from here but also from somewhere else' (TV 5 Panel Discussion 1983; Fraser 1990b; Cordonnier 1995a, 25). He appears to concede that the pro-France Caldoches were indeed from or 'of' the Pacific.

The question came under discussion at the height of regional opposition to France's nuclear testing in French Polynesia, a time when France's assertion of its presence in the South Pacific became a shrill. Régis Debray, speaking as Secretary-General of France's High Council for the Pacific in 1987, demanded that France's right 'as a member of the Pacific family, on an equal footing [to other Pacific states], be recognised' (Chesneaux 1987a, 1). At the same time, Hervé Coutau-Bégarie, while noting that France's Pacific entities returned little revenue to the motherland, underlined that a principal benefit was that they '*allowed France to be present in the Pacific*' (1987. 286).

While Jean Chesneaux acknowledges the undisputed sovereignty of France in the Pacific, its rights over extensive Exclusive Economic Zones (EEZ) there and its permanent presence in its collectivities, he noted that this seemed inconsistent with its commitment to nuclear deterrence, which was at odds with Pacific policies of a nuclear free Pacific. While nuclear testing ensured France's status as a nuclear power, he notes that it did not make it a *Pacific* nuclear power (Chesneaux 1987b,131). He ascribes to France a motivation that was first and foremost political, not economic, given the enormous expense of exploiting the nickel resource, and the relatively small percentages of trade with Australia and the region (French commercial interests were worth less than three per cent in Australia and one per cent of New Zealand markets in 1983). He refers to the irony of France's global nuclear strategy, with its objectives defined thousands of kilometers away, being based on a technical presence in the Pacific, in 'splendid isolation'. He questions the reigning ideas France adduced about the Pacific: that the Pacific was the centre of the world, the technological Pacific myth (nodules, space centres, aquaculture all in foreign or multinational hands), the Pacific as a theatre of Soviet–US confrontation, French–Anglo rivalry, and peaceful island communities subject to the covetous greed of Australia and New Zealand; all of which, according to Chesneaux, were incoherent myths of the mid 1980s (1987b, 208–13). He suggests that this idea of the Pacific did not reflect the reality, a reality France did not want to confront at the time.

While depicting France as an outsider in the region, Chesneaux notes that it was nonetheless a longstanding outsider and, as such, had an ongoing role in the region particularly in the provision of aid (1987a, 17). Indeed, because France is 'in' but not 'of' the Pacific, one could say that France needed to do more than others to provide development assistance. (And, as noted, its record so far has been modest.)

Even after the Matignon Accords were in place, and before the resumption of nuclear testing in the Pacific, regional analysts were drawing the distinction of France being 'in' as opposed to 'of' the Pacific.

In his brief but comprehensive paper on France and the South Pacific island countries, Stephen Bates clearly sees France as an outsider. As in the past, he believes France's approach would primarily be dictated by its national interests, and its interests within Europe. Crucial decisions about the South Pacific would continue to be made on the other side of the globe. He warns about this, noting that 'in any conflict between its national security interests in Europe and regional interest in the South Pacific, the former will inevitably take precedence' (1990, 137). Because of this, France could do and say things that seemed incomprehensible to people in the Pacific. Bates uses the example of France during the vexed 1980s, telling the Pacific island states to stay out of its internal affairs over New Caledonia and French Polynesia, and yet seeing no inconsistency in sending agents to New Zealand to attack a ship in its harbour.

Myriam Dornoy-Vurobaravu begins her 1994 volume *Perceptions of France in the South Pacific* with the observation that France was 'essentially a European power and partner with expertise, not a Pacific country' (1994, 1). She proceeds to illustrate this by examples of Gallicisms, including citing the French Minister for Co-operation in 1975 saying that France must be present everywhere in the world, 'where her thinkers' genius has given her a place without any relation to her demography or resources'; President Valéry Giscard d'Estaing saying 'France is what is best'; President François Mitterrand referring to 'this indefinable genius' of France; and, Charles de Gaulle: 'our action aims at linking objectives, which, because they are French, answer the needs of all men'. Régis Debray is once again cited as applying this kind of thinking to the Pacific, saying in 1986 'To demilitarise the Pacific would deprive it of Francophonie' (Dornoy-Vurobaravu 1994, 1–3). Dornoy-Vurobaravu described Australia as considering itself as a Pacific country, and considering France as an external power (15).

Isabelle Cordonnier took the debate further, writing in 1995 that, while the French collectivities themselves were seen by Pacific island states as part of the region, the *métropole* was not. Taking the cue from Tjibaou's words to Lafleur in 1983, she notes that in South Pacific eyes, you are an insider if you come from there and nowhere else, and that by dint of geography at least, Australia and New Zealand were from the Pacific and, therefore, 'legitimate' Pacific countries (Cordonnier 1995a, 25). Cordonnier sees such differences as explaining some of the critical ambiguities in French policy, for example, how it could support nuclear testing in the region as an instrument of France's *grandeur* and status as a middle global power, in the face of negative perceptions in the region based on fear that testing would provoke a spiral of terror in case of nuclear war (1995a, 20).

The old Gallic–Anglo Saxon distinction often made by France was seen as a factor forever condemning it to being an outsider. In 1998, Nic Maclellan wrote of France's tendency to attribute opposition to it and its policies, variously to Australian and New Zealand's own imperialist ambitions, or even to a 'conspiracy' of customary law of the Pacific islands and the Biblical morality of the London missionaries (Maclellan and Chesneaux 1998). French Admiral Antoine Sanguinetti in 1985 wrote that France's Pacific presence was motivated simply by remaining in the region after the British had left (Sanguinetti 1985, 32). Today it is common for French officials and longstanding French settlers in New Caledonia to dismiss the rest of the Pacific as 'Anglo-Saxon'.

Maclellan sees this kind of defensiveness by France as ignoring the sense of regionalism, of belonging to the South Pacific, that made the settler states in

Australia and New Zealand part of the region, as much as France remained 'an outsider' (Maclellan and Chesneaux 1998, 194). In 2005, he commented that the 'sense of belonging — of looking to the skies, seeing the Southern Cross, and feeling at home — underlies much of the regional opposition to France's nuclear policy', noting this emotion against 'outsiders' from Paris rang just as true in Australia and New Zealand as Pacific countries, as in the islands (Maclellan 2005e, 365). Himself a longstanding opponent to nuclear testing in the Pacific, Maclellan describes regional opposition to nuclear testing as not so much due to quantitative measures of distance but to a qualitative political and cultural unity that had developed in the region. The formation of the PIF showed that this unity was largely cemented as a response to the dissonant French approach. Maclellan sees it as impossible for France, after nuclear testing, to be anything other than an outsider: 'After Mururoa, France can intervene in Pacific affairs, can make a valuable contribution. But it cannot be part of the region — it can only participate from outside the region, as others do ... *France can no longer pretend to be a power of the Pacific, but must act as a power in the Pacific*' (my italics; 1998, 240). In 2005 he wrote that the nuclear issue was not closed, with continuing issues such as dumping of waste; passage of waste ships; uranium mining; testing of missile defence satellite systems threatening the multilateralism of space; and, issues over the long-term effects of past nuclear testing, where French positions were at odds with those of the Pacific (2005e, 365).

Another Australian analyst, Graeme Dobell, when writing in 2007 of China's activities in the region, lumped France along with China and Japan as external powers or outside players who acted as though they wanted a stake in the region (2007, 9). One prominent Australian think tank in 2009 made tentative plans to convene a regional conference on outside powers in the Pacific, specified as France, China and Japan. The perception is, therefore, strong.

Nathalie Mrgudovic, in her major 2008 work on France in the Pacific, notes that while France claimed to have been 'of' the Pacific until the end of the 1980s, France has since pursued a more nuanced approach of claiming simply to be 'in' the Pacific (2008, 37), while working for the integration of its entities 'in *their* region' (her italics, 240). She notes the view of the Pacific islands states that France was not 'of' the region (360) and also that, in the context of the RAMSI force, France was an 'extra-regional' power (314).

Former Prime Minister Michel Rocard writes in his preface to Mrgudovic's work that France had moved from the detested colonising power that detonated bombs in the Pacific to a status more like a 'big sister' to the region, rejecting arbitrary dominations, accompanying 'its former territories' in their progress towards autonomy much to the 'relief' of the bigger powers Australia and New Zealand (13–14). He similarly exaggerates the reaction of regional states, saying that the PIF, which was explicitly created to shun France in the region, had become one 'of the firmest defenders and even seekers of our presence' (15). This idea of being a big sister to the region continues a certain ambiguity about its role: France wanting to project itself as one of the family, but ever conscious of its larger power status.

Perceptions that France is not 'of' the region are not immutable. It is within the power of France, if it so chooses, to change the perception that it is an outsider to the region. For example, in 2008, Maclellan analysed one of the ongoing issues, compensation over the health of those affected by nuclear testing, in terms very damaging to France (pointing out that France, while professing to be compensating for damages, had written legislation which excluded large numbers of potential beneficiaries, see Maclellan 2008a). But in April 2009, France announced compensation measures for those whose health had been affected by its testing in the Pacific, potentially covering 150,000 former workers, and on favourable terms which removed the onus on the worker to prove cause. Chapter 8 examines areas where France might address aspects of its regional involvement.

When viewed against the current and continuing motivation of France to retain its Pacific collectivities, i.e., being able to claim to be a sovereign indigenous power in affairs affecting the Atlantic, Caribbean, Pacific and Indian Oceans, and indeed as the only such European power, representing 'tropical Europe' (Aldrich and Connell 1989, 164 and see Chapter 7), it is important for France to continue to work to alter the widely shared perception amongst non-French and French analysts alike, that it is an outsider in the region, so that it truly can project itself partly as a Pacific power. France appears to be addressing this issue by repeatedly claiming that it wants its *collectivities* to engage more in the region, perhaps seeing its collectivities as proxies for its own interests (a prospect hardly likely to be welcomed by neighbouring Pacific island states), but, as discussed earlier, without giving them the wherewithal to participate effectively in their own right in the region. In this area as in many others, however, it may be that France prefers a certain ambiguity in its position.

Conclusion

In the 1990s and early 2000s, France has directed considerable diplomatic energy towards improving its standing in the Pacific. It has done this first, by developing its own range of regional and relevant international links, conducting regular summit meetings between French and Pacific island leaders; becoming, selectively, engaged in the UN Decolonisation Committee; holding regular annual meetings of its senior regional representatives; and, expanding defence co-operation links. France has increasingly drawn senior Australians into this network of activity, or hitched itself onto existing Australian and New Zealand initiatives (such as fisheries surveillance and coral reef protection), boosting the impact at very little cost. Thus, for example, Defence Minister Hervé Morin, visiting the region in 2008, is cited by *Flash d'Océanie* on 15 September 2008, as saying 'the two main Pacific powers are Australia and France'.

Second, France has said it wants its own Pacific collectivities to participate in the region, in both the SPC and the PIF, and some other CROP organisations, albeit without providing them the training, regular networking and travel, and resources they need to do so effectively. It is encouraging them to work more closely together.

Third, France has funded regional activities, although at an extremely modest level, primarily through the SPC, the PIF and its small, and decreasing, South Pacific Fund.

Finally, France has been a major player in developing EU links with the region, seeking, as Karis Muller describes it, to 'Europeanise' its geopolitical ambitions in the Pacific (Muller 2010, 13). Once again, the results have been mixed (and analysed more fully in Fisher 2012c). Its own collectivities have an ambiguous view of their unique EU connection, largely stemming from their geographic isolation and local preoccupations and sensitivities, thereby leaving to France the shaping of EU activity in the region. In this context, some of the privileges that France has won for the collectivities, within the EU, have been perceived as dubious: their ability to vote in the European parliament is seen as irrelevant, and carrying risky reciprocal consequences in terms of voting rights on their territory; freedom of movement, albeit not completely reciprocal, is seen as risking influxes of Europeans competing with locals for jobs, thereby heightening immigration concerns; economic EU access privileges have limited value given the hold of French custom and capture of the market; pressure to introduce the Euro is seen as a backward step by pro-independence groups, particularly in New Caledonia; and, access to EU development co-operation is limited by the very prosperity the French collectivities enjoy. Dealing with all of this locks the French collectivities into the European system, crowding out the effect of tentative forays into integration within the Pacific region, whatever France's rhetoric promoting regional 'insertion'. One benefit from the local perspective is the recourse the French collectivities have, through the EU association, to EU mediation and political pressure agencies such as the EU parliament and the Human Rights Court. As the successful EU Human Rights Court decision on the restricted electorate for New Caledonia has shown, these instruments are potentially useful for the collectivities in pursuing grievances against the French State.

The EU's direct engagement with Pacific island countries has also been mixed. While funding pledges sound impressive, effective implementation on the ground does not have a good record, and has been geared through bilateral and other initiatives, rather than the regional organisations such as the SPC (though Fisher 2012c, 22 notes a shift in 2010). EU attempts at replacing ACP aid arrangements with economic partnerships have similarly foundered on their inconsistency with other regional ventures and arrangements, such as PACER and PICTA, which are intrinsically not attractive to France or the French entities. Whether these activities are the result of well intentioned but misdirected largesse, or efforts to secure Pacific island co-operation away from existing regional activity, is not clear (and this question is addressed in Fisher 2012c).

The broader response by Pacific island state leaders to France's efforts has not been one of unalloyed enthusiasm. The UN Decolonisation Committee, PIF and MSG — all of whom have overlapping Pacific island memberships — maintain a watching brief on the implementation of the Noumea Accord in New Caledonia. While the PIF has so far stopped short of formally calling for re-inscription of French Polynesia in the UN Decolonisation Committee, its summits have underlined the importance of France and local leaders agreeing to work out self-determination measures, and have provided an opportunity for French Polynesian President Temaru to vent his frustrations about his quashed leadership, and to renew his calls for re-inscription of French Polynesia in the UN decolonisation system.

Just as regional leaders waited for significant policy change (ceasing nuclear testing and negotiation of the Noumea Accord in New Caledonia) from the colonial French power before accepting the French Pacific entities as guests into their Forum, so they are likely to await the outcome of a post-Noumea Accord future in New Caledonia, and democratic handling of instability in French Polynesia, before truly welcoming the French entities as equal partners within their own political organisations. From the regional perspective, as much as for France and its three Pacific entities, New Caledonia has become the pre-eminent French Pacific collectivity, and outcomes in French Polynesia will depend increasingly on solutions in New Caledonia.

The next chapter will examine France's changing motivations guiding its policies, before turning to security risks that may present to the region, along with identifying areas of further regional engagement and possible alternative outcomes in New Caledonia.

Part III — France in the Pacific: Present and future

7. French motivations in the Pacific

France has sought, quietly, to play a greater role in the region, including through maintaining stability in its collectivities and contributing to selected regional activities. It has increasingly sought to pursue this role in tandem with Australia. For its part, Australia has been a willing partner. Australia could rely on the peaceful administration of the French Pacific entities as it grappled with serious governance shortcomings in the Melanesian arc, from Papua New Guinea and Fiji, to Solomon Islands and even a fragile Vanuatu. French military assets have enabled regional burden-sharing in surveillance and emergency assistance across vast areas of the South Pacific. So, an important question for Australia, and for the stability of the region, is: will France stay in the Pacific and if so, why, and how?

There has been very little specific public articulation of French policy on these questions. Chapter 4 referred to institutional factors in Paris working against a coherent strategic approach. As in most key areas of France's presence in the Pacific throughout history, ambiguity is rife. In 2000, a survey of the French overseas presence stated baldly that 'the position of the French government *vis-à-vis* the overseas territories is not always clear' (Doumenge et al 2000, 207).

Just as so often occurred in the past, today France's European and domestic priorities continue to dominate its approach to its Pacific collectivities. Senior French officials note the overriding priority of preoccupations within metropolitan France and Europe, and variously ascribe State action relating to the Pacific collectivities as based on reflex and past approaches, as linked solely to statutory requirements, or as arising simply from the duty to protect French settlers abroad (Personal communications Paris April 2008 and Noumea March 2009).

Pointers to France's continuing motivations in the Pacific are evident in its past motivations, and statements made by the government of Nicolas Sarkozy about its approach to its overseas territories generally, and its practice and policy in the Pacific.

Past motivations

'La grandeur'

As noted in earlier chapters, France's early ventures into the Pacific were based on national prestige and *grandeur* (greatness), to establish its ascendancy as a global power, which was originally based on a quest for knowledge and wealth, accompanied by a competitive objective for its cultural influence to prevail (*rayonnement* and *mission civilisatrice*, or cultural expansion and the civilising mission) particularly over that of Britain. By the late eighteenth and throughout the nineteenth century, there was also a logistical need to support its missionaries and residents and provide *points de relâche* (provision and supply stops) for the presence of its navy; and a temporary motivation in the nineteenth century to relocate its convicts. For the most part, economic or commercial gains were secondary motivators. Charles-Robert Ageron (1978) argues that business interests were notable more for their absence than presence in French colonial adventures to the twentieth century).

For most of this time, too, France was affected by losses of territory in Europe, particularly in the nineteenth century, and sought by its overseas empire to make up for these losses. Chapter 2 shows that this kind of thinking persisted into the twentieth century, after the two world wars and also after its loss of Algeria and Indochina, which shaped its approach to New Caledonia.

At this time an important, but less tangible, motivation was what Robert Aldrich describes as 'an effort to give France a stake in the region and a bet on later uses of the possessions', given the region's potential for the future — its 'strategic centrality' (1990, 32 and 334). Nathalie Mrgudovic describes this as a 'will to be present' ('*une volonté de présence*') rather than a policy of conquest (2008, 73). Hervé Coutau-Bégarie notes the importance for France of simply being present by virtue of its Pacific entities, despite the lack of revenue they brought for France (1987, 286).

Coutau-Bégarie's writings provide some insight into longstanding French beliefs, which continue to inform its approach to the region. He emphasises the preoccupation of France with providing a Gallic leavening to the predominant Anglo-Saxon presence. This was extrapolated from Britain towards Australia, to the point of accusing Australia of being jealous of France. He enumerates instances where Australia had allegedly sought to stymie the French presence: in 1918, apparently succeeding in ensuring France did not get any German islands in the reallocation of colonial possessions; alleged efforts to 'relieve' France of New Caledonia in 1945 and alleged Australian efforts to erase signs of the French presence on Vanuatu's independence in 1980 (1987, 287). This kind of thinking was behind the concerns of Charles de Gaulle's London-based supporters in 1941, to get rid of Governor Henri Sautot, who had worked so assiduously to sustain a loyal pro-de Gaulle New Caledonia, but who had done it in concert with Australia and the Americans, and was thereby suspect (Chapter 1).

Logistical bases and strategic denial

Aldrich describes the strategic motivators for France as changing in the nineteenth century, from supply points for its merchant navy in the 1840s, to coaling stations for steamships in the 1880s and, in the early twentieth century, to airfields for transpacific aviation in the 1930s (1990, 334), to which could be added naval support as World War II approached. Generally, as the nineteenth century gave way to the twentieth, imperial Pacific powers were motivated more by strategic factors in a global context, and focused more on the ocean than on the islands themselves (Alexander 2001, on Japan).

During the world wars the Pacific possessions were seen by European powers, including France, as important assertions of sovereignty and logistical bases from which to defend it. Moreover, during World War II, and throughout the Cold War, France, along with the Western allies, saw its Pacific possessions as an important bulwark from which to keep out hostile powers (for example Guillaud 2003, Henningham 1992, 222). Thus France saw itself, along with the United States, as the principal balance to unwanted Soviet intrusion into the region. Jean Chesneaux sketched in polemical terms the tendency of France to 'only realise its destiny in the Pacific through an adversary which it demonised' (Chesneaux and MacLellan 1992, 91). Again, commercial factors were secondary (Guillaud 2003).

French Polynesia and the independent nuclear deterrent

By the middle of the twentieth century, an initial postwar impulse to free their dependencies gave way to a determination to retain them, albeit within a more democratic framework. As Chapter 1 shows, de Gaulle foresaw, early in World War II, the role of France's overseas empire in bolstering its flagging prestige. As France under de Gaulle sought to build its own self-reliant defence capabilities after its humiliating experiences during the two world wars, the fundamental importance of the nuclear deterrent, the *force de frappe*, meant it was vital to retain testing grounds that were isolated from metropolitan France. Its fevered efforts to retain Algeria, in part for this purpose, failed. These traumatic events underpinned the strength of France's determination to retain the French Polynesian testing site and to continue testing well into the closing years of the twentieth century, despite regional and international opposition.

The coincidence of this commitment with independence demands in New Caledonia also partly explained France's obstinacy there: if New Caledonia were to become independent, it could set a poor precedent for French Polynesia, which was then the more strategically important possession. (Such is the potency of the domino effect argument that one senior New Caledonian pro-France leader as recently as March 2009 expressed his personal belief that it had been the CIA who had instigated the independence movement in New Caledonia, precisely to undermine France's nuclear testing in French Polynesia, (Personal communication March 2009). This thinking is almost incomprehensible to an Australian, or any Western ally, given US support for France as a nuclear power, notwithstanding the latter's desire to be an independent member of the nuclear club.)

France as European *'puissance mondiale moyenne'* (middle-sized world power)

In the 1980s, in an increasingly defensive mode, France made much of the global dimension of its presence. As former Prime Minister Raymond Barre said, 'whatever the cost, our overseas possessions assure us [France] of a global dimension which is fundamental to us' (Chesneaux 1992, 99). Underlying this thinking at this time was France's self-defined role as a *puissance mondiale moyenne* (middle-sized world power), a Fifth Republic concept that grew out of the 'grand design' of the Gaullist years (see Chesneaux 1991).

The importance of the French overseas presence, particularly in the Pacific, to this role was evident in publications of the Institut du Pacifique (such as Ordonnaud 1983). A seminal work of the time on the subject was a paper by French journalist Philippe Leymarie 'Les enjeux stratégiques de la crise calédonienne' ('The strategic stakes in the Caledonian crisis', *Monde diplomatique* 1985). That the work is breathtaking in its articulation of a French/Eurocentric perspective, warts and all (he describes the territorial continuity provided to France by its overseas presence in the Pacific as stretching from Australia 'in the east' to Easter Island in the 'west' (p. 3)), does not diminish the contribution Leymarie has made to enunciating French motivations in the Pacific at the time. Despite, or perhaps because of, his French chauvinist tendencies, his article is illuminating on French motivations, to the modern, non-French reader. Implicit in his paper is a justification or legitimation of the French possessions.

Related domino effect

Leymarie cites a 1985 French armed forces study stating that, at the dawn of the twenty-first century, France was meeting its 'destiny as a middle global power' by its presence in the Pacific (1985, 1 and see also Chesneaux 1987a, 4). He expands on the potential domino effect of a crisis in New Caledonia for France's possessions elsewhere (not only in the Pacific but in the Indian Ocean and beyond, specifically Guyana, Guadeloupe and Réunion, see Leymarie 1985, 1, 3). In this context, he notes that whereas the only questioning (*'contestation'*) of French power for the other overseas territories was internal, this was not the case in the Pacific, especially New Caledonia, where it was the surrounding region that questioned French rule. He cites other specific cases where external claims were being made such as to Clipperton (by Mexico) and Matthew and Hunter (by Vanuatu).

Role in defence of France and Europe

Leymarie notes the importance of the Pacific presence for the defence of France and Europe including through the leverage that France's Pacific entities provided for the Western alliance, particularly for action in advance of that of the United States, which he notes had proved circumspect on any issue in which its own interests were not directly engaged; and for maintaining a role independent of the East–West division in the Third World. The idea of the islands as advance 'aircraft carriers' or 'economic shopfronts' in the Pacific is enunciated, as launching points for penetration of regional markets, cultural *'rayonnement'* (radiation, or influence) and development co-operation as well as sovereign bases from which dissuasion or external intervention could be authorised from Paris (Leymarie 1985, 1 and 2).

In a precursor to the policies contained in France's 2008 defence white paper (see Sarkozy government policy, below), Leymarie extols the virtues of upgrading Noumea as a defence logistics base, for pre-positioning materiel rather than personnel which, he notes, could be landed there in 36 hours. He refers to the value of Noumea in protecting access from the Indian Ocean to the Pacific Ocean via the Torres Strait in the event of conflict to the north, describing it as the only alternative to sea lanes that are flanked by Indonesian and Malaysian waters (sic, given Indonesia's proximity to that strait). This access, he asserts, would be important to protect the New Caledonian nickel resource. Once again he adduces the argument of displacement: France, by its presence, prevents other powers from obtaining a foothold in the region, among which he mentions, revealingly, Australia in company with the then Union of Soviet Socialist Republics.

Exclusive Economic Zone resource base for Europe

Leymarie also refers to the foothold the Pacific presence gave France in the unexploited economic zone resources, including fisheries and minerals, in an ocean touted as the new centre of the world. He argues that it was only at the level of the European Community (EC) that this economic challenge could be met. Still, he notes that the military importance of Noumea should not be exaggerated, citing other examples where relinquishing a presence did not necessarily mean another enemy moving in (Seychelles, Mauritius, Malta, Maldives) and, indeed, asserting that to leave could better ensure a presence (*'s'en aller pour mieux rester'*, to go the better to stay) as France had done in Djibouti, Gabon, Senegal and the Ivory Coast (1985, 4). He claims that even the nickel resource would not be lost, as it would be exploited jointly and 'France would share the revenue with any new state' as its commercial interests made this worthwhile. In any case, he notes that France was concentrating its search for metallurgic nodules more on Clipperton, than elsewhere in its territories at the time.

Post-1990s French policy to retain Pacific collectivities within France

Recent history (see Chapter 2 and 5) shows that successive French administrations in Paris have exercised considerable innovation and ingenuity in developing solutions for the Pacific collectivities, even by changing the French constitution, confirming that they want them to stay with France. They are prepared to underwrite the considerable financial costs of maintaining sovereignty. At the same time, New Caledonia has replaced French Polynesia in primary strategic importance.

French Polynesia

Chapter 5 showed that, in French Polynesia, there was no question of French departure so long as the nuclear testing program had not been completed, which occurred in 1996. But, since then, France has paid a premium to ensure continued sovereignty there by extending its compensation payments to French Polynesia well into the future. It has also invested political energy in statutory change and exerted political pressure to entrench its interests.

As in New Caledonia, France has repeatedly wielded the economic carrot, warning that payments could be at risk if pro-France forces lost out. This threat is the more effective given that French Polynesia has few resources and would be unlikely to survive on its own without French aid. Pro-France groups have frustrated the repeated election of pro-independence forces since 2004. The French State has so far stopped short of extending to French Polynesia the new key powers it has given to New Caledonia (the ability to legislate, special citizenship benefits, and the promise of a vote on independence). Thus France retains leverage over local parties to maintain French sovereignty.

Ascendance in importance of New Caledonia

By the late 1990s, with the end of nuclear testing and the agreement of the Noumea Accord, the relative dominance and importance of the two French Pacific collectivities was inverted, with New Caledonia setting the pace in acquiring increased autonomy (Chapters 4 and 5).

Part of the evolving solution for New Caledonia from 1988 included the development of its rich nickel resource, in ways that were designed to distribute the benefits more equitably to Kanaks and European New Caledonians alike. The prospect of petroleum reserves in New Caledonia's Exclusive Economic Zone (EEZ) heightened the stakes. The commitment to an eventual vote on New Caledonia's future status was made in an innovative transition formula, through the Matignon and Noumea Accords, to buy more time for the French State to build confidence and economic prosperity such that few would wish to take on the responsibilities of independence outside the French republic.

But the day of reckoning is yet to come, and developments to 2018 will be critical in a peaceful ongoing resolution of differences in New Caledonia.

Generally, there has also been an undeniable element of the legacy of history by which France, having held on to its Pacific possessions, had to some extent little choice but to implement its statutory commitments to them. In Wallis and Futuna, for example, there has been little push for change (indeed, the entity still operates on its 1961 statute), and in both New Caledonia and French Polynesia the pro-independence forces have been shown to have used their public stances to pressure France for more support for their groupings at times. But, overall, France has maintained a continuing objective to retain the three Pacific collectivities within the French fold. Did France's motivations change from the 1990s?

France's motivations post 1990s

Continuing strategic importance of France's Pacific presence

While the nuclear deterrent remains a bedrock of French defence policy (see, for example, France's 2008 Defence White Paper), the suspension of the nuclear testing program in French Polynesia altered the contribution that the Pacific entities make to France's global place. France's foothold in the Pacific continued to deliver strategic benefits, but the role of the Pacific is now more indirect in its relation to France. Retaining a presence in the Pacific returns a boost to the strategic weight of France (as part of the chain of Overseas France possessions); real and potential commercial benefits; a negative benefit related to preventing critical public opinion domestically and internationally, as had occurred in the past; and, a claim to new democratic legitimacy and protection of its nationals abroad. Each of these elements will be examined in turn, before considering the approach of the Sarkozy government to the French Pacific collectivities.

Ballast for France's European and global role

France continues to be motivated by its sense of itself as a global power with special privileges and responsibilities. Its leaders no longer use the phrase *puissance moyenne mondiale* in a world where the emergence of China reduces France's status to that of a small power, rather than a medium-sized power. Still, France wants to retain its status as one of the elite five Permanent Members of the United Nations (UN) Security Council, at a time when the composition of that group is under debate. France's presence in every corner of the globe, therefore, remains important. As Jacques Chirac has so succinctly said, 'Without the departments and territories overseas, France would be only a little country' (in Aldrich and Connell 1989, 148).

In the mid 1990s and early 2000s, France was seen as maintaining its overseas possessions to add to its strategic weight (see Firth in Howe 1994, 302: 'France resisted, and continues to resist, the decolonisation of its Pacific territories, because their loss would undermine France's claim to be a world power and create a gap in the global string of French military installations'; Doumenge et al 2000, 205: 'the French overseas collectivities give France a listening post in all the large regions of the world'; Berman 2001, 24: 'Continued presence in New Caledonia projects France's status as a global power').

Elements of Chesneaux's analysis, written in 1987, remain true today. He notes that France is the only power, apart from the United States, capable of establishing military bases worldwide and a communications network that is firmly based on its sovereign possessions including Noumea and Papeete (1987a, 5). A major new listening station was opened near Noumea's international airport, Tontouta, in 2004. The EU's 2009 Briefing Paper on Military Installations lists France's military assets in its Pacific entities (EU Parliament 2009).

Isabelle Cordonnier, in 1995, talked about French military motivations of nuclear dissuasion, exploitation of space; freedom of air and naval mobility; a strategic perception that the presence in the Pacific balanced France's presence in the Atlantic; and the role of the Pacific territories in the *rayonnement* (influence) of France in its global maritime domain, with its vast EEZ deriving from them, its ports, bases and business interests. She also referred to the 'vacuum filling' objective of preventing colonisation of the Pacific by hostile Asian states (1995a,

112). It is partly this concept of denial to outsiders that underpinned the 1990s diplomatic effort to improve France's image in the region as a constructive partner (see Chapter 6).

As late as 2003, Paul de Deckker wrote (2003b, 2) that France went against the current in maintaining its Pacific collectivities to preserve its strategic mining and military interests, the interests of its French nationals, and a nuclear assurance of national defence in French Polynesia.

There was some official acknowledgement of the strategic importance of the French entities in the Pacific. In 2003, the then Minister for Overseas France, Brigitte Girardin, wrote that 'our territorial collectivities of New Caledonia, Polynesia and Wallis and Futuna enable our country to be present in this ocean' (in Cadéot 2003, 7). In his preface to Mrgudovic's 2008 work on France in the South Pacific, former Prime Minister Michel Rocard referred to the South Pacific as a place where France faced the classic contradiction between its 'generous' principles and 'its interests as a great power that it claimed at every opportunity' (Mrgudovic 2008, 13).

Since 2007, Sarkozy's administration has continued to see Overseas France as key to France's global status, which he has described in terms reminiscent of de Gaulle's vision for France (see Sarkozy government policy, below).

Strategic denial/balance

Since Cordonnier wrote of 'vacuum filling' by France in 1995, China has become more engaged in the South Pacific, beginning with competitive chequebook flashing with Taiwan, but also including aid and other investment activities targeted at securing valued fisheries and minerals resources, and simply a strategic presence (see Hanson 2008, especially on China's $US150 million annual aid program; Dobell 2007, on its destabilising effects; Firth in de Deckker and Faberon, 2008, 174, on practical aid and other activity by China including building a headquarters for the Melanesian Spearhead Group (MSG) in Vila, and sending workers to staff a Chinese-owned mine in Papua New Guinea). France retains control in an area that is currently the object of the attention of a future superpower, and contributes to balancing China's presence for the Western alliance.

Stewart Firth argues it is the non-sovereign Pacific states that are of greater strategic importance than the independent Pacific states, and the French entities themselves are no exception (1989, 75). The US dependencies generally lie north of the Equator (the exceptions being the island of Jarvis, the EEZ of Micronesia and Baker Islands). For Australia, France's presence in its three Pacific entities south of the Equator arguably confers wider strategic returns than relations with the independent states, particularly when coupled with the coincidence of France's strategic interests with Australia's own (Firth 1989, 87). Waddell noted in 2008 that France shared with Australia, New Zealand, and the independent Melanesian states, 'a convergence of strategic preoccupations, notably the concern to buttress 'failed' island states and the need to protect the region from what are perceived as destabilising forces originating in Asia' (2008, 12). Australia's Parliamentary Secretary for Pacific Island Affairs, Duncan Kerr, acknowledged France's contribution in working with Australia on issues of mutual security, defence co-operation, control of illegal fishing, and other areas when he visited New Caledonia in November 2008.

By its role in strategic denial alone, France's presence returns strategic benefits not only for France, but also for the Western alliance, and most importantly for Australia. But, as history has shown, these benefits have the potential to turn into negatives should France's presence again become destabilising; for example, by virtue of opposition or dissent by a significant percentage of its local populations who could turn to unwelcome sources of external support, as they have in the past (shown for example when New Caledonia and Vanuatu turned variously to Libya and the Soviet Union, Chapter 2).

Role in supporting space technology within Europe

Part of France's role as a global middle power from the second half of the twentieth century has been its engagement in space technology. Its overseas possessions are an important element of this engagement. Guyana has been the launching site for the French *Ariadne* rocket since 1968 and, from 1975, for the European Space Agency, which co-funds the spaceport and launched the European space shuttle *Hermes*. There has long been recognition of the importance, or at least the potential importance, of a presence in the vast Pacific Ocean in the French space program. On 14 February 1986, Régis Debray, Secretary-General of the High Council for the Pacific, told *Libération* that 'the Pacific may provide opportunities for France and Europe to establish control and treatment stations for geo-stationery and circulating satellites ... the space age will raise the importance of the overseas territories' (Chesneaux 1987a, 4).

And France indeed does derive a leading role within Europe from its role in developing space technology. Apart from hosting the European satellite-launching site in Guyana, France's extensive presence in the Pacific Ocean facilitates space sensoring, monitoring and retrieval. While the Centre d'Expérimentation du Pacifique (Pacific Experimentation Centre, CEP) has closed down, useful infrastructure remains on the French Polynesian islands of Hao and Moruroa (landing strips on each, some staff and scientific monitors measuring underground movements on Moruroa, Personal communications

Noumea, March 2009; also Maclellan 2005e, 372). For example, the United States has signed an agreement with France to use the Hao landing strip for the American space shuttle (see Mrgudovic 2008, 98).

Sarkozy acknowledged the role of Overseas France in France's status as a first-rate space power (*'une puissance spatial de tout premier plan'*) in his November 2009 speech on Overseas France reform (Sarkozy 2009).

Commercial motivations

In recent years, commercial incentives for France to stay in the South Pacific, which were marginal in the past, have strengthened.

Resource base and extended EEZ

France is the second-largest world maritime nation owing to the size of its EEZ, the largest part of which derives from its Pacific collectivities (see Chapter 2 and Sarkozy 2009), with all the potential that extensive EEZ offers in unknown economic resources. While French Polynesia, by its vast extent, contributes the largest portion of EEZ to France, the importance of the EEZ extends to the tiniest element of France's sovereign claims. Mrgudovic describes France's continuing assertion of its claim over the island group of Matthew and Hunter, representing 24,000 square kilometres of EEZ, as illustrating its attachment to a strategy of territorial presence with power deriving primarily an expression from its EEZ rights (Mrgudovic 2008, 219, 261, 397). France's continued scientific research off the Clipperton Islands is another example.

While analysts no longer talk of manganese nodules, as they did in the 1980s, largely because of the continued availability of land-based minerals and the relative expense of seabed extraction, there is little doubt that the seabed is one of the earth's last unexplored frontiers. Almost a third of existing oil deposits come from undersea deposits (Mrgudovic 2008, 95). De Deckker (in Cadéot 2003, 205), notes that the EEZ was not only significant for the resources it may contain, but also in the scope it offered for scientific research and technology transfer. This is an important consideration for a country such as France, which projects itself as a world leader in science and technology. Whereas sovereignty is not a necessary condition for scientific research, it facilitates research at lower cost than such research undertaken on foreign shores. Sarkozy has acknowledged the role of Overseas France in enhancing the role of France in space and in biodiversity (Sarkozy 2009).

As for the French Pacific, François Garde refers variously to fisheries development, scientific research, space interests, new technologies, and hydrocarbons which all give increasing value to the Pacific entities, and which may be worth much more in 20 or 50 years time (2002, 67). De Deckker sees the first decades of the twenty-first century as possibly invalidating the priorities of the past, with economic gain as the major priority (in Cadéot 2003, 205). Coutau-Bégarie, as long ago as 1986, saw the EEZ and nickel resource potential as likely, in the long-term, to outweigh the costly record of the French Pacific collectivities, which were then popularly known as *'les danseuses qui coûtent cher'* (expensive dancing girls) (Coutau-Bégarie and Seurin 1986, 208).

In the Pacific, New Caledonia provides the pre-eminent interest for France, because of its nickel resource and the potential for exploitation of hydrocarbons offshore. France's interest in New Caledonia has been described as a 'geopolitical project', which assists in France's global status and access to the potentially rich seabed and resources (Rumley et al 2006, Chapter 13). As discussed in Chapter 4, New Caledonia's current nickel projects represent France's largest mining activities nationally. In December 2008, Sarkozy told the Noumea Accord signatories committee that Eramet, France's vehicle for participating in New Caledonia's nickel development, was the largest single French mining actor, and wielded strategic responsibilities for the country (*Nouvelles Calédoniennes* 11 December 2008). With global energy demands changing, signs of the presence of large, but currently unviable, hydrocarbon and natural gas reserves represent a significant potential asset.

Link with Pacific as new economic hub

More broadly, reprising the debate of the late 1800s (set out in Aldrich 1988, and see also Chapter 2), there is a view that France's presence in the South Pacific links it to the vibrant economic growth of the northern Pacific (for example, Ordonnaud 1983, Lacour 1987, who argue that the centre of the world inexorably derived from the Pacific Basin, and France's fortuitous presence gave it a chance to take its place amongst the great powers competing for influence there, 17). The idea of the importance of having a presence in this hemisphere persists, despite warnings like that of Chesneaux in 1992 about the risks of confusing the two parts of the Pacific within the fashionable concept of it as the new centre of the world (102). Girardin, then Overseas France Minister, in a forward to Pierre Cadéot's 2003 volume on the French Pacific collectivities states that they 'enable our country to be present in this ocean which has become in the twenty-first century the other Mediterranean. So the Pacific Overseas is an opportunity for France: a gangplank to other civilisations, a gateway to a dynamic economic zone and the place for innovative policies' (7).

So, for the first time, the collectivities in the Pacific represent a positive economic asset for France, notwithstanding France's considerable financial outlay there. This is of interest since, for Australia and New Zealand, 'the importance of the region in defence and security terms … far outweighs its economic importance to them' (Henningham 1992, 219). In a sense, because of these real and potential economic considerations attaching to its Pacific collectivities, France has a greater direct economic motivation than either Australia or New Zealand to be in the region.

Investment requires stability

One consequence of the ascendancy of the economic factor, particularly the importance of large-scale projects such as in nickel mining and the potential processing and exploitation of hydrocarbons, is that investors are necessary, especially in a competitive global environment; and, investors seek political and economic stability. This has injected a new element into the debates about political independence and economic dependence in the French collectivities. It has strengthened France's hand with its overseas communities, as France is better placed than any local government to provide the requisite civil stability and financial inputs. Thus, pro-France leader Jacques Lafleur frequently argued that New Caledonia needed France to negotiate big commercial deals in order to develop (Lafleur 2002; Personal communications 2002, 2009). On the other hand, in New Caledonia in particular, the new players, particularly if they come from metropolitan France, want a say in their community, and expect voting rights (Doumenge et al 2000, 207), which potentially undermines the special electoral arrangements devised to underpin ongoing stability.

France as leader of the EU in the Pacific

France's increasing provision of economic and other types of assistance to the region, and its role in leading EU contributions there, potentially increases its capacity, and that of the EU, to win supportive votes from the numerous Pacific island states in multilateral bodies, most notably the UN, on issues of interest to it. At the same time, France and Europe need to exercise this leverage carefully. As elaborated in Chapter 6, the Pacific island states are aware that EU and French engagement can be a two-edged sword (for example, France threatened New Zealand's access to EU butter markets in the wake of the *Rainbow Warrior* affair; Europe holds the purse strings over sugar with Fiji).

Public opinion

Another recent, unstated motivator for France has been the desire to ensure that its overseas Pacific presence does not become the subject of negative public opinion, either internationally or domestically. One recent senior French official said that his brief before departing for Noumea was succinct: *'pas d'ennuis'* (no problems) (Personal communication April 2008).

As noted in Chapter 2, just as French domestic policy and preoccupations have dictated the pace and direction of policy applying to the French Pacific entities, so too have negative developments in the overseas entities impacted severely on French governments. The starkest example was the effect of the Algeria debacle in bringing down the Fourth Republic government. Another is the role of the Gossanah cave affair on the French presidential elections of 1988. France's Pacific policy engaged the full force of public opinion, not only in France, but internationally, over the nuclear testing issue, the Rainbow Warrior affair, and treatment of New Caledonia, with devastating effect on France's image.

So, France does not want to have its hand again forced by domestic and world focus on what it is doing in the Pacific. On the one hand, this has motivated France to behave more responsibly in the region, but, on the other, it has reinforced a tendency if not to secrecy, at least to non-articulation, or ambiguity, of policy and a desire to avoid international attention. It has also taken firm preventative action, for example by seeking to mute Oscar Temaru's influence in French Polynesia after he raised self-determination and UN reinscription issues in the Pacific Islands Forum (PIF) (Chapter 5).

Relative disinterest of French public

Back home, historically, domestic public opinion neither focused on, nor cared about, the French overseas presence in general, and even less about the Pacific presence. Chesneaux notes that the French at home were too concerned with their own political differences and issues to worry about Overseas France, and that, in any case, France's Pacific entities received less interest and attention than Africa or Indochina (1992, 91). This is true so long as no major disturbance occurs overseas, such as the *événements* in New Caledonia; or, more recently, protests in the mid 2000s in Guadeloupe, spreading to other overseas *Départements*, about the cost of living.

Characteristic of the history of France's overseas presence has been the relatively thin spread of institutional involvement in the overseas empire. As described in Part I, France's overseas possessions were run initially by the navy (which indeed has taken a predominant role right up until the present, see Chapter 4), then by a relatively small Overseas France ministry, which persists until today. Narrow lobby groups have in the past sought to influence policy, including the oceanic lobby of the late nineteenth century. But broad media or public interest in Overseas France has been rare. Such disinterest can be explained by relative ignorance about Overseas France, but also by greater substantive interests; for example, by business people and travellers, in other parts of the world such as Asia.

More recently, René Dosière, French MP for the Aisne, with the special parliamentary role of rapporteur for the Organic Law of 1999, told the colloquium marking the 20th anniversary of the Matignon Accords that 'The National Assembly shows no interest at all in the Overseas, which corresponds to the state of metropolitan public opinion' (Regnault and Fayaud 2008, 159; also see Coutau-Bégarie and Seurin 1986, 40; Chesneaux 1987a, 9 and 1992, 144; Guillebaud 1976, 29; Victor 1990; Doumenge et al 2000, 61; Christnacht 2003, 5; Diémert in Tesoka and Ziller 2008, 239).

Public disinterest seems to apply even to the political issues and lavish expenditures on the Pacific collectivities (demonstrated by Dosière in Regnault and Fayaud 2008, 159–63; Personal communication by members of the Senate Finance Committee 2008). There is no public debate about the collectivities, even when their budgets are under consideration (one New Caledonian representative noted that he often had to remind officials presenting to the Senate Finance Committee to say something about expenditure in the Pacific collectivities, Personal communication March 2009).

Relatively low cost of French Pacific entities

Partly, the French public does not take a close interest in the overseas presence because the costs are not widely known. Moreover, within the overall context of the French budget, the costs are relatively insignificant. The budget for *all* the overseas entities is only .7 per cent of France's GDP, and only 4.6 per cent of its budget. The cost of the three South Pacific entities, totalling EUR2.65 billion ($A4.6 billion) in 2008, represented only .14 per cent of France's GDP or .95 per cent of the French State's budget (figures provided by French Senate Finances Commission September 2008).

In 2000, the costs of Overseas France were considered by some to be relatively cheap (Doumenge et al 2000, 205). Costs per head of the population in the French Pacific collectivities were lower than those per head of the population nationally (23,300 francs per overseas resident ($A6227) as opposed to 28,800 francs nationally ($A7700) in 1999); and an article in *Le Figaro*, 14 September 1999, shows that Corsica, including 'subsidies, fraud and tax exemptions', cost the French State 50 times as much (10 billion francs or $A2.6 billion) as French Polynesia (200 million francs or $A053 million) in 1999 (Doumenge et al 2000, 205).

Chapter 4 described how even reductions in excessive special payments to newcomer retirees in the French Pacific collectivities were motivated more by abuse of the system by newcomers than by a concern about the costs themselves, and these payments are only to be fully phased out by 2027.

Lack of political clout of French entities

It is argued that the Pacific escaped French domestic scrutiny partly because the population of the Pacific collectivities together represented only 20 per cent of the population of all the overseas entities of France in 1999 (Doumenge et al 2000, 61), whereas the four Overseas departments (DOMs) represented over 70 per cent . The non-continental French populations totalled only 2.157 million in the 1999 census, or a mere 3.5 per cent of the entire population of France, overseas and continental (60.9 million); and, according to Internet figures for 2006–2007, this total was even smaller: 2.12 million or 3.25 per cent of a total population of 63.2 million (see Faberon and Ziller 2007, 6). And, from these figures, the South Pacific collectivity populations represented fewer than 500,000 all together, or less than one per cent of France's overall population in either 1999 or 2006–2007.

These figures underpin the political reality that the French Pacific collectivities between them represent limited voting power in the national assembly and senate: two *députés* (MPs) and one senator each from New Caledonia and French Polynesia, and one *député* and one senator from Wallis and Futuna (of a total of 577 *députés* and 343 senators).

This disinterest meant for Doumenge et al that the future of the overseas entities was in question (2000, 61), but it could now be argued that the converse is true. As shown by their own figures, to the extent that the costs were considered, the French do not regard themselves as funding an overseas colonial presence, but rather that the collectivities are part of France. And the French do not have the Australian/Westminster tradition of extensive, broadly based public scrutiny of government costs and efficiencies. Moreover the French public is more occupied with internal mainland and European issues than the overseas possessions. There is also a general feeling that, even if the French Pacific entities were independent, they still would require French handouts (see, for example, Coutau-Bégarie 1986, 208), just as the former African colonies do.

But the lack of a public opinion does not mean that there is no potential for such an interest should things sour, as shown by the damage to France's international image over the Pacific nuclear and decolonisation issues. So it can be said that maintaining a low level of public interest in itself is a motivating factor and an objective for French administrations.

Democracy and the will of the people

With the agreement of the Noumea Accord and statutory evolution in French Polynesia, France's stated motivations began to reflect the new democratic underpinnings these processes had provided for its regional presence. France could now proudly claim, as did the Minister for DOM-TOMs, Louis Le Pensec, in 1990, that it retained its overseas territories first and foremost because it was the wish of their inhabitants to remain French (Henningham 1992, 193). But, as Stephen Henningham pointed out in the early 1990s, Le Pensec did not mention Kanak complaints about the shifts in the population, and therefore the electoral balance, against them in previous decades by government-encouraged immigration, nor that French officials and politicians had worked hard to discourage pro-independence sentiments (1992, 193). And, a few years later, Martine Piquet noted that the underlying assumption of this approach was the familiar *mission civilisatrice*: that, from a republican basis of democratic choice, the civilising mission was 'to progress according to a linear pattern towards absolute perfection and refinement', i.e., to remain French (Piquet 2000, 9–10). Just as much of its activity in the Pacific in the past was hinged upon the presence of its missionaries, France claimed it wanted to preserve and advance the interests of its nationals in the Pacific entities (de Deckker 2003b, 2, and see Protection of nationals, below). In the same vein, senior advisers on New Caledonia indicated that France would proceed to the planned referendums simply because it was statutorily bound to do so through the legal processes set up under the Noumea Accord (Personal communications Paris 2008).

Today, after the extensive modification of statutes and laws to deliver more autonomy and democracy to the two largest French Pacific entities, and continued influxes of metropolitan French, with pro-France views, into New Caledonia, the principal claim by senior French officials continues to be that France is present in the Pacific exclusively because the people of those entities want France to be there, as indicated by their votes in successive elections. This claim is made privately by senior officials, to the point of some denying any other interest in remaining in the Pacific (Personal communications Paris, April 2008 and Noumea March 2009).

But the question of remaining with France has been a vexed one, and indeed, central to political debate in both places.

In 1987, on the only occasion when the question of remaining with France was put to the people of New Caledonia since 1958, a strong boycott by pro-independence forces clouded the result (see Chapter 2). The 1988 Matignon Accords and the 1998 Noumea Accord were specifically designed to defer any referendum on the question of independence or staying with France, at least until 2014–2018.

New Caledonians did vote for what are transitional arrangements in the Matignon and Noumea Accords (see chapter 4, although only 57 per cent of the 63 per cent turnout supported the Matignon Accords; while with a turnout of three-quarters of the population, 72 per cent of them voted 10 years later to accept the Noumea Accord, but this occurred after further inflows of migrants from France and elsewhere in the French Pacific). Since then, some New Caledonians (a restricted electorate, defined precisely as set out in Appendix 1, but generally requiring 10-years residence to 1998) have voted on a proportional basis for a temporary, local, collegial government of transition in provincial elections. The majority of even these restricted electorate voters in these successive provincial elections have supported pro-France parties, but, as noted in Chapter 4, many of these pro-France parties have increasingly adopted policies shared with pro-independence partners. And 2009 provincial elections showed an overall reduction in the pro-France vote, with a clearer polarisation of the pro-independence vote in the Loyalty Islands, where the pro-France groups did not win a seat, even as the pro-independence groups won more representation than in 2004 in the mainly pro-France south (see Chapter 4).

All New Caledonians (i.e., not just a restricted electorate) have been able to vote in French national parliamentary elections (the '*législatives*') and have returned, every time, pro-France *députés* (MPs), but, in the exceptional transitional period, this can hardly be described as representative, as French officials often do in private, as a vote to remain with France. The two legislative districts returning a *député* each, both include substantial proportions of Noumea and therefore more pro-France voters (as opposed to the provincial electorates, two of which are predominantly Kanak). Moreover, in 2007 legislative elections, the pro-France R–UMP's Gael Yanno won easily in the first district (including Noumea proper and small outer islands), whereas Pierre Frogier won in the second district (which includes Noumea suburbs and the interior) with a closer margin (54 per cent as opposed to 46 per cent for his Union Calédonienne (Caledonian Union, UC) competitor Charles Pidjot).

In June 2012, for the first time, the principal pro-France party (in recent years, the R–UMP) did not win both positions. Yanno retained his seat in the first district, but the second *député* position was won by a breakaway rival pro-France group, Philipe Gomès' Calédonie Ensemble, which takes a less hardline pro-France position than the R–UMP.

In the referendum process on the status of New Caledonia to be held after 2014, there will be a broader electorate than that voting in provincial elections. In addition to the latter, i.e., those with 10-years residence to 1998, the referendum electorate will include voters with 20-years residence to 2014, i.e., those arriving in the collectivity up to 1994 as opposed to those who had arrived by 1988 (see Chapter 8 and Appendix 1). As such, that electorate may be expected to include more pro-France newcomers.

In French Polynesia too, the picture is mixed. Frequent floor-crossing and support-bartering between individuals mask the true political affiliations of elected representatives. In entity-wide votes in 2004, however, voters twice returned a leader who propounded independence, and the results were only overturned through procedural means with the complicity of France.

Protection of nationals and the demonstration effect: The 'red line' of independence

In a strand of argument related to the 'will of the people' assertion, French officials claim that France remains in order to do the right thing by its citizens. Although this contention covers all of its citizens, indigenous and otherwise, some senior players point specifically to the responsibilities of protecting longstanding French settlers. Once again, in this respect, they claim that New Caledonia remains key to continuing French motivations in the Pacific because there is a larger France-originating settler population there than elsewhere (Personal communication Paris March 2008 and also Henningham 1989, referring to the 'political ballast' of the majority settler population in New Caledonia that is not present in French Polynesia, 31).

Linked to this idea of defending the interests of its nationals, particularly its settlers, in the overseas collectivities is the idea of preserving the indivisibility of the French republic, to head off a domino effect throughout its entities. Because New Caledonia has been granted the most autonomy of France's overseas possessions, the future fate of New Caledonia is seen as having specific importance as a demonstrator effect for other French collectivities. Thus, a principal motivator for France to succeed in New Caledonia is to retain its possessions elsewhere. Specifically these include French Polynesia, which, as noted in Chapter 5, looks to New Caledonia as a model for its own status; but also Guyana, the vital launch pad for France's space program; and Mayotte (Mrgudovic notes parallels between New Caledonia and Mayotte in France's access to control of petrol-supply routes, 2008, 96).

Closer to home in metropolitan France, the demonstration effect is particularly feared for troubled Corsica. Both Stephen Bates (1990) and Aldrich and Connell (1989) referred to French concern at the implications of actions in New Caledonia for Corsica, Bates quoting then Interior Minister Charles Pasqua as describing the defence of Bastia (northern Corsica) beginning in Noumea (1990). But the domino effect operates both ways: what happens in other possessions also has an effect on the French Pacific collectivities. French handling of the riots and protests in Corsica are equally salutary for New Caledonia. The mainstream New

Caledonian newspaper *Les Nouvelles Calédoniennes*, throughout the early 2000s, regularly reported news of Ajaccio as if to remind the French reader in New Caledonia of the importance of maintaining the French presence.

The outbreak of violent protests against *la vie chère* (high cost of living associated with being tied to the French economy) in Guyana, led to similar protests in Guadeloupe, Martinique and Réunion in February and March of 2009. The speedy chain reaction throughout its West Indies territories and ultimately as far away as Réunion, in the Indian Ocean, confirmed France's fears of the contamination effect of events in one possession influencing developments in the others. In the French Pacific, after the outbreaks on the other side of the globe, arrangements were speedily set in place for local consultations to head off similar reactions. The Sarkozy government response was firm. It included clamping down on violent protests, a major reform of its provisions to Overseas France, and a clear indication of an 'unbreachable' line, that of independence (see Sarkozy government policy, below).

Sarkozy government policy

Strategic importance of Overseas France but declining interest in French Pacific

Sarkozy, elected in early 2007, took little interest in the French Pacific collectivities. He came late to formulating a policy towards Overseas France, only personally addressing the subject when trouble broke out in the French entities in the Caribbean and Réunion in 2009. As a new style of president, of a new generation and with an immigrant background, Sarkozy's views were relatively unknown. His predecessors had all held firmly to the important role of France's overseas possessions in defining the international prestige of France, from de Gaulle, Georges Pompidou, Giscard d'Estaing, and Chirac on the right, to François Mitterrand who, although from the left, had served as Overseas France minister. Sarkozy's early priorities were a special relationship with the United States, and France's role in Europe, including returning France to the high table of the North Atlantic Treaty Organisation (NATO) by rejoining the High Command. In attending to these national priorities, the strategic role of France's string of overseas possessions became clear, as the evolution of thought in official statements shows.

Contribution of Overseas France to France's international status

The early view of the Sarkozy administration about Overseas France emerged over a number of statements by his Overseas France Secretary, Yves Jégo. Speaking to a France–EU seminar in Paris in June 2008, Jégo highlighted the importance of the OCT (overseas collectivities) for Europe, through which, he said, 'Europe has become the first world maritime power' (*Flash d'Océanie* 1 July 2008). In an interview in October 2008, he said that few people understood what the overseas presence meant, for example, that it provided 80 per cent of France's biodiversity, that it made France the second largest maritime power in the world, and that France was present in the three oceans by virtue of its overseas presence. He said the overseas presence was 'an opportunity for France and for Europe in a globalised world' (*Le Parisien* 14 October 2008).

In his response to the troubles in the Caribbean territories, Sarkozy built on these statements. He made two important speeches on Overseas France, one in November 2009 and the other as a New Year message, in January 2010. In his November speech, he referred to France's status as the second maritime nation of the world with an EEZ equal to that of the United States; as a premier space and nuclear power, and one with major diplomatic influence over oceans, and unrivalled biodiversity, all owing directly to Overseas France. '*La France sans l'Outre-mer*', he said, '*ce ne serait plus la France*' (France would not be France without the Overseas France)(Sarkozy 2009). Similarly, in his January 2010 speech, he said that it was because of its overseas possessions that France was '*France des trois océans*' (France of the three Oceans). It was these possessions that contributed to France's identity, '*à notre rayonnement, à notre grandeur et à notre puissance*' ('to our influence, our grandeur and our power') and 'The inclusion of all, across the thousands of kilometers that separate us, in the same national community is one of the multiple facets of the French genius' (Sarkozy 2010a). These are the words of de Gaulle (see 1947). Sarkozy's use of them suggests that, two years into his presidency, he was convinced, as de Gaulle had been, of the role of France's overseas possessions in bolstering France's claim to international status and power.

Sovereignty reinforced: No tolerance for violence or independence

In his speeches, Sarkozy reinforced France's intention of continued sovereignty over its possessions, if necessary backed by force; and announced areas of reform, even innovation, in the governance of its various possessions, but always stopping short of independence. His November 2009 speech was designed to announce a number (137 in total) of reforms primarily targeted at the Caribbean possessions, providing for institutional change including more local participation and greater economic engagement by entities in their geographic regions. But, at the same time, Sarkozy reaffirmed that his government would not tolerate violence or independence.

In his 2009 speech, his comments were focused more on the West Indies ('To be perfectly clear, the question to be put to voters in January will be the appropriate degree of autonomy of Martinique and Guyana in the Republic, and not that of independence. I restate this very simply, but firmly: the question of independence of Martinique and Guyana will not be put. These territories are, and they will stay, French lands', Sarkozy 2009). But, in his early 2010 New Year speech to Overseas France, Sarkozy was more general. He said he was prepared to countenance a range of options for France's overseas *territories* (as opposed to collectivities, as in the Pacific), provided that the unity of the Republic was not called into question. He then noted that the French constitution allowed considerable flexibility, of which he intended to make use, with respect for the will expressed by the relevant populations, 'with only one red line which I will never accept to be breached: that of independence. *The Overseas (France) is and will remain French*' (my italics). This language, i.e., 'the Overseas', includes all French overseas possessions, including the French Pacific entities.

View of the French Pacific

Specific statements and approaches to the French Pacific territories are rare. Sarkozy's comments on the strategic role of France Overseas in the foregoing section can be expected to apply to the French Pacific as well, particularly in view of the vast expanse of the Pacific entities.

French white papers on foreign affairs (July 2008) and defence (November 2008), commissioned by Sarkozy, provide little further insight into the administration's view of the Pacific, which is surprising given France's sovereign presence there. There is no reference to the Pacific region in the foreign affairs paper and the defence white paper simply refers to changing domestic logistical dispositions within its French Pacific entities, which it treats entirely as domestic appendages (see Noumea becomes preeminent base for France's Pacific military presence, below). Apart from a general reference to Australia being a valued partner, no Pacific regional defence priorities or perspectives are identified as stemming from France's resident Pacific presence. Rather, it emphasises exclusively the priority for France of the arc stretching from Mauritania in Africa across the

Middle East to the Indian Ocean (Fisher 2008c). Indeed, the paper speaks of the *'éloignement'* or isolation of Asia, hardly the perspective of a resident Pacific nation (Défense 2008).

Chapter 4 analyses the institutional arrangements and senior appointments that Sarkozy has made, which suggest a continuation of the declining importance of structures and attention devoted to the French Pacific collectivities. Funding allocated to the small South Pacific Fund has declined (see Chapter 6). Sarkozy decided not to head the French delegation to the third Oceanic Summit, in Noumea in late July 2009, which was the first time that the French president did not chair that meeting. He did visit New Caledonia towards the end of his term, in August 2011, to open the South Pacific Games, which it was hosting.

New Caledonia: Commitment and ambiguity

Sarkozy and members of his government say that they are committed to fulfilling the obligations of the Noumea Accord, that their preference is that New Caledonia remain with France and, somewhat ambiguously, that the French State should take an active but impartial approach as the Noumea Accord comes to its end.

The earliest indication of Sarkozy's thinking was set out in a letter he wrote to New Caledonians in March 2007, while he was still a presidential candidate (Sarkozy 2007a). In the Gaullist tradition, his letter begins by recalling that New Caledonia was the first overseas territory to rally to Free France and notes 'your desire to continue to live within our Republic', which he shares. He expresses the hope that, at the appropriate time, New Caledonians would indicate by free choice their wish for a 'French destiny'. He quotes de Gaulle saying 'New Caledonia must be part of a bigger whole. Of what whole could it be part, if not the great French whole?' Implicitly affirming his commitment to the scheduled referendum, he notes that, in the term after the next presidential term, New Caledonians would be called upon to make a decisive vote, as foreshadowed in the Noumea Accord. He writes that some New Caledonians believed that independence could be a solution for the future, but states that, while he respects their choice, 'it is not mine'. Nonetheless, he reaffirms the importance of respecting the Noumea Accord, listing his belief in a policy of consensus, the role of the provinces, the collegial government and, somewhat oddly given his earlier statement of viewpoint, the impartiality of the French State.

He then proceeds to seek to 'persuade' the independentists that staying with France was possible with a 'very large autonomy' for New Caledonia relative to the *métropole*. Further, he asserts that if Noumea Accord partners wanted New

Caledonia to evolve and engage in new perspectives within the Republic, then they could count on his support. He pledges innovative judicial solutions to guarantee the personality and powers of New Caledonia within France.

He then lists French State responsibilities in New Caledonia (justice, public order, defence, foreign affairs, currency, part of national education, tertiary education, immigration control) in all of which he states that he would apply the same commitments to French people in New Caledonia as he had made to those elsewhere in the Republic. He emphasises security measures, which he had introduced as interior minister since 2002 (and which had represented a firm hand on disturbances and, hence, a reminder of the firm control of the French State). And he pledges the State's respect for commitments on development and economic rebalancing under the Noumea Accord, noting support for the nickel project in the south and that at Koniambo.

Finally, he writes that he wants to be president of all the French people (i.e., not just those from the *métropole*) and of the Republic, which would defend with energy and conviction the place of New Caledonia *within France*.

That he had gone a little too far in expressing a preference for New Caledonia within France quickly became apparent. Frogier, the local R–UMP president, apparently taking his cue from the UMP presidential candidate in metropolitan France, proceeded to write his own 'letter to young Caledonians' on 16 May 2008. He notes that it was the independentists who had chosen the path of violence 25 years before, and described the Ouvea (Gossanah) events as an attack on the police brigade in the Loyalty Islands, noting the killing of four policemen without mentioning Kanak losses, and affirming that there was no need for shame at what France had done at that time. He underlines the suffering and memories of that time, which had not healed. He refers to the importance of the handshake between Lafleur and Jean-Marie Tjibaou, the foundation of the Matignon and Noumea Accords. He then states that it is legitimate to question the intentions and motivations of those who wanted to reopen these wounds, and to refuse a 'partisan, erroneous and deformed' vision of history. This letter was seen by the pro-independence groups as provocative.

By December 2007, newly installed as president, Sarkozy shifted tack. In his message to the committee of signatories to the Noumea Accord, he reaffirms his commitment to respect the letter and the spirit of the Noumea Accord (Sarkozy 2007b). He restates the paradoxical active role of the French State 'not only the role of an arbiter', with the State conducting itself 'impartially' in the search for consensus which must prevail in the application of the Accord, as it comes to its conclusion. Bearing in mind the caution of Tjibaou on the primacy of the State's role as an actor rather than judge (see Chapter 2), this reference was one calculated to appeal to both sides. He notes economic rebalancing, social cohesion, and co-operation with the South Pacific countries as essential questions for the future of New Caledonia. He states that the principle of the transfer of responsibilities was provided for in the Noumea Accord, and there was no room for debate about that (putting paid to hopes Frogier had raised that there could be a turning back of the clock). The task remained to devise a timetable and the modalities, while preserving the quality of public services for all Caledonians. He indicates that the State would intervene financially, with tax exemption measures, to support the northern nickel project, and did not mention that of the south.

But, once again, Sarkozy reiterates that, when New Caledonians made their choice with the end of the Noumea Accord, his preference was to continue its path with France, in a new relationship yet to be defined. This 'personal and transparent expression of this preference naturally was not at all contradictory with respect for the Accord and its deadlines in all impartiality. I commit myself to that personally'. He then urges participants not to lose sight of what was at stake in the dialogue process, which was not the victory of one side over the other, but the construction of a common destiny.

More recently, at the seventh meeting of the follow-up committee to the Noumea Accord in December 2008, Sarkozy once again reaffirmed that the French Government would respect its commitments, although reiterating that it was an active player despite claims of impartiality: 'We will go to the completion of this process. The State will not shy away … and will play an active role in this phase of our history, it will not just be a passive referee' (*Flash d'Océanie* 10 December 2008). As High Commissioner, Yves Dassonville restated this approach in his 2009 new year message, saying 'I will work to represent a State as much a participant as arbitrator, firm in the exercise of its powers, but always ready to invite dialogue, a State present without being overbearing …' (*'je m'efforcerai d'être le patron d'un État acteur autant qu'arbitre, ferme dans l'exercice de ses compétences, mais toujours prêt à privilégier le dialogue, un Etat présent sans être pesant …'* New Caledonian government website <http://www.nouvelle-caledonie.gouv.fr> accessed 4 February 2009).

In his New Year's address to Overseas France in January 2010, as outlined above, Sarkozy drew a red line at independence for Overseas France, which, in its application to New Caledonia, was at the least ambiguous, and at worst, begged questions about how he was to implement fully the commitments of the Noumea Accord relating to a self-determination referendum on the future status of New Caledonia (see Fisher 2010a).

In the same speech, Sarkozy made some specific comments about New Caledonia, which were also ambiguous. He noted that transfers of responsibility were under way, and that the vote *'on self-determination'* (my italics) would be organised after 2014. In a new and refreshing tone of impartiality, he remarked that the State would be faithful to all partners of the Accord, whether they were in favour of retaining New Caledonia in France or were independentist. But he said that it was essential that all Caledonians begin discussion so that the *vote foreshadowed in the Accord 'translated into a result approved by a very large majority of voters'* (my italics). Since Sarkozy had ruled out independence, his words suggest that he does not have in mind a vote directly on the independence issue, as envisaged by many pro-independence parties and as implied in the Organic Law (relevant articles appear under the heading 'Vote on the accession to full sovereignty' Titre IX, Organic Law 1999). Sarkozy went on to say that, while the discussions should be between Caledonians, the State would help them and assume to the end its role as signatory to the Accords (Sarkozy 2010a). These discussions began in March 2011, when the French hosted a colloquium in Noumea on the Destinies of the Pacific Political Collectivities. It canvassed a range of alternative models for the future, but skirted the independence option, and included only one session focused on the financial costs of independence.

Through his appointments to key positions in New Caledonia, Sarkozy has also sent mixed messages. He appointed close advisors Christian Estrosi and subsequently Jégo as secretaries for Overseas France, suggesting the importance he attached to the positions. Estrosi did not last long in the job, partly because of heavy-handed response to a protest in Noumea during his first visit there (Chapter 4). But Sarkozy's subsequent appointment to the role of his collaborator Jégo, and of Dassonville (a senior advisor to Estrosi) as High Commissioner in Noumea, underlined his intention to handle protests firmly. Indeed Dassonville said as much on his arrival, when he indicated that the disturbances betrayed an underlying need for better social dialogue (i.e., handling industrial disputes), in which the French State would become involved, although it was not strictly its responsibility, and that it would do so with firmness (*Nouvelles Calédoniennes* 10 November 2007). In his public statements following violence in the Caribbean territories and Réunion, Sarkozy stated unequivocally that he would not tolerate violent protest in Overseas France (Sarkozy 2009, 2010).

Noumea becomes preeminent base for France's Pacific military presence

The Sarkozy government's defence white paper, issued shortly after assuming government, defines significant overarching defence reforms based on reducing personnel, sharpening equipment priorities and enhancing intelligence-gathering (Defence White Paper 2008). The few references to France's South Pacific collectivities imply that their continued possession by France is a given. The paper specifies that it would be New Caledonia that would provide the principal base for France's military presence in the Pacific, including the capacity, mainly aero-maritime, for rapid intervention at times of crisis.

The assignation of this role expressly to New Caledonia was a significant change, in that the entire Pacific naval presence had, to that point, been commanded from Papeete. The changes were proposed take place gradually until 2015. The presence of the strongest contingent of the French regional military presence in New Caledonia would therefore coincide with the most important transition period spelled out by the Noumea Accord, that from 2014 to 2018 when votes would be taken on the future, including, specifically, defence responsibilities.

The shoring up of a defence presence, including construction of expensive French military headquarters in Noumea in 2008, with responsibility for the entire French Pacific military presence, well before the vote on the final five sovereign powers, of which defence is one, as provided for under the Noumea Accord, reaffirms Sarkozy's commitment to meet violence or protests with a firm hand, and raises questions about France's commitment as an Accord signatory (see Chapter 4).

French Polynesia and Wallis and Futuna

Sarkozy has paid only belated attention to French Polynesia, and with limited success. In his 2010 New Year comments to Overseas France, Sarkozy referred to the 'vast comedy' of French Polynesia's political representatives 'where yesterday's enemies become today's allies'. He noted that political stability had still not been found, and that this was intolerable for Polynesians. He foreshadowed a further reform of the voting and institutional system to guarantee more stability to majority elected representatives. But, as shown in Chapter 5, the March 2011 draft reforms submitted to the French Polynesian Assembly for its consideration provoked more controversy, precipitating yet another change of leadership.

Also in 2010 Sarkozy announced he would consider proposals to modernise the organisation of the territory of Wallis and Futuna. No indication of these proposals had been released by mid 2012.

From the foregoing efforts, France clearly wants its collectivities to remain French, and continues to be prepared to back this objective through force. And France derives sufficient strategic benefit, including more recently, actual and potential economic benefit, from its resident presence in the Pacific to continue to pay for them to remain French. Will it continue to do so?

Future motivations

This analysis is being finalised as François Hollande assumes the French presidency in May 2012. There is little to guide a judgement about his stance on the French Pacific possessions, although he flagged in his campaign that he would respond to the wishes of the local people of New Caledonia (rather than publicly advocating retaining New Caledonia within France, as Sarkozy had done). But, historically, there has generally been bipartisanship over issues relating to Overseas France, as exemplified in the disastrous support by both Mitterrand and Chirac over the Gossanah cave attack in the midst of the presidential election campaign (Chapter 2).

Possible future policy motivations can be surmised, drawing from past practice and policy reviewed earlier in this chapter. These are likely to derive from strategic interests, commercial factors, and the protection of domestic interests, including the protection of French citizens.

Strategic motivations

France is likely to see continued strategic advantage deriving from its Pacific presence. First, a Pacific presence will continue to provide justification for its claims to retain its seat as one of the elite Permanent Members of the UN Security Council. In this respect, presiding over a successful decolonisation of New Caledonia under the auspices of the UN would be important. France has already signalled a more forthcoming approach to the Decolonisation Committee.

Second, France, through its Pacific presence will be able also to retain its status as the second largest sovereign EEZ in the world, second only to the United States. Third, a continued sovereign presence in the Pacific will facilitate France's maintaining a self-reliant defence posture within the EU and NATO, based on the nuclear deterrent. Retaining the South Pacific collectivities facilitates the presence of French naval and other armed forces in the region. It also keeps vast areas of the Pacific Ocean under French control, including infrastructure at Moruroa and Hao, all of which are potentially useful contributions to Europe's space program.

Fourth, France will also see its Pacific presence as bolstering its status as a member of the Western alliance beyond that of NATO and the EU in Europe. By virtue of its Pacific presence, France can contribute to prevent or at least balance foreign forays in the region, notably by China. It can also provide a balance to the predominantly Anglo-Saxon influence in the South Pacific. Its military presence supplements those of the allies, particularly Australia and New Zealand, including by providing refuelling and rest and recreation stops;

protecting access to sea lanes in the event of the Malacca Straits being blocked; and enabling emergency assistance, cooperative disaster relief and sharing of regional marine resource intelligence. Its presence also contributes to Western (as distinct from European, mentioned earlier) capabilities for tracking missiles and satellites in space. Finally, France's resident regional presence enables it to promote scientific and technological research in the region (Hage identifies many of these points, 2003, 86–87; and de Deckker and Faberon 2008, 278).

Commercial interests

Whereas commercial returns were secondary for France in its early history in the region, more than ever before, France stands to gain specific future commercial benefits, in the context of global concerns about renewable energy and sustainable development, well into the twenty-first century, as known reserves of key resources decline.

It is here that France's status of sovereignty over the second largest global EEZ is relevant. The extent of economic resources accruing to France by virtue of its extensive EEZ in the Pacific Ocean is as yet unknown. France's intensive research into suspected hydrocarbons offshore from New Caledonia and specific investigations in waters around Clipperton suggest, however, that these resources are of some interest to France.

More immediately, France is expanding exploitation of the nickel resource in New Caledonia. Having incorporated the idea of extending nickel production into the formula for responding to Kanak concerns, and having supplied important fiscal backing and private investment from metropolitan France into the massive nickel projects in New Caledonia, France is already a major producer of a valuable global resource, and is poised for greater production. And, as Sarkozy has signaled, France will not relinquish its control of the major investor, Eramet.

Protection of domestic interests and French settlers globally

France shows a continuing commitment to protect the presence and security of its overseas residents, specifically its overseas settlers from metropolitan France, notably in New Caledonia, the French overseas collectivity where they are the most numerous. France is likely to continue to show a desire to head off a potential domino effect on its chain of other overseas possessions, which is particularly important in Guyana (its space launching site), and Corsica (closer to home) but also, in principle, important to all of its other collectivities. It is likely to continue to ensure a low level of domestic metropolitan public interest in the overseas possessions. It is likely to continue to do this through a policy of *'pas d'ennuis'* (heading off trouble) in the Pacific entities, backed by military force, through a program of consolidating relations with Pacific island neighbours and through appropriate responsible behaviour in the international arena (for example, as UN administering authority in New Caledonia and meeting its nuclear compensation commitments in French Polynesia). It will continue to claim a desire to meet its statutory commitments, particularly in New Caledonia, without prejudicing its other objectives

Future policy implications

On the basis of these motivations, and its past practice, French policy approaches are likely to include continued efforts to meet its legal commitments in New Caledonia under the Noumea Accord. It is likely to seek to do this within UN decolonisation principles, with a minimum of violence, although whether it will offer a genuine independence option as required by UN principles, is less clear. There will be challenges, given the strong possibilities of either a blurring of an independence option, or of rejection of an independence option if it is clearly put, with possible accompanying violence by pro-independence elements. France can therefore be expected to urge local parties to agree on imaginative and innovative solutions, including post-Accord arrangements that maximise autonomy within the French republic.

France can be expected to continue to provide lavish expenditure in all three of its Pacific collectivities, both to encourage their continued commitment to French sovereignty and to head off domestic public interest back home in metropolitan France, which might result from opposition or instability in Overseas France.

France is likely to continue its long-term pursuit of the most valuable of the economic resources in the Pacific, particularly exploitation of nickel, and potentially hydrocarbons, in New Caledonia, and the conduct of aquatic scientific research around all of its Pacific possessions, including the remote ones such as Clipperton.

France will continue to maintain a regional military presence consistent with its other objectives, and the will to exert military pressure when necessary to ensure law and order. It will continue its defence co-operation with large regional powers and selected island states, especially focused on disaster response and the protection of fisheries. France will continue to use its capacity as a western ally to head off intrusion by foreign powers, and this is likely to be accompanied by a tendency to overplay the significance of activities in the region undertaken by foreign powers.

France is likely to continue with the institutions handling its Pacific collectivities in a way that is not commensurate with the strategic return they deliver to France. The domestic affairs of the collectivities will continue to be managed by the interior ministry and its Overseas France secretariat, and military institutions, with the foreign affairs and defence ministries responsible for policy in the wider region. It is not certain that the day-to-day coordination of these various ministries will improve, which carries risks.

France's aid efforts in the wider region are likely to continue to be low-key and modest, multilaterally through the SPC and PIF, and through selective bilateral programs. France will continue to spearhead EU aid and other engagement in the region. There is likely to be continued lip-service to encouraging the regional participation of France's Pacific entities, without building the capacity for them to do so effectively. This will limit the support for, and acceptance of, France and the French collectivities by the region's independent island leaders.

Conclusion

France derives significant strategic advantage from its resident, sovereign presence in the South Pacific. Apart from providing continued credibility to France as a democratic, global power bolstering its claims within the UN, EU and NATO, the French Pacific presence now represents for them a real and potential economic asset, and a resource in future space exploration and exploitation . These are strong motivations leading to France's desire to remain present in the region, even at considerable financial cost and diplomatic and political investment.

Having established France's likely motivations and strategic returns from its Pacific presence, and pointed to likely future policy directions, the next chapter will examine elements of risk undermining its ability to continue to pursue these interests and policies, with the potential to undermine regional stability; and identify actions which might be taken to minimise these.

8. France's future role in the region

France has a long history in the Pacific region (see Chapter 1), and derives strategic benefits from being there. In recent years, France has exercised innovation and flexibility, backed by military force, along with significant economic and political investment in its collectivities and, to a lesser extent, the region, to maintain its presence.

As explored in Chapter 2, just 20 to 30 years ago, France's behaviour created serious disruption and instability in the region. Its resistance to Vanuatu's independence left a legacy of suspicion, resentment and violence, and was an indicator to Pacific neighbours of what might follow should similar circumstances arise in its other Pacific entities. France initially withdrew financial and other resources, supported rebellious forces, and intervened politically in the aftermath of Vanuatu's independence, despite the democratic vote in favour of independence.

Chapter 2 also shows how France's nuclear testing program, which persisted to 1996 despite regional opposition, strengthened negative feeling in the region towards France and, together with its veto of discussions of non-development problems in the Secretariat of the Pacific Community (SPC), resulted in the region forming a new regional grouping, the Pacific Islands Forum (PIF), in 1971. France's mismanagement of Melanesian independence demands in New Caledonia alienated Melanesian and broader Pacific opinion further, resulting in the formation of the Melanesian Spearhead Group (MSG), potentially dividing hard-won South Pacific co-operation and consultation mechanisms. France's policies in New Caledonia also prompted violence, and introduced destabilising extraneous terrorist factors such as Libyan links with Melanesian political parties.

Despite overtures in the 1980s to improve its image (set out in Chapter 3), it was only after France changed its policies, by ending nuclear testing and by concluding the Matignon and then Noumea Accords to address Melanesian independence concerns peacefully, that regional leaders, and the civil society they served, responded more positively towards France (Chapter 6).

As Australia and its immediate Pacific region confront the consequences of failures in governance within the region, against the background of global economic and environmental pressures, including climate change, and a tectonic shift in power relationships between the two great Pacific powers, the United States and China, they may well welcome the energy and resources of France, a significant Western ally present in the region, with similar values and interests here.

But, the history of France's presence, its motivations and recent practices in the Pacific, point to areas of risk to future stability, both within the French collectivities, and the wider region. These risk areas potentially undermine France's ability to achieve its objectives in the region, i.e., to remain present, and to integrate its collectivities there. At the same time, they threaten regional security.

The uncertainties centre around two main areas: continued acceptance of the French presence by Pacific island leaders; and the continued peaceful, workable, democratic status of France's Pacific collectivities, particularly New Caledonia, on which wider regional acceptance hinges.

Regional acceptance

Chapter 6 shows that, at the broadest level, France has succeeded in establishing itself as an accepted presence and major bilateral partner in the region, albeit with some continuing unease, and certainly with perceptions that it is an outside power. In the wider Pacific, France moved beyond its activity, initiated in the 1980s, simply to alter perceptions in the region about itself, by working to change its unpopular policies and to support concrete regional and bilateral aid programs relevant to the region's own needs. It has built up regional credit by stopping nuclear tests, continuing to address some of the lingering issues related to the tests, and introducing responsive change in New Caledonia. It has also engaged itself more productively in regional bodies, including the PIF, SPC, Secretariat of the Pacific Regional Environment Program (SPREP), and in selected bilateral activity. It has presented itself as a close partner of Australia and New Zealand. It claims to want its collectivities to integrate more in the region.

With its dual role as a major Western power, and a vehicle for a greater European Union (EU) presence in the region, France is a strategically important partner to other Pacific powers, notably the United States, Japan, Australia and New Zealand. France supports and complements their own strategic presence in the Asia-Pacific region, and reinforces the balance to the forays that China is making into the region. Facing the heavy demands of governance failure, particularly in Solomon Islands, and ongoing needs of development co-operation in the region, Australia and New Zealand in particular welcome the stability and burden-sharing that have flowed from the French presence (see Chapter 7).

But France has yet to achieve full acceptance of its presence within the region. Partly this derives from its own ambiguous presentation of its interests. As discussed in Chapter 7, there is relatively little high-level articulation beyond its own borders of France's strategic interest in being in or staying in the South

Pacific. The rare references to the South Pacific, or even the French Pacific, in strategic documents such as the 2008 foreign affairs and defence white papers, underline that the priority areas for France lie elsewhere in the immediate geographic vicinity of metropolitan France, and that key policy advisers undervalue the strategic returns the Pacific presence delivers. The language that France uses when talking about the Pacific is at best ambiguous over whether it sees itself as an outsider or as a resident South Pacific power with strategic interests stemming from that presence (Chapter 6). Despite France's proclaimed interest in enmeshing its collectivities more in the life of the region, there is uncertainty, and wariness, about whether France's three collectivities speak for themselves or only channel French views and policy. So, as Chapter 6 shows, perhaps it is not surprising that others in the region do not see or welcome France clearly as a *resident* power.

In Australia's 2009 defence white paper, France is mentioned along with other North Atlantic Treaty Organisation (NATO) countries such as Spain, Germany, Italy and Sweden, as a co-operative European partner, with a brief reference to practical co-operation in the Pacific and southern oceans and Afghanistan; and as a donor in the South Pacific to support capacity building (Defence White Paper 2009, 98 and 100). No mention of France is made in sections on interoperability, intelligence, and science and technology, nor even when the paper discusses coalitions with others in military operations, disaster and humanitarian relief in the Pacific and Timor Leste, where France has specifically played a role (in FRANZ and in INTERFET, International Force for East Timor) (Australian Defence White Paper 2009, 50, 54 and 105). The paper does not indicate that France is considered other than as a co-operative European partner and donor, and certainly not as a *regional Pacific* power.

Chapter 6 suggests that many regional island country leaders remain cautious about France. Some remember the period of French opposition to, and frustration of, Vanuatu's independence process; French nuclear testing; and the long refusal to respond to Kanak independence demands. Their caution is not allayed by France's assertion of its claim to the Matthew and Hunter Islands, contested with Vanuatu (Chapter 4). France's own efforts in the region have been well received, but remain modest in financial terms, fitful (for example, President Nicolas Sarkozy's non-attendance at the French Oceanic Summit, the desultory holding of bilateral talks between Australia and New Caledonia under the 2002 Trade Arrangement, Chapter 6), and generally involve joining existing, longstanding initiatives by Australia and New Zealand with low budgetary outlays. While working for an accepted role for its collectivities within the PIF, which the Forum acceded to, France has only reluctantly acquiesced in the Forum mechanisms to monitor its policies, such as the regular Forum ministerial committee visits to New Caledonia in 1999, 2001 and 2004, but with none since then. French officials privately claim that Pacific island leaders themselves are no models of good governance and should not be judging France's performance in the Pacific. But they overlook the fact that regional leaders have been fair and balanced in their conclusions from these visits, and restrained in responding to calls by French Polynesian and New Caledonian indigenous pro-independence leaders for the Forum to take positions on French policy. At the same time, regional leaders expect more of a Western sovereign power and will judge French action in its collectivities by higher standards than they apply to themselves, however unfair this might seem.

So long as France sees itself as an outside power in the region, regional countries know that ultimately France will pursue its own national interests, to which their interests, and those of the French collectivities located in the Pacific, will always be secondary. The bigger states, Australia and New Zealand, know that France sees them as useful regional allies and information sources, but only up to a point, the point where France's overriding national interests as a UN, EU, NATO and global player become engaged. France seems to undervalue the leverage these regional relationships can provide for it in pursuing its own interests; for example, with China and the United States. Thus, France can probably not expect to do much more with the big Pacific countries in the defence and intelligence area than participate in exercises and exchanges to promote interoperability, and exchange intelligence in practical areas such as fisheries, as it is currently doing. The regional powers will continue to be wary of closer co-operation in sensitive areas such as intelligence exchanges so long as they perceive France may use these resources to further interests and relationships different to those of the region.

Island leaders have successfully used regional and international mechanisms to influence French policy in the past. The UN Decolonisation Committee, the PIF and the MSG have been useful, and remain potential instruments should differences with France arise. In May 2008, UN Secretary-General Ban Ki-moon urged administering authorities to discharge the UN's mandate on decolonisation, arguing that 'Colonialism has no place in today's world' (Ban Ki-Moon 2008). The UN Decolonisation Committee has the mandate to send visiting investigatory missions to New Caledonia, although it has not exercised this mandate to date (mid 2012), not even when the Committee agreed to host its regional Pacific seminar there in May 2010. Through the PIF, regional leaders have a watching brief on how France deals with Melanesian and Polynesian demands for independence (see Chapter 6). They have an ongoing mandate to send visiting missions to the French collectivities should they wish to do so. The MSG has remained active, reminding the Forum of Kanak concerns related to New Caledonia, such as French handling of the restricted electorate and the ethnic category of the census, sending a visiting team there in 2010, and supporting New Caledonia's Melanesians on important issues such as Vanuatu's Matthew and Hunter claim. All three mechanisms remain safety valves for the expression of Kanak and French Polynesian frustrations (for example, Roch Wamytan continues to make submissions to the UN Committee; Oscar Temaru and the MSG have respectively raised self-determination concerns in the Forum, and Temaru in the UN Decolonisation Committee, see Chapter 6) and are tools that remain available to Pacific leaders, should France transgress (see also Mrgudovic 2008, 390).

Chapter 6 shows how France has sought to insert itself and its supporters into these mechanisms in recent years, presumably in order to neutralise their potential to be used against it. Having secured a special status of associate membership for the two larger Pacific French entities in the PIF, France and its pro-French supporters are now seeking full membership, even before the full status of New Caledonia is decided. The pro-France President of New Caledonia, Philippe Gomès, has called for New Caledonia to become a full member of the MSG, in a bid to displace or weaken the voice of the current member, the Kanak coalition Front de Libération Nationale Kanak et Socialiste (Kanak Socialist National Liberation Front, FLNKS). And France has begun to report as administering authority for New Caledonia to the UN Decolonisation Committee, and has hosted the Committee's May 2010 regional Pacific seminar in Noumea (and treated Kanak protestors and the French Polynesian President dismissively when they set up protests there), thereby diluting the effect of petitions to the Committee by Kanak groups. Whether France is successful in its efforts to head off future criticism from these various organisations remains to be seen.

More broadly, the adoption by the UN General Assembly (UNGA) in October 2007 of a Declaration on Indigenous Rights (A/Res/61/295 of 2 October 2007) has set the stage for another avenue of pursuit of grievance by aggrieved Melanesian people. The declaration specifically provides for the right of *indigenous* peoples to self-determination (Declaration on Indigenous Rights, Article 3), and enshrines their right to control their education (Article 14) and not to be forcibly displaced from their lands arbitrarily (Article 10).

In the international and Pacific regional context, debate is under way over the rights of indigenous peoples to self-determination, as distinct from rights of non-self-governing territories. Jan Furukawa, Guam's Decolonisation Commissioner, has argued that the right of Guam's colonised people, however few they might be, to 'forge their own permanent, political identity' was not dismissable but 'inalienable' (Furukuwa 2003) and US-administered Guam has prepared legislation for a future self-determination referendum for the minority indigenous Chamoru people.

New Caledonia's own Sarimin Boengkih in 2010 made a distinction between the voting rights of the 'colonised peoples', as opposed to immigrant settlers in New Caledonia (Boengkih 2010), referring to the requirements of UNGA 35/118, which, as noted in Chapter 6, calls for member states to discourage the systematic influx of outside immigrants and settlers into territories under the Committee's auspices.

Against this background, whatever bilateral arrangements France works out within its sovereign borders, indigenous peoples may, in theory, continue to raise their grievances and receive support in an international context. Given the untested nature of the relatively new Declaration on the Rights of Indigenous Peoples, which France supports, there may be considerable scope for differences to arise in New Caledonia over indigenous rights. The 2011 Report of the Special Rapporteur for the Rights of Indigenous Peoples, after his February visit to New Caledonia, which was critical of elements of France's implementation of the Noumea Accord, is an initial sign of this.

Within the region, France will need to continue to work hard to build confidence in the Pacific in its policies and presence.

Facilitating closer links in the South Pacific

The history of France's presence in the South Pacific suggests that there remain ways in which France could improve its regional links.

Institutional factors in Paris

From an outside observer's perspective, aspects of France's inchoate institutional arrangements in Paris relating to its Pacific collectivities are not compatible with the best management of its own strategic interests, many of which are shared by Australia and New Zealand.

France's wish to remain as a sovereign presence in the South Pacific suggests that there would be value in continuing to build expertise on the Pacific within its bureaucracies which deal with the region (foreign affairs and defence ministries, offices of the President and the Prime Minister) and those dealing with its Pacific collectivities (the secretariat for Overseas France and its posted officials in the South Pacific from the interior ministry); and to provide for sound, ongoing coordination between the two, and between them and the rest of the French domestic bureaucracy (environment, health, education and other ministries).

As the disastrous, but relatively recent, experiences of the Gossanah cave crisis and the *Rainbow Warrior* affair show, maintaining the most effective Paris-

8. France's future role in the region

based decision-making apparatus relative to the Pacific entities is critical to France's international image and prestige. As these incidents and the *événements* themselves recede in history, and as new challenges arise (see New Caledonia outcomes, below), the idea of continuing to administer the French Pacific entities on the basis of past policy reflexes, is risky.

We have seen how, from its first foray into the region, France's policy on the South Pacific and towards its possessions there has been subject to the ebbs and flows of its domestic and European preoccupations. It goes without saying that France's direct national interests must come first for France. Given occasional talk of reorganisation of the French Overseas structures (such as Jégo's suggestion to abolish the Overseas France secretariat itself, Chapter 4), retaining a distinct, effective institutional unit for the French Pacific collectivities will be all the more important to ensure that their political, cultural and regional circumstances are understood and not subsumed in large domestic bureaucratic structures.

In view of the strategic value of the French Pacific entities, and the desirable ongoing engagement of the most senior of the ministries such as defence and foreign affairs, it is anomalous that the Overseas France secretariat is a junior ministry. If the office is to remain headed by a secretary of state or junior minister, as has been the case to date, then moving the office to the office of the Prime Minister, or the President, would enhance its bureaucratic weight relative to the ministries it needs to consult. Its senior officials should desirably have a history and experience in Overseas France, particularly, as critical deadlines fall due in New Caledonia.

Specific, ongoing, inter-agency steering committees in Paris on the French Pacific collectivities, coordinated by an appropriately senior Overseas France minister or secretary reporting direct to the Prime Minister or President, as New Caledonia's deadlines approach, would keep communication lines open and minimise the potential for a repeat of past disasters. Such a committee would desirably include, apart from the Pacific unit of the Overseas France secretariat; the foreign affairs ministry, especially its oceanic division; the defence ministry; and, from time to time, the Paris-based offices of the French Pacific entities, and other ministries such as environment, health and education. Sarkozy's temporary interministerial committee for Overseas France, (see Chapter 4), with its focus primarily on France's Caribbean entities, has not taken on this role. What is known, from the past subsuming of France's Pacific collectivities into the Overseas France structures (whether an Overseas France ministry or secretariat under the interior minister), is that French Pacific issues can get lost in the mix.

Policy ambiguities

The policy ambiguities enshrined in France's behaviour, sometimes as a power 'in', and sometimes as a power 'of', the Pacific, outlined in Chapter 6, reflect inadequacies of the inter-agency consultation process. They also reflect the understandably Eurocentric character of French policy-making, which has generally served French interests well, albeit on occasion leading to disruption in the Pacific. In recent years, France is both 'of' the region, by virtue of its collectivities, and 'in' the region as a European country with sovereignty in the Pacific. France can, in some ways, be all things to all interests: European to Europe, French to its citizens in the region, a helpful, but not extravagantly so, external donor to the Pacific, a benign supporter to its collectivities' regional engagement, all without much cost.

The dualities of this position are unlikely to be resolved until New Caledonia has expressed itself democratically on the question of independence. The implementation of credible democratic principles in French Polynesia will also be important, but the unsatisfactory 2011 statutory reforms there give no room for confidence. If New Caledonia were to endorse staying with France by a vote before 2018, without dissension, and if French Polynesian electoral outcomes are respected, then France could consider identifying itself more as a rightful regional presence 'of' the Pacific, with a unique identity, similar to that of Australia and New Zealand. France might then reasonably expect that it and its collectivities be accepted fully into regional organisations. Even in this case, it is not clear that France would be prepared to project itself unambiguously as a resident regional player, for example in playing its full role as an aid and trade partner.

If, however, there is political opposition and unrest in New Caledonia as the Noumea Accord application period comes to a close, and/or if France's role in French Polynesia continues to appear partisan with associated political instability and disturbance, then regional leaders may well continue to be hesitant to embrace a more fulsome French/French collectivity presence in their regional structures. This hesitancy would be compounded should such instabilities again lead to the engagement of external powers hostile to Western alliance interests.

France supporting its collectivities in regional engagement

France's effectiveness in engaging constructively for its own benefit in the region would be enhanced not only by more financial support to the region, but by more concrete practical assistance to the three French Pacific collectivities to participate in the region in their own right, an objective which France openly espouses but to which it has devoted few resources.

Fundamental to regional integration of the French collectivities is a letting go of any idea of cultural competition in the region.

History has shown how emphasising the 'Anglo-Saxon' distinction has contributed to misunderstanding and instability in the region. Just as France has made large gestures towards the indigenous people in its collectivities and in the region, French authorities could lead a change in how it views what is undeniably an Anglophone neighbourhood. Accepting the realities of the Anglophone region around the French collectivities means accepting at face value that the bigger regional governments, Australia and New Zealand, are no longer mere ciphers for their former British colonisers and, indeed, that they have not been so for most of the last century. Even in recent years, both in Canberra and in the French collectivities, European diplomats and officials in private communications continue to assume that Canberra's policies reflect British policy. French analysts have made revealing references to Australia and New Zealand as 'dominions' in their academic writings, a quaint throwback to pre-federation (1901) status in the case of Australia (see for example Cordonnier 1995a). Sweeping comments that Australian and New Zealand policy positions are 'Anglo-Saxon' mean little in these countries, which have been built on immigration from all over the world, with multicultural populations and leadership. France has taken great pains in recent years to cement closer relations with Australia and New Zealand. Better efforts to understand regional positions on their own terms would ensure continued partnership within the region on an equal basis.

Equipping the leaders and officials of its own collectivities with the appropriate language training would enable them to participate confidently, in ongoing communication with neighbouring governments. In the Pacific, as elsewhere, France has handicapped itself with its insistence on the use of French when English is the international language. Despite the SPC having provided full interpretation facilities for the benefit of the three French entities and France for over 60 years, it is not realistic to expect the South Pacific region, with all its underdevelopment and multiplicity of languages of its own, to provide French language interpretation to facilitate integration of the French Pacific collectivities in the many Council of Regional Organisations of the Pacific (CROP) bodies and working committees. The practice, implemented when the full New Caledonian government delegation visited Australia in March 2010, of French Pacific delegations travelling in the region with their own interpreters and portable interpretation equipment is an impressive sign of genuine willingness to participate in the region.

Such an approach would not undermine the important process of retaining, and indeed promoting, the exquisite and unique French language and culture at home in the collectivities. For the collectivities, there is nothing to be lost, and much to be gained, by actively engaging with the wider region in the English language. Regional island country leaders, most of whom are multilingual themselves in indigenous languages, would recognise and welcome the gesture. One can envisage useful exchange programs whereby indigenous Pacific island state officials and researchers work side by side with their French collectivity counterparts in work exchanges in the collectivities, in Pacific island states, and in Australia and New Zealand.

A key element contributing to regional stability and understanding is the capability and effectiveness of a professional regional affairs unit in each collectivity, appropriately resourced and staffed with personnel trained in diplomacy and the English language, to provide day-to-day guidance for the collectivities' participation in regional affairs, to monitor and participate actively in regular regional meetings. Provision for exchanges between the regional affairs unit staff and diplomatic officers of the island governments would substantially boost understanding in both the collectivities and Pacific island governments of their respective contributions and potential contributions to the region. An active role by the English-speaking Pacific governments, including Australian and New Zealand, in funding and supporting such inter-PIF exchanges, and funding expanded English-language training for personnel of the French collectivities, perhaps with co-funding by France, would maximise the benefits of such regional co-operation.

Such a unit would simplify interactions by foreign interlocutors with the French entities. Currently, in New Caledonia alone, outsiders such as officials from neighbouring foreign governments and regional bodies, need to deal with three critical layers of government: the French State authorities, in areas of their power and also for courtesy's sake; the New Caledonian government; and the provincial governments in their areas of responsibility. Australia and New Zealand, and to a lesser extent, Indonesia, as countries with resident representation in Noumea, understand this. But other governments, particularly Pacific island governments with their own capacity constraints, regional organisations and other potential interlocutors such as non-governmental organisations, do not. Simplifying the government structures through an effective, professional, one-stop regional affairs unit would facilitate interchange with neighbouring governments. The unit could provide valuable support for officials and leaders of the collectivities when they travel throughout the region. It would facilitate integration of the French entities in the region. It would also enhance understanding by island governments of French motives and actions in the region. There is currently very little knowledge in the region of innovative French practices of potential interest elsewhere in the Pacific, such as the involvement of customary indigenous authorities in judging civil law cases, the presence of central officials in remote areas, the application of gender parity law which has significantly boosted the representation of women in the assemblies and congress (Berman 2005), and the implementation of collegial government in a multi-ethnic society.

Visits by metropolitan, collectivity and island government leaders and politicians

The regular regional meetings of senior French officials in the region (French regional ambassadors, High Commissioners of the collectivities, and Paris-based officials) are a valuable input into informed policymaking in Paris. More visits by young French politicians from the hexagon to the Pacific collectivities, and to the Pacific region; and by Pacific leaders from the collectivities and the Island countries to Paris to meet French politicians and officials, could assist in informing members of the French national assembly and the Paris-based French administration about issues, history and preoccupations, and in enabling the appointment of responsible ministers or permanent secretaries with a background knowledge of the region. A tailoring of the rhetoric during these visits, which places less emphasis on the fact of French sovereignty and focuses, rather, on the particular needs and experiences of the islanders, would be beneficial.

Development co-operation, economic engagement and investment

France's development assistance to the region has grown in recent years, and it has contributed to increased assistance by the EU. But France's annual financial contributions to the region outside its own sovereign territory remain minuscule, at most EUR103 million or $A146 million (converted May 2010) in 2008, some of which is EU aid, see Chapter 6). This compared poorly to its expenditure in its own Pacific collectivities ($A4.6 billion), and its expenditure elsewhere (it was two per cent of its overall aid effort compared with 43 per cent to sub-Saharan Africa). And it compares poorly with the aid expenditure in the region by Australia ($A1.092 billion in financial year 2009–2010, Minister for Foreign Affairs press release 12 May 2009) and New Zealand ($NZ205.5 million in 2007–2008, NZAID website accessed 25 June 2009).

Its relatively low expenditure in the region reinforces the view that France, with a sovereign presence in the Pacific, does not see the region as part of its own area of responsibility.

One could argue that France's own effort to engage more in the region in the last few years, itself increases expectations, and the potential for misunderstanding and retrograde thinking, towards France. Its encouragement of exchanges and visits to its entities by regional figures, which is desirable, while impressing them with the prosperity in the French collectivities and in Paris, heightens expectations about potential aid in the minds of officials from countries, almost all of whose entire GDP is less than what the French spend in New Caledonia alone each year (see Chapter 6). It would be helpful if such visits were matched by more visits in the other direction, by leaders and officials of the French collectivities, and French officials from Paris, to other island countries.

The EU activity that France has encouraged, although welcome, is not large, averaging a planned $A90 million per annum for the five years to 2013, of which approximately 20 per cent comes from France and is included in France's regional aid figure above (see Chapter 6). While some changes are being made, in the past this aid has proven at odds with existing mechanisms. The EU process of shifting from an aid donor/Africa–Caribbean–Pacific (ACP) basis to new trade partnerships through EPAs, was complicated by initial disregard for the region's own evolving trade arrangements. Despite its proclaimed 2006 Strategy for the Pacific, the EU's endemic bureaucratic requirements and a tendency to a one-size-fits-all approach in a varied and disparate group of archipelagos has resulted in delayed and inefficient aid delivery, generally outside of existing regional mechanisms such as the SPC. These efforts are complicated by the growing gap between the way the EU treats its Overseas Countries and Territories (OCT) and the way it treats ACPs (Chapter 6). Pacific leaders remember, too, that EU aid is a two-edged sword, bringing with it unflinching standards of human rights standards and the threat of economic sanction. The EU has used its muscle to sanction Fiji, and France threatened to cut off New Zealand's access to EU markets in the post-Rainbow Warrior period (see Chapter 2).

The increased presence of the EU in the region has the further strategic consequence for France that any opprobrium attaching to France amongst regional leaders will, by extension also attach to the EU, and vice versa. Whereas in the past, pressure on France came from the regional island countries and the UN, in any future situation of concern to the region, France is likely also to come under pressure from the EU itself (as indeed it did when the European Court of Human Rights endorsed the restricted electorate in New Caledonia). Thus, France's European engagement can act as a helpful brake in its wielding of power within the region. On the other hand, action by the EU, for example in its dealings with Fiji, which might be perceived as negative, will also have an accompanying residual effect on regional attitudes to France.

In the grand scheme of things, the reality is that the Pacific islands are low in the pecking order of Europe's foreign policy priorities. In this context, as a major EU and Pacific power, France is in a privileged position to promote the regional economic efficiencies, which the PIF countries aspire to, enunciated in the Pacific Plan. It could facilitate better information flows between the Pacific island states, the French Pacific collectivities, and Paris and Brussels, on trade matters to ensure that the EU, in pursuing its Pacific strategy, works within the Pacific Plan, Pacific Agreement on Closer Economic Relations (PACER) and Pacific Island Countries Trade Agreement (PICTA) (for example, in implementing its EPA arrangements); and to ensure better communication and understanding between its Pacific EU OCTs and the Pacific island ACP states. Again, equipping local officials in its collectivities with training and a working external affairs secretariat would be important.

Apart from increased funding more commensurate with the needs and status of the Pacific island states as neighbours to France in the region, France could also do more to encourage the EU to work through regional mechanisms which have proven to be effective, such as the SPC, the CROP organisations, and bilaterally, in consultation with the government and non-government aid organisations of Australia and New Zealand, which are experienced in working in the small and remote communities of the Pacific islands.

Just as France devotes considerable expenditure to supporting commercial activity within its Pacific collectivities, regional integration of its collectivities would benefit from France providing funding to examine economic links between the Pacific island states and the French Pacific collectivities, and to promote private French investment in there. So long as the collectivities' dependence on European and French imports is unlikely to change substantially, given tastes and preferential tariff arrangements, true economic integration is unlikely to occur without a re-examination of the high tariff protection the French collectivities maintain against regional imports. Whereas full PICTA and PACER participation might be too large a concession to make by the French collectivities, some review of their high tariff walls would be a welcome gesture.

One of the most valuable targets for any increased expenditure by France and the EU would be increasing people-to-people links, both ways, between the French entities and the rest of the region. Apart from promoting training exchanges in the field of diplomacy to address the desire of France to integrate its collectivities into the life of the region, such exchanges could take place in areas of regional trade, engaging for examples the officials of Agence de Développement Économique de la Nouvelle-Calédonie (New Caledonia Economic Development Agency, ADECAL), New Caledonia's trade promotion arm, with those of neighbouring counterparts. Exchanges involving regional organisations could also be helpful.

Greater funding and engagement by France and its national and regional experts could build on France's solid start in focusing on the big challenges for the Pacific region, those of climate change and sustainable development, food security and the protection of the environment, particularly marine resources and fishing stock management, in which France has expertise.

There is scope for France to engage regional neighbours more in its technological and scientific activities, which are second to none within the region but often little known about and under utilised. Institutions such as the Institut Français de Recherche pour l' Exploitation de la Mer (French Research Institute for Marine Exploitation, IFREMER), Institut de recherche pour le développement (Development Research Institute, IRD), and agricultural institutions (Institut Pasteur, Institut agronomique de Nouvelle-Calédonie) are represented in the French entities and have a valuable role to play in the region in hosting more workshops and exchanges at the grassroots, working level, which would be welcomed, if language issues are seriously addressed. The cultural context of exchanges needs to be recognised. Pacific island researchers themselves have valuable expertise. Many good intentions, and considerable financial expenditure, can be wasted by seminars in the European tradition, for example the idea of '*Assises*', or stocktakes of existing European research, which is alien idea to the Pacific island researcher, and involves presentation formulas that can appear to be talking *at*, rather than talking *with*, regional experts.

As indicated in Chapter 6, France or its collectivities have formal links with all the CROP organisations except the three specifically involving tertiary institutions. Whereas there are systemic differences in the operation of French education institutions, with changes to the European tertiary system of the last few years aligning European degrees more closely with those of the Anglophone system, there may be opportunities for further collaboration between the two French Pacific universities and regional tertiary institutions.

France has supported ongoing cultural links between the indigenous peoples of its collectivities and their neighbouring peoples. New Caledonia hosted the Melanesian Arts Festival in 2011, which is held every four years under the auspices of the MSG. It supported the meeting of Polynesian royal families in Tahiti in 2007. It promotes sporting participation by the French collectivities in regional sporting events, which is valued in the region. The Pacific island state participants could benefit from more training funds to ensure more equal competition with the well-funded French athletes who have tended to scoop most events.

In the cultural context, France has understood the need to proceed gently. The explicit use of expressions and concepts such as *rayonnement*, or the national mission to expand cultural influence, has notably reduced in recent years, perhaps in response to the sensitivities of the small island states. The role of French culture is an idea unique to French people. The justified pride and emotion with which the French approach their culture and intellectual heritage, and their feeling of the responsibility to share it, can be misunderstood. Introducing others to a body of literature, culture and thought not accessed without an understanding of the French language and thinking, is a valuable contribution to the region that only France can make. It can be achieved through more two-way exchanges, visits, scholarships, sport sponsorships, promotion of Alliances Françaises (French clubs) and other study opportunities, building on existing programs that France is funding. France is also in a unique position to expand exchanges to enhance understanding of the indigenous Pacific cultures in its collectivities, for example exhibitions and visits to highlight Kanak and Polynesian culture in other parts of the Pacific, including Australia and New Zealand.

Further French underwriting of the tourist industries in its Pacific collectivities would enhance regional understanding of its presence. New Caledonia, French Polynesia and Wallis and Futuna each represent unique cultural showcases, and yet are considerably more expensive tourist destinations than other Pacific islands and therefore out of reach for travellers from most other Pacific countries.

Building on France's own development co-operation, and on EU activities, its cultural links, and its investment and trade links, would balance France's projection of itself as a defence player, along with Australia and New Zealand, an aspect which Pacific leaders find disquieting (see Chapter 6).

Successful outcomes in French collectivities

By far the most important medium-term outcome that France can continue to provide for the region is continued democracy, stability and economic prosperity in the French collectivities. France faces particular challenges in achieving this outcome within the next 10 years. The key to France's success lies in New Caledonia, to whom the other French collectivities, French Polynesia and Wallis and Futuna, look as a guide to their future.

Within the Melanesian 'arc of instability', New Caledonia has, to a degree, been a shining light of democratically based stability, at least for much of the period of the Matignon and Noumea Accords (a period that was marred by the assassination of Jean-Marie Tjibaou in 1989 and ethnic problems in Saint-Louis). As the critical deadlines under the Noumea Accord fall due from 2014,, new uncertainties arise within the Melanesian arc. Transitional arrangements in Bougainville in Papua New Guinea, which were themselves based partly on the Noumea Accord model, fall due from 2011 to 2016. In Indonesia, West

Papuan issues remain a potential trouble spot, and West Papuan independence leaders have links with New Caledonian counterparts. The Solomon Islands will be reconsidering the mandate for the Regional Assistance Mission to the Solomon Islands (RAMSI), which will have been in operation for a decade. Fiji is a military dictatorship. Democracy in Vanuatu is also fragile.

Against this background, Pacific island leaders and Australia and New Zealand will be alert to any new difficulties or instabilities in the French Pacific collectivities, particularly in New Caledonia, where the terms of continued French control are yet to be agreed.

French Polynesia

In French Polynesia, we have seen that democratic expression in a personality-dominated political culture with an economy bankrolled generously by France has led to constant changes of leadership, and shifts of alliances around increasingly French Polynesian local interests, as distinct from pro-France interests. This coalescence of local interests has in part been brought about as a reaction to the French State's own intervention, through statutory and other means, to favour pro-France political outcomes (Chapter 5). Such actions, with accompanying corruption and frequent changes of government, hardly help French credibility in the region.

In real terms, such instability has had a low level of impact locally since it is the French sovereign power that delivers budgetary support, all services, and a flow of high quality consumer goods. And France controls law and order. The lack of any substantial economic resource means that few see long-term benefit in pushing for true independence. So long as that continues, and France is prepared to pay, stability is assured. The implementation of the latest reforms of French Polynesia's statute applying to elections will, however, be a test. If the reforms are used to favour the pro-France group, as has occurred in the past, they may exacerbate rather than reduce political volatility. And already, the mere terms of the reforms have provoked controversy (Chapter 5).

In the best of times, it is a difficult, expensive, and thankless task for French authorities to foster democratic processes, while maintaining first world standard services and civil law and order in the remote archipelagoes of French Polynesia. If there were a significant downturn in French economic support, local protests and heavy-handed responses by French security services could create further instability. With global financial pressures and the weakened eurozone, French systems and processes, already under pressure from shifting local groupings, may be tested further.

French Polynesia, like New Caledonia, has a record of recent violence (1987, 1991 and 1995). The influence of Gaston Flosse who, through his personality and close relationship with the now departed Jacques Chirac, had been able to secure increasingly favourable autonomy measures, has faded. Young French Polynesians are well aware that the big changes occurred in New Caledonia only after the violence of the 1980s. A French Polynesian participant at a colloquium on New Caledonia in Paris in May 2008 noted that there had been no Rocard-type mission to French Polynesia because there had been no violence there (Comments to Colloquium 2008). Nathalie Mrgudovic (2008, 244) signals that, of the many statutory changes applying to New Caledonia since 1958, only the 2004 statute was negotiated, suggesting that it was violence which was the factor leading to a negotiated outcome. In a contracting global economy, which inevitably impacts on the one resource employing French Polynesians, tourism, the possibility of French Polynesians seeking further political autonomy through violence cannot be ruled out.

Unlike Flosse, whose record in the region was mixed, Oscar Temaru has a strong network amongst regional island leaders, many of whom have supported his cause. This can be an asset for France. Respect for Temaru has meant some regional tolerance even for his recent temporary alliances with pro-France groups, and the dilution of his demand for independence. But, should Temaru up the ante on independence or autonomy issues, he would find ready support in the PIF and the region. He has shown he is prepared to use the Forum card, regularly calling for reinscription of French Polynesia on the UN decolonisation list in recent years (and meeting strong French official reaction) and advancing ideas on further autonomy at the 2007 Forum summit (Chapter 6), including his idea of a Tahiti Nui Accord for autonomy for French Polynesia, based on the Noumea Accord. His quiet but protesting presence outside the SPC headquarters in Noumea, the venue for the UN Decolonisation Committee's regional pacific seminar in May 2010, reflected his continuing determination to use UN avenues to put his case where possible. And the support he secured from the subgroup of Pacific island leaders on the eve of the 2011 PIF summit (Nadi Communiqué 2011) suggests that he is likely to have some success, even as successive Forum communiqués, including in 2012, continue to use non-controversial language in referring to the issue.

French Polynesia will continue to look to the treatment of New Caledonia as a model for its own future. An unstable long-term outlook for New Caledonia will have repercussions there.

Wallis and Futuna

For the time being, there are few forces for change in Wallis and Futuna. France has done virtually nothing to connect the collectivity with its near neighbours. Despite its location neighbouring Fiji and Samoa, Wallis and Futuna remains isolated, with more flights to and from New Caledonia, 2500 kilometres away, than from Fiji, 800 kilometres away, and none from Apia, just 500 kilometres away. There are no ferry services to any of these places. The archipelago has little infrastructure, including roads, shipping and air services, both within the collectivity and to other parts of the Pacific. The potential for tourism has not been developed.

Sarkozy's promise of a review of the 1961 statute (Sarkozy 2010a) that still governs the collectivity has yet to be implemented. The dependence and remoteness of the archipelago suggest few problems for the French administering authority, which works closely with the two other pillars of Wallisian society, the Catholic Church and the three Kings (one on Wallis and two on Futuna). Events surrounding the succession of the King of Wallis, Kulimoetoke, in 2008 suggest, however, some strain on the existing system. Kulimoetoke reigned for 40 years and signed the 1961 pact with France on which the statute is based. Perhaps it is not surprising that, after such a lengthy period of stability, the succession procedures were time-consuming and initially divisive. Moreover, in 2005, the King had sought to protect his son, who was involved in a manslaughter case, from French law, claiming that customary law should apply. At that time, the King's supporters rioted in the streets and successfully foiled attempts to replace him. After his death in 2007, a successor was agreed upon, following the traditional lengthy processes of consultation, and notwithstanding the opposition of the two other kings, in Futuna, who abdicated over the issue. A successor to one of the Futuna kings was agreed in 2010. The other had not been replaced by mid 2012. This suggests that old systems may not necessarily measure up to future challenges. And prosperity and peace in Wallis and Futuna rest largely on the continued ability of the bulk of its citizens to find work in New Caledonia. So, what happens in New Caledonia matters in a real sense for Wallis and Futuna and could provide a model for it as well.

Long-term solution for New Caledonia

In New Caledonia, the first test for France will be in fulfilling its Noumea Accord commitments, respecting its *parole*, or word, and being seen by Kanak and regional leaders alike to be doing so. This is a critical prerequisite given France's history of dealing with autonomy provisions, revising and often breaking promises from 1956 to 1988 (Chapters 2 and 4). The current generation of Kanak and regional leaders are aware that the most recent, post-1988 French promises, were obtained under the duress of civil war and loss of life on both sides, for and against independence. Tjibaou was murdered only 23 years ago, within a year of negotiating the Matignon Accords, by Kanaks who felt he had sold them out and succumbed to France's manipulation. Already the Noumea Accord, deferring the vote promised by the Matignon Accords for a further 10 years, has been seen by some as simply a delaying tactic. In the years to come, the test for France will be to respond to the frustration expressed by Kanak leader Roch Pidjot in his last speech to the National Assembly in Paris, in 1984, when he said:

> France's sole preoccupation is to maintain its presence in the Pacific. In order to do this, it privileges the interests of Europeans and of other immigrants … convinced that New Caledonia must be governed at the centre, you play into the hands of the most reactionary elements in this country and those of small political groups, thereby providing an unexpected chance for them to appear much more important than they are in reality. … it is a classic strategy: you divide to rule …. Our human dignity is profoundly wounded by declarations to the effect that Kanak independence would be racist …. Our wish is that the referendum be held and that New Caledonia becomes independent …. *You have hurt us too many times. So we have become skeptical, and we will judge the Government not on its declarations but on its actions.* (my italics, Waddell 2008, 128).

For his part, Sarkozy, when he addressed Overseas France in January 2010 repeatedly underlined that 'the State would keep its word' in undertakings that it made ('we don't just say something, we do it', Sarkozy 2010a). But, in the same speech, he said he would not allow independence (see Chapter 7), although Françoise Hollande in May 2012 pledged to respect the wishes of the New Caledonian people.

As Chapter 4 shows, the record of the French State in keeping its commitments under the Noumea Accord has been mixed. It has a positive report card in the areas of setting up relevant institutions, innovative democratic systems and financial support for increasingly autonomous government, engaging all political groupings, Melanesian and Caldoche, pro-independence and pro-France alike. These are themselves major achievements. But the French State has recorded serious minuses in its handling of the sensitive restricted electorate promise; allowing, if not encouraging, continued immigration of French nationals from elsewhere; altering the basis of entity-wide censuses to obfuscate the ethnic composition of the population. It has also sought decisions on one of the five sovereign powers which are reserved for treatment only by referendum after 2014, that of currency, before time. And it has also acted to entrench its presence in another, similarly reserved, sovereign power, defence, well before the Noumea Accord deadline. There have also been delays in the scheduled transfer of important responsibilities.

Moreover, on sensitive economic rebalancing promises, despite all of France's considerable inputs to facilitate better production and distribution of the nickel asset across the peoples of New Caledonia, the pace of progress has been slow. So, to date, the only producer of the valuable commodity remains in French hands and in the European-dominated south, and there has been increasing French control of investment in the critical northern project. France has reasserted its intent to maintain control of the principal investor, Eramet (Sarkozy 2011).

France itself faces difficult dilemmas, injecting their own uncertainties into the situation, as it shepherds New Caledonia to its next stage. France claims to be impartial arbiter at the same time as it is an active participant in the transition process (see Chapter 7). But it was this dual and conflicting role that impeded implementing the Pons and Pisani proposals in the mid 1980s, a role that led to Tjibaou's prescient warning that France was not a judge but an actor (Chapter 2). Despite these early lessons, France has been open in its support for New Caledonia remaining within France, and supporting the pro-France political groups, undermining any claim to impartiality. Its record in French Polynesia, of blatant partiality for particular pro-France groupings (see Chapter 5), despite electoral outcomes supporting the pro-independence groups, with serious effect on political stability, suggests what lies ahead for New Caledonia if the final stages of the Noumea Accord are frustrated by pro-independence activity.

A practical problem for France arises from statutory arrangements which provide for the French State to be responsible for law and order in New Caledonia, while many of the decision-making powers underpinning stability are in the hands of the New Caledonian government. For example, congress decides the regulations and legislation that may give rise to workers' grievances leading to strikes and disruptive barricades and burning of tyres; but it is the French authorities who are responsible for imposing order. Procedurally, the common link between development of the policies (in many key areas the responsibility of the New Caledonian government) which will impact on security, and the security responsibility of the French State, is the French High Commissioner, who is present at all meetings of the New Caledonian executive and the implementer of law and order as senior representative of the French State. But, since the Noumea Accord, he no longer has executive power in the areas of responsibility of the New Caledonian and provincial governments. These considerations have become more relevant with the emergence of the Labour Party and its capacity to stage violent industrial protest, and the tendency, particularly since Sarkozy's presidency, for the French State to treat protest with a firm hand.

Possible radicalisation of pro-independence demands

As New Caledonia looks ahead to the final denouement of the Noumea Accord processes, local political forces are divided, not only between the pro-France and pro-independence groups, but within each side as well. There has been some effort on the part of the pro-France groupings to unite around the idea of holding discussions on the future of New Caledonia after the Noumea Accord (*l'après Accord*), but divisions persist. And the pro-independence groups include a raft of viewpoints within the mainstream FLNKS grouping that signed on to the Accord. The mainstream FLNKS itself, the more influential because of its status as signatory to the Accord, has responded mutely to pro-France overtures to consider an 'association with France' style outcome, and has accused the French State of meddling. One of its constituents, the UC, has frustrated the signature of a framework for the further transfer of responsibilities and called for a review of progress in transfers to date (Chapter 4), while playing into the hands of divided pro-France groups over the flag issue. These are hardly promising signs for the future.

Many analysts have signalled that a major risk to the continued stability of New Caledonia in its transition phase under the Accord could arise from the rift between the young and the older generations, with the emergence of a new, possibly young, idealistic Kanak leader to lead a new push for full independence (see Maclellan 2005b, 412; Faberon 2002, 57; Dornoy-Vurobaravu 1994, 28; Christnacht 2003, 10; Personal communication, senior official May 2008). The emergence and effect of the avowedly pro-independence, mainly Kanak, Labour Party, with a capacity to mobilise large numbers of people, including the young (see Chapter 4), and with a record of violent strategic protest, including blocking flights at the international airport, create worrying uncertainty and the potential for instability and even violent protest. Whether the Labour Party will provide a radical leader, or whether the pro-independence mainstream groups will become radicalised, remains to be seen. Much will depend on the inclusiveness and realism of the negotiation process. As a commentator warned in 2006, the '*status quo*, or the no-change' option 'will heighten the intensity of that [Kanak] resistance and lead to increasing local and regional instability' (Rumley 2006, 241).

Another, related, question on which future stability will rest in New Caledonia is whether or not, given a certain commonality of interest between long-term European residents and Melanesian leaders, social, economic and generational cleavages might assume greater importance than ethnic ones. Such divisions have the potential to bolster the support for the traditional pro-independence group and break down traditional pro-France loyalties, as has been evident in the political realignments of the early 2000s (see Chapter 4).

Next steps for New Caledonia

Chapter 4 sketches the next steps under the Noumea Accord process, which include the continued transfer of responsibilities followed by the holding of a referendum on three questions: the transfer of the sovereign responsibilities, access to an international status of 'full responsibility' for New Caledonia, and organisation of citizenship into nationality (Noumea Accord Article 5), described as a vote on 'accession to full sovereignty' in the Organic Law (Titre IX). The scheduled transfer of specified responsibilities has already slipped, with some significant responsibilities, such as education and aspects of civil law, still to be transferred (at the time of writing, mid 2012).

Non-acceptability of deferring a referendum beyond 2018

The holding of a final referendum, specifically on the independence issue, became a contentious issue during the 2009 provincial election campaign. Chapter 4 outlines the demographic and psephological pointers to any vote on independence probably resulting in a 'no' vote. The unique electorate for the final referendum, suggesting more pro-France voters (as it includes more newcomers, i.e., those with 20 years residence to December 2014, than the electorate for provincial elections, who have residence from 1988), the decline in relative numbers of Kanaks (from whom the largest numbers of pro-independence support come) and the record of the greater weight of the pro-France vote in provincial elections to date, suggests that the likelihood of any pro-independence outcome is slim. The most recent provincial election in 2009 nonetheless showed a sizeable, and growing, part of that electorate supported the pro-independence groups. But, so far, the restricted electorate has applied to the *provincial* (local) elections within the Noumea Accord process. How the (differently defined) restricted electorate for a *referendum* (i.e., those with 20-years residence to 2013 or 2014) might vote on post-Accord issues has not been tested. Moreover, demographic trends show a majority of the population (at least 57 per cent, see Chapter 4) are Pacific Islanders. While many of these are from the Polynesian French collectivities, who have tended to vote pro-France in provincial elections, there is no guarantee that they would vote that way in a referendum on New Caledonia's future.

Recent history has shown that holding a vote on independence, which would be likely to result in a 'no' vote, would rouse sensitivities on the part of extreme pro-independence voters, with the risk of violence and civil war once more. It was for these reasons that the Matignon Accord deferred a vote for 10 years from 1988, and that the Noumea Accord deferred a vote, yet again, for 20 years. And, as Chapter 4 notes, it was this thinking that led pro-France leaders Jacques Lafleur and Harold Martin to propose yet another deferral of a vote. In early 2009, seasoned leader Lafleur, who was a signatory to the Accords and who remembers the civil war of the 1980s, proposed a deferral by up to 50 years, reflecting the gravity of his concern. But these proposals did not meet with general approval. Indeed, the results of the 2009 provincial elections showed that not proceeding to a referendum as provided under the Noumea Accord was not an option. In that election, parties arguing for an early referendum (from amongst the pro-France and pro-independence groups alike) attracted strong support, highlighting the paradoxical polarisation around the issue.

Arguably, one reason why the deferral option was not viable related to the poor record of the French State over the years in delivering on its promises. Its early track record was one of successive statutory measures bestowing then revoking various powers (Chapter 2), and delays in meeting the deadlines of its own complex, scheduled transfer of responsibilities under the Noumea Accord, generous though the promised transfers might be (Chapter 4). In particular, the French State's perceived early reneging over the central 'fixed' restricted electorate issue, allowing continued inflows of migrants from other parts of France and frustrating the census process applying to ethnic categories, was not well received by pro-independence groups. Deferring a vote would raise the difficult question of the continued application of a restricted electorate beyond 2018. It is inconceivable that the pro-independence side would accept abolishing the hard-won concept of a restricted electorate for the final vote, given the swelling of the non-indigenous population. At the same time, it is difficult to see the pro-France side agreeing to prolong the application of the restricted electorate after 2018, given the influx of many pro-France supporters in recent years who, as French citizens, would expect the right to vote.

So, in a sense, either choice — that of deferring a referendum as in the past, or proceeding to a referendum resulting in the rejection of independence — risks serious negative reactions and possibly violence. While it is impossible to predict the future, developments to date, outlined in Chapter 4 and 7, suggest that the French State will encourage all parties to agree to a referendum focused on a result that will be acceptable to all in the long-term. The stakes in ensuring stability in coming years by seeking to promote a successful, peaceful referendum are high.

A referendum, on what?

With the idea of deferring a referendum, or not holding one at all, ruled out by the May 2009 provincial election result, by late 2009 and early 2010 political debate began to focus on the *subject* of the referendum.

Thus, as set out in Chapter 4, in October 2009, pro-France leader Frogier shifted from a position advocating an early referendum to floating a proposal for an 'in association with France' option. He received a mixed response, even from within the pro-France camp, the Avenir Ensemble supporting him with Philippe Gomès' Calédonie Ensemble preferring discussions on a more general idea of 'shared sovereignty'. The pro-independence group, too, were divided. Palika aligned itself more with Gomès' ideas, and the mainstream FLNKS chose not to make a public comment specifically on the 'association' idea, and instead questioned the motives of the French State.

By January 2010, the French State acknowledged the growing importance of the terms of the referendum itself. Sarkozy exhorted both sides to hold discussions, so that the result of the vote 'for self-determination' provided for by the Noumea Accord would translate into a result approved by 'a very large majority of voters' (Sarkozy 2010a, and Chapter 7). As pointed out in Chapter 7, Sarkozy was vague and ambiguous as to the subject of the referendum. He had, earlier in his speech, ruled out independence for Overseas France, so his comments exhorting a result approved by a large majority suggests that he was not expecting the vote to focus on an independence option. And yet, the Organic Law implementing the Accord specifies a vote 'on the accession to full sovereignty' (Titre IX), and pro-independence signatories expect that the independence option will be put.

The terms in which a referendum question is cast, and careful inclusive negotiation, will be the more critical, since the Organic Law provides for repeated votes, up to three, from 2014 to 2018, if the initial vote results in a 'no' vote (Article 217). Three successive votes against independence over three years would conceivably heighten the potential for prolonged violence. No doubt Sarkozy calculated that it would therefore be preferable to pose a different question, in such a way as to receive an overwhelming endorsement the first time round.

Despite the flexible interpretations of some of the mainstream pro-independence coalition about what true independence and sovereignty mean (Chapter 4), not all pro-independence forces may be convinced to set aside the specific option of independence. For some pro-independence supporters, a vote on independence *per se* would alone be seen as fully implementing the spirit and letter of the Noumea Accord. Supporters of the new Labour Party would fall into this category, and that party, and the union that forms its base, have a record of violent disruption. And France is bound, now that it has taken on responsibilities within the UN Decolonisation Committee, to consider independence as an option (see below).

A further note of caution arises from the conclusion by one senior legal advisor to the French Government in March 2011 that technically, given the Organic Law provisions for up to three referendums with associated specified time frames, a referendum could be held as late as 2023. He noted that this would entail an added complication of election of another congress in 2019 (Christnacht 2011). This writer notes that such a further congressional mandate was not foreseen by the Accord or Organic Law and would be likely to raise bitter divisions.

Options and risks for New Caledonia's future

The Noumea Accord specifies that the final 'vote will be concerned with the transfer to New Caledonia of the *régalien* [sovereign] responsibilities, the access to an international status of full responsibility, and the organisation of citizenship into nationality' (Article 5). So, it is these matters that will be the subject of debate and negotiation between the various parties.

By recommencing its reporting responsibilities as administering authority from 2004, France has seemingly committed itself to working within the context of the UN decolonisation provisions. The language of many of the pro-independence groups has also begun to centre on 'decolonisation' as opposed to 'independence' (see Chapter 4). As noted in Chapter 6, relevant UN General Assembly resolutions provide that a non-self-governing territory may reach a full measure of self-government in one of three ways: emergence as a sovereign independent state, free association with an independent state, or integration with a metropolitan state (for example, UNGA Resolution 1541 (XV) 1960). Within the Pacific region itself, there exist already all of these three, and numerous other models. Examples include fully independent states (the independent Pacific island states), total integration in another state (Hawaii), attachment to another state while retaining significant autonomy (Norfolk Island, Marianas), and association (Cook Islands, Palau) (see Robert Aldrich, in Regnault and Fayaud 2008, 199; Firth 1989; *New Pacific Review* 2003).

For New Caledonia, using the UN decolonisation framework as a basis for comparison, some of the options might include, in ascending degrees of retained links with France:

- Formal independence. France's commitment to retain its Pacific collectivities, recently enunciated by Sarkozy, while at the same time being a party principal in the negotiations; its economic support and careful management of grievances of pro-independence forces since 1988; demographic trends shaped by policies over many years; the apparent dominance of the pro-France groupings recent voting patterns in New Caledonia; and, ultimately, France's control over immigration and law and order backed by civil and military power, reduce the likelihood of an independence scenario. Despite its mineral wealth, an independent New Caledonia would still require substantial support by a number of donors, no doubt including France (although this is not guaranteed, given its history and warnings about the costs of independence). The new state would be vulnerable to the same factors the other Pacific island countries face, but with the added complication of its own resource wealth: reduced economic resources, inadequate or non-existent defence and local law enforcement, shifting alliances and rapidly changing governments, and pressure from foreign benefactor governments; in New Caledonia's case this is compounded by competing interests for its rich nickel resources and the need to adjust speedily from dependence on France and Europe to engagement with regional economies. This outcome would deliver new vulnerabilities to the region, potentially negatively affecting security and economic development. Inevitably an independent New Caledonia, on the basis of the Vanuatu experience, would demand an input of economic support and political and diplomatic investment by Australia, additional to the large Australian commitments elsewhere in the region.

- Some kind of free association with France. Pro-independence leaders reacted unenthusiastically to this idea when floated by pro-France leader Frogier in 2009. Because of associations with the doomed 1988 Pisani proposal, another name such as 'partnership' might make the idea more palatable to these groups. Various models already exist in the Pacific region:
  * Compact of free association, such as Palau has with the United States, with its own UN seat, and defence taken care of by the United States for a defined period (50 years in Palau's case).
  * Compact of free association as in Federated State of Micronesia, and the Marshall Islands, which has its own UN seat, with defence taken care of by United States.
  * The 'in association' option of Cook Islands or Niue with New Zealand, with full participation in regional organisations but no UN seat. Freedom to vote to change its status.
- 'Commonwealth' option of the Northern Marianas with the United States, with no UN seat, no responsibility for foreign relations, and the status loosely of an unincorporated dependent territory.
- A form of integration, perhaps either:
  * Federation within France. New Caledonia could become a federated 'state' or province of France (see arguments on this possibility by Faberon, *L'idée fédérale en Nouvelle-Calédonie*, in Regnault and Fayaud 2008, Chapter 2). This would require amendment to the French constitution. New Caledonia would retain its rights acquired under the Noumea Accord, for example, to foreign relations with its immediate region, some civil aviation matters, etc.
  * New status, making permanent the status quo at the time, i.e., 2018 or before, under the Noumea Accord and implementing Organic Law. This would mean a continued consultative collegial government, with ultimate

majority (pro-France) votes on important legislation. Current provisions for a restricted electorate, however, would be unlikely to continue (see citizenship discussion below). The government could be elected on a basis of proportional representation, with declining influence of the Kanak ethnic group over time, in the absence of a specially defined restricted electorate. Still, as under the Noumea Accord, Kanak parties would be likely to continue to administer the Northern and Island provinces and to be represented in the European-dominated Southern Province. Thus there may be scope to negotiate greater powers for the provinces as opposed to the central congress, particularly on administering economic resources such as nickel, as the Northern Province project develops, to accommodate Kanak concerns.

(Note: A further theoretical option would be that of partition, under which conceivably the generally pro-independence Northern and Loyalty Island Provinces could attain full sovereignty; while the Southern Province, dominated by pro-France supporters, could remain with France. This option has been specifically ruled out by the Noumea Accord, which provided at Article 5 that the results of any final referendum will apply globally to New Caledonia, spelling out that one part of New Caledonia cannot accede to full sovereignty or preserve different links with France on the basis of different results in different parts of the electorate.)

Each of the above options provides a basis for implementing the provisions of the Noumea Accord (Article 5) to focus on the five remaining sovereign powers (justice, public order, defence, currency and foreign affairs), international status, and citizenship and nationality. The way in which these issues might be handled is also guided by the Noumea Accord provision that 'so long as the referendums provided for do not result in new political arrangements, then the political arrangements set in place by the 1998 Accord will remain in force, in its last iteration, without possibility of regression, this 'irreversibility' being constitutionally guaranteed' (Article 5). That is, New Caledonia will never revert to what it was before 1998; it will retain the powers transferred by 2018 under the Accord.

Under the Noumea Accord, it is assumed that all but the five *régalien* or sovereign powers would be transferred to New Caledonia before 2018 (even though experience to date shows considerable slippage in these transfers). Of the options set out above, New Caledonia would take over all five remaining sovereign powers in the independence option. France would retain all these powers under an integration option, although New Caledonia would retain those elements of foreign affairs that it received under the Noumea Accord (for example, regional representation, see Chapter 4). In the 'in association' option, negotiations would centre on elements of the remaining sovereign powers which might be traded, for example, responsibility for certain foreign relations and civil law and enforcement elements. Apart from these five powers specified in the Accord, for any non-independence scenario, as demonstrated in Chapter 4, important questions remain about the future responsibility for control over external immigration (both from other parts of France and from other parts of the world), and mining, central issues that have been blurred in the Accord.

With respect to the access to international status, in all three options New Caledonia would retain the responsibilities that it has already been accorded under the Accord to representation in regional organisations. Under the independence option, New Caledonia would clearly, as an independent country, take over all foreign affairs powers and gain full membership of international organisations such as the UN. Under the integration option, France would retain these responsibilities. Negotiations for an 'in association' option can be expected to focus on the nature of New Caledonia's regional relations and representation in regional and other bodies, i.e., factors such as whether New Caledonia could set up its own diplomatic representation in regional countries, and whether it would have delegations of its own as opposed to being subsumed in French delegations. A central question would be whether or not it could be a member of the UN, as are those Pacific island states in forms of association with the United States.

New Caledonia would clearly take over entire responsibility for citizenship and nationality questions in an independence option. For the other options, discussion of these questions is likely to be thorny, since it is here that the question of immigration from other parts of France, non-continuation of the restricted electorate beyond 2018, and the application of employment protection and preferences, would be addressed, all of which have been core elements of the Kanak pro-independence groups' claims from the 1970s. Negotiations in these areas, because they touch on employment in a nickel-dominated economy, would necessarily be linked with discussion and compromise over the future delineation as between the French State and the New Caledonian congress and three provinces over minerals and hydrocarbon resources, and distribution of the benefits, along with difficult sustainable environment issues.

In both the integration and association with France options, because the Noumea Accord states that there can be no regression to the status quo ante the Accord, both pro-France and pro-independence groups would expect to retain those citizenship protections New Caledonia has currently, and will have refined by 2018. These include preserving the rights of longstanding residents over newcomers permanently beyond 2018 in areas such as employment protection for long-term residents and even the idea of a restricted electorate. For example, a residency qualification period could be defined after which newcomers would attain these rights. As described in Chapter 4, France was obliged to devise special legislative constitutional amendment for the relevant provisions of the Noumea Accord, and this was a controversial issue only resolved by constitutional amendment in 2007, nine years after the Accord was signed. Whether France would do so for a permanent future arrangement is open to question, although Sarkozy has spoken of using the flexibility of the constitution to the full (Sarkozy 2010), which suggests an open approach.

France's commitments to comply with UN decolonisation principles also come into play. These principles provide for equal status and rights of citizenship between the peoples of the erstwhile territory and the independent territory into which it is to become integrated (UN Resolution 1541 December 1960, Annex), seemingly at odds with the idea of a restricted electorate. Whereas, as we have seen (Chapter 4), the UN Human Rights Committee upheld the idea of a restricted electorate in 2002 and denied the appeal brought by pro-French supporters, nonetheless the committee specifically linked the idea to the Noumea Accord and the Organic Law 'in particular for the purpose of the final referendum' (UN Human Rights Committee 2002). But again, whether long-term ongoing provisions for special rights would be similarly interpreted as consistent with UN principles could be in question in the future. This could prove vexatious and even inflammatory for frustrated Kanak and pro-independence supporters who could then see themselves as having been betrayed by the UN and the French State.

France would also need to address implications for the non-reciprocal arrangements it has negotiated with the EU, namely the one-way rights for citizens of its Pacific entities to travel to European countries, and to work there (see Chapter 6). Like the UN Human Rights Committee before it, the EU Human Rights Court in 2005 endorsed the idea of a restricted electorate in an appeal hearing brought by pro-France residents, but only owing to the 'local necessities' of the time (see Faberon and Ziller 2007, 394). It may not make the same judgement about permanent special citizenship arrangements.

It is unlikely that pro-independence forces, who have sacrificed much on these particular issues, would agree to dispense with immigration controls, the restricted electorate and employment protection for long-term residents without significant progress in their other expectations (international status, but especially the mining dividend). Differences over these questions between newly arrived residents and longstanding Caldoche residents and the indigenous people; and between pro-France and pro-independence groups may be exacerbated. This would be a factor for ongoing instability.

In all but the independence option, it is likely that the Euro would be speedily introduced, and that inflows of French settlers from other parts of France would continue and probably increase. These developments would work against the greater integration of New Caledonia (and potentially the other French Pacific collectivities) into the Pacific region.

The most likely direction for the future is discussions centring on some kind of future 'in association' with France. The violent history of the referendum issue and the expectations of the pro-independence group about a referendum, suggest that these discussions, and the holding of a referendum in coming years, are likely to be painstaking and sensitive processes, with risks of violence and disruption. The discussions initiated by the French authorities, in the March 2011 Colloquium on the Destinies of the Pacific Political Collectivities, were a start, albeit seeming to concentrate almost exclusively on sovereignty-within-France options.

Whatever the subject of the referendum, because of the sensitivities and potential for disturbance, France, and New Caledonian leaders, including FLNKS leaders like Paul Néaoutyine and Roch Wamytan, would benefit from keeping regional leaders informed, through the UN, PIF, and MSG mechanisms, about the processes under way.

Conclusion

France has earned a long and respected place in the South Pacific region. Its presence has been characterised variously by a sense of enquiry, mission and adventure; strategic interest, national pride and global power; the imposition and maintenance of its military weight; and, more recently, commercial interest. In the past, France's presence has brought strong elements of stability, but also some elements of instability, to the Pacific region.

This work has sought to identify the remaining elements of risk to stability. Australia sees France as a valuable ally in the region at a time of strategic change. It is in Australia's interest to understand the nature of the challenges before France and its Pacific collectivities in the future.

The challenge for France is to respect its own commitments to its entities and the international community, and its responsibilities as a resident neighbour to regional governments and leaders, particularly as it handles difficult governance issues in French Polynesia, but more importantly in the momentous definition of a long-term status for New Caledonia acceptable to all of its people. The solutions will carry implications not only for France's other Pacific entities, but for its necklace of overseas possessions around the world. France's Pacific neighbours understand the complexities of this governance process, one with which they are themselves constantly grappling in their own ways. They will continue to welcome and support genuine, unflinching democratic effort on the part of France and its collectivities.

Appendix 1
Wording of Noumea Accord and 1999 Organic Law on Restricted Electorates

Relating to local (provincial and Congress) elections

Article 2.2.1 of the Noumea Accord:

> "*le corps électoral aux assemblées des provinces et au Congrès sera restreint: il sera réservé aux électeurs qui remplissaient les conditions pour voter au scrutin de 1998, à ceux qui, inscrits au tableau annexe, rempliront une condition de domicile de dix ans à la date de l'élection, ainsi qu'aux électeurs atteignant l'âge de la majorité pour la première fois après 1998 et qui, soit justifieront de dix ans de domicile en 1998, soit auront eu un parent remplissant les conditions pour être électeur au scrutin de la fin de 1998, soit, ayant eu un parent inscrit sur un tableau annexe justifieront d'une durée de domicile de dix ans en Nouvelle-Calédonie à la date de l'élection.*"

> "The electoral body for the assemblies of the provinces and the Congress will be restricted: it will be confined to voters who fulfilled the conditions to vote in the 1998 vote, to those who, registered in the annex table, would fulfill the residency requirement of ten years at the date of the election, as well as voters who have reached majority age for the first time after 1998 and who, either with ten years residency in 1998, or with a parent fulfilling the conditions to vote in the election at the end of 1998, or, having a parent registered on the annex table would be resident for ten years in New Caledonia at the date of the election."

Article 188 of the 19 March 1999 Organic Law:

> "*Le congrès et les assemblées de province sont élus par un corps électoral composé des électeurs satisfaisant à l'une des conditions suivantes:*
>
> *(a) Remplir les conditions pour être inscrits sur les listes électorales de la Nouvelle-Calédonie établies en vue de la consultation du 8 novembre 1998;*

(b) Etre inscrits sur le tableau annexe et domiciliés depuis dix ans en Nouvelle-Calédonie à la date de l'élection au congrès et aux assemblées de province;

(c) Avoir atteint l'âge de la majorité après le 31 octobre 1998 et soit justifier de dix ans de domicile en Nouvelle-Calédonie en 1998, soit avoir eu un de leurs parents remplissant les conditions pour être électeur au scrutin du 8 novembre 1998, soit avoir un de leurs parents inscrit au tableau annexe et justifier d'une durée de domicile de dix ans en Nouvelle-Calédonie à la date de l'élection."

"The Congress and the provincial assemblies are elected by an electoral body composed of voters satisfying one of the following conditions:

Fulfilling conditions to be registered on the electoral role of New Caledonia established for the referendum of 8 November 1998;

Being registered on the annex table and resident for ten years in New Caledonia at the date of the election to the Congress and the provincial assemblies;

Having attained the age of majority after 31 October 1998 and either with ten years residence in New Caledonia in 1998, or having had one of their parents fulfilling the conditions to be a voter in the 8 November 1998 vote, or having one of their parents registered on the annex table and with ten years residence in New Caledonia at the date of the election."

Relating to the final referendum(s)

Article 2.2.1 of the Noumea Accord:

"Le corps électoral pour les consultations relatives à l'organisation politique de la Nouvelle-Calédonie intervenant à l'issue du délai d'application du présent accord (point 5) comprendra exclusivement: les électeurs inscrits sur les listes électorales aux dates des consultations électorales prévues au 5 et qui ont été admis à participer au scrutin prévu à l'article 2 de la loi référendaire, ou qui remplissaient les conditions pour y participer, ainsi que ceux qui pourront justifier que les interruptions dans la continuité de leur domicile en Nouvelle-Calédonie étaient dues à des raisons professionnelles ou familiales, ceux qui, de statut coutumier ou nés en Nouvelle-Calédonie, y ont eu le centre de leurs intérêts matériels et moraux et ceux qui ne sont pas nés en Nouvelle-Calédonie mais dont l'un des parents y est né et qui y ont le centre de leurs intérêts matériels et moraux.

Pourront également voter pour ces consultations les jeunes atteignant la majorité électorale, inscrits sur les listes électorales, et qui, s'ils sont nés avant 1988 auront eu leur domicile en Nouvelle-Calédonie de 1988 à 1998 ou, s'ils sont nés après 1988, ont eu un de leurs parents qui remplissait ou aurait pu remplir les conditions pour voter au scrutin de la fin de 1998. Pourront également voter à ces consultations les personnes qui pourront justifier, en 2013, de vingt ans de domicile continu en Nouvelle-Calédonie."

"The electoral body for the referendums on the political organisation of New Caledonia at the end of the period of application of this agreement (Point 5) will include exclusively: voters registered on the electoral role at the dates of the referendums foreshadowed at 5 and who would be able to vote in the vote foreshadowed at Article 2 of the referendum law, or who fulfilled the conditions to vote in this vote, and those who could prove that interruptions to their continued residence in New Caledonia were due to professional or family reasons, those who, by customary status or born in New Caledonia, have the centre of the material and moral interests there, and those not born in New Caledonia but for whom one parent is born there and who has the centre of their material and moral interests there.

Also able to vote in this vote in these referendums are young people of majority age, registered on the electoral role and who if born before 1988 would have their residence in New Caledonia from 1988 to 1998 or if born after 1988, have a parent fulfilling or who could fulfill conditions to vote in the vote at the end of 1998. Also able to vote in these referendums are people who can prove, in 2013, twenty years of continued residence in New Caledonia."

Article 218 of the 19 March 1999 Organic Law:

"Sont admis à participer à la consultation les électeurs inscrits sur la liste électorale à la date de celle-ci et qui remplissent l'une des conditions suivantes:

a) Avoir été admis à participer à la consultation du 8 novembre 1998;

b) N'étant pas inscrits sur la liste électorale pour la consultation du 8 novembre 1998, remplir néanmoins la condition de domicile requise pour être électeur à cette consultation;

c) N'ayant pas pu être inscrits sur la liste électorale de la consultation du 8 novembre 1998 en raison du non-respect

de la condition de domicile, justifier que leur absence était due à des raisons familiales, professionnelles ou médicales;

d) Avoir eu le statut civil coutumier ou, nés en Nouvelle-Calédonie, y avoir eu le centre de leurs intérêts matériels et moraux;

e) Avoir l'un de leurs parents né en Nouvelle-Calédonie et y avoir le centre de leurs intérêts matériels et moraux;

f) Pouvoir justifier d'une durée de vingt ans de domicile continu en Nouvelle-Calédonie à la date de la consultation et au plus tard au 31 décembre 2014;

g) Etre nés avant le 1er janvier 1989 et avoir eu son domicile en Nouvelle-Calédonie de 1988 à 1998;

h) Etre nés à compter du 1er janvier 1989 et avoir atteint l'âge de la majorité à la date de la consultation et avoir eu un de leurs parents qui satisfaisait aux conditions pour participer à la consultation du 8 novembre 1998.

Les périodes passées en dehors de la Nouvelle-Calédonie pour accomplir le service national, pour suivre des études ou une formation ou pour des raisons familiales, professionnelles ou médicales ne sont pas, pour les personnes qui y étaient antérieurement domiciliées, interruptives du délai pris en considération pour apprécier la condition de domicile."

"Those allowed to vote in the referendum are voters registered on the electoral role at the date of the referendum and who fulfill one of the following conditions:

Having been able to vote in the referendum of 8 November 1998;

Not being registered on the electoral role for the referendum of 8 November 1998, but fulfilling the residence condition required to vote in that referendum;

Not having been able to be registered on the electoral role for the referendum of 8 November 1998 because of not fulfilling the residence requirement, by proving that the absence was due to family, professional or medical reasons;

Having had customary civil status or, born in New Caledonia, having there the centre of their material and moral interests;

Having one of their parents born in New Caledonia and having there the centre of their material and moral interests;

Being able to prove a continual residence of twenty years in New Caledonia at the date of the referendum and at the latest to 31 December 2014;

Born before 1 January 1989 with residence in New Caledonia from 1988 to 1998;

Born after 1 January 1989 and having reached majority age at the date of the referendum and having had one parent fulfilling conditions to participate in the referendum of 8 November 1998;

Periods passed outside New Caledonia to complete national service, to pursue studies or training, or for family, professional or medical reasons are not, for persons with prior residence, deemed to interrupt the period taken into consideration to fulfill the residence requirement."

Appendix 2
Principal statutory measures and proposals: New Caledonia and French Polynesia

Year	Title	Key Features	Status
New Caledonia			
1957	Defferre Law	Administrative autonomy. Territorial Assembly based on universal suffrage, Council of Government of 6–8 ministers.	Law 56-619, 23 June 1956 Decree, 22 July 1957
1963	Jacquinot Law	Reduced autonomy. Removed title of Ministers; Governor the unequivocal head of territorial services.	Law 21 Dec 1963
1969	Billotte Law	Reduced autonomy. Local municipalities replaced by communes run by Paris; confined control over tax exemption for minerals, and other controls over minerals, to French state.	Laws (3) 3 Jan 1969
1976	Stirn Statute	Increased autonomy. High Commissioner shares control of government with Assembly. Members of government council have responsibilities.	Law 28 Dec 1976
1979	Loi Dijoud	Weakened autonomy. Minimum threshold 7.5% for parties to win seats in assembly. Council of Government elected by majority rather than proportional vote; Council can dissolve Assembly.	Law 79-407, 24 May 1979

Year	Title	Key Features	Status
1984	Lemoine Law	Internal autonomy. Referendum within 5 years. Allows distinctive identity signs. Local President of the Territorial Assembly who controlled administration. Consultative mine and credit councils; Assembly including customary representatives.	Law 6 Sept 1984
1985	Pisani Plan	Independence-in-association. Referendum July 1985, if yes: transfer of sovereignty January 1986. Citizenship of new state for all. Non-Kanaks rent from traditional Kanak owners. Retention of French nationality. France to provide defence, expertise, funding for development and training.	Law 23 Aug 1985 Not implemented
1985	Fabius Plan	Reduced autonomy. Introduced regionalisation. French High Commissioner takes on executive power aided by smaller Council. French Government takes ordinance issuing powers. Customary Council created. Referendum on independence-in-association to be held by 31 December 1987.	Law 23 Aug 1985
1986	Pons I Statute	3-year residence rule for self-determination vote in September 1987; powers of regions weakened; new Land Agency created.	Law 17 July 1986
1988	Pons II Statute	Revised demarcation of regions, more autonomy. Executive Council of 10 members, High Commissioner participates without right of vote. Territory freely determines identity signs.	Law 22 Jan 1988 Never implemented

Appendix 2. Principal statutory measures and proposals: New Caledonia and French Polynesia

Year	Title	Key Features	Status
1988	Statut Rocard Matignon/ Oudinot Accords	Created three provinces, each with assembly; a Congress including representatives from the provinces, a Consultative customary council; referendum on self-determination in 1998 by restricted electorate of voters resident in 1988 and descendants; direct rule from Paris for one year; French state takes control of Land Agency and French High Commissioner assumes executive control.	Law 9 Nov 1988
1998	Noumea Accord	Collegial government and Congress based on proportional vote in provinces by one restricted electorate; phased handover of all but five sovereign powers by 2018; up to 3 votes between 2014–2018 on these powers, on international status and on citizenship, by different restricted electorate; work for agreed identity signs; protection of employment for defined New Caledonian citizens.	Agreement to 2018 Organic Law No 99-209 19 Mar 1999
French Polynesia			
1957	Defferre Law	Application of the Defferre Law to French Polynesia (formerly EFO), providing more autonomy.	Law 56-619 23 June 1956
1958	Ordinance	Reduced autonomy and local freedoms. Reaffirmed pre-eminence of French Governor. Removed individual ministerial responsibility in favour of collegial responsibility. Reduced Governing Council from 6–8 to 5 members.	Ordinance 58-1337 23 Dec 1958

Year	Title	Key Features	Status
1977	Management Autonomy Law	Some increased autonomy in management. Reinstates Vice-President of Governing Council with some collegial management powers. French Governor becomes High Commissioner with executive power.	Law 77-772 12 July 1977
1984	Law	More internal autonomy, executive power devolving to the Assembly rather than French High Commissioner; Tahitian flag and official language. Local President created. French State sovereign responsibilities but some shared responsibilities, return to territory of some responsibilities (post and telegraphs, secondary education) taken by State in 1960s.	Law 84-820 6 Sept 1984
1990	Law	Modifies internal autonomy. More powers to Territory over direct foreign investment budget; exploration and exploitation of seabed, marine and subterranean resources; and regional relations; consultative committee on immigration and foreign residence.	Law 90-612 12 July 90
1996	Organic Law	Statute of autonomy.	Law 96-313 12 April 1996
2004	Organic Law	Reinforces 1996 Law after constitutional review.	Law 2004-193 27 Feb 2004
2007	Organic Law	Modifies Organic Law as it applies to election.	Law 2007-223 21 Feb 2007
2007	Law	Modifies the February 2007 Law applying to elections.	Law 2007-1720 7 Dec 2007

Sources: Faberon and Ziller, 2007; Henningham, 1992; <http://www.legifrance.gouv.fr>

References and bibliography

Ageron, C. (1978) *France coloniale ou parti colonial*, Paris, PUF.

Ah Choi, Y. (2006) *Discourse Analysis: A Linguistic Study of the French Press's Representation of the Political Crisis in Tahiti (2004–5)*, French Department, University of Canterbury.

Al Wardi, S. (2009) 'Twenty years of politics in French Polynesia', *The Journal of Pacific History*, 44, 195–208.

Aldrich, R. (1988) *The French View of the Pacific: A Critique of Geopolitical Analysis*, Occasional Paper No. 3, Research Institute for Asia and the Pacific, University of Sydney.

—— (1990) *The French Presence in the South Pacific, 1842–1940*, Basingstoke, Macmillan.

—— (1991) *France, Oceania and Australia: Past and Present*, Department of Economic History, University of Sydney.

—— (1993) *France and the South Pacific since 1940*, Honolulu, University of Hawaii Press.

—— (1996) *Greater France: A History of French Overseas Expansion*, London, Macmillan Press Ltd.

—— and Connell, J. (1989) *France in World Politics*, London, Routledge.

—— —— (1998) *The Last Colonies*, Cambridge University Press.

Aldrich, R., and Merle, I., (eds) (1997) *France Abroad: Indochina, New Caledonia, Wallis and Futuna, Mayotte: Papers Presented at the Tenth George Rude Seminar*, Department of Economic History, University of Sydney.

Alexander, R. (2001) *Japan and the Pacific Island Countries*, Japan-South Pacific Forum Summit Meeting, April 2000, Tokyo, 123–42.

Anaya, J. (2011) *The situation of Kanak people in New Caledonia*, Report of the Special Rapporteur on Indigenous Rights, France, UN Human Rights Council, UN Document A/HRC/18/35/Add. 6, 14 September.

Angleviel, F. (2002) *Le Pari d'Intelligence: From the Matignon Accords to the Noumea Accord 1988–2002*, SSGM Discussion Paper series Current Politics in New Caledonia.

—— (2006) *Brève histoire politique de la Nouvelle Calédonie contemporaine (1945–2000)*, Noumea, Groupe de Recherche en histoire océanienne contemporaine.

Asian Development Bank (2008) *Working in Fragile Environments: Mid-term Review of the Pacific Strategy 2005–2009*, Manila.

Assemblée Nationale De La République De La France (1985) *Journal Officiel*, Débats parlementaires 2 December 1985.

—— (1996) *La France et les États du Pacifique Sud*, Paris, National Assembly.

Ausaid (2009) *Tracking Development and Governance in the Pacific*, Canberra.

Bachimon, P.(1990) 'Le continentalisme et l'exploration du Pacifique Sud', in P. de Deckker and P. Toullelan (eds) *La France et le Pacifique*, Paris, Société d'histoire d'outre-mer, 13–44.

Ban Ki-Moon (2008) 'Message to Decolonisation Seminar', Indonesia, 14 May 2008.

Bates, S. (1990) *The South Pacific Island Countries and France: A Study in Inter-State Relations*, Canberra, Department of International Relations, Research School of Pacific Studies, Australian National University.

Bélorgey, G. (2002) 'Le ministère de l'outre-mer: les raisons de la permanence et les besoins de réforme', *Revue Française d'Administration Publique*, ENA Paris, 101, 83–96.

Bély, L. (2001) *The History of France*, Paris, Éditions Jean-Paul Gisserot.

Berman, A. (2001) 'The Noumea accords: Emancipation or colonial harness?', *Texas International Law Journal*, 36, 277–97.

—— (2005) 'The law on gender parity in politics in France and New Caledonia: A window into the future or more of the same?' *Oxford University Comparative Law Forum 2*, at <http://www.ouclf.iuscomp.org>

Bernardel, G., Lafoy, Y., Van De Beuque, S., Misseque, F. and Nercessian, A. (1999) 'Preliminary results from AGSO Law of the Sea Cruise 206: An Australian/French collaborative deep-seismic marine survey in the Lord Howe Rise/New Caledonia region', *AGSO Record* 1999/14, Commonwealth of Australia, Australian Geological Survey Organisation.

Bertram, G. (2004) 'On the convergence of small island economies with their metropolitan patrons', *World Development*, 32, 343–64.

Boengkih, S. (2010) 'Who constitutes the "people" of a non-self-governing territory?' *Overseas Territories Review* at http://overseasreview.blogspot.com.

Bougainville, L.-A. de (1772) *A Voyage Round the World Performed by Order of His Most Christian Majesty, in the Years 1766, 1767, 1768, and 1769 by Lewis de Bougainville, Colonel of Foot, and Commodore of the Expedition, in the Frigate La Boudeuse, and the Store-Ship L'Étoile*, John Reinhold Forster (trans), London, Eighteenth Century Collections Online, Gale.

Brown, A. (2007) (ed.) *Security and Development in the Pacific Islands: Social Resilience in Emerging States*, London, Lynne Rienner Publishers.

Brown, P. (2008a) 'Les Dieux sont borgnes et la question de l'histoire', in E. Wadrawene et F. Angleviel, *La Nouvelle-Calédonie: Les Kanaks et l'histoire*, Paris, Les Indes Savantes.

—— (2008b) 'Récit fondateur et culture politique en Nouvelle-Calédonie: "Téa Kanaké", de Mélanésia 2000 au Festival des Arts du Pacifique (1975–2000)', *International Journal of Francophone Studies*, 11, 539–57.

Bullard, A. (2000) *Exile to Paradise: Savagery and civilization in Paris and the South Pacific, 1790–1900*, Stanford University Press.

Burchett, W.G. (1941) *Pacific Treasure Island: New Caledonia*, Melbourne, F.W. Cheshire Pty Ltd.

Cadéot, P. (2003) *L'Outre-mer français dans le Pacifique Sud: Nouvelle-Calédonie, Polynésie française, Wallis et Futuna*, Noumea, Artypo.

Carleton, F.R.L. (1995) *Terre de France a la Pérouse: A Study of the Historical Foundations of a Local Myth*, Kensington NSW, Carleton.

Cazaux, Y. (1995) Dans le sillage de Bougainville et de Lapérouse, Paris, Albin Michel.

Chappell, D. (1998) 'New Caledonia', *The Contemporary Pacific*, Fall 1998, 441–46.

—— (1999) 'The Noumea Accord: Decolonization without independence in New Caledonia?', *Pacific Affairs*, 72, 373–91.

—— (2005a) '"Africanization" in the Pacific: Blaming others for disorder in the periphery?' *Comparative Studies in Society and History*, 47, 286–317.

—— (2005b) 'Political review of French Polynesia', *The Contemporary Pacific*, 17, 193–203.

—— (2006) 'New Caledonia', *The Contemporary Pacific*, 18, 399–413.

—— (2009) 'New Caledonia. Melanesia In review: Issues and events, 2008', *The Contemporary Pacific*, 21, no. 2, Fall 2009, 352–64.

Chauchat, M. (2006) *Vers un développement citoyen — Perspective d'émancipation pour la Nouvelle-Calédonie*, Libre Cours Presses Universitaires de Grenoble.

Chesneaux, J. (1987a) *France in the Pacific: A Tentative Analysis*, Canberra, Peace Research Centre, Research School of Pacific Studies, Australian National University.

—— (1987b) *Transpacifiques: Observations et Considérations diverses sur les terres et archipels du Grand Océan*, Paris, Éditions La Découverte.

—— (1991) 'Grand design: Theory and practice of the "Puissance mondiale moyenne"', *Journal of Pacific History*, 26, 256–72.

—— and Maclellan, N. (1992) *La France dans le Pacifique: de Bougainville à Moruroa*, Paris, Découverte.

Chirac, J. (2003a) 'Discours', Place des Cocotiers 23 July 2003, <http://www.gouv.nc>

—— (2003b) Speech to France–Oceanic Summit, Papeete, 28 July.

Christnacht, A. (2003) 'L'avenir de l'accord de Nouméa', Revue Juridique, Politique et Economique de Nouvelle Calédonie, 2, 2–11.

—— (2004) *La Nouvelle-Calédonie*, Paris, Documentation française.

—— (2011) 'Quelles Perspectives Institutionnelles Pour La Nouvelle-Calédonie?' unpublished presentation to Colloquium, Destins des collectivités politiques d'Océanie, Noumea, Centre National de la Recherche Scientifique, 10 March 2011.

Christopher, A.J. (2002) 'Decolonisation without independence', *GeoJournal*, 56, 213–24.

Cleland, L. (2008) 'From the archives', *The Journal of Pacific History*, vol. 9, no. 1, 164–71.

Colchester, C.(Ed.)(2003) *Clothing the Pacific*, New York, Oxford.

Colloque (2008) A l'occasion des vingt ans de la signature des Accords dits de Matignon-Oudinot, Paris, see also Regnault and Fayaud 2008.

Comptes Economiques Rapides De L'outre-Mer (2008) *Les défis de la croissance calédonienne*, Paris.

Connell, J. (1987) *New Caledonia or Kanaky? The Political History of a French Colony*, Canberra: National Centre for Development Studies.

2003) 'New Caledonia: An Infinite Pause in Decolonisation?', *The Round Table*, 92, 125–43.

Consulat-Général D'australie (2010) *70 Ans De Relation Bilatérale: Fraternité, Animosité, Amitié*, Noumea: Artypo.

Cooper, R. (1996) *The Post-modern State and the World Order*, London, Demos.

Cordonnier, I. (1993) 'La France dans le Pacifique sud: Perspectives pour les années 1990', *Politique Etrangère*, 3, 733–46.

—— (1995a) *La France dans le Pacifique Sud: Approche Géostratégique*, Paris, Editions Publisud.

—— (1995b) 'The French Government and the South Pacific during cohabitation 1986–1988', *Pacific Studies*, 18, 79–102.

Courtin, P., Capitaine de Corvette (1999) 'La stratégie maritime de la Chine', *Bulletin d'études de la Marine*, 15, 49–50.

Coutau-Begarie, H. (1987) *Géostratégie du Pacifique*, Paris, Institut français des relations internationales, Economica.

—— and Seurin, J.-L. (1986) *Nouvelle-Calédonie, Les antipodes de la démocratie*, Paris, Lieu Commun.

Cugola, U. (2003) 'Perspectives pour une décolonisation en Nouvelle-Calédonie', *Journal de la Société des Océanistes*, 117, 273–80.

Dalton, J. (1986) 'French national interests and military policies in the South Pacific', Paper presented to the Australasian Political Studies Association, Brisbane.

Daly, H. 'L'opportune assistance de l'Australie à la Nouvelle-Calédonie pendant la seconde Guerre Mondiale (1940–1945)', *Bulletin de la Société d'Études Historique*, no. 113.

Danielsson, B. and Danielsson, M.-T. (1986) *Poisoned Reign: French Nuclear Colonialism in the Pacific*, Ringwood, Victoria, Penguin Books.

de Brosses, Charles (1756) *Histoire des navigations aux terres australes*, Paris, Durand.

de Brouwer, G. (2000) 'Should Pacific island nations adopt the Australian dollar?', *Pacific Economic Bulletin*, 15, 161–69.

de Deckker, P. (1983) *The Aggressions of the French at Tahiti and Other Islands in the Pacific, George Pritchard, 1796–1883*, Auckland University Press.

—— (1996) 'Decolonisation processes in the South Pacific islands: A comparative analysis between metropolitan powers', *Victoria University of Wellington Law Review*, Special Issue, Comparative Law, 26, 355–71.

—— (2002) 'Le Pacifique à la recherche du développement dans un espace émietté', *Revue Française d'Administration Publique*, ENA Paris, 101, 157–68.

—— (2003a) 'France in the Pacific: Colonial administration and policy', *The New Pacific Review*, 2, 59–70.

—— (2003b) 'L'arc mélanésien: l'état des états', *Géoéconomie*, 27, Autumn, 1–8.

—— (2004) 'New Caledonia: Yesterday, today and tomorrow', Paper presented to 39th Foreign Policy School, Otago University, Dunedin.

—— (2005) 'Pour une géopolitique de l'Arc mélanésien', *Revue juridique, politique et économique de Nouvelle-Calédonie*, 5, 2–9.

—— (2006) *Figures de l'État dans le Pacifique Sud*, Paris, L'Harmattan.

—— (2007a) 'Dépendances et indépendances dans le Pacifique insulaire', *Bulletin des Historiens et des Géographes de Polynésie Française*, 111–17.

—— (2007b) 'Development and self-determination in New Caledonia', in A. Brown (ed.) *Security and Development in the Pacific Islands: Social Resilience in Emerging States*, London, Lynne Rienner Publishers.

—— and Toullelan, P.-Y. (1990) *La France et le Pacifique*, Paris, Société française d'Histoire d'Outre-mer et L'Harmattan.

—— Faberon, J.-Y., Le Guillou G., and Steinmetz, L. (2003) *L'outre-mer France du Pacifique*, Noumea, CDP L'Harmattan.

—— and Faberon, J.-Y. (ed.) (2008) *La Nouvelle-Calédonie pour l'intégration mélanésienne*, Paris-Noumea, L'Harmattan.

Defence, Department of, (2009) *Defending Australia in the Asia Pacific Century: Force 2030*, Defence White Paper, Canberra, Commonwealth of Australia.

Défense, Ministère de la, (1994) *Livre Blanc*, Paris.

—— (2008) *Livre Blanc*, Paris.

De Gaulle, C. (1947) Strasbourg Speech, 7 April 1947, website charles-de-gaulle.org.

Deladrière, B. (2004) 'La France, la Nouvelle-Calédonie et le Pacifique Sud', *Revue Juridique, Politique et Économique de Nouvelle-Calédonie*, 4, 5–9.

Delbos, G. (2000) *The Catholic Church in New Caledonia*, Paris, CEPAC.

Dening, G. (1980) *Islands and Beaches: Discourse on a Silent Land, Marquesas, 1774–1880*, Melbourne University Press.

Deschanel, Paul (1884) *La Politique Française en Océanie à propos du Canal de Panama*, Paris: Berger-Levrault et Cie.

Deschanel, Paul (1888) *Les Intérêts Français dans l'Océan Pacifique*, Paris: Berger-Levrault et Cie.

Dillon, Peter (1829) *Narrative and Successful Result of a Voyage in the South Seas Performed by Order of the Government of British India, to Ascertain the Actual Fate of La Pérouse's Expedition Interspersed with Accounts of the Religion, Manners, Customs and Cannibal Practices of the South Sea Islanders*, London, Hurst, Chance and Co., vols 1 and 2.

Diver, C. (2004) 'La Nouvelle-Calédonie dans l'exercice de ses relations internationales', *Revue Juridique, Politique et économique de Nouvelle-Calédonie*, 4, 10–19.

Dobbins, J., Jones, S.G., Crane, K. and Degrasse, B.C. (2007) *The Beginner's Guide to Nation-building*, National Security Research Division, Rand.

Dobell, G. (2007) *China and Taiwan in the South Pacific: Diplomatic Chess versus Pacific Political Rugby*, Lowy Institute Policy Brief.

Dommel, D. (1993) *La Crise Calédonienne: Rémission ou guérison?*, Paris, L'Harmattan.

Dornoy-Vurobaravu, M. (1994) *Policies and Perceptions of France in the South Pacific: New Caledonia and Vanuatu / Objectifs et interprétations de la politique française dans le Pacifique Sud: la Nouvelle-Calédonie et le Vanuatu*, Suva, Institute of Pacific Studies, University of the South Pacific.

Doumenge, J.-P. (1987) 'Les Mélanésiens et la société pluriethnique en nouvelle-calédonie', *Hérodote*, 37–38, 123–29.

—— (2002) 'La France confrontée au trou noir du Pacifique, la face inconnue de la question calédonienne', *Conflits actuels Revue d'étude politique*, 10, 101–12.

——, Doumenge, F., and Faberon, J.-Y. (2000) *L'Outre-mer français*, Paris, Armand Colin.

Du Prel, A. (1996) 'Dur, dur de réintégrer le pacifique sud', *Tahiti Pacifique*, 9–11.

Dunmore, J. (1978) *Les Explorateurs Français dans le Pacifique*, vol. I, Tahiti, Éditions du Pacifique.

—— (1997) *Visions and Realities: France in the Pacific, 1695–1995*, Waikanae, N.Z., Heritage Press.

Duzer, A.R. (1991) Closing speech France in Pacific Seminar, Australian National University.

Estrosi, C. (2007) Discours au Haut-commissariat de la République en Polynésie, Post Forum Tonga, 18 October 2007.

European Commission (1998) 'The European Union and the overseas countries and territories / L'Union européenne et les pays et territoires d'outre-mer', *Development DE99*, December, Brussels.

—— (2006) 'EU relations with the Pacific Islands — A atrategy for a atrengthened partnership', Communication from the Commission to the Council, the European Parliament, and the European Economic and Social Committee, Brussels.

—— (2007) *The European Union and the Pacific*, Brussels.

—— (2008) *Green Paper: Future Relations between the EU and Overseas Countries and Territories*, SEC (2008) 2067, Brussels, Commission of the European Communities.

European Union (2009) *Briefing Paper: The Status and Location of the Military Installations of the Member States of the European Union and their Potential Role for the European Security and Defence Policy*, European Parliament Policy Department, External Policies, Brussels.

—— (2010) Brochure, Delegation to the Pacific.

Faberon, J.-Y. (1997) *L'avenir statutaire de la Nouvelle-Calédonie, l'évolution des liens de la France avec ses collectivités périphériques*, Paris, Collection les Études de la Documentation française, Revue "Institutions".

—— (2001) 'L'évolution du droit de vote en Nouvelle-Calédonie', *Revue Juridique de Polynésie*.

—— (2002) 'La Nouvelle-Calédonie: vivre l'Accord de Nouméa', *Revue Française d'Administration Publique*, ENA Paris, 101, 39–57.

—— (2004) *L'outre-mer français: La nouvelle donne institutionnelle*, Paris, La Documentation française, Études.

—— and Auby, J-F., (1999) *L'Évolution du Statut de département d'outre-mer*, Montpellier, Presses Universitaires d'Aix-Marseille.

——, Gautier, Y., and Doumenge, J-P. (eds) (1999) *Identité, nationalité, citoyenneté outre-mer*, Colloque, Paris, La Documentation française.

—— and Hage, A. (2010) *Mondes Océaniens*, Paris, L'Harmattan.

—— and Ziller, J. (2007) *Droit des Collectivités d'Outre-Mer*, Paris, Libraire générale du droit.

Faivre, J.P. (1953) *L'expansion française dans le Pacifique de 1800 à 1842*, Paris, Nouvelles éditions latines.

Firth, S. (1989) 'Sovereignty and independence in the contemporary Pacific', *The Contemporary Pacific*, 1, 77–83.

—— (ed.) (2006) *Globalisation and Governance in the Pacific Islands*, Canberra, State Society and Governance in Melanesia, Australian National University E Press

—— (2007) Security in the Pacific Islands, 2007–2027, unpublished manuscript.

Fisher, D. (2003) Interview, *France–Australie*, Sydney, French Australian Chamber of Commerce and Industry.

—— (2004) Address to visiting French Minister for Research, M. François d'Aubert, Noumea, drawing on material provided by Australian Department of Foreign Affairs and Trade.

—— (2008a) 'Searching for Pacific solutions', *Courier Mail* (Brisbane), 14 January.

—— (2008b) New Caledonia: What now after twenty years of peace? *Interpreter* blogsite, Sydney, Lowy Institute, 16 June.

—— (2008c) The South Pacific in France's Defence White Paper, *Interpreter* blogsite, Sydney, Lowy Institute, 9 July.

—— (2009a) Industrial strife as New Caledonia goes to the polls, *Interpreter* blogsite, Sydney, Lowy Institute, 16 March.

—— (2009b) 'Riots in French territories will impact on Australia', *Canberra Times*, 23 March.

—— (2009c) New Caledonia election: reduced pro-France majority, *Interpreter* blogsite, Sydney, Lowy Institute, 15 May.

—— (2009d) France all but ignored in Defence White Paper, *Interpreter* blogsite, Sydney, Lowy Institute, 28 May.

—— (2010a) France's mixed messages for the Pacific, *Interpreter* blogsite, Sydney, Lowy Institute, 28 January.

—— (2010b) 'France in the South Pacific: An Australian perspective', presentation to George Rudé Conference: Histoire et Mémoire, University of Sydney, 16 July 2010.

—— (2010c) 'Supporting the Free French in New Caledonia: First steps in Australian diplomacy', *Explorations*, 49, 1, December, 18–37.

—— (2011) 'France and the South Pacific', Annual Fonds Pacifique lecture, Australian National University School of Asia and the Pacific, Podcast 16 March 2011.

—— (2012a) 'France: "in" or "of" the South Pacific? *Journal de la Société des Océanistes*, 2012, 2, 35,185–99.

—— (2012b) 'The Need to Remember: L'ordre et la morale (*Rebellion*)', film review, *Fiction and Film for French Historians*, vol. 2, iss. 5, April 2012, H-France website http://h-france.net/fffh/.

—— (2012c), 'France, the EU and the South Pacific', briefing paper, Centre for European Studies, Australian National University, vol. 3, no. 9, August.

—— (2012), France in the Pacific: Countdown for New Caledonia - Options for the future, Briefing Paper, Centre for European Studies, Australian National University Vol 3 No 1, March.

—— (2012), France in the Pacific: Countdown for New Caledonia - Review of implementation of the Noumea Accord, Briefing Paper, Centre for European Studies, Australian National University, Vol 3 No 2, May.

Floyd, N, (2007), 'An Expedition in Regime Change: Australia's party to the ralliement of New Caledonia during World War II', *Journal of the Australian Naval Institute*, 124, Winter, 8-16.

Foreign Affairs And Defence, Departments of, (1987) 'Submission to the Joint Parliamentary Committee on Foreign Affairs and Defence Enquiry into Australia's relations with the South Pacific', Canberra.

Foreign Affairs And Trade, Department of, (1997) *The South Pacific Commission: The First Fifty Years*, Canberra, Paragon Printers.

—— (2000) *Statement of Service: Appointments and Biographies*, Canberra, Commonwealth Government, June.

—— (2003) *Advancing the National Interest: Australian Foreign Affairs and Trade Policy White Paper*, Canberra.

Fraenkel, J. (2006) 'Power sharing in Fiji and New Caledonia', in S. Firth (ed.) *Globalisation and Governance in the Pacific Islands*, Canberra, State Society and Governance in Melanesia, Australian National University E Press.

Fraser, H. (1990a) *Your Flag's Blocking our Sun*, Melbourne, Australian Broadcasting Corporation.

—— (1990b) *Man of the Decade*, Pacific Island Monthly, 60, 9–12.

Frogier, P. (2008) Lettre aux jeunes calédoniens, 16 May 2008.

Fromion, Y. (2003) *Défense, espace, communication et renseignement*, Assemblée Nationale de la République de France, Paris.

Fry, G. (1981) 'Regionalism and International Politics of the South Pacific', *Pacific Affairs,* 54 3 455–84.

Furukawa, J. (2003) 'Educate the public about the decolonization issue', *Pacific Daily News*, October.

Garde, F. (2002) 'L'Administration des Îles désertes', *Revue Française d'Administration Publique*, ENA Paris, 101, 59–67.

Gaszi, M. (2006) 'Sommet France-Océanie 2006', in Ministère des Affaires Étrangères website <http://www.diplomatie.gouv.fr/>

Gay, J.-C. (2003) *L'outre-mer français*, Paris, Belin.

Geoffroy, J. (2006) *Le nickel calédonien: Modèle industriel et changement social du milieu du XIXe siècle au milieu du XXe siècle. Les mutations d'une filière économique*, Lycée A. Kela, Poindimié.

Girardin, B. (2002) 'Avant-propos — La Réforme constitutionnelle et l'outre-mer', *Revue Française d'Administration Publique*, ENA Paris, no. 101, 3–5.

Gohin, O. (2002) 'La citoyenneté dans l'outre-mer français', *Review of Institute of Public Affairs*, 101, 69–82.

Gomane, J.-P., Guibert, J.-L., Martin-Pannetier, A., and Ordonnaud, G. (eds.) (1983) *Le Pacifique: "Nouveau Centre Du Monde"*, Berger-Levrault (see also under Ordonnaud).

Gonnot, F.-M. (1995) 'Australie, Nouvelle-Zéland: les nouveaux 'dragons' du pacifique Sud?' *Information report No 2009*, Paris, National Assembly.

Gonschor, L. (2009) 'Polynesia in review: Issues and events, 1 July 2007 to 30 June 2008: French Polynesia', *The Contemporary Pacific*, 21, 151–62.

Gorce, de la, X. (2007) Letter to the Secretary-General, Law of the Sea, 18 July 2007, <http://www.un.org/Depts/los/clcs_new/submissions_files/fra07/fra_letter_july2007_english.pdf>

Gorman, L. (1997) 'Australia and Vichy: the impact of divided France, 1940–1944', *The Australian Journal of Politics and History*, vol. 43.

Gorodey, D. (2004) *The Kanak Apple Season*, Peter Brown (trans. & ed.), Canberra, Pandanus Books.

Green, M.H. (1990) *The South Pacific Nuclear Free Zone Treaty: A Critical Assessment*, Canberra, Australian National University.

Greenpeace International (1990) *Témoignages essais nucléaires français: des Polynésiens prennent la parole (Testimonies: witnesses of French nuclear testing in the South Pacific)*, Auckland.

Guiart, J. (1992) 'A drama of ambiguity: Ouvea 1988–89', *Journal of Pacific History*, 85–102.

—— (1999) *Les Mélanésiens devant l'économie de marché*, Noumea, Éditions du Rocher-à-la-Voile.

Guillaud, D., Huetz De Lemps, C., and Sevin, O. (2003) *Iîes rêvées: territoires et identités en crise dans le Pacifique insulaire*, PRODIG: Presses de l'université de Paris-Sorbonne.

Guillebaud, J.C. (1976) *Les Confettis de l'Empire*, Paris, Editions du Seuil.

—— (1980) *Un Voyage en Océanie*, Paris, Editions du Seuil.

Guillou, J. (2000) *Peter Dillon: Capitaine des mers du sud*, Beauvoir-sur-Mer, L'Étrave.

—— (2002) *L'Odyssée d'Ann Smith*, Beauvoir-sur-mer, L'Étrave.

—— (2007) *Échos du grand océan*, France, L'Étrave.

Hadj, L. (2009) 'Wallis et Futuna: Recensement de la population de 2008', *INSEE Première*, no. 1251.

Hanson, F. (2008) *The Dragon Looks South*, Lowy Institute Analysis Paper, Sydney, 1–46.

Haut-Commissariat (1999) *Le programme '400 cadres' principales données statistiques bilan 1989-1999*, Haut-Commissariat de la République en Nouvelle-Calédonie, Nouméa.

Heffer, J. (1995) *Les États Unis dans le Pacifique — Histoire d'une frontière*, Paris, Albin Michel.

Henningham, S. (1989) *France and the South Pacific: Prospects into the 1990s*, Parliament of Commonwealth of Australia, Canberra, Legislative Research Service Discussion Paper Number 2.

—— (1992) *France and the South Pacific: A Contemporary History*, Sydney, North, Allen and Unwin.

Horner, F. (1987) *The French Reconnaissance: Baudin in Australia 1801–1803*, Melbourne University Press.

Horner, F.B. (1996) *Looking for La Pérouse: D'Entrecasteaux in Australia and the South Pacific, 1792–1793*, Melbourne University Press.

Horowitz, L. (2004) 'Toward a viable independence? The Koniambo Project and the political economy of mining in New Caledonia', *The Contemporary Pacific*, 16, 287–319.

Howe, K.R., Kiste, R.C., and Lal, B.V. (1994) *Tides of History: The Pacific Islands in the Twentieth Century*, Honolulu, University of Hawaii Press.

Huffer, E. (1993) *Grands Hommes et petites îles*, Paris, ORSTOM.

Hughes, H. (2003) 'Aid has failed the Pacific', *CIS Issue Analysis*, 33.

Institut De La Statistique Et Des Etudes Economiques Nouvelle-Calédonie (2008) *Tableaux de l'économie Calédonienne Edition Abrégée 2008*, Noumea.

Institut National De La Statistique Et Des Etudes Economiques (2008) , Paris.

Institut Polaire Français (2006) *Les rapports de campagnes à la mer : MD153/ AUSFAIR-Zonéco 12 et VT 82/GAB on board R/V Marion Dufresne*, OCE/2006/05, Plouzané.

Jégo, Y. (2009) Interview, *Outre-Mer, Guadeloupe*, France 24, 19 February 2009.

Kerr, D. (2008) 'Australia strengthens relations with France and New Caledonia in the Pacific', trranscript of a media conference, Department of Foreign Affairs and Trade, 15 November 2008.

Kochenov, D. (ed.) (2011) *The EU Law of the Overseas: Outermost Regions, Associated Overseas Countries and Territories, Territories Sui Generis*, The Netherlands: Kluwer Law International BV.

La Pérouse, J.-F. de G. (1832) *Voyage de La Pérouse*, Paris, Lecointe.

Lacour, P. (1987) *De L'Océanie au Pacifique: Histoire et Enjeux*, Paris, Éditions France-Empire.

Lafargue, R. (2002) 'La Justice Outre-Mer: Justice du lointain, justice de proximité', *Revue Française d'Administration Publique*, ENA Paris, 101, 97–109.

Lafleur, J. (2000) *L'Assiégé*, Paris La librairie Plon.

—— (2002) *Ce que je crois*, Imprimeries Réunies de Nouméa.

Lafoy, Y., Brodien, I., Vially, R, and Exon, N.F. (2005) 'Structure of the basin and ridge system west of New Caledonia (Southwest Pacific): A synthesis', *Marine Geophysical Researches*, 26, 37–50.

Latham, L. (1978) *La révolte de 1878 : étude critique des causes de la rébellion de 1878, en Nouvelle-Calédonie*, Noumea, Publications de la Société d'études historiques de la Nouvelle-Calédonie.

Lawrey, J. (1982) *The Cross of Lorraine in the South Pacific: Australia and the Free French Movement 1940–1942*, Canberra, ANU Printing Service.

Le Borgne, J. (2005) *Nouvelle-Calédonie 1945–1968 La confiance trahie*, Paris, L'Harmattan.

Le Pensec, L. (1990) 'Une politique pour l'Outre-Mer Français', *Défense Nationale*, August–September, 9–23.

Leenhardt, M. (1937) *Gens de la Grande Terre: Nouvelle-Calédonie*, Paris, Gallimard.

Lefebvre, J.C. (1999) 'La marine dans le nouveau paysage stratégique', *Bulletin d'Etudes de la Marine*, 15, 17–20.

Lepot, H. (2010) 'Recensement: Nous sommes bien 245,580', *Nouvelles Calédoniennes*, 14 February.

Leymarie, P. (1985) 'Les enjeux stratégiques de la crise calédonienne', *Le Monde diplomatique*, 1, 13.

Maclellan, N. (1990) 'Liberty, Equality, Fraternity? French military forces in the Pacific', *Interdisciplinary Peace Research*, 2.

—— (2005a) 'Conflict and reconciliation in New Caledonia: Building the Mwâ Kâ', *State Society and Governance in Melanesia Discussion Paper* 2005/1,

—— (2005b) 'From Eloi to Europe: Interactions with the ballot box in New Caledonia', *Commonwealth and Comparative Policies*, 43, November, 394–418.

—— (2005c) 'New Caledonia: An uncertain marriage: Merger to change the face of New Caledonian mining', *Pacific Magazine*, 1 December.

—— (2005d) 'New Caledonia: Building a common destiny', *Pacific Magazine*, 1 December.

—— (2005e) 'The Nuclear Age in the Pacific Islands', *The Contemporary Pacific*, 17, 263–372.

—— (2006) 'Radiating heat: Report blows open French nuclear testing in the Pacific', *New Internationalist*, May.

—— (2008a) France continues to avoid responsibility for nuclear compensation, Personal communication to author.

—— (2008b) 'Under one flag: Will a new flag, anthem unite New Caledonia?', *Pacific Magazine*, November 13, 2008.

—— (2009a) 'New government in New Caledonia — The May 2009 elections in a French Pacific territory', *State Society and Governance in Melanesia Briefing Paper* 3/2009, 1–12.

—— (2009b) 'The Australia–France Defence Co-operation Agreement: Implications for France in the South Pacific', Nautilus Institute Australia, Austral Policy Forum 09-19, 2 November.

—— (2009c) 'Noumea takes control of education', *Islands Business*, December.

—— and Boengkih, S. (1996) *France's Decolonisation Process in New Caledonia: Conflict on the Path to Self-Determination*, Melbourne, Victoria University.

—— and Chesneaux, J. (1998) *After Moruroa: France in the South Pacific*, Melbourne and New York, Ocean Press.

Marlaud, J.-M. (2006) 'France, EU and the Pacific', seminar presentation to University of Canterbury, Christchurch, New Zealand, 7 April 2006.

Marles, R. (2012) Interview with Girish Sawlani, Radio Australia *Pacific Beat*, 17 April.

Matsuda, M.K. (2005) *Empire of Love, Histories of France and the Pacific*, New York, Oxford University Press.

Mcintyre, A. (2003) 'Independence in the Pacific should be a positive process', *Review of Institute of Public Affairs*, 55, 19–20.

Mcphail, A. (2007) 'John Howard's leadership of Australian Foreign Policy 1996 to 2004: East Timor and the war against Iraq', Department of Politics and Public Policy, Griffith University.

May, R. (2011) 'The Melanesian Spearhead Group: testing Pacific island solidarity', *Policy Analysis*, Australian Strategic Policy Institute, 8 February 2011, 1–8.

Menzies, R.G. (1939) 'Ministry's policy', *Sydney Morning Herald*, 27 April 1939, 9.

Merle, I. (2010) 'La creation de la route du Pacifique, HG/NC la site académique d'histoire-géographie de Nouvelle-Calédonie', 17 Juillet.

Methven, P. (1986) *The French Approach to Regional Security in the South Pacific 1962–1986*, Canberra, Australian National University.

Michal, E. J. (1993) 'Protected states: The political status of the federated States of Micronesia and the Republic of the Marshall Islands', *The Contemporary Pacific*, 5, 303–32.

Michalon, J.-P. (1982) 'La République française, une fédération qui s'ignore?', *Revue du droit Public et de la Science Politique*, 623.

Michener, J. (1946) *Tales of the South Pacific*, The Curtis Publishing Company.

Miles, J., Shaw, E.(1996) *Chronology: the French presence in the South Pacific 1838–1990*, Auckland, Greenpeace.

Mohamed-Gaillard, S. (2009) 'Les relations franco-australiennes en Océanie', *Journées d'études: Images et pouvoirs dans le pacifique*, Rochefort, France.

Mokkadem, H., Poingam, É., and Veyret, M.-P. (1999) *L'Échec scolaire en Nouvelle-Calédonie*, Noumea, Éditions Rond Point.

Mrgudovic, N. (2002–2003) 'Nouvelle-Calédonie ou Kanaky: perceptions régionales du Caillou', *Journal de la Société des Océanistes*, 117, 281–99.

——(2004) 'New Caledonia's struggle for independence: A regional perspective', *The New Pacific Review*, 105–24.

—— (2006) 'La France dans le Pacifique Sud 1966–2006: Enjeux et mutations', Thèse, Bordeaux, Université Montesquieu-Bordeaux IV.

—— (2008) *La France dans le Pacifique Sud: les enjeux de la puissance*, Paris, L'Harmattan.

Muckle, A. (2009) 'No more violence or war: 20 years of nation-building in New Caledonia', *The Journal of Pacific History*, 54, 179–94.

Muller, K. (1999) 'Problems of European Union citizenship rights at the periphery', *Australian Journal of Politics and History*, 45, 35–51.

—— (2010) 'Europe as a Pacific power', unpublished work presented as 'The Europeanisation of the Pacific' to the European Studies Centre, Australian National University, 6 July 2010.

Munholland, K. (1986) The Trials of the Free French in New Caledonia, 1940–1942, *French Historical Studies* XIV, 4, 547–79.

—— (2005) *Rock of Contention: Free French and Americans at War in New Caledonia, 1940–1945*, New York and Oxford, Berghahn Books.

Nadi, Communiqué of, (2011) Engaging with the Pacific Leaders Meeting, Fiji, 1–2 September.

National Gallery Of Australia (2000) *Les sauvages de la mer Pacifique: manufactured by Joseph Dufour et Cie 1804–05 after a design by Jean-Gabriel Charvet*, Canberra.

Néaoutyine, P. (2001) 'Les Kanak dans l'économie: Entretien avec Paul Néaoutyine', *Mwà Véé Revue Culturelle Kanak*, 32, 5–13.

—— (2006) *L'indépendance au présent*, Paris, Édition Syllepse.

—— (2009) Interview, *Nouvelles Calédoniennes*, 8 April 2009.

—— (2011) Interview, YouTube, 8 July 2011.

New Pacific Review La Nouvelle Revue Du Pacifique (ed.) (2003) *Pacific Island States Today, L'État des états*, Paris Noumea Papeete Canberra, Pandanus Books.

Newbury, C.W. (1980) *Tahiti Nui: Change and Survival in French Polynesia, 1767–1945*, Honolulu, University Press of Hawaii.

Newman, H.R. (2001) 'The mineral industry of France', in *US Geological Survey Minerals Handbook*.

Nichols, M. (2007) *The Impact of France on Conflict and Stability in the South Pacific*, University of Canterbury.

Nouzé, H., Cosquer, E., Collot, J., Foucher, J-P, Klinghoefer, F., Lafoy, Y, and Géli, L. (2009) 'Geophysical characterization of bottom simulating reflectors in the Fairway Basin (off New Caledonia, Southwest Pacific), based on high resolution seismic profiles and heat flow data', *Marine Geology*, 266, 80–90.

OECD (2008a) *France*, Committee of Development Cooperation, Peer Review, Brussels

—— (2008b) 'Is it ODA?', factsheet, November 2008.

Ordonnaud, G., Coulmy, D., Gomane, J-P., and Guibert, J.L. (1983) *Le Pacifique, "Nouveau Centre du Monde"*, Paris, Berger-Levrault.

Panoff, M. (1989) *Tahiti Métisse*, Paris, Denoël.

Papon, P. (1999) 'Mieux gérer l'Océan mondial', *Bulletin d'Etudes de la Marine*, 15, 55–59.

Parker, G. (2000) 'Ratzel, the French school and the birth of alternative geopolitics', *Political Geography*, 19, 957–69.

Perret, C., (ed.) (2002) *Perspectives de dévéloppement pour la Nouvelle-Calédonie*, Presses Universitaire de Grenoble.

Piquet, M. (2000) *Cold War in Warm Waters: Reflections on Australian and French Mutual Misunderstandings in the Pacific*, Carlton, Victoria, Contemporary Europe Research Centre, University of Melbourne.

Plomley, N.J.B. (1983) *The Baudin Expedition and the Tasmanian Aborigines, 1802*, Hobart, Blubber Head Press.

Politique Etrangère (1987) *La France et le Pacifique Sud 1/87*, Paris, Institut français des relations internationales.

Pons, X. (1988) *Le Géant du Pacifique*, Paris, Economica.

Quanchi, M. (2004) 'A name that featured once or twice a year: Not noticing French New Caledonia in Australia in the mid-twentieth-century British Australia', 16th Pacific History Association Conference, University of New Caledonia, Noumea.

Queyranne, J.-J. (2000) 'The South Pacific: A new frontier?', *New Zealand International Review*, 25, 7.

Raoult, E. (2005) *Rapport No 2451 sur l'approbation de l'accord de siège entre le gouvernement de la République française et la Communauté du Pacifique*, Paris, Assemblée nationale.

Regnault, J.-M. (2005a) *Le Pouvoir confisqué en Polynésie française*, Paris, Les Indes Savantes.

—— (2005b) ,Une zone d'instabilité méconnue, le Pacifique insulaire (No peace in the pacific)', *Le Monde diplomatique*, 26–27.

—— and Fayaud, Viviane (2008) *La Nouvelle-Calédonie Vingt années de concorde 1988–2008*, Paris, Publications de la Société Française d'Histoire d'Outre-Mer.

Reilly, B. (2000) 'The Africanisation of the South Pacific', *Australian Journal of International Affairs*, 54, 261–68.

Rivoilan, P. and Broustet, D. (2011) *Synthèse — Recensement De La Population 2009*, website of Institut National de la Statistique et des Études Économiques, accessed 12 May 2011.

Royer, J.-F. (2011) 'Les flux migratoires externes de la Nouvelle-Calédonie de 1989 à 2009', Rapport De Mission, *Série des Documents de Travail*, No F1103, Direction des statistiques démographiques et sociales, Département de la démographique, Centre de recherche en économie et statistique.

Roynette, J. (2009) *Le piège calédonien*, Paris, Editions l'Harmattan.

Rumley, D., Forbes, V.L. and Griffin, C. (2006) *Australia's Arc of Instability: The Political and Cultural Dynamics of Regional Security*, Springer Netherlands.

Sanguinetti, A. (1985) 'La Calédonie, summum jus summa in juria, *Politique aujourd'hui*, 22–35.

Sankey, M. (1991) 'La mission impossible: l'abbé Paulmier et les terres australes', in *Essays in Honour of Keith Val Sinclair*, Capricornia, Department of Modern Languages, James Cook University of North Queensland.

Sarkozy, N. (2007a) Lettre aux calédoniens.

—— (2007b) Message, Comité des signataires de l'Accord de Nouméa, December 2007.

—— (2009) Discours sur l'Outre-Mer, Conseil Interministériel de l'Outre-Mer, Paris, 6 November.

—— (2010a) Discours de M. Le Président de la République: Voeux à la France d'Outre-mer, Saint-Denis, 19 January.

—— (2010b) *Discours à la reception des signataires de l'Accord de Nouméa*, Paris, 24 juin.

—— (2011) *Déclaration sur le présent et l'avenir de la Nouvelle-Calédonie*, Païta, 28 August.

Satineau, Maurice. (1987) *Le Miroir de Nouméa*, Paris, L'Harmattan.

Sautot, H. (1949) *Grandeur et Décadence du Gaullisme dans le Pacifique*, Melbourne and London, F.W. Cheshire.

Schéma De Cohérence De L'agglomération De Nouméa (SCAN) (2009) Période de 1996 à 2002. Plan de déplacement de l'agglomération de Nouméa. Noumea.

Secretariat of the Pacific Community (2001) *New Caledonia Population Profile Based on 1996 Census*, Noumea.

—— (2007) 'Financial statements and audit reports for the year ended 31 December 2007', *SPC Annual Reports and Financial Statements*, Noumea.

—— (2009) 'France support to SPC: 1993 to 2009', *Annual Reports and Financial Statements*, Noumea.

—— (2010) *Annual Reports and Financial Statements*, Noumea.

Sénat (2006) *Projet de loi de finances pour 2006: Outre-mer*, Paris.

—— (2008) Figures on Costs of Overseas Collectivities, Paris, Senate Finance Commission, conveyed by email correspondence to author, September 2008.

Sevaistre, C.A. (1986) 'Le nouveau droit de la mer, la France et les départements et territoires d'outre-mer', *Défense Nationale*.

Shineberg, D. (1983) 'Un nouveau regard sur la démographie historique de la Nouvelle-Calédonie', *Journal de la Société des Océanistes*, 39.

—— (1986) *French Colonisation in the Pacific: With Special Reference to New Caledonia*, Sydney, H.V.Evatt Memorial Foundation.

Smith, N.C. (2001) *Robin Force: The Australian Defence of New Caledonia*, Gardenvale Victoria, Mostly Unsung Military History Research and Publications.

Spencer, M., Ward, A., and Connell, J., (eds.) (1988) *New Caledonia: Essays in Nationalism and Dependency*, St Lucia, University of Queensland Press.

Strokirch, K.V. (2001) 'French Polynesia', *The Contemporary Pacific*, 13, 225–35.

Surville, J. (1981) *The Expedition of the St. Jean-Baptiste to the Pacific, 1769–1770: From Journals of Jean de Surville and Guillaume Labe*, (John Dunmore, trans & ed.), London, Hakluyt Society.

Sydney Morning Herald (1853) 'The French in New Caledonia', 2 November.

Symonds, P.A. and Willcox, J.B. (1989) 'Australia's petroleum potential in areas beyond an exclusive economic zone', *Journal of Australian Geology and Geophysics*, 11, 11–36.

Tatou, M.E. (2009) 'Les Victimes polynésiennes des essais nucléaires français devant le Tribunal du travail de Papéete, Tahiti'.

Tesoka, L. and Ziller, J. (2008) *Union Européenne et Outre-Mers Unis dans leurs diversités*, Aix-en-Provence, Presses Universitaires d'Aix -Marseille.

Thakur, R. (1995) *The last bang before a total ban: French nuclear testing in the Pacific*, Canberra, Peace Research Centre, Australian National University.

Themereau, M.-N. (2006) Speech of the President of the Government of New Caledonia, 37th meeting of the Pacific Islands Forum.

Thomas, M. (1998) *The French Empire at war 1940-45,* Manchester University Press.

—— (2005) *The French Empire between the Wars, Imperialism, Politics and Society*, Manchester University Press.

Tjibaou, J.-M. (2005) *Kanaky*, Canberra, Pandanus Press.

——, Bensa, A., and Wittersheim, E. (1996) *La présence Kanak*, Paris, Editions Odile Jacob.

Tschoegl, A. E. (2003) 'Foreign banks in the Pacific: Some history and policy issues', paper for University of Pennsylvania, Wharton School, Financial Institutions Center.

Tcherkezoff, S. (2003) 'On cloth, gifts and nudity: Regarding some European misunderstandings during early encounters in Polynesia', in Chloë Colchester (ed.) *Clothing the Pacific*, New York, Oxford, 51–78.

Vially, R., Lafoy, Y., Auzende, J-M., and France, R., (2003) 'Petroleum pPotential of New Caledonia and its offshore basins', AAPG International Conference, Barcelona, Spain.

Victor, J.C. (1990) 'France in the Pacific', *The Pacific Review*, 3, 343–48.

Waddell, E. (2008) *Jean-Marie Tjibaou: Kanak Witness to the World: An Intellectual Biography*, Honolulu, University of Hawai'i Press.

Wadrawene, E. and Angleviel, F. *La Nouvelle-Calédonie: Les Kanaks et l'histoire*, Paris, Les Indes Savantes.

Wall, S. (2009) 'Jean-Marie Tjibaou, statesman without a state: A reporter's perspective', *The Journal of Pacific History*, 44, 165–78.

Weeks, C. (1989) 'Hour of temptation: American interests in New Caledonia 1935–45', *Australian Journal of Politics and History*, 5, 2, 185–200, August.

White, H. (1985) 'Pisani lays the foundation for a compromise solution', *Sydney Morning Herald*, 26 January 1985.

Wittersheim, E. (1998) 'Melanesian elites and modern politics in New Caledonia and Vanuatu', *State Society and Governance in Melanesia Discussion Paper* 98/3.

Wolton, D. (2002) 'La France et les Outre-mers', *L'enjeu multiculturel*, Paris, CNRS Editions.

Wolton, D. (2006) *Demain la francophonie*, Paris, Flammarion.

Woolner, D. (1995) 'Raison d'état and popular response: The resumption of French nuclear testing in the South Pacific', Canberra, Department of the Parliamentary Library.

World Council Of Churches (2012), Statement on the re-inscription of French Polynesia (Maohi Nui) on the United Nations List of Countries to be Decolonised, WCC Central Committee Meeting, Crete, 4 September

Periodicals and media

Depêche de Tahiti, la <http://www.ladepeche.pf>

Figaro, le <http://www.lefigaro.fr/international>

Flash d'Océanie/Oceania Flash <http://www.newspad-pacific.info>

France 24 <http://www.france24.com>

Islands Business <http://www.islandsbusiness.com>

Interpreter <http://www.lowyinterpreter.org/>

Mwà Véé <http://www.adck.nc/patrimoine/mwa-vee/archives>

Nouvelles Calédoniennes, les <http://www.lnc.nc>

Nouvelles de Tahiti, les <http://www.lesnouvelles.pf>

Parisien, le <http://www.leparisien.fr>

Post Courier <http://www.postcourier.com.pg>

Radio New Zealand <http://www.rnzi.com>

Réseau France Outre-Mer (Overseas France Network) <http://www.rfo.fr/>

Tahiti Pacifique (Pacific Tahiti) <http://www.tahiti-pacifique>

Television New Zealand <http://tvnz.co.nz>

TV5 <http://www.tv5.org>

Websites

Ausaid <http://www.ausaid.gov.au>

Australian Department of Foreign Affairs and Trade <http://www.dfat.gov.au>

Australian Department of Defence <http://www.defence.gov.au>

Asian Development Bank <http://www.adb.org>

Baudin Legacy Project <http://setis.library.usyd.edu.au/baudin/index.html>

Bourse interministerielle de l'emploi public en polynésie française <http://www.polynesie-francaise.biep.fonction-publique.gouv.fr>

Euroinvestor website <http://www.euroinvestor.co.uk>

European Union <http://www.http//europa.eu>

French Ministry of Foreign Affairs <http://www.diplomatie.gouv.fr>

French Embassy in Australia <http://www.ambafrance-au.org>

French Embassy in Fiji <http://www.ambafrance-fj.org>

French Embassy in Papua New Guinea <http://www.ambafrance-pg.org>

Institut d'Émission d'Outre-Mer <http://www.ieom.fr>

INCO Goro website <http://www.inco.com/global/goro>

Institut de la statistique et des études économiques <http://www.isee.nc>

Institut national de la statistique et des études économiques <http://www.insee.fr/en>

Institut statistique de la Polynésie Française <http://www.ispf>

New Caledonia official website <http://www.nouvelle-caledonie.gouv.fr>

New Zealand's Ministry of Foreign Affairs and Trade <http://www.nzmfat.gov.nz>

New Zealand Aid <http://www.nzaid.govt.nz/programmes/c-pac-countries.html>

Organisation for Economic Cooperation and Development <http://www.oecd.org>

Pacific Islands Forum <http://www.forumsec.org.fj/>

Palika http://<http://www.journal.kanak.org>

President of France <http://www.elysee.fr/president>

Secretariat for the Pacific Community <http://www.spc.org>

Société le Nickel <http://www.sln.nc>

Service Territorial de la Statistique et des Études Économiques STSEE (Statistics and Economic Studies Institute Wallis and Futuna) <http://www.spc.int/prism/country/wf/stats/index.html>

United Nations <http://www.un.org>

Official documents

Department of Foreign Affairs and Trade, Historical Documents (DFAT HD) series website <http://www.info.dfat.gov.au/historical>

—— (2010) 'Parliamentary Secretary visit to Pacific', media release, Canberra, 13 October.

High Commission of France in French Polynesia (2007) '*159.1 milliards de F CFP ont été dépensés par l'Etat en Polynésie française en 2006*' press release, 7 August.

ISEE *Situation Démographique 2008.*

ISEE *Recensement de la Nouvelle-Calédonie 2009 (résultats provisoires)* see isee.nc website

ISEE–INSEE (2004) *Recensement de la Population de la Nouvelle-Calédonie au 31août 2004* (Census of the Population of New Caledonia of 31 August 2004).

ISEE TEC (2008) *Tableaux de l'Économie Calédonienne 2008 édition abrégée.*

Joint press conference Australian and French Defence Ministers Joel Fitzgibbon and Hervé Morin, 17 September 2008.

Joint press statement Australian and French Foreign Ministers Kevin Rudd and Alain Juppé, 11 September 2011

Journal Officiel du Sénat de la République française, response to question 10070, 15 October 1998.

Letter from the French Prime Minister François Fillon to UN Secretary-General Ban Ki-Moon, on Law of the Sea, 18 July 2007.

Ministère de la Défense (2008) *Livre Blanc sur la défense et la sécurité nationale*, Paris.

Ministère des Affaires Étrangères (2008) *Livre Blanc sur la politique étrangère et européenne de la France,* Paris.

PIF communiqués, <http://www.forumsec.org.fj>

PIF (2005) Agreement Establishing the Pacific Islands Forum, Port Moresby, 27 October.

Press Release, 'Enhanced Pacific Engagement', Australian Minister for Foreign Affairs Stephen Smith, Department of Foreign Affairs and Trade, 12 May 2009

Relevé de conclusions, VIIeme Comité des signataires de l'Accord de Nouméa, (Conclusions, Seventh Meeting of the Noumea Accord Committee of Signatories), 8 December 2008

Relevé de conclusions, VIIIeme Comité des signataires de l'Accord de Nouméa, (Conclusions, Eighth Meeting of the Noumea Accord Committee of Signatories), 24 June 2010

Relevé de conclusions, IXeme Comité des signataires de l'Accord de Nouméa, (Conclusions, Eighth Meeting of the Noumea Accord Committee of Signatories), 9 Juillet 2011

Senate of France, Document no. 180, Ordinary Session 1998–1999, vol. 1.

STSEE (2008) Wallis and Futuna, Recensement de la Population.

Vœu (2010) Congress of New Caledonia 1 13 July.

Republic of France, legislation and agreements

Relating to New Caledonia:

The texts of the following laws are available at <http://www.legifrance.gouv.fr> and <http://www.congres.nc/textes-fondamentaux>

Defferre Laws 1956 and 1957 — *Loi No 56-619 du 23 juin 1956 dite Loi-cadre Deferre et le décret du 22 juillet 1957 pris pour son application.*

Jacquinot Laws — *Loi du 21 décembre 1963 dite Loi Jacquinot.*

Billotte Laws — *Lois du 3 janvier 1969 dites Lois Billotte.*

Stirn Statute — *Loi du 28 décembre 1976 dit statut Stirn modifiée par la loi du 24 mai 1979.*

Dijoud Law — *Law No. 79-407 of 24 May 1979.*

Lemoine Statute — *Loi du 6 septembre 1984 dit statut Lemoine.*

Pisani Statute — *Loi du 23 août 1985 dit statut Pisani.*

Pons I Statute — *Loi du 17 juillet 1986 dit statut Pons I.*

Pons II Statute — *Loi du 22 janvier 1988 dit statut Pons II2.*

Referendum Law — *Loi Référendaire du 9 novembre 1988, Loi No 88-1028.*

Les Accords de Matignon-Oudinot (Matignon Accords), 1988.

L'Accord de Nouméa (Noumea Accord), 1998.

La loi organique (Organic Law) No 99-209 and related *Loi ordinaire No 99-210*, 19 March 1999.

Loi No 88-1028 of 9 November 1988 — Statutory dispositions preparatory to self-determination of New Caledonia in 1998 — (*Loi No 88-1028 du 9 novembre 1988 portant dispositions statutaires et préparatoires à l'autodétermination de la Nouvelle-Calédonie en 1998*).

Trade and Economic Relations Arrangement, Australia and New Caledonia, March 2002.

Relating to French Polynesia:

The texts of the following laws are available at <http://www.legifrance.gouv.fr>

Ordonnance n°58-1337 du 23 décembre 1958

Loi n°77-772 du 12 juillet 1977 relating to the organization of French Polynesia.

Loi n°84-820 du 6 septembre 1984.

Loi n 90-612 du 12 juillet 1990.

Loi n°96-313 du 12 avril 1996.

Organic Law, French Polynesia, February 2004 — Loi n°2004-193 du 27 février 2004.

Organic Law relating to Overseas France — *Loi organique n° 2007-223 du 21 février 2007.*

Loi n°2007-1720 du 7 décembre 2007.

Relating to Wallis and Futuna:

Law No 61-814 of 19 July 1961 conferring on the Wallis and Futuna Islands the status of Overseas Territory (*Loi No 61-814 du 19 juillet 1961 conférant aux îles Wallis et Futuna le statut de territoire d'outre-mer*)

Personal communications/meetings

Aisi, Mr Robert, H.E., Permanent Representative for Papua New Guinea to the United Nations, New York, 7 January 2010.

Aldrich, Dr Robert, Professor of European History, University of Sydney, Paris, 6 May 2006.

Alla, M. Pierre, Directeur Général, SLN, Noumea 24 February 2009.

Angleviel, Dr Frédéric, historian, Noumea, 22 February 2009.

Baudchon, M. Gérard, Director, ISEE, Noumea, 23 February 2009.

Beustes, Annie, Member, Government of New Caledonia, 24 February 2009.

Bieuville, M. François-Xavier, Conseiller technique auprès du Secrétaire d'Etat à l'Outre-Mer, Ministère de l'Intérieur, de l' Outre-Mer et des Collectivités territoriales, Paris, 5 May 2008.

Buguet, M. Jacques, Adjoint diplomatique, French High Commission, Noumea, 26 February 2009.

Butler, Ms Anita, Australian Consul General, Noumea, 4 March 2009.

Christnacht, M. Alain, former French High Commissioner, Noumea and Conseiller d'État, Paris, 7 May 2008.

Cohen, Dr Eliot, Counsellor, State Department, Washington DC, 7 April 2008.

Colin, M. Christian, Director, IRD, Noumea, August 2004.

Dassonville, M. Y., Haut-Commissaire de la République, Noumea, 23 February and 6 March 2009.

Dauth, H.E. Mr John, LVO, Australian Consul General Noumea 1986–1987, email 14 March 2009.

de Braquilanges, Général, Commandant Supérieur, French Forces in New Caledonia, 3 March 2009.

de Zuniga, H.E. Mr Javier Ortez, Chargé, EU mission, Noumea, 27 February 2009.

Décamp, Mme Janine, Présidente, Syndicat des Industries de la Mine, 25 February 2009.

Downer, The Hon. Alexander, Australian Minister for Foreign Affairs 1996–2007, communication 2003; telephone 5 January 2008; Canberra, 10 July 2009.

Faberon, J.-Y., Directeur, Adjoint de l'Institut de droit d'outre-mer, Université Paul Cézanne Aix-Marseille III, Noumea, 18 March 2009.

Faure-Tournaire, M. Jean-Luc, Sous-directeur Océanie, Ministère des Affaires Étrangères, Paris, 2 May 2008.

Frogier, M. Pierre, Président, R-UMP, Noumea 24 February 2009.

Gorodey, Mme Déwé, former Vice-President of New Caledonia and Member, Government of New Caledonia, numerous meetings Noumea 2001–2004 and Paris, 26 April 2008.

Kazeriou, M. Emmanuelle, Director, Centre Culturel Tjibaou, 4 March 2009.

Kotra, M. Wallès, former director, RFO, French Polynesia, Paris, 26 April 2008.

Lafleur, M. Jacques, former president of Southern Province and Noumea Accord signatory, 2 March 2009, and meetings 2001–2004.

Lataste, M. Thierry, former high commissioner, Nouméa, 2001–2003, and general secretary, Noumea, 1991, Chief of Staff, Secretaire d' État de l'Outre-Mer, 1997, Paris, 26 April 2008 and La Roche Sur Yon, 17 May 2008, and numerous meetings 2001–2002.

Leader, Dr Malcolm, Australian Consul General, Noumea, 1980–1983, Canberra, October 2009.

Lèques, M. Jean, Mayor of Noumea, Noumea, 6 March 2009.

Loueckhote, Senator S., Sénateur and Président, Mouvement pour la Diversité, Noumea, 3 March 2009.

Mackay, Ms Freda, Executive Secretary, UN Decolonisation Committee, Department of Political Affairs, United Nations, New York 14 April 2008 and 5 January 2010.

Maclellan, Mr Nic, freelance journalist, Canberra, 1 October 2008.

New Caledonian Government delegation, visit to Australian National University, Canberra, 10 March 2010.

Mann, Dr R., Deputy Director General, SPC, Noumea, 27 February 2009.

O'Leary, Mr David, Australian Consul General, Noumea 1987–1990, Canberra, September 2009.

Ritchie, H.E. Mr David, Australian ambassador to France 2008–2010, Paris, 12 May 2008.

Rogers, Dr Jimmie, Director-General, SPC, 2 March 2009.

Roussel, H.E. M. Patrick, Ambassadeur, Secrétaire Permanent pour le Pacifique, Paris, 5 May 2008.

Tuheiava, M. Richard, Sénateur for French Polynesia in the French Senate, 12 July 2011.

Tutugoro, Mr Victor, FLNKS Spokesman, Noumea, 2 March 2009 and email 30 October 2009.

Washetine, Mr Charles, Member, New Caledonian Government, 24 February 2009.

Wamytan, Roch, UC/FLNKS leader and representative for Youth on the Sénat Coutumier, Paris, 26 April 2008 and Noumea 5 March 2009.

Wensley, H.E. Ms Penny AO, Australian Ambassador to France 2005–2007, Brisbane, 6 May 2009.

White, Dr Hugh, Head, Strategic and Defence Studies Centre, Australian National University, Canberra 13 August 2009.

And the countless French and New Caledonian, French Polynesian, and Wallis and Futuna based government officials, military officers, politicians, academics, journalists, business people, *anciens combattants*, and residents from all ethnic backgrounds who helped me to understand the politics of France in the South Pacific from November 2001 to November 2004 as Australia's consul-general in Noumea.

United Nations documents

United Nations Charter, 1945.

UNGA Fourth Committee (1987) A/C.4/42/SR.17, 21 *Summary Record of the 17th Meeting*, October, 10–12.

—— (2006) A/AC.109/2006/20 *Report of the United Nations Mission to observe a referendum on self-determination of Tokelau, February 2006*, 30 May.

—— (2008) A/AC.109/2008/9 Special Committee on the situation with regard to the implementation of the Declaration on the Granting of Independence to Colonial Countries and Peoples, *New Caledonia: Working Paper* prepared by the Secretariat, 5 March.

—— (2012) A/AC.109/2012/15 Special Committee on the situation with regard to the implementation of the Declaration on the Granting of Independence to Colonial Countries and Peoples, *New Caledonia: Working Paper* prepared by the Secretariat, 22 March.

—— (2009) A/AC.109/2009/L.6 Draft resolution submitted by the Chair, *Question of sending visiting and special missions to territories*, 3 June.

UNGA (1995) 'Environmental impact assessment of France's Nuclear Testing in South Pacific called for in Second Committee', press release, GA/EF/2693, 1 November.

United Nations Human Rights Committee (2002) 'Views', Antonin *et al. v. France*, 75th Session, UN Document CCPR/C/75/D/932/2000, 15 July.

United Nations Human Rights Council, (2011) A/HRC/18/35/Add.6 *The situation of Kanak people in New Caledonia, France*, Report of the Special Rapporteur on Indigenous Rights, 14 September.

UNGA resolutions:

744 (VIII) Association of representatives from non-self-governing territories in the work of the committee on information from Non-Self-Governing Territories, 27 November 1953.

1514 (XV) Declaration on the Granting of Independence to Colonial Countries and Peoples, 14 December 1960.

1541 (XV) Principles which should guide members in determining whether or not an obligation exists to transmit the information called for under Article 73e of the Charter, 14 December 1960.

2625 (XXV) Declaration on principles of international law concerning friendly relations and cooperation among states in accordance with the Charter of the United Nations, 24 October 1970.

3477(XXX) Establishment of a Nuclear Weapons Free Zone in the South Pacific, 11 December 1975.

35/118 Plan of Action for the full implementation of the Declaration on the Granting of Independence to Colonial Countries and Peoples, 11 December 1980.

40/41 Implementation of the Declaration on the Granting of Independence to Colonial Countries and Peoples, 2 December 1986.

A/RES/50/65, Comprehensive Test Ban Treaty, 12 December 1995.

A/57/23 Report of the Special Committee on the Situation with regard to the implementation of the Declaration on the Granting of Independence to Colonial Countries and Peoples, 2002.

57/140 Implementation of the Declaration on the Granting of Independence to Colonial Countries and Peoples, 20 February 2003.

A/Res/59/129 Implementation of the Declaration on the Granting of Independence to Colonial Countries and Peoples by the specialised agencies and the international institutions associated with the United Nations, 25 January 2005.

A/Res/59/136 Implementation of the Declaration on the Granting of Independence to Colonial Countries and Peoples, 25 January 2005.

A/Res/61/295 United Nations Declaration on the Rights of Indigenous People, 2 October 2007.

UNGA resolutions on the question of New Caledonia:

A/Res/42/79, 4 December 1987.

A/Res/43/44, 22 November 1988.

A/Res/44/89, 11 December 1989.

A/Res/45/22, 20 November 1990.

A/Res/46/69, 11 December 1991.

A/Res/47/26, 25 November 1992.

A/Res/48/50, 10 December 1993.

A/Res/49/45, 9 December 1994.

A/Res/50/37, 6 December 1995.

A/Res/51/144, 13 December 1996.

A/Res/52/76, 10 December 1997.

A/Res/53/65, 3 December 1998.

A/Res/54/88, 6 December 1999.

A/Res/55/142, 8 December 2000.

A/Res/56/70, 10 December 2001.

A/Res/57/136, 11December 2002.

A/Res/58/106, 9 December 2003.

A/Res/59/132, 10 December 2004.

A/Res/60/115, 8 December 2005.

A/Res/61/126, 14 December 2006.

A/Res/62/117, 17 December 2007.

A/Res/63/106, 5 December 2008.

A/Res/64/102, 19 January 2010.

A/Res/65/113, 20 January 2011.

A/Res/66/87, 12 January 2012.

www.ingramcontent.com/pod-product-compliance
Lightning Source LLC
Chambersburg PA
CBHW060930180426
43192CB00045B/2861